Only two were privileged actually to walk to Emmaus with the risen Lord Jesus, but for every reader of this marvelous book the values of the Emmaus experience are made available. . . . [Ideal for] study by the pastor-preacher, as a handbook for all would-be clued-up Christians, or for home-group leaders and their groups.

*J. Alec Motyer*
*Former Principal of Trinity Theologial College, Bristol, England*
*Review in* Evangelicals Now

This is theology which has been preached. . . . It warms and informs, lifting heart and mind to the grandeur of Christ and to humanity's place within God's purposes for this world.

*David Atkinson*
*Fellow and Chaplain of Corpus Christi College, Oxford, England*

Rich material from a preacher-theologian.

*R. T. France*
*Former principal of Wycliffe Hall, Oxford, England*

# THE GLORY OF CHRIST

Peter Lewis

**MOODY PRESS**

CHICAGO

Originally published in London, England, by Hodder & Stoughton Ltd. This is an adaptation of that book.

ISBN: 0-8024-3029-5

1 3 5 7 9 10 8 6 4 2

*Printed in the United States of America*

*To the elect lady whom I love*

# CONTENTS

# PREFACE

This is a book of theology for everybody. It is written by a pastor who believes that "theology" and "everybody" go together, that biblical doctrine warms as well as informs, and that such teaching belongs in the churches, not just in the seminaries.

More specifically, it is written for those who may have read briefer introductory material on this subject and want to move deeper into the doctrine but who do not want highly technical discussions. Many readers whose expertise is in other fields want to explore Christian doctrine in greater depth but without the barbed wire of in-house vocabulary ("existential" this and "ontological" that and "eschatological" the other). They do not want the "five reasons why Jesus may not have said this and six reasons why He probably did" treatment of the Scriptures. This book also may be a bridge to scholarly works; it includes the insights of more than two hundred scholars.

*The Glory of Christ* has been written in the midst of a busy preaching and teaching ministry at home and abroad, and I must record my gratitude to Edward England and my British publishers, who first approached me to write a book on Jesus, for their great patience and enthusiastic cooperation. I wish to thank those "friends in high places" who have read, corrected, and advised on various parts of the book: Drs. John Balchin, Peter Cotterell, R. T. France, John Goldingay, and Stephen Travis.

Special thanks are due to Barbara Walters of Stapleford, Notts, my kind and long-suffering typist who should easily manage a doctorate in hieroglyphics. Without her this book might still have been written, but it would never have been read! My gratitude to the elders and members of Cornerstone Evangelical Church, who free me for such work and who love their pastor faithfully, should be written across the sky. Lastly my wife, Valerie, to whom this book is dedicated, deserves a thousand times the love and praise and honor in which she is held by myself and our two sons, Calvin and Justin.

On such a theme as the glory of Christ the best of books are inadequate and the largest of treatments incomplete. This study is neither among the former for excellence nor the latter for thoroughness, and I am painfully aware of its faults. I can only ask the readers to learn what they can from me, and go on to others for more. I find myself recalling the words of the devout seventeenth-century Anglican, Bishop James Ussher of Armagh, who, on his deathbed, was heard to pray, "Lord, forgive me my sins, especially my omissions."

# INTRODUCTION

I once saw a restless congregation stilled and then thrilled by one of the most moving and powerful testimonies I have heard.

On a holiday Sunday in a remote, rural spot in West Wales thirty visitors, including myself, had gathered at a local chapel that had organized an English service for summer guests. We were all easily distinguishable from the prim and well-dressed "regulars" by our multicolored anorak jackets. (It was an English summer!)

The preacher was a respected and somewhat cultured local figure. His integrity and sincerity were immediately apparent, and he led the worship in a deeply spiritual manner. However, as the hands of the chapel clock reached the half-hour after his sermon had begun, the anoraks began to rustle. Then, even as he announced the close of his sermon, he leaned over the old-fashioned pulpit and asked if he might end with a personal testimony. This is what he said:

"When I was a boy of about twelve I had a great hero. My hero was a local sportsman who achieved the rare distinction of gaining a cap in rugby for playing for his country, and who played cricket to county standard. I so admired this man that I papered the walls of my bedroom with press-cuttings and photographs of him, and loved to talk and hear about his exploits on the field. He was my great hero.

"Then, when I was in my fourteenth year, I actually got to know my hero personally! He was a keen angler and I used to go fishing with him. On these occasions I was able to observe him from an entirely different viewpoint and got to know the man and not merely the image."

At this point the preacher paused, looked closely at his congregation, shook his head slowly from side to side, and with an air of considerable authority, said in emphatic tones, *"And the nearer I got, the smaller he became."*

In a few brief sentences he sketched the young boy's disillusionment as he discovered the true character of the man whose public image had so captivated him. No doubt everyone in the congregation that morning recognized the experience and sympathized with the preacher. But attentive as we now were, we were hardly prepared for what followed.

Suddenly, in a rising voice and with arms outstretched, voice breaking with emotion, he cried out: "But God eventually led that downcast schoolboy to a new hero. And I have walked with *my Jesus* for thirty-five years now. In that time I have often disappointed him, but he has never disappointed me! I have got to know him better, and *the nearer I get the* bigger *he becomes!"*

My wife and I (and, I trust, many others that morning) went out of that quaint old chapel walking on air. It was so utterly true: Jesus was getting bigger and bigger for us all, undiminished by the years. Not dwarfed by any crisis, not regulated by any gain, not lessened by any intimacy; always with us, always before us, always leading us on. We growing daily in admiration and gratitude; He revealing more and more of His majesty and love. We had been awed and elevated by seeing just how big our Lord and Savior is.

This book is an attempt to show something of the stature of Jesus Christ to the reader. To explain Him, but not to explain Him away; to listen to His voice, not to drown it; to admire Him, and to urge His uniqueness and His lordship upon a world so short of heroes and upon a church that has put away childish things.

It is written for Christians who want to know more clearly and more thoroughly what the Bible says about Jesus, and it is written so that as we get nearer He might get *bigger*—in our minds, in our hearts, and in our lives!

## JESUS AND HIS CHURCH

For almost twenty centuries the church has placed one historic figure where it has placed no other man. It has taken the carpenter from first-century Nazareth, Jesus, and ranged Him on the side of deity: making His teaching the absolute authority in our knowledge of God. Jesus' work has become the ground of our salvation, and His person the object of our faith and worship. And church members, drawn from "every tribe and language and people and nation" (Revelation 5:9), have known Him and served Him, loved Him and hymned Him, preached Him and praised Him.

Yet the same church has resolutely refused to worship "man" and has repeatedly suffered for it! The early Christian martyrs, for instance, were not tortured and put to death for worshipping Jesus, *but for refusing to worship anyone else—* including the Roman emperor. The thought of deifying a mere man, even the best and greatest, revolted the conscience of the first-century Christians no less than it revolted the minds of the Jews with their long history of monotheism. Moreover, in the long centuries since His earthly ministry the true church has never been tempted to exchange Jesus for another. No one has ever suggested placing an Augustine, or a Luther, or a Wesley where the church has previously placed Jesus.

Why is it, then, that Jesus occupies not only a place in the church which no one else occupies, but a place which is forbidden to the best and greatest men the church will ever produce?

Jesus occupies a unique place in the mind and heart of the church because Jesus insisted on that unique place. The church has made many claims for the carpenter from Nazareth, but none higher than He made for Himself. The church has not been extravagant in its devotion to Him; it has only been loyal and faithful in responding to the devotion He claimed and still claims.

Jesus of Nazareth preached as no prophet preached, as no apostle or preacher since the days of the apostles has ever preached. Isaiah did not preach Isaiah, Paul did not preach Paul, Augustine did not preach Augustine, Martin Luther did not preach Martin Luther. But Jesus Christ preached Jesus Christ! Paul said, "We do not preach ourselves" (2 Corinthians

4:5). Jesus could not say that! He was integral to His gospel, indeed He was central to it. It had no life or power without Him. He was its form and content. From the beginning Christianity has been not a philosophy, not a mysticism, not even an ethic, but "the good news about Jesus Christ, the Son of God" (cf. Mark 1:1).

The Christian church has said many remarkable things about Jesus in its creeds and councils and theological writings. But the question arises: Did *He* give rise to them? Did He initiate them and prompt them by what He claimed for himself and by His attitudes and by the demands He made upon His followers? Is the church's reaction to Him the response of effect to cause? Is Jesus responsible for the church He produced?

I want to show in the first part of this book that it is precisely Jesus' claims about Himself that distance Him from every other religious leader and which make impossible a respect that stops short of worship. C. S. Lewis has made the point as well as anyone. He notes the dilemma in which Jesus leaves admiring believers:

> People often say . . . "I'm ready to accept Jesus as a great moral teacher, but I don't accept His claim to be God." That is the one thing we must not say. A man who was merely a man and said the sort of things Jesus said would not be a great moral teacher. He would either be a lunatic—on a level with the man who says he is a poached egg—or else he would be the Devil of Hell. You must make your choice. Either this man was, and is, the Son of God: or else a madman or something worse. You can shut Him up for a fool, you can spit at Him and kill Him as a demon; or you can fall at His feet and call Him Lord and God. But let us not come with any patronising nonsense about His being a great human teacher. He has not left that open to us.[1]

The dilemma not only confronts the man or woman of no religion: it also confronts the adherents of every other religion also. This Jesus simply will not stand alongside even the greatest leaders of world religions and philosophers. Lewis puts the case memorably:

There is no half-way house and there is no parallel in other religions. If you had gone to Buddha and asked him: "Are you the son of Bramah?" He would have said, "My son, you are still in the vale of illusion." If you had gone to Socrates and asked, "Are you Zeus?" he would have laughed at you. If you had gone to Mohammed and asked, "Are you Allah?" he would first have rent his clothes and then cut your head off.[2]

But if with Thomas you kneel and adore Jesus as "My Lord and my God," you will receive only the beatitudes of approval and love (John 20:28–29).

However, in the last 150 years or so new trends of thought have made radical reassessments no only of previous beliefs of the church, but of her foundational documents themselves—the Scriptures.

## JESUS AND HIS INTERPRETERS

In some circles within the world of biblical scholarship, it has long been fashionable to regard the Jesus of our New Testament as being largely the creation of the various writers and schools of thought within the early church. We are told that Jesus' virgin birth, His miracles, His claims to divinity and pre-existence, His bodily resurrection, and other supernatural elements have been "creatively added" to earlier and much more rudimentary accounts of Jesus' life and sayings in order to make some important spiritual and theological points.

John's gospel in particular (when seen as the product of a Johannine school rather than an original disciple) does not, it is said, give us reliable access to the original words of Jesus, or indeed to the original Jesus Himself: a high Christology is simply put into His mouth as a literary device. The enthusiasm of Jesus' early admirers and followers has wrapped the carpenter-preacher from Nazareth in supernatural myths that, while meaningful in their time, now have to be stripped away so that modern man may meet the original Jesus and discover the original Christianity.

Similarly Paul's cosmic Christ is believed to be a far cry from the original Galilean prophet who, it is confidently said, went about preaching not Himself, but the kingdom of God. No one, we are assured, would have been more surprised than Jesus to see the way His teaching was transmitted (or transmuted) by "John" and Paul.

In his book *The Person of Christ,* David Wells surveys some of these views, which have been enormously influential in this century, and asks: "Why is it that only now, two thousand years after the event, we are at last beginning to understand what Christianity is all about?"[3] He registers his concern about a new kind of priesthood that is developing, under which ordinary Christians are urged to set aside the full Scriptures they once had and attempt to understand Christian truth only by means of those parts of the Bible these particular scholars allow them. "To suppose such a thing," he protests, "is to subject the meaning of Scripture to a far more restrictive 'tradition' than anything proposed by Rome in the sixteenth century and to invest our new magisterium—the coterie of learned scholars—with an authority more stifling and far-reaching than the Roman Catholic magisterium ever exercised."[4] God gave the Scripture to the church so that "the believer might exercise his or her priestly obligation in reading and learning of Him through His Word." He concludes: "The Scriptures must, therefore, be returned to the church."[5]

Far from being the creation of His disciples, as some critics argue, the Jesus of the Gospels clearly overturned and made havoc of His followers' expectations. Left to their own devices, the gospel writers would have given to the world a very different Messiah than the one they eventually came to portray. Their "Messiah" would have been at once more nationalistic, more political, and more predictable. *Their* Christ would never have shared divine honors in the way Jesus claimed to do.

R. T. France has written:

It is perhaps impossible for us, with nearly twenty centuries of familiarity with Christian doctrine, to grasp the shocking nature of this belief. But it is important to realise that no Jew would calmly listen to a man being described as divine, and it can only have been with utmost reluctance that Jesus' Jewish followers, however great their respect and love for their leader, could be brought to use such language. We are told today that incarnational language is incredible and offensive to modern man. If he with his cultural conditioning cannot take it, how hard it must have been for the first-century Jews to speak like this![6]

If the Jesus whom the world has admired for nearly two thousand years is not the real Jesus, but the creation of the early church, then what we have is a church that is greater than its Master; early committees of first-century admirers who had enough religious and literary genius for half a dozen Augustines and Shakespeares; in a word, an exciting church and a boring Jesus! However, all the evidence indicates that Jesus was not the creation of the church, but that the church was the creation of Jesus. He shaped His followers; they did not shape Him. He towered over all their later preaching and worshipping and theologizing. They lived and died proclaiming a unique life, not a splendid philosophy. And they proclaimed the "good news" about Jesus Christ the Son of God, as reliable witnesses of these things (Acts 2:32; 1 Corinthians 15:3–19; 1 John 1:1–4).

This does not mean that the true and proper New Testament revelation stops with the gospel accounts. The New Testament writers were far from thinking that Jesus' revelation was confined to His earthly words. John records Jesus telling His disciples, shortly before His passion, that His deepest, fullest teaching was yet to be given to them: "I have much more to say to you, more than you can now bear. But when he, the Spirit of truth, comes, he will guide you into all truth . . . He will bring glory to me by taking from what is mine and making it known to you" (John 16:12–14). And it is a fact which issues from this that the letters of Paul and Peter and John, for example, are not covered with quotations from Jesus' sermons and do not take the form of homilies on His parables, etc. They write fully aware of their unique status and authority in the early church, and aware too of the Spirit by which they speak and write (e.g., 1 Corinthians 2:12–13; 2 Peter 3:2, 15–16). Moreover, the burden of their message and the center of their thinking is the death and resurrection of Jesus. Jesus Himself spoke only a little on those things in His public ministry, keeping back their full significance, even from His disciples, until after the event. Thereafter, following those marvelous seminars immediately after His resurrection (e.g., Luke 24:27, 44), it is by His Spirit that Jesus deepens their understanding of His divine person and atoning work.

The ministry to which the apostles are commissioned by Jesus (Matthew 28:19–20) is open proclamation. They preach on the housetops what Jesus taught in private; they explain the Cross and what Christ's resurrection means for them and for all believers; and they preach the Son of David as the Savior of the world. What enables them to do so is their knowledge of the Jesus of the Gospels in His historic presence, the Jesus of Calvary and His meaningful death, the Jesus of Easter in His demonstrable resurrection, and their possession of the Spirit of Jesus in their ministries and His divine witness to this same Jesus as Savior and Lord. As Peter put it to the Jewish leaders: ". . . we are witnesses to these things, and so is the Holy Spirit, whom God has given to those who obey him" (Acts 5:32).

In all this Jesus remains central for reflection upon the past, for announcement in the present, and for preparation for the future. The Jesus of apostolic Christianity, and of the New Testament as a whole, is not simply a starting point, subject to later refining, but the testing point for all thinking about God, man, sin, and salvation. As P. T. Forsyth put it: "The New Testament is not the first stage of the evolution but the last phase of the revelationary fact and deed."[7] The apostolic witness in its fullness—its teaching as well as its testimony—is crucial both for the knowledge of the Christ-event and for the true understanding of that event, for "the fact without the word is dumb; and the word without the fact is empty."[8]

This book takes the New Testament writings as they stand and tries to draw together their content and their message, convinced that the Jesus of history is also the Christ of today and, as ever, the hope of the world.

As Jesus Himself is at the center of the gospel accounts, so Jesus Himself is at the beginning of the writers' testimony and reflection. We should begin, therefore, with Jesus' witness to Himself, His own self-understanding and self-revelation, and in fact this will occupy the early chapters of this book.

For Matthew, writing very much from within a Jewish mind-set and culture, the starting point is the Old Testament and Jesus' place in the historic work of God. For the Gentile Luke it is a matter of collecting materials which give an orderly account of Jesus' life (Luke 1:3), beginning with His birth and its attendant circumstances. For John, also writing for fellow Jews (John 20:31), what has already been written about Jesus' origins on earth needs to be supplemented with a statement about His origins in heaven. For Mark's brief gospel, written (like Luke's) for Gentiles, the starting point is Jesus' entrance upon His public ministry and its attendant circumstances. And here too (since this book is by a Gentile) we shall begin: namely with Jesus' baptism, temptations in the wilderness, and earliest preaching.

# PART 1

# THE DIVINE
# REVELATION

# 1

# JESUS STANDS
# AMONG US

Between Jesus' birth at Bethlehem and His passion at Jerusalem there is no more crucial or revealing incident in His recorded life than that of His baptism. In one event, and at the outset of His public ministry, God sets Him forth, though in a veiled way, as Messiah, as Son of God, and as suffering servant.

## THE BAPTISM OF JESUS

John the Baptist has been preaching "a baptism of repentance for the forgiveness of sins" (Mark 1:4). He announces that his baptism is a preparation for the appearance of the Messiah who already stands among them, unknown but ready to be revealed (John 1:26). He is greater than John, both in His person (John 1:27, 30) and in His work as baptizer with the Spirit (Mark 1:8), and as judge (Matthew 3:7–12) and Savior (John 1:29).

To this baptism Jesus comes. John, his cousin, must surely have heard from his parents, Zechariah and Elizabeth, something of the circumstances surrounding Jesus' conception and birth, which were even more remarkable than his own (Luke 1). Perhaps he also knew about Jesus' precocity in the things of God (Luke 2:46–49). Yet clearly he does not realize Jesus' full identity until it is revealed by the vision and the voice at Jesus' baptism (John 1:31–34; Matthew 3:17). Still, John feels unworthy to baptize Jesus; he does so only when Jesus insists on it as the will of God for them both (Matthew 3:14–15).

Jesus' understanding of His baptism is best approached

from the words spoken by the voice from heaven: "Thou art my beloved Son; with thee I am well pleased" (Mark 1:11, RSV). Most commentators detect in these words echoes of two Old Testament passages. The first is Isaiah 42:1, "Here is my servant, whom I uphold, my chosen one in whom I delight; I will put my Spirit on him . . ."; the second is Psalm 2:7, "I will proclaim the decree of the Lord: He said to me, 'You are my Son; today I have become your Father.'"

D. A. Carson says that Psalm 2 was "not regarded in the first century as messianic," but was clearly Davidic and "recalls other 'son' passages where David or his heir is seen as God's son. . . ." At the same time, he notes, the earlier account of the virginal conception in Matthew and Luke has already suggested "a more than titular or functional sonship."[1] William Lane writes:

> In this context "Son" is not a messianic title, but is to be understood in the highest sense, transcending messiahship. It signifies the unique relationship which Jesus sustains to the Father. . . . The first clause of the declaration (with the verb in the present tense of the indicative mood) expresses an eternal and essential relationship. The second clause (the verb is in the aorist indicative) implies a past choice for the performance of a particular function in history.[2]

The remaining phrases, "my beloved" and "with thee I am well pleased," are taken from the point in the prophecy of Isaiah where he begins his collection of "servant" prophecies that trace the course of an increasingly personalized figure from obedience and suffering to final vindication and honor (a series of "songs" that extends from chapter 42 to chapter 53).

Those prophecies, and especially the final climactic "suffering servant" song of 52:13–53:12, will recur at a number of points in Jesus' life and ministry (for example, Mark 10:45; 14:24), and will be particularly evident in some of the later apostolic teaching (e.g., Acts 8:32–35; Philippians 2:6–11; 1 Peter 1:10; 2:21–24).

The original text has "my servant . . . my chosen one in whom I delight" (Isaiah 42:1), but "my chosen" is not far from "my beloved" since in biblical language "to choose" and "to love" lie very close together (e.g., Amos 3:2). Lane notes that "beloved" can mean "only" or "unique" (e.g., Genesis 22:2, 12, 16), and believes its use in regard to Jesus indicates "an eternal and essential relationship."[3] G. R. Beasley-Murray, commenting on John 1:14, suggests that *agapētos* (*beloved*) here, is comparable with *monogonēs* (*only begotten* or, better, *only one of its kind*) there.[4] Lane connects the ideas thus: "Because you are my unique Son, I have chosen you for the task which you are about to enter."[5]

It is against the background of these words that the descent of the Spirit should be understood. In the Isaiah prophecy and the other "servant songs" that follow (Isaiah 42–53), it is because Yahweh puts His Spirit upon the chosen one that he is able to fulfill his task to "bring justice to the nations"; that is, to subdue and reconcile the whole world to God (Isaiah 42:1; cf. 11:2–4; 61:1; Luke 4:16–21). The kingdom does not come without God's king, but neither does the king extend the kingdom of God without the Spirit of God. The Spirit does not simply touch Him, it descends and remains on Him (John 1:32).

Only in the light of the Spirit's descent and the Father's words can we fully understand the messianic act of Jesus' baptism. He has come to undergo John's "baptism of repentance" not because He is a sinner needing repentance, but because He is the Servant-Son whose decreed task is to identify with sinners and to bear their sins in His own person (Isaiah 53:6–10; hence Matthew 3:15). This is the climactic revelation in the Servant Songs of Isaiah (Isaiah 52:13–53:12), and here, in the waters of an alien baptism, the sinless Son of God takes His place alongside sinners as He will one day take His place instead of them. As James Denney writes, in His baptism Jesus numbers "Himself with the transgressors, submitting to be baptised with their baptism, identifying Himself with them in their relation to God as sinners, making all their responsibilities His own." He adds, "In that hour, in the will and act of Jesus, the work of atonement was begun."[6]

In the waters of John's baptism, Jesus is *acting* Isaiah 53, even while His Father is *announcing* Isaiah 42. Jesus leaves the waters of a public baptism to begin a public ministry as God's

Servant-Son and Israel's Messiah for whom "the time leading up to the kingdom is finished, the time of the kingdom has begun" (cf. Mark 1:15). But what kind of kingdom is it, and what kind of Messiah will He be who brings it and dominates it? These are the questions that will be asked and decisively answered at the time of Jesus' temptations in the wilderness.

## JESUS' TEMPTATION IN THE WILDERNESS

The sonship announced at Jesus' baptism is both tested and vindicated at His temptation; for Jesus' sonship implies obedience as well as honor, suffering as well as joy. Matthew records that after His baptism "Jesus was led up by the Spirit into the desert to be tempted by the devil" (Matthew 4:1). Mark, in his brief notice of it, stresses the powerful, deliberate, and urgent nature of the Spirit's activity: "At once the Spirit sent him out into the desert" (Mark 1:12). Luke makes clear the Spirit's continued activity and tells us that Jesus, "full of the Holy Spirit," was not only *led up* but also *led in* the wilderness for the duration of the forty-day test (Luke 4:1).

This forty-day period obviously has symbolic significance. Moses had spent forty days on Mount Sinai (Exodus 24:18), and Elijah had trekked for forty days and forty nights to Horeb, "the [same] mountain of God" (1 Kings 19:8). However, there is a richer symbolic significance implied here. For forty years Israel as a nation had wandered in the wilderness because of the people's refusal to trust God (Numbers 14:33; Hebrews 3:17). Against that background God's Son Jesus comes to meet a test that God's son Israel (cf. Deuteronomy 8:5) failed.

The account of His temptation period in the desert could only have come to the disciples from Jesus Himself, since no one else was present. It thus gives us an early insight into Jesus' own sense of unique sonship, since He hears Satan begin the temptations with the words, "If you are the Son of God . . ." (Matthew 4:3; cf. v. 6, but for obvious reasons kept back in the last temptation, v. 9). The temptation here is not for Jesus to doubt His sonship. Satan's temptations are from the start based upon Jesus' awareness of His sonship (with its privileges and possibilities), and he seeks to use this to give them force. We would therefore translate his words, "Since you are the Son of God . . . ."

The temptations are both personal and vocational; that is, they relate both to Jesus' relationship with the Father and to His messianic task. In each of the temptations Jesus is urged not to abandon His messianic vocation, but to perform it independently, in self-will, without waiting for the Father's direction and the Spirit's guidance.

For Jesus there could be no more radical temptation than this. To yield to it would fracture the perfect unity with the Father's heart and will that Jesus maintained in all of His words and works, thoughts, and deeds. He Himself would later disclose something of that harmony and cooperation that existed between Himself and God who sent Him, His reliance upon and obedience to the Father: "I tell you the truth, the Son can do nothing by himself; he can do only what he sees his Father doing, because whatever the Father does the Son also does. . . . By myself I can do nothing; I judge only as I hear, and my judgment is just, for I seek not to please myself but him who sent me" (John 5:19, 30).

In the first temptation we have a repetition of Israel's early wilderness testing, where they were faced with hunger and no visible means of relief (Deuteronomy 8:3). This, Moses explained, was not only to teach the people to rely on God for food, but further, to teach them to recognize that even in times of plenty they were sustained not by the food (whether miraculous or natural) which God's commanding word provided, but by the powerful word which produced that food. That is, they were sustained by God, without whose will to bless nothing sustains. The provision can never substitute for the Provider, at any level. But they murmured and rebelled and missed the full blessing of the divine provision that God had prepared (Exodus 16:1–36). Jesus recognized in His hunger a repeat of the test to put one's trust in things-in-themselves, considered apart from God. But without God's blessing, life's most necessary things lose their real value and ultimate good. God must be put before food as the Provider is before the provision. For Jesus it was "God first"—God before opportunity, God before ministry, God before life itself.

In the second temptation Jesus is tempted to test God as Israel did in the wilderness at Massah (Deuteronomy 6:16), where, demanding water, they "put the Lord to the test" by saying, "Is the Lord among us or not?" (Exodus 17:2–7). This was a display not of faith, but of its opposite. So now Jesus is tempted to throw Himself down from the pinnacle of the temple (Matthew 4:5–7), to provoke a crisis that would force God's hand, to manipulate God into a display of presence and power in which the Son would dictate to the Father who sent Him, in which the Servant would control the Master and in which the onus would be placed on God to prove His reliability. However, the harmony between the Son and the Father could be maintained only in a relationship of trust which needs no test, of obedience which does not provoke (Hebrews 3:6, 10–16).

The third temptation was not, I think, as crude or as obvious as it may at first appear. To have any real force where Jesus was concerned, it must have had at least the appearance of compatibility with His messianic calling and destiny, which was to achieve world dominion (Psalm 2:7–9; 110:1; Daniel 7:14; Matthew 28:18) and consequent *shalom*. Here, in return for a certain recognition (in its first-century use *worship* may mean no more than "respect"), Satan offers to step aside, to drop all opposition to the kingdom Jesus wants to bring in, to allow the Prince of Peace unhindered sway. This is a temptation to bypass God's way of the cross for another route to world dominion, and to make the end justify the means. But the end would then not in fact be God's intended end: sin as guilt, as liability to punishment, would not have been dealt with. Some of the symptoms may have been removed by benevolent dictatorship, but the disease would have remained—and its consequences, death and hell. Jesus, however, repudiates this offer (Matthew 4:10; cf. Deuteronomy 6:13, 16), and goes on to achieve by way of the Cross the victory over sin and guilt, and all its consequences.

In choosing each of His replies from the same section of Scripture (Deuteronomy 6–8), it is clear that Jesus sees Himself not only as the Son of God in a private and personal sense, but as in some way embodying what Israel stood for in God's purposes, representing in Himself the people of God. This is the first, but not the last glimpse we will have of Jesus as more than individual in His significance. He sees Himself as God's other Israel, just as Paul will see Him as God's other Adam (Romans 5:12–21; 1 Corinthians 15:20–22, 45–49); He recapitulates in His own life the history of the chosen people, even as He begins a new history for the whole people of God (Galatians 6:15–16; Ephesians 2:11–22; 1 Peter 2:9). Where God's son Israel failed, God's Son Jesus succeeds.

## THE SINLESS LIFE

One of the most striking features of Jesus' character as we see it in the Gospels is the complete absence of any sense of personal sin. He teaches His disciples to pray, "Forgive us our trespasses . . . ," but He Himself is never found joining them in the plea. When confronted by the unbelief and hostility of His critics, He could say to them, "Can any of you prove me guilty of sin?" (John 8:46). And there the most important thing is not that they failed to contradict Him but that He challenged them to do so! No one was more sensitive to human sin or the divine holiness; yet in the same breath He affirms His truthfulness and asserts His sinlessness.

Not once do we find Him confessing, regretting, or repenting or even lamenting any moral or spiritual inadequacy. Everywhere He seems deeply content with His obedience and fully confident of the Father's complete approval of Him (e.g., Luke 2:49; John 5:17, 19, 30; 8:28, 38, 49, 54; 10:17). His guiltless conscience before God was not a peak He had climbed but a character He had maintained. Holiness was at the foundation of His being (Luke 1:35; Acts 3:14; 4:27, 30).

Even where God the Father is referred to or communed with we never find Jesus abasing Himself before the divine holiness as one unworthy to approach it: He only relates to it as one who is compatible with it (e.g., John 17). Indeed, this comprises one of the evidences that in the Gospels we do *not* have a Jesus who is the mere creation of hero-worshipping disciples and an adoring church. For in this matter, as in so much else, Jesus does not fit the conventional picture of an "ideal" saint.

All this does not mean that Jesus' obedience was mechanical or effortless. On the contrary: He grappled with temptation

(Matthew 4:1–11), He learned obedience (Hebrews 5:8), and He wrestled with the horror of Calvary as one who knew its full implications (Matthew 26:36–46). Yet in all this His saying held good, "I always do what pleases him" (John 8:29; see also John 14:30). His weapon in temptation was the Word of God (Matthew 4:4, 7, 10), and prayer showed Him the way forward in obedience (Luke 3:21–22; 9:28–29) and conflict (Luke 22:31–32, 39–46).

It is interesting that the writer of the book of Hebrews, who is unequivocally clear about our Lord's sinlessness, is equally emphatic about His qualification to minister to us in His priestly work (Hebrews 2:17–18; 4:14–16). There is no inconsistency here. Only one who has continually resisted temptation can know its maximum pressure, and on the other hand only one whom sin has not desensitized in any way can sympathize fully with us in our sufferings and failures. For our comfort we need one who knows temptation. Perhaps that is why the disciples who walked with Him left us a testimony, artless in its truthfulness, of one who was different without being distant; who does not join us on our knees as a penitent, but who can lift us off our knees as forgiven sinners—Jesus, our righteousness and our atonement.

I said earlier that in choosing the Deuteronomy texts for His replies to Satan, Jesus was indicating a consciousness that in Him, as in a new Israel, God's purposes for His people would be fulfilled. This sense of not only being *at* a new point in history, but of being *in Himself* a new point in history, is found throughout His ministry.

## JESUS AND HISTORY

However cursory, any study of the Gospels must see that Jesus assumed a role in human history that was extraordinary. For instance, He saw the entire history of His own people, Israel, as leading up to His coming, and stood forth as the one whose advent brought centuries of prophecy to its summation. He assured His disciples: "For I tell you the truth, many prophets and righteous men longed to see what you see but did not see it, and to hear what you hear but did not hear it" (Matthew 13:17). To His critics who so revered Moses' law, but who challenged Jesus at every turn, He said, "If you believed Moses, you would believe me, for he wrote about me" (John 5:46). After His resurrection He instructed His disciples in the whole matter of prophecy and fulfillment in a way He could not do until all had been fulfilled at Calvary and the empty tomb: "And beginning with Moses and all the Prophets, he explained to them what was said in all the Scriptures concerning himself" (Luke 24:27).

Jesus also saw Himself as not only summing up the past, but also determining the future. What remains to be fulfilled will be fulfilled by Him and through Him (Matthew 5:17–18). The most momentous example of this is the final day of judgment at the end of world history as we know it. Throughout the Old Testament, universal judgment had been the prerogative of God, who alone could assume the role of "judge of all the earth." However, in Jesus' teaching the Old Testament "Day of the Lord" becomes the "day" of the "coming of the Son of Man": "Therefore keep watch, because you do not know on what day your Lord will come . . . because the Son of Man will come at an hour when you do not expect him" (Matthew 24:42, 44).

On that awful day *He* will sit on the judgment seat of God: "When the Son of Man comes in his glory, and all the angels with him, he will sit on his throne in heavenly glory. All the nations will be gathered before him, and he will separate the people one from another . . ." (Matthew 25:31–32). On that day men will be judged according to their relationship with Him. By the presence or absence of such a relationship they will be justified or condemned: "I tell you, whoever acknowledges me before men, the Son of Man will also acknowledge him before the angels of God. But he who disowns me before men will be disowned before the angels of God" (Luke 12:8–9).

Such was Jesus' view of the past and the future in relation to Himself that He did not so much see Himself as having a destiny in the world as the world having a destiny in Him. In this, as in so much else, His self-understanding surpasses our categories. He certainly had a mission (Luke 12:50), but ultimately it was not so much that He *had* a goal as that He *was* the goal. To quote the ringing words of C. F. D. Moule, Jesus confronts each generation in the same way—"familiar yet startling, recognizable yet always transcending recognition, always ahead, as well as abreast: the ultimate from whom each generation is equidistant."[7]

Jesus' sense of His own uniqueness in human history and in the history of God's dealings with the entire human race comes out in a variety of ways in His teaching about the kingdom of God. Mark informs us that after John the Baptist was arrested, "After John was put in prison, Jesus went into Galilee, proclaiming the good news of God" (Mark 1:14); Matthew (Matthew 4:17, 23) and Luke (Luke 4:43) make the same point. John had also preached the good news of the imminent coming of the kingdom of God (Matthew 3:1–2; Luke 3:18), but what was quite distinctive about Jesus was the way He linked the kingdom to His own person. We will consider this subject in some detail, but first we must take note of Jesus' announcement of the arrival and nature of the kingdom that had come with Himself.

## JESUS ANNOUNCES
## HIS PROGRAM AT NAZARETH

In the synagogue at Nazareth Jesus sounds the keynote and character of His public ministry. There He reads—with certain modifications—from the opening verses of Isaiah 61:

> The Spirit of the Lord is on me, because he has anointed me to preach good news to the poor. He has sent me to proclaim freedom for the prisoners and recovery of sight for the blind, to release the oppressed, to proclaim the year of the Lord's favor.

These words have been called a sort of manifesto, a programmatic statement. They announce how far the salvation that is proclaimed will extend, into how many areas of human need and human failure. As elsewhere in Luke's gospel, Jesus speaks of a salvation that touches and transforms every aspect of life so that what has been corrupted, damaged, or disjointed becomes cleansed and healed and set free. The poor, the oppressed, and the outsiders are particularly in view here as illustrating what happens to a spoiled world in the "year of the Lord's favor" (Isaiah 61:2).

"The year of the Lord's favor" is an allusion to the Levitical law concerning every fiftieth year in Israel. It was to be known as the year of Jubilee, a year in which fields were to be fallow, property alienated by debt was to be restored to its original owner or his heirs, debts were to be canceled, and slaves were to be set free (Leviticus 25:8–55). Thus was every Israelite to have access again to his birthright in God.

It was the perfect picture of restoration and a new beginning for a world that sin had spoiled, in which the whole human race had lost its privilege in God, and where hope could come only from the outside and from a power that made "all things new." It spoke of a salvation that restored men and women to lives of dignity and purpose in spiritual and physical and socioeconomic terms. Jesus had come to achieve in principle and to initiate in practice a new order in which His followers would participate: loving their enemies, sharing with the needy, taking the side of the oppressed, and giving a share to the outsider. In this way His followers could become agents of reconciliation and restoration.

However, in a fallen world even Scripture is not safe from misunderstanding and misuse, and Jesus' hearers in the synagogue at Nazareth may well have understood His Old Testament text in a very different way and expected a very different sermon on it. Palestine at this time was no pastoral idyll, filled with kindly spiritually minded heirs of the prophets. Under Roman domination it was a cauldron seething with social tension and political unrest, and Galilee in particular was rife with revolutionaries and apocalyptic thinkers. And the villagers of Nazareth were no exception. Consequently, when the synagogue congregation sat down to hear Jesus' application of a well-known passage from the prophet Isaiah, they had certain expectations. And Jesus disappointed every one of them—and more!

Isaiah lived at a time when other Gentile superpowers dominated the earth. His words in the later chapters of his prophecy are given to comfort the Jews who would return from their Babylonian exile, restored to their promised land, but still mourning a lost freedom, still under a foreign yoke. Isaiah prophesies a complete reversal of this situation: a time that would be not only "the year of the Lord's favor," but also "the day of vengeance of our God" (Isaiah 61:2), and a time when foreigners would serve the people of God. Against this background, what sentiments would this prophecy evoke in Jesus' audience? Probably "the text would be heard in a similar way in the first century A.D.; [however] the audience would be expecting release from Roman, not Babylonian, domination."[8]

It is this expectation that would have made the passage Jesus chose so acceptable to His Galilean congregation ("The eyes of everyone in the synagogue were fastened on him," Luke 4:20). However, what follows confounds all expectations and outrages all popular instinct.

First of all, as well as adding a line from Isaiah 58:6 ("to set the oppressed free")—which in its context ("and break every yoke") must have increased political expectations—Jesus ends the larger quotation from Isaiah 61 halfway through a statement, stopping short of the very words political extremists used to justify their violence. The original prophecy reads, "to proclaim the year of the Lord's favor and *the day of vengeance of our God*," and according to the rules of Hebrew parallelism this second clause belongs essentially to the first. However, not only does Jesus omit any reference to God's judgment on Israel's enemies, He goes on to remind His hearers of God's compassion towards those considered outsiders (Luke 4:25–27). The result, as recorded by Luke, has often been found puzzling. In verse 21 we have rapt attention, in verse 22 we *seem* to have admiration, but by verse 28 we have opposition, and furious opposition at that! D. J. Bosch writes:

> These circumstances have prompted B. Violet and particularly Joachim Jeremias to suggest that the key to the entire enigma of interpreting the Nazareth episode should be looked for in the dramatic way in which the reading from Isaiah 61 is terminated just before the reference to the day of vengeance and the portrayal of the hoped-for-reversal— for which the entire congregation must have been waiting. Jesus does the unimaginable by omitting this . . . Jeremias

therefore takes a fresh look at verse 22—which is usually interpreted in terms of a very positive response to Jesus—and retranslates it as follows, "They protested with one voice and were furious, because he only spoke about (God's year of) mercy (and omitted the words about the Messianic vengeance)."[9]

Such retranslation of Luke 4:22 is not so drastic as might at first appear. The Greek verb generally translated "all spoke well of him" is literally "all bore witness to him," and the verb can mean either to affirm or praise someone or to witness against him, to condemn. Hence we might understand it, "And everyone condemned him."

I. H. Marshall notes: "The parallel narrative in Mark suggests that the attitude at Nazareth was one of uniform hostility."[10] He notes too that the verb "were amazed" (Gk. *thaumazō*) "can express both admiration (7:9) and opposition" (John 7:15; cf. Luke 11:38), and agrees with others that "the point may be that Jesus' words were purely gracious; he omitted reference to the vengeance of God."[11] Then the point would be that everyone heard Him and was horrified that He announced the revolution but spoke nothing about judgment, vengeance, and retribution on the Roman oppressors. It was all mercy, peace, and blessing, to Roman as well as to Jew. It was presumptuous and utterly unpatriotic—an insult to His class and upbringing ("Isn't this Joseph's son?"), and "they got up, [and] drove him out of the town . . ." (4:22, 29). Jesus' preaching nearly cost Him His life at the very beginning (v. 29), but the time was not yet come (v. 30).

Unusual as Jeremias's rendering is, Bosch remarks that it is "probably the only translation that helps us make sense of what Luke writes about the events in the Nazareth synagogue,"[12] where the crowd, if the usual English translations are followed, moves unaccountably from pleasure to fury in a very short space of time. Bosch further notices that elsewhere in Luke Jesus sets aside references to vengeance when quoting Old Testament passages that contain a mixture of grace and judgment (e.g., 7:22, quoting Isaiah 35:5–6; 29:18 and 61:1).[13] It was not *this* coming of Jesus that was intended to fulfill such warnings of impending judgment (see John 3:16–18; 5:22, 28). For Jesus'

hearers, and for those who had yet to hear, this was a year of
grace, a time of amnesty and reprieve. He had come "not to
condemn" the Gentile world, including the Romans, but "that
the world might be saved through him" (John 3:17, RSV). It was
not *this* kind of universal Messiah that the revolutionaries of
first-century Palestine wanted. However, for Luke and for us,
gospel ministry is a ministry of reconciliation and peace; it is
good news (Luke 3:18); and it is good news to all men (Luke
2:10, 14). The first words of Jesus' public ministry are words of
forgiveness and healing. The day of grace has dawned, the
"year of the Lord's favor." The kingdom of God is come.

# 2

# JESUS AND
# THE KINGDOM OF GOD

Today it is hard for us to talk about kings and kingdoms. We find the notion of absolute rule questionable, even repugnant, because it is generally linked in our minds with tinpot dictators or with revolutionary tyrants or with monarchs and warmongers of the past. We are perhaps willing to speak of national sovereignty because that has a democratic flavor: it is a shared sovereignty. However, democracy too has its evils and only works effectively insofar as men and women share, at least to some extent, the same fundamental standards and the same ultimate goals. Because we are taught to look no higher than mankind and its own resources, we are content to make do with this.

God, however, disturbs our complacent satisfaction and reminds us that He is king, lord, and judge, that we must all be judged by Him, by His truth, and by His standards. He challenges our whole world *now*, by the presence and power (and persistence, against all odds) of His kingdom, which is in fact His own kingly activity in salvation and judgment by Jesus Christ. This activity began with the first coming of Christ, is maintained by His present life "at the right hand of God," and will be consummated by His second coming in full and final judgment and salvation.

It is of great importance, then, that as Christians who want to understand God's ways in Christ we hear the biblical teaching about the kingdom of God.

The term "the kingdom of God," and its more Jewish equivalent "the kingdom of heaven," occurs some sixty times in the first three Gospels. It is obviously at the center of Jesus' message and ministry. The actual term "the kingdom of God" is not used in the Old Testament, but what does occur very clearly and frequently is the idea that God, Yahweh, is king: He, and He alone, not only in Israel but throughout the earth. This is its hope and its judgment (Psalm 97:1; 99:1). It is this which gives meaning to life, even in a world where chaos and tyranny seem to reign. Hence even in Babylon, where the chosen people are in exile and the heathen have power, the sovereignty of God is known to Daniel and vindicated in his visions (Daniel 2:21, 31–35, 44–45; 7:13–14).

However, we live in a world in open rebellion against God, a place where His rule is often exercised in a hidden manner: guiding those who do not acknowledge Him, overruling those who do evil, sustaining a damaged creation, and calling men and women to repentance and faith. In such a situation the rule of God has a future aspect which is "not yet" and which is not easily seen, even in its beginnings.

## "THE DAY OF THE LORD"

The prophets of the Old Testament period received promises about the time when Yahweh would affirm and establish His rule in a new way; when He would reign in a new situation in the world; one where sin would finally be judged and harmony be fully restored to His world. Here something of the essential content of the term "the kingdom of God" appears vividly and frequently in the term "the Day of the Lord" and in related phrases such as "in that day."

That "day" will be a time of particular and personal intervention by God in human affairs and in Israel's history (Isaiah 40:3–5, 9–11): a time of widespread judgment (Isaiah 2:12–21; Amos 5:18–20; Zechariah 14:1–9) and worldwide renewal (Isaiah 65:17–25; 66:10–24). It will be a day in which the nations also turn to Him, a day and a time characterized by righteousness and peace. Present and interim judgments and deliverances (also called "the Day of the Lord"; e.g., Isaiah 13; Ezekiel 30; Joel 1, 2) anticipate this final settlement and remind men that the God of history will one day wind up history, and is even now working towards that end.

*[handwritten margin note: maybe, 6 days of creation also]*

The term *day* should not be misunderstood. What is meant is an event rather than a date. It is used to single out the whole period of which it speaks, to mark it off and to set it apart from other times, to give it a specific identity because of what will be specially done in that time. The length of the day is not important. The Hebrews saw time in terms of content rather than duration, in terms of what was done rather than how many weeks or months or years passed. "The Day of the Lord" is therefore a period of time characterized by God's special activity: it is the day of His coming, the day of His power in judgment and blessing.

The ultimate purpose of the Day of the Lord is the establishment of the kingdom of God on earth, and its supreme characteristic is that Yahweh comes *in person* to do this. The coming of the kingdom is unthinkable without the coming of the king. It is by God's intervention, not man's evolution, that the age of peace and prosperity dawns. G. R. Beasley-Murray writes: "There could never have been a stage in Israel's history when the kingdom of God was looked for apart from the coming of Yahweh," and notes the widespread conviction of Old Testament scholars that the coming of Yahweh is the central idea of Old Testament eschatology and the final character of all salvation.[1]

However, along with this there gradually emerges the revelation that an anointed King, a Messiah, will appear who is uniquely related both to God and men, the representative of Yahweh and the instrument of his rule (Isaiah 7;14; 9:6–7; 11:1–10). This does not seem to diminish the personal element in God's involvement. Beasley-Murray notes:

> If we further ponder such statements as that in Zechariah 9:9 ("Behold, your king comes to you") in relation to Isaiah 40:9 ("Behold your God . . . comes with might"), there seems some justification for the view of H. H. Wolff that *the Messiah is the form of the appearance of Yahweh the Lord* [emphasis added].[2]

Finally, the emphasis is clearly on kingship rather than kingdom; that is, on the *activity* of ruling rather than denoting a restricted *area* that is ruled. The idea is of a dynamic sovereignty rather than a limited geographical sphere. R. T. France observes: "It is remarkable how often in Jesus' teaching 'the kingdom of God' is the subject of an active verb—it is in itself a dynamic agent, not the result of someone else's action."[3] It is "near" and "at hand"; it "has come upon you"; it "does not come with observation"; it is "in power"; the disciples are taught to pray "your kingdom come"; elsewhere it is likened to yeast spreading, a seed growing, a new trawling, and the general impression is that *we* do not bring in the kingdom of God, but rather the kingdom of God brings *us* in. We can see it, enter it, receive it, belong to it, but we do not manufacture it or produce it, either by social or by spiritual programs. It is not an achievement of man but an activity of God in which we are the achievement.

When Jesus appeared in public He began His ministry by announcing: "The time has come. . . . The kingdom of God is near"(Mark 1:15). "The time" is of course the time of Old Testament expectation, the time of promise before fulfillment, the time of waiting for the kingdom to come. "Accordingly," concludes Beasley-Murray, "if the time leading up to the kingdom is *finished*, the time of the kingdom has *begun*." He continues:

> It is important to stress that it is the beginning of the kingly rule, the royal working of God, that is in view in the saying. Jesus is not so much proclaiming an end as a beginning in the initiation of that sovereign action of God which brings with it salvation, and is to end in a transformed universe. The royal rule of God has begun, because God has "come" to do his saving work.[4]

Jesus' statement, says France, is a "declaration of arrival, not just of imminence."[5] The main point "is not the precise timescale, but the fact that it is in the coming of Jesus that we are to see God's revolution taking place. Indeed, it is in Jesus that we are to see God coming as king."[6]

When we understand this we can see why Jesus saw the kingdom of God as both *present* in His ministry of mighty works and preaching (Matthew 11:5–6; 12:28) and *future*, at the harvest of the world at the end of the age (Matthew 13:24–30), when He, the Son of Man, would come again in His glory (Matthew 25:31). In Jesus God had already come to establish and work out His reign in grace: it was from the start, and would be until the final judgment, "the acceptable year of the Lord" (Luke 4:19, RSV). Its fullness, however, lies in the future (Matthew 19:28–30), the church's goal and her inheritance (Acts 14:22; 1 Corinthians 15:50; 2 Timothy 4:1).

## THE KINGDOM OF GOD AS PRESENT

"The foundational element in the teaching of Jesus relating to the kingdom of God," writes Beasley-Murray, is that Jesus "affirms its presence in the world in and through his word and work."[7] What God had long since promised to do by His coming, Jesus had begun by His coming and appearance. The sovereign work of Yahweh, which was to defeat all evil and overcome all opposition and achieve a transformed earth, had been decisively inaugurated by Jesus in His powerful deeds and authoritative words.

Hence Jesus could say to His critics, "If I drive out demons by the Spirit of God, then the kingdom of God has come upon you" (Matthew 12:28). In His power over the demons, as in His preaching of emancipation and redemption to those oppressed by sin and sickness and deprivation—preaching that was accompanied by effective deed (Matthew 11:4–5; Luke 4:18–21)—Jesus demonstrated the rule of God in salvation and judgment. The kingdom of God had begun even in the world of the Fall and its consequences: the restoration of all things was at hand; the hope of generations was now a present reality (Matthew 13:16–17).

However, there was a shadow side even to this, a shadow cast by unbelief and rejection. From the start Jesus warned that even among the custodians of God's age-old promise there would be many who would never taste the sweetness of the kingdom about which they had boasted, and that it would be enjoyed by others, long dismissed as unworthy: Gentiles, publicans, and sinners (Luke 4:23–30). From the least expected quarters, as well as from the world at large, it would be violently opposed (Matthew 11:12). To Pharisees who questioned His claims about the kingdom of God, Jesus replied: "The kingdom of God is within you" (Luke 17:20–21). The Greek word commonly translated "within" or "in the midst" or "among" probably means, as G. R. Beasley-Murray argues, that the kingdom of God was "within their reach."[8]

Despite His repeated and solemn warnings to those who turn the word of grace into a word of judgment by their unbelief, Jesus presented a kingdom message essentially of joy. It is the "good news" of the kingdom, and the good news is that it is offered to "the poor." It is the treasure hidden in a field, the pearl of great value, and those to whom it is offered are happy to pay any price for it (Matthew 13:44–46). The joy of receiving it is a joy shared by God Himself: indeed it is *His* joy in us becoming one with our joy in Him (Luke 15:7, 10, 23–24).

Yet even in this high key of joy, the harsh realities of resentment and unbelief cannot be ignored, and those who are offended by Jesus' eating with "tax collectors and 'sinners'" (Luke 15:1–2) are warned by the self-exclusion of the elder son who "refused to go in" (Luke 15:28) that they too will be excluded at the messianic banquet at the end of the age—an event that is already anticipated by Jesus' action as the representative of God eating and drinking with the "unworthy," who nevertheless receive His word of salvation gladly (Luke 7:34). These people, though late in repentance and faith, are met with all the rich grace of God. They *are* "last"; they *shall* be "first." A full day's wages will be given to them though they come late in the day (Matthew 20:1–16). Such people are being effectively called into God's great marriage feast, whatever others do with their invitations (Matthew 22:14).

What runs through all these parables and sayings is the implication that the kingdom of God, so long promised and expected, is *even now* present in Jesus' words and deeds, and Jesus' hearers are being challenged to appropriate its blessings now. If they do not do so now, they never will. It is now or never, for it is Jesus or no one. Hence when an enthusiast cries out, "Blessed is he who shall eat bread in the kingdom of God!" (Luke 14:15, RSV), Jesus immediately tells a parable about temporizing and procrastination. This is the parable of the great banquet where those originally invited to the feast excused themselves in various ways and were replaced by "the poor and maimed and blind and lame" (Luke 14:16–24, RSV; cf. Matthew 22:1–14). The point, not to say the sting of the story, is well made by E. Linneman:

> The Pharisees do not believe that the kingdom of God is beginning *now*, and see no connection between this event and Jesus' table fellowship with the lost. But Jesus places the situation in the light of a parable in which some people are not prepared to respect the fact that *the meal has already begun*, and have to put up with the consequences. Anyone who is not willing to be summoned to the first course does not get to taste the meal proper.[9]

The growth and spread of the kingdom is related in the twin parables of the mustard seed that became a great bush and the leaven that filled the dough with its energy (Matthew 13:31–33). The small beginnings of the kingdom and its unlikely form must not be allowed to obscure the fact that God has begun a work of unstoppable energy and force. The very important parable of the sower (Matthew 13:1–9), explained so clearly by Jesus to His disciples (Matthew 13:18–23), recognizes the indifference and unbelief, the distractions and the temporary enthusiasm with which the preaching of the gospel of the kingdom (the seed sown) will be met. But because God is at work in unvanquishable and sovereign grace, the full harvest at the end of the age will abundantly make up for all lost effort (Matthew 13:23; Mark 4:20; Luke 8:8).

## THE KINGDOM OF GOD AS FUTURE

It is clear from many of Jesus' sayings and parables already touched upon that the present manifestations of the kingdom of God do not exhaust its power or potential. On the contrary, they point to a future coming of the kingdom when God's reign of grace shall be more widely, even universally demonstrated, unhindered and fully victorious. Yet the kingdom of God spoken of in future terms is still the same kingdom as that inaugurated by Jesus at His first coming. The future must not be thought of as superseding Jesus Christ in any way or as setting aside His present work. In that future He Himself will bring to a climax what He has already begun. For that climax the whole New Testament church is taught to look and pray and work.

At the center of the Lord's Prayer is the central petition of the waiting church: "Your kingdom come" (Matthew 6:10). The entire prayer may be seen as ordered around that petition. D. A. Carson notes that Jews of Jesus' day

> recited "Qaddish" ("Sanctification"), an ancient Aramaic prayer, at the close of each synagogue service. In its oldest extant form, it runs, "Exalted and *hallowed* be his great name in the world which he created according to his will. *May he let his kingdom rule* in your lifetime and in your days and in the lifetime of the whole house of Israel, speedily and soon. And to this, say: amen." . . . But the Jew looked forward to the kingdom, whereas the reader of Matthew's Gospel, while looking forward to its consummation, perceives that the kingdom has already broken in and prays for its extension as well as for its unqualified manifestation.[10]

As the petition in this way unites present and future, so it looks forward to a uniting of heaven and earth. Of this Beasley-Murray writes:

> Heaven has already invaded the earth in the mission of Jesus; here he is praying for a completion of what God has begun in him, for a securing of this purpose to unite heaven and earth. As H. Traub has expressed it, "Not only does the Mathaean formula comprehend heaven and earth, it also implies a new interrelation of heaven and earth effected by God's saving action . . . [by which] the saving work of Jesus Christ has replaced the division of heaven and earth."[11]

This future gaze is prominent in the Beatitudes too. The children of the kingdom are variously described as "the poor in spirit," "the meek," "the pure in heart," "those . . . persecuted because of righteousness," etc. The promise of the kingdom at its coming is that they "will be comforted," "will inherit the earth," "will see God," and will receive their reward (Matthew 5:3–12).

That final consummation of what has already begun is also described by Jesus as a feast (Matthew 8:11) at which believing Jew and believing Gentile alike shall share with Abraham, Isaac, and Jacob, but from which the unbelieving, even among the Jews, even though they be leaders of Israel, will be excluded (Matthew 8:11–12; cf. Luke 13:28–30; Matthew 21:31; 23:13–14, 34–36). This "belief," in the context in which Jesus is speaking here, is clearly and necessarily oriented around Himself (see Matthew 8:5–10). It is impossible to "believe" in the kingdom of God while rejecting the one God has sent to inaugurate it: "I say to you that many will come from the east and the west, and will take their places at the feast with Abraham, Isaac and Jacob in the kingdom of heaven. But the subjects of the kingdom will be thrown outside, into the darkness, where there will be weeping and gnashing of teeth" (Matthew 8:11–12). "The shock of this saying is difficult for us to imagine," says Beasley-Murray. He explains why it was such an unexpected thing to say:

> It was axiomatic for the Jews of Jesus' time that the kingdom of God belonged to them. It was an exercise of charity on their part to contemplate the possibility of Gentiles being admitted to the kingdom promised to them, but to think of the Gentiles *replacing* them in the kingdom of God was incomprehensible.[12]

Jesus frequently points to a future climax in history that intensifies His urgent calls to decision and action. The coming of the Son of Man will be unexpected and unpredictable, like a thief in the night (Matthew 24:42–44). Elsewhere, and changing the focus and metaphor, Jesus urges His church to be ready as the friends of the bride are alert for the coming of the bridegroom (Matthew 25:1–13). Those who are not shall have no part in the joy to come. Elsewhere the lesson is taught that those who receive the gifts of the kingdom must accept its obligations too. If the good of the kingdom is like treasure in a field or a pearl of great price, then when it is possessed it must be used well and wisely. To utterly neglect or abuse it is not truly to possess it at all. These are the lessons of Matthew's parable of the talents (Matthew 25:14–30) and Luke's parable of the pounds (Luke 19:11–27). Like others, they speak of the presence of the kingdom in the light of the future of the kingdom.

From its climactic future, however, the kingdom reaches backward into the present with extraordinary signs. After warning of future judgment when the Son of Man comes "in his Father's glory" (Mark 8:38), Jesus adds: "I tell you the truth, some who are standing here will not taste death before they see the kingdom of God come with power" (Mark 9:1). To those who interpret this and similar statements to mean that Jesus mistakenly thought the kingdom of God was going to come in its fullness within His own generation, D. A. Carson makes the shrewd point: "If Matthew believed that . . . was what Jesus meant, we would expect a Gospel full of the Thessalonian heresy, loaded with expectation of the Second Coming because few of the first generation would still be alive."[13] Instead, we have hints of delay in the very parables which urge watchfulness (e.g., Matthew 25:5, 19), and we have Jesus' promise that he will be with those who "make disciples of all nations . . . to the very end of the age" (Matthew 28:19–20).

The future aspect of the kingdom of God is strikingly brought out in a number of the Son of Man sayings, many of which we examine more closely elsewhere in this book. The Son of Man who feasts with "sinners" (Matthew 11:19; Luke 7:34) and who is introduced as a glutton and a drunkard is in fact anticipating the coming feast of the kingdom. In this inauguration of that final blessedness He shall sit "on his glorious throne" in heavenly splendor, with His apostles sitting as assessors in court as Israel is judged (Matthew 19:28). Now the mediator of the kingdom of God appears in lowliness and humiliation; then He will appear in the glory of divine sovereignty (Mark 14:62; cf. Daniel 7:13–14).

## THE KINGDOM AND THE CHURCH

It should be clear by now that the church is not identical with the kingdom of God: nor is there anything the church can do or achieve. The kingdom of God is a larger (and another) concept than the church. The church is the *product* of the kingdom, the *channel* of the kingdom, and the *community* of the kingdom. In the church the kingdom demonstrates its presence and its potency. In the church it also proclaims the future. As D. A. Carson writes: "So far as the kingdom has been inaugurated in advance of its consummation, so far also is Jesus' church an outpost in history of the final eschatological community."[14]

Because of all this, the church finds itself at all times speaking of the kingdom of God under two aspects. In the first sense it is here "already," and in the second it is still in the future and "not yet." It is in the world and moving *through* the world, but it has not *filled up* the world. It is changing lives and building a church; it is also touching the world at many points, yet not transforming the world, which remains stubbornly the world of the Fall, resisting its Savior and refusing His kingdom. As the kingdom grows in the world, it brushes against institutions, law-making bodies and societies, and "salts" them with its influence, stemming their corruption and fostering their sense of responsibility. Still, it does not yet sweep the earth clean of corruption. If it did, it would sweep the world clean of mankind!

As yet, we live in "the times between" the first and second coming of our Lord Jesus Christ: a time of patience and entreaty (2 Peter 3:9); a time when a new church is being built, but not yet a new world; new people, but not yet a new society at large. The effects of the kingdom of God in society point men and women to God's future, but they do not substitute for God's future. Even the effects of the kingdom in the church do not do that.

For the church and in the church, which is the community of the kingdom and its agent in the world of men, the kingdom is "here" to a greater extent—that is, in greater intensity and power—than in the world at large. Its powers are available to the church and put forth in her more consistently and more largely than anywhere else on earth. Yet even for the church the kingdom has not yet come in fullness, and every day those of the church pray, "Your kingdom come," with longing and with expectation.

The kingdom of God must not be divorced from history, confined within history, nor confused with history. It is not constructed from the materials of this world (its politics, sociology, resources, changes, etc.). Indeed, its origins are in another world. But it does come into this world and touches its people and its politics, its societies, and its sociologies. It does this through the salting and lighting influence of its own people (Matthew 5:13–16): the people of God, the followers of Christ, the sons and daughters of the kingdom.

Yet these people, however closely identified with people in the world at large, are also separate from the world (John 15:19; 17:15–18); identified with its needs, but separate from its conspiracy to keep God out of its solutions! Hence, at one and the same time, we are the world's friends and its critics. We must make the best of what is and what is not, and still cry, "This is not enough!" We are indeed to be occupied in this world, but not preoccupied with it, "For this world in its present form is passing away" (1 Corinthians 7:31).

In his book *The Bible in Politics*, Richard Bauckham sums up Jesus' work during His public ministry in this way: "Jesus in his ministry proclaimed the coming Kingdom of God and *practised its presence.* That is, he anticipated the future hope of the unrestricted, uncontested sovereignty of God, by extending God's rule in the present and inviting people to live within it."[15]

The effects of God's rule practiced in this way were, in relation to :

- demonic oppression, conquest;
- misrepresentation of God's rule, sharp rebuke;
- selfish complacency, warning;
- sin and failure, forgiveness and assurance of love;
- sickness, healing;
- material need, provision of daily bread;
- exclusion, welcoming inclusion;
- desire for power, an example of humble and loving service;
- death, life;
- false peace, painful division, but in relation to enmity, reconciliation.[16]

These are to be the relationships that characterize the church in the world: touching the untouchables, including the excluded, confronting the powers that keep people from God, modeling the life of the kingdom of God in our church communities—communities of reconciled people in societies of alienated people; communities of caring people in a world of individuals too preoccupied to care; communities of love and peace, encouragement and strength, commitment and loyalty. As Eddie Gibbs puts it: "The Church is more than the herald announcing the message, it is a demonstration model which gives credence to the effectiveness of that message."[17] This is the life of the kingdom. Such a life may at present be only partially and imperfectly grasped and lived; it might appear weak and irrelevant to the world. But it was and is a mustard-seed beginning of a mighty future, a parable of what would be; small steps towards a great destiny—for "the meek" shall "inherit the earth" at the coming of their King.

# 3

# JESUS AND
# THE HOLY SPIRIT

The Holy Spirit is God-next-to-us. Every time in sensitivity and faith we hear God speaking, it is the Spirit who is working. Every time we respond to God's love in the gospel with joy and faithful obedience, it is the Spirit who is blessing. Every time we take that gospel—the good news about Jesus—to others with courage and love, it is the Spirit who is moving out into the world—through us!

The story of the church is the story of the Holy Spirit's presence and activity. It is, I know, the story of much else too: of hypocrisy and apathy, of corruption and cowardice, of high ideals and low achievements. Yet it is the continuing story of the Holy Spirit's power and persistence, without which there would be no church. And the story of each believer is, similarly, the story of the undeserved privilege of being "the place wherein the Holy Spirit makes His dwelling," living in closest proximity and infinite patience with us in our slight faith and poor obedience. However, we tend to respond to this with a diminishing sense of wonder and an increasing accommodation to the standards of the world around us, looking to "the main chance" instead of "looking to Jesus the pioneer and perfecter of our faith" (Hebrews 12:2, RSV). As John V. Taylor has put it:

Few are they who, after their first awakening, dare trust the Spirit to carry them by way of the wilderness and the dark night into a widening freedom and availability until the manhood of Christ Himself is formed in them. . . . He has made us little lower than gods, while our highest ambition is to be a little above the Joneses.[1]

In Jesus, however, we see the Spirit's willing and perfect agent, even as we see Jesus Himself work by the Spirit as His willing and mighty instrument. The cooperation between the Son and the Spirit is the counterpart of the cooperation between the Father and the Son. And by the grace of the now-exalted Christ and the fellowship of the Holy Spirit, even as we look "with unveiled faces" upon "the Lord's glory" in the historical Jesus, we, even we, can still be "transformed into his likeness with ever-increasing glory" (2 Corinthians 3:18).

The question has often been asked: Why is there so little about the Holy Spirit in the Gospels when so much attention is given to Him later in the New Testament? Why is so little said about the Spirit's work in the life of Jesus when the early church was intoxicated with the experience of the Spirit? The question is a valid one, but it should certainly not be allowed to obscure the very important material that we have not only in John's gospel, but also in that of Luke, who has been called "the theologian of the Holy Spirit" and who portrays the earthly ministry of Jesus in terms of the initiative and guidance of the Spirit from the start (Luke 3:22; 4:1, 14, 18, etc.).

There are a number of reasons why the Spirit is less prominent in the Gospels than in Acts or in the Epistles. Firstly, the undisputed focus of attention has to be Jesus Himself. He is God's mightiest act in human history because he is God's personal and unique entrance into human history. He is Immanuel—"God with us"—sent for our salvation (Matthew 1:23). He is not, therefore, to be understood simply as a man full of the Holy Spirit of God. As C. K. Barrett points out, the ancient world had any number of "spiritual men," whether Hebrew prophets or Greek seers.[2] Jesus understood Himself to be far more than a man filled with the Spirit. He, in His own person, was God's decisive deed, the fulfillment of prophecy and the hope of the world.

Furthermore, as Barrett notes:

Direct emphasis upon the Spirit had to be avoided also because Jesus was keeping His Messiahship secret; to have claimed a pre-eminent measure of the Spirit would have been to make an open confession of Messiahship, if, as seems to have been the case, there was a general belief that the Messiah would be a bearer of God's Spirit.[3]

Thirdly, as we shall see later, the gift of the Spirit is crucially related to Jesus' glorification at the right hand of God, and is part of the reward of His sufferings. That is why in the Upper Room discourse, where Jesus speaks most fully about the Holy Spirit, His references are repeatedly to a future coming. Correspondingly, as far as the church after Pentecost is concerned, the Spirit "had not been given" in the time of Jesus' earthly ministry—that is, it had not been poured out fully and universally upon the church—because Jesus had not yet been glorified (John 7:39). Hence Jesus Himself has little to say about the Spirit until near the time of His passion. There is, indeed, a sense of timing about much of the Lord's teaching in the Gospels. Many things wait to be explained, because only after the critical events of His death and resurrection are they capable of full explanation (John 16:12–15).

However, what references we do have in regard to the earthly life of Jesus are of such significance that it becomes immediately clear that we cannot understand His life apart from the Holy Spirit. This is true right from the start.

## THE HOLY SPIRIT'S WORK
## AT THE CONCEPTION OF JESUS

We learn from both Matthew and Luke that the Holy Spirit was personally and uniquely active at the conception of Jesus. It was by His creative activity that Mary conceived without any other human participation in the procreative act. In Luke's account, Gabriel announces to Mary: "The Holy Spirit will come upon you, and the power of the Most High will overshadow you. So the holy one to be born will be called the Son of God" (Luke 1:35). In Matthew's account of the appearance of "an angel of the Lord" to Joseph, the angel (presumably Gabriel again) explains to the worried Joseph: "Joseph son of David, do not be afraid to take Mary home as your wife, because what is conceived in her is from the Holy Spirit" (Matthew 1:20).

Both accounts of the virginal conception of Jesus are clear and emphatic on this. The prediction in Luke that the Holy Spirit will *overshadow* Mary recalls the reference in Genesis 1 to the Spirit of God "moving over the face of the waters" of the original chaos, about to create life and growth and form at God's command. This leads Barrett to write:

> Just as the Spirit of God was active at the foundation of the world, so that Spirit was to be expected also at its renewal. . . . The part played by the Holy Spirit in the birth narratives is thus seen to be the fulfillment of God's promised redemption in a new act of creation comparable with that of Genesis chapter one.[4]

In Luke 1 and Matthew 1 we have, however mysterious the matter may be, the clear revelation that Jesus is both "of Mary" and "of God." He is *conceived* in her (Matthew 1:20), not simply *created* in her. That is, the Son of God did not assume a duplicate human nature, but shared our humanity (Hebrews 2:14). His humanity was taken from Mary, but creatively enlivened and critically conditioned by the divine Spirit. He really is a member of the human race, renewing the old and not simply starting a new. Mary had her part in the procreation or generation of the human nature of our Lord. She did not merely incubate a *separately* produced fetus or even zygote.

The creative work of the Holy Spirit in the process is as mysterious as it is unique. To speculate on the biological processes may not be wise. However, it is that human nature which is *of Mary* and *of God* which the divine Logos personally "assumes," takes up and makes His own, from the start of its existence and forever.

Much of this must inevitably remain a mystery to us. Yet what is revealed must be believed. Jesus' critics once flung at Him the mysterious circumstances of His origins, saying with a meaningful emphasis, "*We* were not born of fornication" (John 8:41, RSV, emphasis added). The alternative to what is implied there is the revelation given from God concerning Mary's virginal conception of Jesus: "what is conceived in her is from the Holy Spirit" (Matthew 1:20). In that discovery we move from earth-bound cynicism to hope. For God has come! The divine Spirit has done a new and decisive thing in the material world of the Fall; the supernatural has claimed the natural, and along with that, the person of the Son has entered human History by means of "a body . . . prepared" (Hebrews 10:5).

## THE HOLY SPIRIT'S WORK
## IN JESUS' HUMAN DEVELOPMENT

In the created world the Holy Spirit is "the divine executive" of all the works of God. He brings to pass daily and at ground level, as it were, all that is decreed and directed "from above." He is the personal activity of God working upon us and among us; He is God next to us. There are more than one hundred references to the Spirit of God in the Old Testament alone that express this. His work in the world at large ranges from bestowing mental and moral abilities and artistic and technical skills upon man in general, to the unique and saving work of softening the heart, sanctifying the penitent and comforting the people of God.

Here too the infinite Son personally takes up this finite humanity in the womb of Mary. However, the Son maintains the divine order of creation and works in and upon that human nature of His only through the Holy Spirit. We cannot, therefore, understand Jesus as we see Him in the Gospels apart from an understanding of the work of the Holy Spirit in Him. There was no area of the human nature of the divine Son which was not molded and developed and conditioned by the divine Spirit. There was a perfect and wonderful harmony here. As it was the Father who sent the Son into the world, so it was the Spirit who assisted Him into it and in it at every step. Nothing that the Son did in His human nature was done solely from His own divine power: everything He did at that level was by and through and with the Spirit.

The seventeenth-century Puritan theologian John Owen explains the regular order of working of the Trinity this way:

The Holy Ghost . . . is the immediate, peculiar, efficient cause of all external divine operations. . . . And hence he is the immediate operator of all divine acts of the Son Himself even on His own human nature. Whatever the Son of God wrought in, by or upon the human nature, he did it by the Holy Ghost, who is His Spirit as he is the Spirit of the Father.[5]

If this should seem at first reading rather abstract, it is not. It is a crucial aspect of our Lord's entire earthly life, His inner development as a man, and His public ministry. We must realize that although the baby in Egypt and at Nazareth was the eternal Logos, the Word of God, the divine Son in human nature, yet that human mind was not aware of all of which the divine person was aware. The Son did not live in and through His created human nature in such a way that the human became divine. What was finite did not become infinite; what was conditioned by age and circumstances, time and culture, did not become at any point totally unconditioned by anything outside itself, as the divine nature is totally unconditioned by anything outside itself.

Here is a *real* incarnation, a true and full entry into our humanity; a profound humiliation in which the Creator becomes a creature. Here in Bethlehem we have a baby; there in Nazareth we have a little boy growing up: not God *pretending* to be a little boy growing up, but God *becoming* a little boy growing up; God experiencing, through an assumed humanity, dependence, growth, and discovery, the perplexities of ignorance and the joy of discovery. And a crucial factor in that is the work of the Holy Spirit in the human development of Jesus.

In his book *The Doctrine of the Holy Spirit*, the nineteenth-century Scottish theologian George Smeaton sees the place of the Holy Spirit as central to the whole development of Jesus, including His self-consciousness. On Luke's words, "And the child grew, and waxed strong in spirit, filled with wisdom" (Luke 2:40, KJV), he writes:

We must ascribe to the Spirit all the progress in Christ's mental and spiritual development, and all His advancement in knowledge and holiness. . . . The Spirit was given to Him in consequence of the personal union in a measure which no mere man could possess, constituting the link between the Deity and humanity, perpetually imparting the full consciousness of His personality, and making Him inwardly aware of His divine Sonship at all times [Luke 2:49].[6]

There must have been a number of stages in the growth of our Lord's awareness of who He was in relation to God, though whether this growth was gradual or by critical discoveries and experiences we can hardly say—probably it was both. Most likely, Jesus' self-awareness as divine would have grown together with His self-awareness as human, developing from His relationship with God. In other words, Jesus would have been conscious first of all of a relationship with God, which only later would He have discovered to be unique. His self-consciousness as divine could certainly not have appeared or grown in any independent way (Matthew 11:27; John 5:19–20). From the start, an abiding relationship preceded and undergirded a growing understanding of that relationship. Out of a growing awareness of a unique relationship proceeded a growing awareness of a unique identity.

In time a fuller self-awareness would have passed from the Logos to the human mind, by means of the Holy Spirit, integrating self-awareness with intellectual understanding in such a way that Jesus could hold in balance the knowledge of divine and human factors in His makeup. Consider, for example, Jesus' statements "No one knows the Father except the Son" (Matthew 11:27) and "No one knows about that day or hour, not even the angels in heaven, nor the Son, but only the Father" (Mark 13:32).

There is great mystery involved here (1 Timothy 3:16), yet we may assume that the growth of Jesus' self-awareness would not take place in a vacuum, but together with prayer and much reflection on the Old Testament Scriptures as the Holy Spirit unfolded to the human mind of the young Jesus a growing awareness of His identity, place, and destiny.

The one passage that breaks the privacy of "the silent years" at Nazareth shows us the twelve-year-old Jesus in the temple courts, interacting with some of the senior teachers of Jerusalem. These were probably scribes of considerable learning, occupied with answering questions about the law for the many pilgrims who came from all over the Roman world to Jerusalem for the Passover. They would not have been village preachers! Yet, in the question-answer-question method of teaching adopted by the rabbis, Jesus' probing questions, and His answers to their own responsive questions, astonish everyone: "Everyone who heard him was amazed at his understanding and his answers" (Luke 2:47).

Jesus' response to His parents' protest is itself revealing: "Didn't you know I had to be in my Father's house?" (Luke 2:49). Three elements in that reply may be significant. First, Jesus refers to God as "my Father." As we shall see when we consider the title "Son of God," such an awareness of God as "*my* Father" is particularly striking against a Jewish background that emphasized the transcendence, majesty, and grace of God. We may wonder, in the light of Luke 1:32–35, if Mary had told Him more of His origins as He approached His bar mitzvah year of manhood. The angelic designations "Son of the Most High" and "Son of God" would tally with His deepest experience and confirm His growing self-consciousness.

Secondly, behind the intense sense of purpose and destiny implied by the words "I *must be* in my Father's house" may well lie a deepened conviction that the prophets had spoken of Him and of His destiny under God: a conviction which had grown in the young Jesus' mind as He prayed and pondered over the synagogue readings at worship and in His Nazareth home.

Thirdly, His reply intimates that His Father's house is the obvious and proper place for Him of all people to be: His true home is not in Nazareth, but in Jerusalem, the city of the King of Peace; not in the carpenter's shop, but in the place of God's particular dwelling; not in the familiar securities of an earthly family, but in the service and companionship of God.

## THE HOLY SPIRIT'S WORK
## AT THE BAPTISM OF JESUS

"When all the people were being baptized, Jesus was baptized too. And as he was praying, heaven was opened and the

Holy Spirit descended on him in bodily form like a dove. And a voice came from heaven: 'You are my Son, whom I love; with you I am well pleased'" (Luke 3:21–22).

All four Gospels refer to the descent of the Spirit upon Jesus at this time—even John, who does not record the baptism itself—and its importance cannot be doubted. Something so crucial occurred at Jesus' baptism that after it, according to Luke (who has a special interest in the Spirit's work), Jesus went up from Jordan "full of the Holy Spirit," returned to Galilee "in the power of the Spirit," and announced in His first synagogue sermon: "The Spirit of the Lord is on me, because he has anointed me to preach good news to the poor" (Luke 4:1, 14, 18).

We can hardly doubt that Jesus was filled with the Spirit from the start of His earthly life, since as much is said of His cousin and forerunner, John the Baptist (Luke 1:15), and is implied in what Luke has said of Jesus' conception (Luke 1:35) and His early development (Luke 2:40). There is no incompatibility in saying on more than one occasion of the same person or persons that they were "filled" with the Spirit or that the Spirit then "descended" or "fell" upon them (e.g., Acts 2:4; 4:31), since the terms are fluid and signify not so much entering into a fixed state as enjoying or experiencing a particular divine filling of knowledge (e.g., Acts 4:31) or power (e.g., Acts 13:9) in varying degrees and for longer or shorter periods.

However, it is interesting to note John's record of John the Baptist's testimony: "I saw the Spirit come down from heaven as a dove *and remain* on him" (John 1:32, emphasis added). Leon Morris sees this as indicating that "the whole of Jesus' ministry is accomplished in the power of the Spirit."[7] Jesus Himself indicates this when He warns that the scribes' slander that He operates by means of a demonic power is a blasphemy against the Holy Spirit (Mark 3:29), for it is by the Spirit of God that Jesus casts out demons and reveals the presence of the kingdom of God (Matthew 12:28). On this point Herman Ridderbos writes:

All these things are not merely based on a few utterances but form the presupposition of Jesus' action. As the Messi-

ah sent by God, Jesus is guided and prompted by the Holy
Spirit in everything. . . . This investiture with the Holy Spirit as Jesus' messianic privilege is one of the basic motives of
the gospel, although it is not explicitly mentioned every
time. . . . His being endued with the Spirit is the principle
and the power of Jesus' entire activity.[8]

This qualifies our earlier question about why so little is said
about the Spirit in the Gospels, because it reminds us that the
Spirit's presence and power is everywhere presupposed and
demonstrated (Luke 11:20). Yet the Holy Spirit's power is
demonstrated with Jesus' person and in His works in such a
way that it is primarily Jesus and not the Spirit who defines
and initiates the kingdom of God which has "come upon" men.
    The descent of the Spirit upon Jesus at His baptism was His
inauguration into His messianic task rather than His inauguration into the messianic age. The Spirit is the effectiveness of
Jesus' messianic presence; it conditions the kingdom in its
coming, but it is not the condition on which the kingdom
comes. Jesus' own presence is that condition: where He is, the
kingdom is. Hence Jesus announced *Himself*, and throughout
His ministry His emphasis was not "the Spirit has come" but "I
have come."
    It is, then, Jesus Himself who is foremost, decisive, and
definitive for the new age. At Jesus' baptism, and accompanying the Father's voice, the Spirit in His own way manifests
Jesus' significance in the kingdom of God; at the same time the
Spirit releases others into the new life of the kingdom which
Jesus' coming and ministry is inaugurating (Luke 4:18–19;
7:22; Acts 10:38). The baptism is itself the crucial turning point
in which the Spirit leads Jesus from obscurity to prominence.
    A whole cluster of Old Testament prophecies gather around
this event, and a feature of them all is the publicity with which
God introduces His Servant-Son. He is God's king who will
make the ends of the earth His possession (compare Luke 3:22
with Psalm 2:6–8); God's servant who will bring justice to the
nations (compare Luke 3:22 with Isaiah 42:1). The Spirit of
Yahweh is on Him to preach good news to the poor and to proclaim God's Jubilee for those in bondage (compare Luke

4:18–19 with Isaiah 61:1–2). As he moves out from Nazareth, an earlier Isaianic prophecy begins to be fulfilled, according to Matthew: "the people living in darkness have seen a great light; on those living in the land of the shadow of death a light has dawned" (cf. Matthew 4:16 with Isaiah 9:2).

## THE HOLY SPIRIT
## IN THE PUBLIC MINISTRY OF JESUS

Although we have already discussed the main aspects of the Holy Spirit's role in Jesus' ministry, the following points need to be made.

First, the Holy Spirit was crucial to the ministry of Jesus at every point. After the baptism and its singular endowment we read that it was "in the power of the Spirit" that Jesus taught, healed the sick, and cast out demons (Luke 4:14–21, 31–36, 38–44). His baptismal experience not only *inaugurated* Jesus' ministry, but *empowered* Him for that ministry. The apostle Peter would later speak of a time when "God anointed Jesus of Nazareth with the Holy Spirit and power, and . . . he went around doing good and healing all who were under the power of the devil, because God was with him" (Acts 10:38). Out of His deity Jesus would not and out of His humanity Jesus could not perform the mighty works that later marked His ministry. The Spirit signaled the time and gave the power for such a ministry to begin. As we saw earlier, the divine Logos did not immediately act upon the human nature, but did everything *mediately*, that is, with and by the Spirit.

Jesus' references to the Spirit during His public ministry are very few, so His words in Luke 11:20 are revealing: "If I drive out demons by the finger of God [i.e., Spirit of God; see Matthew 12:28], then the kingdom of God has come to you." Here Jesus is forced to break His reserve regarding His possession of the Spirit, with its implication of messianic status, much as He has to break His reserve in His trial before the high priest when confronted with a direct question as to His identity (see Mark 14:61–62). Here He confronts the work of Satan, owning His possession of the divine Spirit only in order to preserve the honor of God in His work among men.

A further point is worthy of note here. This perfect correspondence and cooperation between Christ and the Spirit is the immediate counterpart of the ultimate correspondence between the Son and the Father. Jesus speaks more freely of this in John 5:16–19, where He makes it clear to His critics that He waits for and works with His Father in all that He does, and in John 14:10–11, where He tells His disciples that He does His mighty works because He is "in the Father" and the Father is "in Him." This is to be understood in terms of the Spirit's working, at least for its dynamic.

Not only His miraculous healings, but also the enlightening and life-giving effect of His words were the result of Jesus' dependence upon and work by the Spirit. In John's gospel we read that He told Nicodemus, "That which is born of the flesh is flesh, and that which is born of the Spirit is spirit" (John 3:6 RSV). Later we find Jesus telling His disciples, after many had left Him, being disillusioned by some "hard" words: "The Spirit gives life; the flesh counts for nothing. The words that I have spoken to you are spirit and life" (John 6:63). This means, says Leon Morris, that "Jesus' words are creative utterances (note the words of God in Genesis 1). They bring life. They do not only tell of life" (see John 5:24).[9] This is indeed true, but it is also clearly implied that it is by the corresponding work of the Holy Spirit that Jesus' words are life-giving. As R. E. Brown comments: "The Spirit is the divine principle from above which alone can give life."[10] Jesus cannot rightly be explained simply as a man specially endowed with the Spirit—His words about Himself and His authority preclude that. But neither can He be considered apart from the Spirit. The Spirit is crucial to Him in all His earthly life, from the cradle to the cross.

## THE HOLY SPIRIT'S ROLE
## IN THE EXALTATION OF CHRIST

In the New Testament the resurrection of Jesus is repeatedly attributed to the Father. The fact that God raised Jesus up was seen to be crucial for reasons we shall consider later in this book. Still, it is clear that we are not to take this attribution to God in an exclusive sense. Jesus Himself has an active part in it (John 10:17–18), and the Holy Spirit is clearly inseparable from the Father's work at this point (Romans 8:11; 1 Timothy 3:16).

However, it would be superficial to see the Holy Spirit's work merely as the revivifying of the body of Christ. Paul has something far more profound to teach us in the following statements:

> . . . declared with power to be the Son of God by his resurrection from the dead: Jesus Christ our Lord . . . (Romans 1:4)

> "The first man Adam became a living being"; the last Adam, a life-giving spirit. (1 Corinthians 15:45)

> Now the Lord is the Spirit, and where the Spirit of the Lord is, there is freedom. (2 Corinthians 3:17)

In the Romans passage the resurrection is identified as the point at which Christ in His humanity passed from a stage of humiliation conditioned by flesh to one of exaltation conditioned by Spirit, from a mode of existence that was weak and space-bound to one that was, as John Murray puts it, "all-pervasively conditioned by pneumatic powers."[11] Moreover, the Spirit who now conditions His incarnate state is so closely related to Christ that the Spirit is functionally one with Him; it is His potency in the world of men.

Richard B. Gaffin concludes His close study of 1 Corinthians 15:45 thus: "The Spirit who raised Him up as the firstfruits, indwells Him so completely and in such a fashion that in their functioning he [Christ] *is* the Spirit who will be instrumental in the resurrection of the full harvest" (emphasis added)[12] Gaffin, like others, sees here a "functional identity" between the risen, exalted Christ and the Holy Spirit who at the resurrection of Christ inaugurated the eschatological era, "the new and final world-order, . . . the commencement of the age-to-come."[13] This "functional, dynamic identity" Gaffin sees as "most explicit and intimate"[14] in 2 Corinthians 3:17, and especially in the statement, "Now the Lord is the Spirit." He comments: "In terms of the efficacy of the new covenant, they are one . . . in terms of their redemptive activity they are identified."[15] The result of the Spirit's work at the resurrection of Jesus is that the "Son of God

in power" (Romans 1:4, RSV) becomes a life-giving Spirit to a
dying humanity (1 Corinthians 15:45), imparting a life that can
be experienced more and more as "we all . . . beholding the
glory of the Lord, are being changed into his likeness from one
degree of glory to another; for this comes from the Lord who is
the Spirit" (2 Corinthians 3:18, RSV).

## THE HOLY SPIRIT,
## THE HOLY SON, AND THE HOLY CHURCH

For us, here and now, everything that Christ communicates
to us of His grace, His love, His joy, and His gifts He communicates by the Holy Spirit, and everything that the Holy Spirit
works in us and brings to us He brings from the Son in His
exalted humanity. The Spirit is the means of His presence and
the mediator of His blessing: it is by the Spirit as *His* Spirit that
Christ shares with us His life and its richness.

This notable theme of New Testament preaching and teaching has profound theological implications. Peter announces in
his Pentecost sermon that Jesus, "exalted to the right hand of
God," has "received" from God the Father the promised Holy
Spirit spoken of by Joel and has poured Him out upon the
church (Acts 2:33). M. M. B. Turner understands this to mean
that Jesus now has "the power to administer the operation of
the Spirit"; He now "has lordship over the gift of Spirit given to
the Church."[16] This, says Turner, goes far beyond traditional
messianic expectations or honors. Jesus is no longer only
empowered by the Spirit: from the right hand of God He directs
the activity of the Spirit. "To speak of Jesus directing God's
Spirit," says Turner, "would surely be tantamount to calling
Him God," and he asks: "Could Jesus be less than God if he is
Lord of the Spirit?"[17] The Spirit of God has become the Spirit
of Christ (cf. Acts 16:7; Romans 8:9; Galatians 3:5; Philippians
1:19).

Henceforth the Spirit is Christ-centered in His whole ministry. The outpouring of the Spirit awaits the achievement of
Christ, mediates the results of that achievement, and draws
attention to that achievement (John 7:39; 16:5–15; 20:22; Acts
1:4–5; 2:1–4, 32–33). The life the Spirit gives is a share in
Christ's endless life (Romans 8:2, 10), the gifts of the Spirit are

the exalted Christ's gifts (1 Corinthians 12:5; Ephesians 4:7–11), and the goal of the Spirit's work is to transform us into His likeness (2 Corinthians 3:18). By means of His Spirit Jesus is *effectively* present in His church (Matthew 18:20; 28:20); and it is the gravitational pull of that same Spirit that leads us to Jesus' feet and that worship which belongs to God alone.

The implications of this are no less personal than theological. By means of the same Spirit who filled Him, the Lord Jesus conforms us to His character and image (Romans 8:28–30), sharing with us that life that is with Him and the Father (1 John 1:1–3), fulfilling in us the fellowship with the Godhead that Jesus promises: "If anyone loves me, he will obey my teaching. My Father will love him, and we will come to him and make our home with him" (John 14:23). It is by the Spirit that we know the truth (1 Corinthians 2:6–16; 1 John 2:20–21, 26–27), which in His hands bring us the life of Jesus (1 John 5:7–12).

Finally, as God is a missionary God and Christ is a missionary Son, so the Spirit is a missionary Spirit, communicating both the desire and the power necessary for the church to complete its mission in the world (Acts 1:4–5, 8). This is Luke's understanding and emphasis. The only Gentile author of a New Testament book, Luke has the church's mission at the center of his writings. David J. Bosch, quoting F. Hahn, calls it "the dominating theme" for Luke, who, he reminds us, wrote his gospel with his Acts in mind, reserving an explicit Gentile interest for his second book, but fully aware of its connection with the public ministry of Jesus. Bosch writes of the two periods:

> Jesus and the church belong to one and the same era. The historical life of Jesus was not purely and simply related to the past. The church lives in continuity with the life and work of Jesus.[18]

The church that confesses Christ therefore must ever be the church that lives by His Spirit. Without it she is simply another institution that will crumble and fade; an organization rather than an organism, grouped around Jesus Christ as an idea rather than joined to Him as her Lord and life. But joined to

Him by His Spirit, the church is what the world needs in every age—able to say, like Paul: "our gospel came to you not simply with words, but also with power, with the Holy Spirit and with deep conviction" (1 Thessalonians 1:5).

# 4

# THE SON OF MAN

As we read the Gospels we come across the term "Son of Man" again and again, and always on the lips of Jesus Himself or those quoting Him. It is His favorite self-designation and appears eighty-one times. It puzzles His hearers (John 12:34), not because the term is unknown to them, but because of the bewilderingly different uses Jesus makes of it.

The phrase "Son of Man" is not a Greek idiom, but a literal rendering of the Aramaic *bar-nash* or *bar-nasha*. "This expression," writes William Lane, "was in common use, both as a noun [meaning *man*] and as a substitute for the indefinite pronoun [meaning *someone, anyone,* or *a certain one*]."[1] Geza Vermes has shown that the idiom sometimes functioned as a circumlocution for "I," either in humility or in emphasis ("I and nobody else").[2]

The expression "Son of Man" would also have been known from the Old Testament book of Ezekiel, where it occurs over ninety times, and from its occurrence in Psalm 8:4 and Psalm 80:17. In all of these references the term emphasizes the weakness and frailty of man, and its suitability in many of Jesus' references to His suffering is obvious.

Most surprisingly, and for His hearers most confusing, is the way Jesus allied His messianic identity and task and future glory with this term. There is no clear evidence that at this time anyone ever used it as a title for the coming Messiah, but Jesus used it in preference to more obviously messianic titles and, especially towards the end of His ministry, vested the term with its most awesome significance.

Among the Old Testament occurrences of the term there is one passage, a passage of singular mystery and importance (which the rabbis later *did* connect with the Messiah), in which "Son of Man" occurs in a unique connection. In the book of Daniel "one like a son of man" appears who stands between God in heaven and His suffering people on earth, and who receives and mediates an everlasting kingdom for them (Daniel 7:9, 13–14). He is by far the most profound figure in the Old Testament in connection with the coming kingdom of God.

## DANIEL 7 AND THE SON OF MAN

C. F. D. Moule notes that in its many occurrences in the Gospels the title almost invariably carries the definite article when Jesus uses it. It is never simply "Son of Man" or "a Son of Man," but always "*the* Son of Man." This emphasis is so regularly made that Moule sees behind it an Aramaic phrase the equivalent of "*that* Son of Man,"[3] and takes it to be a specific reference to the impressive and mysterious figure of Daniel 7. The Daniel passage therefore demands our close attention at the start of this study.

The dominant theme of the whole book of Daniel is the kingship of God: how He intervenes from heaven to establish and increase that kingdom on earth, overturning all opposition and perfectly fulfilling his purposes. Daniel 7 summarizes that message.

The scene is the majestic throne room of heaven. God, the Ancient of Days, is seen enthroned in His eternal glory, surrounded by the host of heaven, sitting in judgment over this fallen world and its rebellious powers (Daniel 7:9–12). Then there approaches a figure, strangely human, "like a son of man," yet coming "with the clouds of heaven." To this divine-human being is given dominion, both for Himself and for the people He represents:

> In my vision at night I looked, and there before me was one like a son of man, coming with the clouds of heaven. He approached the Ancient of Days and was led into his presence. He was given authority, glory and sovereign power; all peoples, nations and men of every language worshiped him.

His dominion is an everlasting dominion that will not pass away, and his kingdom is one that will never be destroyed. (Daniel 7:13-14)

R. D. Rowe, in a study of this figure and its later messianic connections, notes that "in each of the chapters of Daniel 2-7, God is shown as intervening in human affairs" via various instruments or agents, such as the stone cut without hands in chapter 2; the figure in the fiery furnace "like a son of the gods" in chapter 3; the "watcher" from heaven in chapter 4; the fingers of a man's hand in chapter 5. In chapters 8-12 "Daniel is visited by various heavenly beings and told of the doings of others."[4] However, what is singular about the figure of chapter 7 is, as verse 9 implies, that He is to sit with the Ancient of Days (*thrones* are plural) and, as Rowe remarks, "Nowhere is the heavenly host represented as seated beside God."[5] Hence we are taken beyond the supposition that we have here an angelic being. Indeed, the angelic beings here appear to take a subordinate place as they present this august figure who, though "like a son of man," yet has the glory of God Himself about Him as He comes "with the clouds of heaven" (Daniel 7:13b).

The fact that Daniel's manlike figure is located in the heavenly court, rather than on earth with the saints, and approaches Yahweh "with the clouds of heaven" is also important. Throughout the Old Testament clouds are repeatedly associated with the glory of God. They are His tent (Psalm 18:11) and His chariot (Psalm 104:3), and the day of His activity in judgment will be a day of clouds (Ezekiel 30:3; cf. Joel 2:2). Yahweh comes to Moses "in a thick cloud" (Exodus 19:9, RSV), and "The glory of the Lord settled on Mount Sinai, and the cloud covered it six days" (Exodus 24:16, RSV). The Lord descends in the cloud to speak to Moses (Exodus 34:5), appears in the cloud upon the mercy seat to Aaron (Leviticus 16:2), and leads Israel day by day through the desert "in a pillar of cloud" (Exodus 13:21).

Leon Morris states that "clouds are linked with the divine in both the classical writers and the Old Testament. It is thus significant that in the New Testament clouds are most often associated in some way with Jesus Christ." For instance, he observes that all three of the Synoptic Gospels tell of the cloud at the transfiguration "which was plainly linked with the presence of God and from which the heavenly voice greeted Jesus as 'my beloved Son.'" He points out that at the Ascension a cloud received Jesus out of the sight of the disciples (Acts 1:9), and that when He comes again there will be clouds (see 1 Thessalonians 4:17 and Revelation 1:7).[6]

The Jews themselves, in Jesus' day and later, saw in Daniel 7 a mysterious but mighty figure who would appear on behalf of the Jewish people to deliver them from their enemies and restore to them the kingdom intended for them. As R. T. France says, "the figure in Daniel 7:13 was interpreted consistently from at least as early as the time of Jesus as an individual Messiah, but . . . he was not generally dubbed 'Son of man', this title being restricted to the (later) Similtudes of Enoch, and perhaps a few similar circles."[7] Instead, the title "Son of Man" was passed over by the rabbis for the more impressive title "the son of the clouds."

Faced with this situation, our Lord took a term that no one understood to be a title of their great Messiah and he allied it with new and remarkable associations. This was calculated at once to reveal and to conceal His full identity. It caused people to ask in bewilderment, "Who is this 'Son of Man'?" (John 12:34), as Jesus' Son of Man sayings moved on from authority to suffering to enthronement. The title corresponds, says Beasley-Murray, "with the obscurity of Jesus as representative of the divine sovereignty (despite his unparalleled authority in the exercise of its powers) and with the hiddenness of the kingdom that is to give way to manifest splendor at the revelation of the Son of Man."[8]

The title, understood against the background of the various Old Testament uses, would be used to integrate all the main elements of Jesus' character and mission, His suffering and His glory, His earthly work and His heavenly destiny, His own destiny and that of His people. Richard Longenecker observes that an important, indeed essential part of Daniel's message is glory through suffering, with vindication following humiliation.[9] Jesus' use of the title, and the things He associates with it, is dominated by precisely these themes.

Traditionally, Jesus' Son of Man sayings have been divided

into three categories: those that relate to His public ministry, those that relate to His sufferings, and those that relate to His future glory.

## THE SON OF MAN IN HIS PUBLIC MINISTRY

While the term *Son of Man* may at times be understood in a number of ways (e.g., possibly as a substitute for "I" in Matthew 8:20; John 6:27), in Jesus' public ministry again and again it carries undertones of authority, even when it seems to be most self-effacing. Sometimes the element of authority is challengingly prominent.

In Luke 12:8–9 we read that Jesus said, "I tell you, whoever acknowledges me before men, the Son of Man will also acknowledge him before the angels of God. But he who disowns me before men will be disowned before the angels of God." Similarly in Mark 8:38, "If anyone is ashamed of me and my words in this adulterous and sinful generation, the Son of Man will be ashamed of him when he comes in his Father's glory with the holy angels."

For Jesus' followers these words had a present significance. Someone was in their midst who not only preached the kingdom of God, but played a decisive role there and then in determining who should enter it. The future kingdom of God was already present in His words and works; He was its representative and mediator. It was impossible to enter the kingdom in the future if one did not enter it now, and it was impossible to enter it now if one refused its one entry point—Jesus.

Beasley-Murray quotes H. E. Todt on Mark 8:38: "He by no means appears as the lowly one, the sufferer, but demands with supreme authority that allegiance which detaches the disciple from this generation. In demanding this, Jesus utters an unsurpassable claim. No prophet in Israel ever claimed that men should confess Him."[10]

Very early in Jesus' ministry we come across the use of the term *Son of Man* in connection with His authority to forgive sins. The idea that a man, even the best of men, has the authority to forgive sins was, says Vincent Taylor, "alien to the mind of Judaism and early Christianity."[11] However, the manner in which Jesus exercised such authority is highly significant. To the cripple let down from the roof by his friends (Mark 2:10), Jesus does not say, "*I* forgive you," and thus appear to invade the prerogative of God; nor does he say, "The Lord has forgiven you" (note 2 Samuel 12:13), as one who has merely heard the divine decision and is authorized to declare it. Rather, as Taylor notes, "Jesus in his own person says 'Your sins are forgiven' with the conviction of One who sees the paralytic through the eyes of God."[12] It is not that the man Jesus sees *into* the heart of God, but that as the Father sees, so does the Son; as the Father speaks, so does the Son; what the Father does, that the Son does likewise (cf. John 5:17, 19, 22–23, 30; 6:38, 45–46). His authority does not stand alongside God's authority; it proceeds from it. There are profound subtleties present here from the start of Jesus' ministry which both reveal and conceal the full significance of His person and the final dimension of His work.

At this point the sign that the Son of Man has unique authority to forgive sins will be the freeing of this man from both his guilt and his paralysis. Soon, however, another sign will be given: the resurrection of the one who dies as an atonement for all sin.

The Son of Man also has authority over the Sabbath day: "The Sabbath was made for man, not man for the Sabbath. So the Son of Man is Lord even of the Sabbath" (Mark 2:27–28). Donald Guthrie argues that this statement implies far more than that man can treat the Sabbath as he wishes:

Not man in general, but the Son of man in the person of Jesus has that power. It is clear from his statement about the sabbath that . . . Jesus would superintend the sabbath for man's good, and not in the legalistic manner of the Pharisees. Since it was God who instituted the sabbath, the claim of Jesus to be Lord of the sabbath was another claim to exercise divine authority.[13]

Beasley-Murray, however, understands it differently. Closely following C. H. Dodd, he sees the reference as an echo of man's original lordship over creation (Genesis 1; Psalm 8), lost in the Fall (Hebrews 2:8) but fulfilled in Jesus for man's sake: "The sabbath was made for *man*, the crown of God's creation, and sovereignty over the sabbath, which belongs to man, is exercised now by *the Son of Man,* since he is representative and mediator of the divine rule, and so the one through whom man may experience it."[14]

In Luke 19:9–10 we find Jesus saying to Zacchaeus, who represents a whole class of rejected sinners in Israel, "Today salvation has come to this house, because this man, too, is a son of Abraham. For the Son of Man came to seek and to save what was lost." The note of authority here is obvious. Where Jesus comes, salvation comes with Him, for the Son of Man is the Good Shepherd, gathering in the strays of the flock of God (see Luke 15:1–7).

John has his own distinctive collection of Son of Man sayings in which the element of authoritative revelation of God is prominent. Only the Son of Man who "came from heaven" (John 3:13; cf. 5:27; 6:27, 53, 62) can speak with supreme adequacy and authority of heavenly things. D. A. Carson comments: "The Judaism of Jesus' day circulated many stories of bygone saints who had ascended into heaven and received special insight into God's ways and plans." In contrast, he continues, quoting B. F. Westcott, Jesus came from heaven, which was His home in the first place, and therefore He has "inherently the fullness of heavenly knowledge."[15]

Jesus does not simply have authority as a prophetically well-endowed "Son of Man"; He has unique, unchallengeable authority in the matter of heavenly things because, as Guthrie observes, "the real sphere of the Son of man is in heaven and not earth" (John 1:51; 3:13; 6:62). Moreover, John's language of descent "is integral to John's whole approach to Jesus as the connecting link between earth and heaven" (see John 6:33, 51, 53).[16]

As the heavenly Son of Man, Jesus breaks into the world of men with both the offer of life (John 6:27, 53) and the threat of judgment (John 5:27). The two great prerogatives of God lie within His domain (Genesis 18:25): "For as the Father has life in himself, so he has granted the Son to have life in himself. And he has given him authority to judge because he is the Son of Man" (John 5:26–27). Here Jesus takes us straight to the heavenly figure of Daniel 7:14, to whom such dominion and judgment and glory is given. "In this context," writes Carson of Jesus' authority to judge in John 5:27, "three strands come together":

> Jesus is the apocalyptic Son of Man who receives from the Ancient of Days the prerogatives of Deity, a kingdom that entails total dominion. At the same time he belongs to humanity and has walked where humans walk. . . . It is the combination of these features that make Him uniquely qualified to judge. Third, judgment in the Fourth Gospel is often linked with revelation (3:19; 8:16; 12:31; 16:8, 11). Judgment descends because men love darkness rather than light.[17]

## THE SON OF MAN IN HIS SUFFERING

Peter had confessed Christ's divine Messiahship at Caesarea Philippi (Mark 8:29; cf. Matthew 16:16), and the disciples had a clear understanding that Jesus was indeed God's promised Messiah. Now Jesus begins, in a series of statements, to prepare them for His death as a necessary precondition of the coming in fullness of the kingdom (see Mark 8:31; 9:31; and 10:34). Each time He calls Himself the Son of Man.

While Peter has spoken of Jesus as the Messiah ("You are the Christ"), Jesus refers to Himself as the Son of Man. True, Jesus had drawn forth Peter's confession of faith and had accepted it (Matthew 16:17). However, the title *Messiah* had, for the disciples as for their countrymen in general, almost exclusive connotations of national glory and political, even military, triumph among the nations. Jesus, in contrast, interpreted *Messiah* in terms of a theology of suffering, and of glory through suffering, best expressed by reference to the psalmist's rejected stone (Psalm 118:22; Mark 12:10), Isaiah's suffering servant (Isaiah 42–53), and His own Son of Man title.

This is given further emphasis by Jesus immediately after the breathtaking experience of His transfiguration: "As they were coming down the mountain, Jesus gave them orders not to tell anyone what they had seen until the Son of Man had risen from the dead" (Mark 9:9). Only through His unique sufferings will the Son of Man gain His unique position of glory and power. As Jesus goes on to intimate (v. 12), John the Baptist, notwithstanding his suffering, was the Elijah who was to come, and Jesus, the Son of Man, notwithstanding *His* sufferings, is the Messiah who was to come. His kingdom will not be won by easy conquest, but by suffering and rejection. As with Isaiah's suffering servant, the exaltation of the Son of Man will be inseparably bound up with His humiliation.

In His repeated predictions of His sufferings, our Lord reflects a deep awareness of the absolute necessity of an atoning death for the world's salvation: "The Son of man *must* suffer" (see Mark 8:31; 9:11–12; 14:21, 41); "Just as Moses lifted up the snake in the desert, so the Son of Man *must* be lifted up" (John 3:14; cf. 12:23, 27; emphasis added). He sees it as a thing long-decreed and also an event long-since prophesied in the Old Testament Scriptures, which He had come to fulfill. The lesson He teaches here for the first time—that such suffering is inextricably linked with His messianic person and task—will fall on deaf ears at first, but after His passion and resurrection it will be clearly understood (e.g., Luke 24:25–27, 44–48; Acts 26:22–23).

In the passion predictions of Jesus, and in particular in the great saying of Mark 10:45, the closest and clearest background is that of the servant sayings of Isaiah. Particularly in the song of the suffering servant of Isaiah 52:13–53:12, we find the themes of the suffering of the Son of Man and of the righteous man who suffers at the hands of ungodly men. Earlier we meet with the servant whose tongue, prophetlike, is made by Yahweh a sharp sword (Isaiah 49:2), whose mission is to restore Israel to be a light to the nations (Isaiah 49:5–6), and who receives continuous revelation to speak the right word (Isaiah 50:4). But he becomes "despised and rejected by men" (Isaiah 53:3), "oppressed and afflicted," "led like a lamb to the slaughter," and delivered up "by oppression and judgment" (Isaiah 53:7–8).

Isaiah's suffering servant provides a compelling background to many of Jesus' passion predictions, but especially to Jesus' greatest Son of Man passion saying: "For even the Son of Man did not come to be served, but to serve, and to give his life as a ransom for many" (Mark 10:45; cf. Matthew 20:28; Luke 22:27). Here Jesus sums up His predictions of rejection and death in words that echo the central disclosure of the most important of the servant songs: "when he makes himself an offering for sin . . . he shall . . . make many to be accounted righteous" (Isaiah 53:10–11, RSV). Indeed, Joachim Jeremias has said that Mark 10:45 "relates word for word to Isaiah 53. 10f, and indeed to the Hebrew text."[18]

In Isaiah 53 the death of the suffering servant is accepted as "an offering for sin" (Isaiah 53:10), literally, "a guilt offering." Similarly, in Mark 10:45, states Lane, "Jesus, as the messianic Servant, offers Himself as a guilt-offering (Leviticus 5:14–6:7; 7:1–7; Numbers 5:5–8) in compensation for the sins of the people."[19] He will be, to use His own figure of speech, "a ransom for many" which, by the payment of a price, will free them from bondage to sin and guilt and death. The Greek preposition *anti* (*for*, as in "a ransom for many") normally denotes equivalence, exchange, substitution, states M. J. Harris,[20] and on Mark 10:45 he writes: "The life of Jesus, surrendered in sacrificial death, brought about the release of forfeited lives. He acted on behalf of the many by taking their place. As in 1 Timothy 2:6 ["a ransom for all"], the notions of exchange and substitution are both present."[21] Thus Jesus sees His death as an atoning substitute in the place of "the many" who would otherwise have no hope of a place in the kingdom of God.

The sheer scope of His redeeming work also links the Son of Man of Mark 10:45 with the suffering servant of Isaiah 53:10 and gives it a unique character. Isaiah announces that the servant of Yahweh will bear the sin of *many* and "make *many* to be accounted righteous" (Isaiah 53:11–12, RSV, emphasis added). As Messiah, He will enter His kingdom through suffering, and the whole people of God will enter His kingdom through the atoning value of His death. Isaiah declares: "He shall see the fruit of the travail of his soul and be satisfied' (Isaiah 53:11, RSV). In Lane's words: "His death has infinite value because he dies not as a mere martyr but as the transcendent Son of Man."[22] We see, then, that under this term *Son of Man* Jesus fuses together the august figure of Daniel and the suffering servant of Isaiah 53.

A number of the Son of Man sayings in the Gospel of John reflect both the sufferings and the glory of the Son of Man

together: "The hour has come for the Son of Man to be glorified" (John 12:23); "Now is the Son of Man glorified and God is
glorified in him" (John 13:31). Twice in John the reference to
the Son of Man being "lifted up" has an ambiguity about it
which is intentional—denoting both His cross and His exaltation to heaven: "Just as Moses lifted up the snake in the desert,
so the Son of Man must be lifted up, that everyone who believes
in him may have eternal life" (John 3:14); "But I, when I am lifted up from the earth, will draw all men to myself" (John 12:32).
The importance of these words is not simply that glory will *succeed* suffering, but that it will *begin* there.

Carson emphasizes this at many points in his commentary
on John's gospel. The Cross is "the supreme moment of divine
self-disclosure"[23] and revelation in the Son of Man (John 1:14;
8:28–29). It is not merely the first stage on the way to the real
exaltation, rather "the cross itself is the glorification of
Jesus."[24] Nowhere is God more glorified in the Son of Man than
here (John 13:31); "the greatest moment of displayed glory was
in the shame of the cross."[25]

It is no wonder that the crowds, who have begun to see in
Jesus associations between *their* Messiah and *His* Son of Man,
become quite bewildered when they hear from Jesus of His
expectations of death: "We have heard from the Law that the
Christ will remain forever, so how can you say, 'The Son of Man
must be lifted up'? Who is this 'Son of Man'?" (John 12:34). Carson informs us,

> The Palestinian Judaism of the time expected the Messiah
> to be triumphant; most expected Him to be eternal. Jewish
> sources amply attest this (e.g. 1 Enoch 49:1; 62:14; Psalms
> of Solomon 17:4). A slightly later Judaism speculated that
> the Messiah would be defeated and destroyed before the
> consummation (e.g. 4 Ezra 7:28–29), but that perspective
> had not invaded the thinking of Jesus' interlocutors. [26]

As were the disciples at an earlier period, so now the
crowds are thoroughly confused at what appear to be conflicting signals from Jesus: signs of power and predictions of weakness, rejection, and death.

## THE SON OF MAN IN HIS FINAL GLORY

The final glory of the Son of Man is especially in view in Matthew's collection of Jesus' Son of Man sayings, where thirteen of the thirty occurrences speak of this. It also is clearly present in Mark and Luke. While Jesus' awareness of Himself as Daniel's heavenly being lies behind His Son of Man sayings as a whole, it is those Son of Man sayings of Jesus that point to future vindication, judgment, and glory that our Lord alludes directly to Daniel 7.

This class of sayings covers these three distinct but related events in Jesus' destiny. And within this class of sayings, Mark 14:62—and its parallels, Matthew 26:63–64; Luke 22:67–69—is the most obvious, and in some ways the most important.)

Firstly, consider the element of *vindication* by God. When asked, "Are you the Christ, the Son of the Blessed One?" Jesus replied to the high priest and his court, "I am. And you will see the Son of Man sitting at the right hand of the Mighty One and coming on the clouds of heaven" (Mark 14:61–62). The phrase "at the right hand of the Mighty One" is a typically Hebrew way of saying "at the right hand of God," and Jesus is rebutting their charge of blasphemy by saying that His rightful and predestined place as the Son of Man is not in any opposition to God, but at His "right hand"; in a place of ultimate intimacy and privilege.

Most scholars agree that in this statement Jesus is bringing together allusions to Psalm 110:1 and Daniel 7:13. The psalm is as important as the vision, messianically, and was widely recognized in our Lord's day as relating to the Messiah: "The Lord said to my lord: 'Sit at my right hand, until I put your enemies under your feet.'" It is outstanding among the Old Testament prophecies since it places the mysterious subject (the psalmist's "lord," see Matthew 22:45) in a position of supreme honor and glory above all the kings of the earth, and even above Israel's greatest king. Consequently H. Schlier can say, "The glory of Christ is so great that beside it the title 'son of David' denotes his humiliation."[27]

Psalm 110:1 is quoted or referred to indirectly no less than nineteen times in the New Testament, and was used repeatedly by the apostles in their preaching to convince the Jews that the one whom they had rejected as unfit to be their Messiah was, after all, God's anointed Son and Servant, His king whom He had exalted to His own throne. (See, for example, Acts 2:34; 5:31; 7:56; Hebrews 1:3; 8:1; 10:12; 12:2; 1 Peter 3:22.) Walter Grundmann concludes from this, "Jesus in the place of honour at the right hand of God has share in the glory and power and deity of God."[28]

Secondly, there is the element of *judgment* in these words of Jesus at His trial. The Jewish leaders are told that they will see "the Son of Man . . . coming on the clouds of heaven" (Mark 14:62). These words are often thought to refer to Christ's second coming, and would certainly be true of that final demonstration of His power and glory when "every eye will see him, even those who pierced him" (Revelation 1:7). However, R. T. France, like many contemporary scholars, maintains that

> the sitting at God's right hand and the coming with clouds are not . . . two events separated by an indefinite period of time, but two figures for the single idea of the vindication and exaltation of the Son of Man. His "coming" is not a coming to earth, but, as in Daniel 7:13, a coming to God in heaven to receive power and glory.[29]

This, Jesus says, is something which will be true "from now on" (i.e., from the time He is exalted by His Father, as the risen Christ, to the right hand of the Mighty One) and is something that they will "see" in the succeeding events that will take place around them. "New Testament exegesis," France observes, "has increasingly recognized this perspective, and there has been 'a considerable shift of opinion' towards the interpretation of Mark 14:62 as an enthronement text, not a parousia prediction."[30]

By "you will see" (Matthew 26:64, RSV, adds "hereafter," i.e., "from now on"—*not* "in the future," as in the *New International Version*), Jesus indicated no single event in the near or distant future. Instead He indicated a continuous state of vindication and authority, which would succeed Jesus' present state of humiliation. His judges will be faced with a Christ whom they rejected and who has become *their* judge, "the Son of Man sitting at the right hand of the Mighty One." They will experience this as they see for themselves: the empty tomb and the preaching of the Resurrection (Acts 2:22–24, 32); the unstoppable spread of the gospel (Acts 5:14, 39; 6:7, etc.); the terrible judgment upon Jerusalem in A.D. 70 (Matthew 24:2, 15–34; Luke 23:26–31); and, at the end, as the climax of all judgments, the second coming of Christ as judge of all the earth (John 5:25–29; Revelation 1:7).

France takes the words "you will see" to include in particular one event that would happen within the lifetime of Jesus' accusers—an event that the risen Christ Himself would bring about in an act of self-vindicating judgment and which He repeatedly predicted in terms similar to the ones used here.[31] That event would be the terrible destruction of Jerusalem by the armies of Titus in A.D. 70. Other passages in the Gospels may well refer to this, though they are often taken by other scholars (as well as most preachers!) to refer to the Second Coming: Mark 8:38 (cf. Matthew 16:27; Luke 9:26); Matthew 10:23 and Mark 13:26 (cf. Matthew 24:30; Luke 21:27); and Mark 14:62 (cf. Matthew 26:64; Luke 22:69). They are closely examined by France. In each and all of these passages, he argues, however highly colored and dramatic the language, Jesus speaks of a *"coming" within the lifetime of His hearers* (see, e.g., Mark 9:1; 13:30).

Other Son of Man sayings, however, lead to a scene of even greater devastation and judgment. In Matthew 24:37–44 Christ warns of a coming *after* the ruin of Jerusalem. Here again I agree with France in his division of the chapter.[32] The disciples have earlier asked Jesus when the destruction of the temple, which He has just predicted, will be and (as if it were to happen at the same time) when "the end of the age" would take place (v. 3). Although to them all this will be the same event, Jesus answers their first question (vv. 4–35) by describing the judgment upon Jerusalem (A.D. 70) in typical apocalyptic language (vv. 20–32). But then, in verse 36, He refers to their questions about the close of the age and begins to speak of that further day, the Day of the Lord for the entire world. Then, He says, men and women will be "eating and drinking, marrying and giving in marriage" until, as suddenly and as devastatingly as

the great flood of Noah's day, the Son of Man will come personally and in final judgment (vv. 32–51).

Thirdly, there is the element of *glory* in Jesus' dramatic
courtroom saying (Matthew 26:64). A little earlier in Matthew's
gospel, Jesus begins to paint one of His most vivid and dramatic scenes of coming judgment for the world: "When the Son of
Man comes in his glory, and all the angels with him, he will sit
on his throne in heavenly glory. All the nations will be gathered
before him . . ." (Matthew 25:31). Here we clearly have the
Daniel passage recalled: we have again the Son of Man figure,
the retinue of angels, the coming in glory and the throne of sovereignty and judgment. But, in contrast to some of the earlier
Son of Man sayings, we also have the last stage of fulfillment,
including the final overthrow of all opposition and the ushering
in of the kingdom prepared for God's people from the foundation of the world.

Another Son of Man saying in Matthew takes us beyond
even this, to a final statement about this future glory. It is Jesus'
statement to His disciples: "I tell you the truth, at the renewal
of all things, when the Son of Man sits on his glorious throne,
you who have followed me will also sit on twelve thrones, judging the twelve tribes of Israel" (Matthew 19:28). It is interesting
to note that here, Jesus gives a corporate significance to the
Daniel 7 prophecy: the "saints of the Most High" will indeed
receive the kingdom, but they will receive it in association with,
indeed through the mediation of, the Son of Man. France
points out that

> whereas in Daniel 7 it is Israel who thus rules over the
> nations, here it is Jesus' twelve followers . . . who judge
> (probably in the Old Testament sense of ruling, Jdg. 3:10,
> etc.) the twelve tribes of Israel. This remarkable transfer of
> imagery graphically illustrates the theme of a "true Israel"
> of the followers of Jesus who take the place of the unbeliev-
> ing nation, a theme which runs through much of the teach-
> ing of Jesus in this Gospel (cf. 8:11–12; 21:43).[33]

The central figure of the Daniel vision is an individual in
His own right, and an august one; but He, though distinct, is

not to be divorced from the people for whom He appears in the heavenly courts. Here the perspective takes our gaze beyond the Second Coming as an event to the endless and glorious reign in the new world that follows. The Son of Man is thus seen to be no interim figure, but an eternal reality, governing and guiding the final state of God's redeemed people. From the heavenly courts of Daniel 7 to the new earth of Revelation 21 He stands: an abiding and dominating figure.

# 5

# THE ONLY REVEALER
# OF THE FATHER

Many regard Matthew 11:25–30 as one of the most important and profound of all Jesus' statements about Himself and His significance in the world. Luke, in his gospel, tells us that Jesus was "full of joy through the Holy Spirit" as He uttered these words (Luke 10:21). Jesus was in fact rejoicing in the dawn of a new age: the age of the kingdom of God in which the gospel of the kingdom, announced in word and deed (Matthew 4:23; 9:35; 24:14), and centering on Jesus Himself, would open the kingdom to those without earthly advantages or worldly backing. Here are Jesus' words:

> At that time Jesus said, "I praise you, Father, Lord of heaven and earth, because you have hidden these things from the wise and learned, and revealed them to little children. Yes, Father, for this was your good pleasure.
>
> "All things have been committed to me by my Father. No one knows the Son except the Father, and no one knows the Father except the Son and those to whom the Son chooses to reveal him.
>
> "Come to me, all you who are weary and burdened, and I will give you rest. Take my yoke upon you and learn from me, for I am gentle and humble in heart, and you will find rest for your souls. For my yoke is easy and my burden is light."

In the final words, Jesus declares that God, through His Son Jesus, was building a new church (Matthew 16:18) with a people of His own choice: the least likely people in human terms, but the elect of God nonetheless. Later, the apostle Paul will glory in the same thing and in the same manner (1 Corinthians 1:26–29).

Jesus knows the Father's ways in His ministry and rejoices in them. He approves them; He approves all the decisions and purposes of God with a complete oneness of mind and judgment: "Yes, Father, for this was your good pleasure." (Matthew 11:26). Moreover, Jesus Himself has an essential and crucial part in this. He is the supreme executor of the divine will, He Himself brings to pass the divine decrees and secret purposes of God. He is in His own person the key to the fulfillment of the Father's eternal plan of salvation: "All things have been committed to me by my Father" (v. 27). Eternal realities accompany Him, eternal issues rest on Him, and eternal destinies center upon Him. As men hear Him they hear God; as men receive Him they receive the Father; as men reject Him they repudiate forever the God who sent the Son to be the Savior of the world.

## WHAT THE SON KNOWS

There follows one of Jesus' most tremendous utterances: "No one knows the Son except the Father, and no one knows the Father except the Son and those to whom the Son chooses to reveal him" (v. 27). B. B. Warfield described this utterance of Jesus as "in some respects the most remarkable in the whole compass of the four Gospels." He continued: "Even the great Gospel of John contains nothing which penetrates more deeply into the essential relation of the Son to the Father."[1] Indeed the saying has been called "a bolt from the Johannine blue." However, it would be a mistake to think that other passages in the synoptics do not teach just as high a Christology. Herman Ridderbos calls Matthew 11:27 (and its parallel, Luke 10:22), "the climax of the synoptic tradition" and insists that "the ontological relationship between the Father and the Son indicated here ... presupposes the pre-existence of Jesus' person."[2]

The first part of the utterance, "no one knows the Son except the Father," has to be read, for its full impact, in the light of the second part, "and no one knows the Father except the Son." This indicates a mutuality, a reciprocity about the relationship between Father and Son which shows that in His own self the Son is as much a mystery as the Father, who alone is capable of knowing Him. In the statement "no one knows the Son except the Father" Jesus is saying, in effect, "Only God is big enough to comprehend Me; only God is wise enough to understand Me; only God is great enough to direct Me."

The assumption underlying the statement "and no one knows the Father except the Son" is vast, and the implications staggering. D. A. Carson writes:

> Verse 27 is a christological claim of prime importance. . . . The text places enormous emphasis on Jesus' person and authority. The thought is closely echoed both in John (3:35; 8:19; 10:15; 14:9; 16:15) and in the Synoptics (Matt. 13:11; Mark 4:11—Jesus makes known the secrets of the kingdom; cf. Matt. 10:37–39; 11:25; Luke 10:23–24; ch. 15 *et al.*). What is made clear in this passage is that sonship and messiahship are not quite the same. Sonship precedes messiahship and is in fact the ground for the messianic mission.[3]

There is no higher knowledge than the knowledge of God. There is no greater claim than the claim to know God. But Jesus here surpasses every other claimant, for He claims to have a unique and absolute knowledge of God. Notice that He does not say, "No one knows the Father as well as I know Him"; He says, "No one knows the Father *except* the Son." As Carson comments: "There is a self-enclosed world of Father and Son that is opened to others only by the revelation provided by the Son."[4] He is the only one among men who "knows" the Father without distortion and without limitation.

It is important to read the two statements together: "No one knows the Son except the Father, and no one knows the Father except the Son." Jesus says, in effect, that He knows God as well as God knows Him! His knowledge of God is unique precisely because His knowledge of God is exhaustive. And His knowledge of God is exhaustive because He is not one among the many (not even the chief "one" among the many), but one apart from the many. As "the Son," Jesus' knowledge of the Father is no acquired thing, but a knowledge based upon an identity of nature and an eternity of communion. That is why Jesus does not say here, "Only God knows Me and only I know God," but uses the terms "the Father" and "the Son." He is speaking of an inter-Trinitarian relationship: coequal, coeternal, infinite. Because of that relationship the Son knows the Father as well as the Father knows the Son; and each knows the other as well as each knows Himself!

In a word, Jesus Christ is part of the *self*-knowledge of the Godhead. He is part of God's self-consciousness! That is the core truth of this unsurpassed revelation of Jesus' full identity. (We shall come to study this more closely when we examine the one passage in the Gospels that equals this passage in explicitness and depth, namely John 1:1–4.)

Looking at this utterance simply as a declaration of Jesus' dignity, we might have expected a full stop after these last words: "No one knows the Father except the Son." But our Lord did not stop there. He did not come merely to throw our darkness and alienation from God into deeper shadow by asserting His oneness and intimacy with the Father. He was sent "not to condemn the world, but that the world might be saved through him" (John 3:17, RSV). Hence Jesus continues: ". . . no one knows the Father except the *Son and those to whom the Son chooses to reveal him*" (emphasis added). The Son has come to earth not merely to assert this knowledge, but to share it; and not simply to share it as information, but as salvation. He has come to tell a fallen world that a holy and outraged God has decreed to love it and to call a people out of it to be the sons of the kingdom.

Earlier in Matthew 11:27 Jesus had said that all things had been "committed" to Him by His Father. What had been "committed" to the Son was not the knowledge of the Father (which He had by nature), but the messianic right to reveal the Father's plan for salvation to sinful, needy men (Matthew 10:37–39; 13:11; Mark 4:11; Luke 10:23–24). In this revelation the Father has His own originating part (Matthew 11:25; cf. 16:17), but the Son is the great agent of it (John 3:35; 10:15; 16:15). It is a revelation of the Father given by the only one competent and sufficient to mediate it (John 8:19; 14:19). Indeed, were this knowledge not given, it could never be acquired, for, as Herman

Ridderbos points out, in these verses "the mystery of the Son is placed on an equal basis with that of the Father, and the communication of the revelation concerning the Father and Son is the exclusive privilege of both."[5]

## WHAT THE SON'S FOLLOWERS CAN KNOW

Consequently, even from the distance set up by our creatureliness and sinfulness, we may know the infinite, eternal, and holy God in Jesus Christ and through Jesus Christ, with the knowledge Christ Himself has of God. He mediates to us a knowledge of God that is as authentic as His own, though not as exhaustive as His own. Such knowledge is not the playground of the religious philosopher nor the lofty purview of the intellectual nor the native intuition of the mystic. Such knowledge is a given thing; it is given now, as then, by the risen Jesus, and it is given still to the "little children" of Matthew 11:25 and the "weary and burdened" of verse 28.

There could hardly be a more relevant or urgent truth for our times than this. We know so much and yet we know so little—and all because our starting point is wrong. We have made man the measure of all things and He is busy taking the measure of all things even while He is losing the measure of all things. Our data banks are loaded with technical know-how, while our century had become bankrupt of know-why. Even as we solve the problems we remain our greatest problem. We can control colossal forces but we cannot control ourselves. Even as we see the possibilities we fail to reach them, and indeed they seem to recede. Having locked God out of a scientifically determined universe, we now find ourselves lost in a spiritually empty universe: one with no higher purpose and in which life has no ultimate meaning.

One response to this, ancient and modern, has been to people our universe with "gods," projections of our own hopes and fears, mystic philosophies and occult experiences that are intended to give greater value or meaning to the world of brute facts and physics. Once again man becomes the starting point, and inevitably His creation is as flawed as its creator.

Jesus calls us to a new starting point. He offers help from the outside. It is help that will not fail us. If we will leave our learned limitations, our stunted wisdom; if we will in the things of God "become little children" and learn from Him, then, in the busyness of our days and the excitement of our discoveries and the disappointment of our failures, we shall find "rest for our souls."

# 6

# THE "I AM" SAYINGS OF JESUS

No examination of Jesus' revelation of Himself could pass over the great "I am" sayings of John's gospel, which are as prominent and as significant as the Son of Man sayings throughout the four Gospels.

The phrase "I am" may seem to us, at first sight, entirely commonplace. After all, we use it all the time at the beginning of statements about ourselves. However, if we examine closely the way Jesus uses the phrase, and especially the Old Testament background of His usage, we shall see that in a number of remarkable sayings of Jesus it carries the most momentous and profound message concerning His self-consciousness and identity. It is, in such cases, says Leon Morris, "the style of deity";[1] for in the Old Testament the declaration "I am" is the signature of Yahweh of Israel, an expression He uses repeatedly to describe His uniqueness as the God and Savior of His people.

## THE "I AM" OF YAHWEH

When God appeared to Moses at a crucial time in Israel's history, Moses asked God for a special revelation of Himself that would authenticate Moses in His mission as leader of the people of Israel (Exodus 3:13). In response God made to Moses a new and awesome disclosure of His essential being, as well as of His saving purposes for His chosen nation. Out of the strange fire of the burning bush God identified Himself in the mysterious and yet profoundly impressive announcement, "I am who I am" (Exodus 3:14).

To understand the significance of this profound statement

we must concentrate not only on the form of words used, but also on the covenant context in which they are made. God is not merely placing before His people an intriguing piece of religious information; He is telling them something about Himself that is momentous for them. Notice that He does not say "I am this" or "I am that," but simply, "I am who I am." That is, He is conditioned and defined by nothing outside Himself. He is the unconditioned God: eternal in His being and unbounded in His freedom and resources. Yahweh is the self-existent deity who can be to His people all that He chooses and all that they need. In this covenant context His "I am who I am" really means, "All that I am, I am for you." God in His unfathomable and unlimited being was putting Himself at the disposal of His beloved people: He who was all things in Himself would be all things to them.

This epoch-making self-disclosure of God was, for all time, to give a new insight into His ancient name "Yahweh" (Exodus 3:15), a name which gathers up some of the sounds of the great phrase, "I am who I am." The phrase itself appears to come near to defining the meaning of the name. This was Israel's God, her covenant God, her Savior God: His name was "Yahweh" and His nature was "I am."

God's revelation given to Moses here is essentially retained in a host of Old Testament announcements containing, in different forms, echoes of the monumental "I am" formula. For example, we have "I am Yahweh," "I am God," "I am the Lord your God," or even, simply, "I am He."

Nor does it appear as a piece of philosophical information. Again and again, notably in the later chapters of Isaiah, it confronts men and women with a claim and a challenge. God stands before a wayward people or a discouraged people or a seeking people and says, "Stop, turn, look at me. Come to me. Trust me fully for I am yours wholly" (cf. Isaiah 41:10, 13). God's "I am," "I am the Lord, and there is no other" (Isaiah 45:5, 18, 22), is God's being *in action:* revealing (Deuteronomy 32:39), saving (Isaiah 43:25), judging (Ezekiel 33:29). God is asserting Himself, confronting the people and calling them to Himself, challenging them to find a better God, and provoking them to an immediate reaction of penitence, hope, and worship.

D. A. Carson agrees with the majority of interpreters who see as the proper background to Jesus' "I am" sayings in John 8:24, 28, 58 the use of "I am" in Isaiah 40–55 (especially Isaiah 41:4; 43:10, 13, 25; 46:4; 48:12; cf. also Deuteronomy 32:39). Isaiah 43:10, Carson notes,

> is especially close to Johannine language: "You are my witnesses," declares the Lord, "and my servant whom I have chosen, so that you may know and believe me and understand that I am He." In Isaiah, the contexts demand that *I am He* means "I am the same", "I am forever the same", and perhaps even "I am Yahweh", with a direct allusion to Ex. 3:14 (cf. Is. 43:11–13). For others to apply this title to themselves was blasphemous, an invitation to face the wrath of God (Is. 47:8; Zp. 2:15). For Jesus to apply such words to Himself is tantamount to a claim to deity.[2]

## THE "I AM" OF JESUS

God's "I am" had enormous relevance for Israel. It has no less relevance for us as Christians. For the point God made in the burning bush He made more clearly than ever in the ministry of Jesus. In the one He said to an ancient people, "All that I am, I am for you"; in Jesus God said it again, not in a bush that burned, but in a man who came and spoke and died. In the bush it is a momentous message to Moses and to Israel; in Jesus of Nazareth it is a definitive statement to the human race.

In John 8:23–24 we read that Jesus warned His critics, "You are from below, I am from above. You are of this world, I am not of this world. I told you that you would die in your sins; if you do not believe that I am the one I claim to be, you will indeed die in your sins." Again, in verse 28 (RSV), He says, "When you have lifted up the Son of man, then you will know that I am he . . ." Finally, in verse 58, He contradicts His critics' challenge that He was far inferior to Abraham in time and significance by warning them, "Truly, truly, I say to you, before Abraham was, I *am*" (emphasis added).

The first of these sayings explicitly points to the context of His heavenly pre-existence. Jesus comes "from above," a being of a higher order than man, and bids men to acknowledge Him in an act of faith as the divine "I am" in their midst: "You will die in your sins unless you believe that I am he" (v. 24, RSV; cf. Isaiah 43:10). At first the significance of all this is lost on His hearers, who asked in puzzlement, "Who are you?" (v. 25). They think the saying of verse 24 was incomplete, failing to realize that it was in fact absolute!

However, knowing their total failure to see Him in His true character, and His life among them in its true significance, He tells them in the second passage that when they have "lifted up," that is, crucified, their Messiah, they will at last realize that God has come among them in the person of His Servant-Son. His full identity will be known when He has borne the sin of the world and taken His place, triumphant over death, at the right hand of the Father: "When you have lifted up the Son of man, then you will know that I *am He*" (v. 28, emphasis added).

When He tells them that their illustrious ancestor Abraham, whose faith they are failing to imitate, was but His forerunner, and He finally says, plainly, "Before Abraham was born, I am" (v. 58), the full significance of Jesus' self-disclosure bursts upon them. As R. E. Brown notes, "No clearer implication of divinity is found in the gospel tradition."[3] In one single statement the supreme truth about the supreme Man is made known—His pre-existence, His absolute existence. Jesus Christ was present in history "before Abraham was born," and Jesus Christ is Lord of eternity, "I am." In His perfect oneness with God, Jesus has always been the revealer and the revelation. What He was to men in His earthly life He always had been in His heavenly one: all that Yahweh had been to them *He* had been to them.

There is hardly a more dramatic or decisive moment in Jesus' ministry for the Jewish leaders. It is a moment of real unveiling, of profound self-disclosure on the part of Jesus. He is Yahweh-Jesus, the Savior-God in their midst! But the Jewish leaders see this announcement only as a blasphemy, a confirmation of their worst fears. In a moment of supreme and crucial opportunity, the leaders of Israel reject their calling. They are in fact standing where Moses stood on the memorable day He turned aside to see the bush that burned. They, however, do not take off their shoes from their feet, but trample the holy ground looking for stones to hurl at the voice which says "I am."

## THE SEVEN GREAT "I AM" SAYINGS

Besides this absolute use of the "I am" formula there are in John's gospel a series of "I am" sayings that are no less significant. In seven outstanding utterances Jesus says that He is the bread of life, the light of the world, the door of the sheep, the good shepherd, the resurrection and the life, the way and the truth and the life, and the true vine.

G. R. Beasley-Murray, observes that the primary feature of the "I am" sayings is that they point "to an aspect of the salvation which Jesus is and brings." Quoting W. G. Kummel, He remarks that in these sayings "Jesus bestows life as only God can."[4] Any one of them would be unthinkable on the lips of a mere man. In each of them there is an emphasis on the "I" that places Jesus alone in these various roles. He, and He only, is this to mankind. Moreover, the "I am" form of announcement implies that He is these various things *at a divine level.* Jesus is to men what only God can be to them, and He can do for men what only God can do for them (cf. Isaiah 43:10–13).

### "I Am The Bread Of Life" (John 6:35)

Here Jesus follows a remarkable miracle, the feeding of the five thousand, with an even more remarkable sermon. The crowd who follow Him are obsessed with the spectacular feat He has recently performed. They utterly fail to look beyond the miraculous sign to the thing it signified. Jesus therefore begins to press upon them their need to seek heavenly realities rather than earthly gains: "Do not work for the food that spoils, but for food that endures to eternal life, which the Son of Man will give you. On him God the Father has placed his seal of approval" (v. 27).

But the crowd fail to see that the whole point of the miraculous supply of food had been that Jesus, and Jesus only, was the source of the greater thing to which it pointed. They immediately respond to His call to seek eternal life from God by asking, "What must we do, to be doing the works of God?" (v. 28), failing to see what the miracle signified—that Jesus alone can give eternal life (v. 27).

Jesus then plainly tells them that God's great command to men and women, and the crucial and fundamental "work" pleasing to Him is to believe in Jesus, "whom he has sent" (v. 29). It is at this point that the mood of the crowd changes, or at any rate this is the point at which the critics among them come to the fore. They quickly ask Jesus to prove that He is quite as significant as He now claims. They acknowledge that He has miraculously fed a great crowd in the desert but point out that Moses did that with the "manna" to an entire nation—and kept it up almost daily for forty years (v. 31). Indeed it was among their legendary expectations of the Messiah that He would renew the miracle of the manna. Jesus must do more than He has so far done to gain their support.

Jesus knows it is not in fact more signs that they need (for which the current Jewish appetite was insatiable, 1 Corinthians 1:22), so He matches their stubborn refusal to receive *Him*, above and beyond His gifts, with the insistence that in fact He, in His own person, is the higher manna, the "true bread" to which the Old Testament manna pointed. When they had witnessed His miraculous provision on the previous day they should have looked from the bread He gave to the bread He was. Hence He tells them, at first ambiguously (v. 33) but then plainly (v. 35): "I am the bread of life. He who comes to me will never go hungry, and he who believes in me shall never be thirsty."

Notice that He does not now say He *gives* spiritual bread, but that He is spiritual bread. What He is, He shares; what He gives is from Himself. He is the bread of life because He has life within Himself—the life of the kingdom, the life of God. Moreover, He is so with such completeness and all-sufficiency that those who believe in Him shall never hunger or thirst again. What Yahweh in His all-sufficient "I am" character was to Moses and the people of Israel, Jesus will be to the believer and to the entire new Israel of His church.

Towards the end of His sermon Jesus makes a further striking statement: ". . . This bread is my flesh, which I will give for the life of the world" (v. 51)—not "my teaching" nor "my life," but "my flesh." Beasley-Murray comments: "It is characteristic of this Gospel . . . that the emphasis in the passage falls not on Christ's death *for sin* but on His death for *life:* "my flesh . . . for the life of the world."[5]

### "I Am the Light of the World" (John 8:12)

This famous saying of Jesus was spoken shortly after the end of the Jewish Feast of Tabernacles. That feast was a great time of celebration for the people, and for its duration the court of women in the temple precincts was dominated by two gigantic candlesticks that needed ladders to reach their tops and that were surmounted with large reservoirs of oil feeding huge wicks made out of the cast-off garments of the priests. It was said that by their light every roof and courtyard in Jerusalem was illuminated, and in their brilliance godly men and priests danced in the temple courts to the praise of Yahweh—the God of their salvation.

If that feast is over, as the absence of crowds in this chapter would indicate, then Jesus, again facing His critics, may well be pointing to the smoldering tops of the extinguished candlesticks and saying in stark contrast: "I am the light that never goes out! I am the true light, the light of Jerusalem—and of the world" (cf. Zechariah 14:5–7; John 8:12).

There is a considerable Old Testament dimension to His words. Throughout John's gospel Jesus' words link Him in a striking way to the activity of Yahweh in that great redemptive event in Israel's history—the exodus from Egypt to the Promised Land. In chapter 3, for instance, He refers to Himself as the true brazen serpent (John 3:14; cf. Numbers 21:9); in chapter 6 as the true manna from heaven (John 6:33–35, 50–51; cf. Exodus 16:1–36); in chapter 7 as the true rock from which living water flows (John 7:37; cf. Exodus 17:6) and in chapter 10 as the good shepherd (John 10:11; cf. Ps. 78:52).

Here in John 8 Jesus is recalling the luminous cloud that led the Israelites in their wilderness wanderings (Exodus 40:34–38). That pillar of cloud by day and fire by night was the Shekinah glory of God. It was God in action leading His people into full salvation. Here again our Lord is saying that what God Himself is, Jesus is.

As in all the "I am" passages, Jesus does not stop with a statement about who He is, but goes on to unfold its relevance for us: "Whoever follows me will not walk in darkness, but will have the light of life" (John 8:12). The whole message of His incarnate state is that He is what He is *for us*. Notice that He does not lead us *to* the light, but *is* the light who leads us.

Beasley-Murray shows the connection between Jesus' words at this point and the Old Testament background of the wilderness wanderings led by the pillar of cloud and fire (Exodus 13:21–22):

> When the original setting of 8:12 is seen in the Feast of Tabernacles, it is understood why the imagery of "following" the Light is employed instead of receiving it, or walking in it, or the like: this is what Israel did in the wilderness! The people followed the Light as it led from the land of slavery through the perilous wilderness to the promised land.[6]

Carson, moreover, reminds us of the wider background and allusions implicit here:

> The light metaphor is steeped in Old Testament allusions. The glory of the very presence of God in the cloud led the people to the promised land (Exodus 13:21–22) and protected them from those who would destroy them (Exodus 14:19–25). The Israelites were trained to sing, "The LORD is my light and my salvation" (Ps. 27:1). The word of God, the law of God, is a light to guide the path of those who cherish instruction (Ps. 119:105; Pr. 6:23); God's light is shed abroad in revelation (Ezk. 1:4, 13, 26–28) and salvation (Hab. 3:3–4). "Light is Yahweh in action, Ps. 44:3" . . . Isaiah tells us that the servant of the LORD was appointed as a light to the Gentiles, that He might bring God's salvation to the ends of the earth (Is. 49:6). The coming eschatological age would be a time when the LORD Himself would be the light for His people (Is. 60:19–22; cf. Rev. 21:23–24).[7]

## "I Am the Door" (John 10:9)

The saying "I am the door" is part of a discourse spoken by

Christ at the Feast of Tabernacles, as was His "I am the light of the world" saying. This was the last year of His public ministry, and opposition against Him was assuming dangerous dimensions (John 7:1). Jesus' appearance late in the feast (John 7:14) and His temple-preaching there, especially on its last day (John 7:37–38), marked the beginning of a drawn-out series of skirmishes with the Jewish authorities, who attempted in different ways to out-argue Him (John 8:13ff.), to insult Him (John 8:48–49), to slander Him (John 9:24–25), and even to stone Him (John 8:59). Because of His popularity, however, they failed to arrest Him (John 7:30–31, 44–46). Still, it was clear that their hatred of Him and opposition to Him was implacable.

John 10 follows all this, and, in particular, it follows Jesus' final rejection of the religious leaders at Jerusalem (John 9:35–41). In this chapter He warns the people against these false shepherds and announces that He, the good shepherd, is gathering the messianic flock, God's true people.

Jesus first uses a short, simple picture to illustrate the profound personal relationship He has with His people (John 10:1–6). Such a relationship is entirely absent between His critics and the people. The picture seems to be of a communal sheepfold where several flocks belonging to different shepherds would be kept overnight: "Truly, truly, I say to you, He who does not enter the sheep-fold by the door but climbs in by another way, that man is a thief and a robber" (v. 1, RSV). In contrast to them Jesus is a legitimate shepherd who can go straight to the door of the communal fold that encloses His sheep and who can call them out to follow Him with familiar voice and real authority: "but He who enters by the door is the shepherd of the sheep. To Him the gatekeeper opens; the sheep hear His voice, and He calls His own sheep by name and leads them out" (vv. 2–3).

It was because His hearers found His parable obscure (v. 6) that Jesus decided not only to repeat it but also to expand and develop its images. He does this by comparing Himself to two things in the earlier parable and in the shepherd-life of Palestine. First He compares Himself to the door or gate of the sheep-pen (vv. 7–10), and then He compares Himself to the shepherd Himself (vv. 11–18). Finally He compares His own people to the sheep of the parable (vv. 26–30), as we shall see in the next "I am" saying.

Various suggestions are given as to the background to verse 7, but that of Beasley-Murray seems the most straightforward.[8] He sees Psalm 118:20 as the most likely precedent for the figure of Jesus as the door: "This is the gate of the Lord; the righteous shall enter through it." A very familiar verse to the temple pilgrims! Jesus is saying, then, that He, and He alone, is the way to God: one can "enter" into salvation only by Him.

Here we encounter a clear note of exclusivism. It is sharply intensified in the ensuing words of Jesus: "All who came before me are thieves and robbers; but the sheep did not heed them" (v. 8). Carson thinks that reference is being made here to "messianic pretenders who promise the people freedom but who lead them into war, suffering and slavery."[9] However many are entranced by them, the real sheep do not listen; they know only one voice (v. 5); they enter the one and only gate (vv. 7, 9).

This element of exclusivism is common to all the "I am" sayings of Jesus. It is significant in terms of Jesus' divine self-awareness. Ethelbert Stauffer speaks of the powerful exclusivism of the formula and points to the sixfold "I" of God's self-revelation in Deuteronomy 32:39: "See now that I, even I, am he, and there is no god beside me; I kill and I make alive, I wound and heal . . . (RSV)" This is developed and repeated in the later chapters of Isaiah, as we have seen: "I, I am the Lord, and besides me there is no savior" (Isaiah 43:11); "I am the Lord, and there is no other, besides me there is no God" (Isaiah 45:5). As Stauffer says, "This 'I am' of God will not tolerate any second subject, any other god."[10]

Verse 9 presents us with the picture of a sheep-pen in the countryside, set in rich pasture-land where the sheep are, under the shepherd's eye, free to move in and out at will: "If any one enters by me, He will be saved, and will go in and out and find pasture." Brown presses through the parable to its message when He writes: "We have heard previously that Jesus supplies the living water and the bread of life; now He offers the pasture of life, for verse 10 makes it clear that in speaking of pasture He is really speaking of fullness of life."[11]

## "I Am The Good Shepherd" (John 10:11,14)

"I am the good shepherd." Popular as this beautiful saying of Jesus is, there was far more behind it than the familiar Eastern sight of shepherds tending sheep, and Jesus is claiming far more than a pastoral care for the people of God. The title He gives Himself, and indeed the passage as a whole, has strong Old Testament resonances. The most familiar verse from the most famous of psalms, for instance, declares, "The Lord [Yahweh] is my shepherd," and goes on to develop the metaphor in detail.

However, Jesus is not merely recalling the opening words of Psalm 23, or indeed any single Old Testament passage. The Old Testament is rich in allusions to Yahweh as the great Shepherd of His people and to Israel as the flock of God (e.g., Ps. 78:52; 80:1; 95:7; 100:3). As far back as the time of the patriarchs He was known as "the Shepherd" (Genesis 49:24).

Two prophecies in particular may have been in Jesus' mind. In the celebrated fortieth chapter Isaiah comforts God's distressed people with the words: "See, the sovereign Lord comes . . . He tends his flock like a shepherd: He gathers the lambs in his arms and carries them close to his heart; he gently leads those that have young" (Isaiah 40:10–11). There is also an outstanding prophecy in Ezekiel, which has remarkably clear echoes in Jesus' discourse in John 10. During a time of national corruption, calamity, and exile God assures Israel that He will be their true Shepherd, in contrast to the false shepherds who are abusing their trust (echoed perhaps in the words of John 10:12–13):

> "I myself will search for my sheep and look after them. . . . I will bring them out from the nations and gather them from the countries, and I will bring them into their own land. . . . There they will lie down in good grazing land, and there they will feed in a rich pasture on the mountains of Israel. I myself will tend my sheep." (Ezekiel 34:11, 13–15).

It seems clear, therefore, that Jesus' words about the future church in John 10:16 are a conscious recall of the Ezekiel passage: "And I have other sheep, that are not of this fold; I must bring them also, and they will heed my voice. So there shall be one flock, one shepherd (RSV)." And that Shepherd will be Jesus.

An important part of Jesus' teaching here is His exclusive claim as the Shepherd and His exposure of and rejection of all rivals. He alone can lead His people to the life of the kingdom of God: "The thief comes only to steal and kill and destroy; I have come that they may have life, and have it to the full" (v. 10). On these words Carson offers some powerful contemporary applications:

> This is a proverbial way of insisting that there is only one means of receiving eternal life . . . only one source of knowledge of God, only one fount of spiritual nourishment, only one basis for spiritual security—Jesus alone. The world still seeks its humanistic, political saviours—its Hitlers, its Stalins, its Maos, its Pol Pots—and only too late does it learn that they blatantly confiscate personal property (they come "only to steal"), ruthlessly trample human life under foot (they come "only . . . to kill") and contemptuously savage all that is valuable (they come "only . . . to destroy").[12]

Quoting Roy Clements, he continues: "It is not the Christian doctrine of heaven that is the myth, but the humanist dream of utopia."[13]

Jesus does not say, "I am a good shepherd" (in contrast to a bad one), nor does He say, "I am *like* the good shepherd of Israel's history." But He says, without qualification, "I am the good shepherd" (v. 11), and the definite article combined with the divine signature leads us to the recognition that Jesus is consciously and deliberately taking the name and the claim of Yahweh, the Shepherd of Israel (Psalm 23:1; 78:52), and applying it to Himself. What Yahweh was to the old Israel, Jesus is to the new. The Lord is our Shepherd—and Jesus is that Lord.

Jesus might have gone on to draw out the analogy in many ways (as for instance Psalm 23 does). But instead He singles out the unique, distinguishing feature of His shepherd-role which strains and perhaps even leaves behind His analogy. He does not say simply that He is willing to risk His life for the sheep. He says it is integral to His work that He "lays down" His life for the sheep (v. 11). Carson points out that we have here an "emphasis on the intentionality of Jesus' sacrifice,"[14] and that the words "for (Gk. *hyper*) the sheep" suggest sacrifice (*hyper* being repeatedly used in this way in John's writings, e.g., John 6:51; 10:11, 15; 18:14).[15] Before He can live for them and lead them to their destined place He must die for them, and the result of His self-sacrifice will be their eternal security (vv. 27–28).

Furthermore, His death is not for a few, nor for God's people out of Israel only, but for the whole flock of God, including the "other sheep" not yet called and still far away from God on Gentile hills: "I have other sheep that are not of this sheep pen. I must bring them also. They too will listen to my voice, and there shall be one flock, and one shepherd" (v. 16). Such a worldwide work had formed part of the Old Testament hope for the future (e.g., Psalm 96 and Isaiah 2:1–4), but God Himself could not fulfill the deeper implications of the ancient prophecies apart from the obedience to the death of His Son Jesus; therefore Jesus immediately adds, "The reason my Father loves me is that I lay down my life—only to take it up again" (v. 17). At Calvary He will purchase His sheep, and from the uttermost ends of the earth He will gather them, so that the life He will take up at the resurrection may be shared with the whole people of God.

## "I Am the Resurrection and the Life" (John 11:25)

No saying of Jesus has been more precious to Christians than "I am the resurrection and the life." It reveals His lordship even over death. He who leads us will not lose us (John 10:27–29). He does not stand helpless at the deathbed or the grave. We do not leave Him behind as we leave others behind, but He takes us to His Father's house (John 14:1–3). We change our place but not our company!

These words are uttered against the background of the death and burial of Jesus' friend Lazarus and the confession of Lazarus' sister Martha that her brother would "rise again in the resurrection at the last day" (v. 24). The late doctrine of the bodily resurrection (Daniel 12:2–3, 13) was vigorously defended by the Pharisees but was denied by the Sadducees (Acts 23:6–9). Jesus firmly held to it (Matthew 22:23, 31–32), and it is not surprising to find Martha, one of His followers, confessing it.

However, Jesus, unlike Martha, connects the resurrection of the dead with Himself and orients the orthodox doctrine around Himself in unique ways. He really speaks of two things here. He first says, "I am the resurrection . . . he who believes in me, though he die, yet shall he live" (v. 25, RSV); and then He says, "[I am] . . . the life," followed by "whoever lives and believes in me shall never die" (v. 26, RSV).

Thus the first clause of the saying is a promise of future resurrection even after death, and the second clause is an assurance that the life that is found in and comes from Jesus (hence the otherwise superfluous clause "lives and believes") will never under any condition die. (The Greek is a double negative, "will never, no never die.") The life-for-us of Jesus is the life-for-us of God, who is eternal; it is therefore "eternal life," a frequent term in John. It is the imperishable kingdom life of God, and it is found in, and only in, Jesus, who not only gives the water of life (John 4:1–15; 7:38) and the bread of life (John 6:50–51), but is Himself that life for all who believe—and is that life *now*.

On this last point Morris writes:

> This transcends the Pharisaic view of a remote resurrection at the end of time. It means that the moment a man puts His trust in Jesus He begins to experience that life of the age to come which cannot be touched by death. Jesus is bringing Martha a present power, not the promise of a future good.[16]

The doctrine of the bodily resurrection of the dead is given a special emphasis in this saying and will shortly be vividly illustrated in the raising of Lazarus. But it must be made clear to Martha, and then to all who see and hear with faith (vv. 41–42), that the resurrection of the dead at the last day will not be an isolated event or one issuing from an independent power, even from God. Jesus has been sent into the world (v. 42) not only to proclaim resurrection and life, but to *be* resurrection and life in His incomparable person and by His unsurpassable work (John 12:23–33; I Corinthians 15:20–22).

### "I Am the Way and the Truth and the Life" (John 14:6)

Three of the verses in John 14 emphasize the idea of Jesus as the *way* to God (vv. 4, 5, 6). Therefore, in His declaration of being "the way and the truth and the life," Jesus may be using the other two words, *truth* and *life,* to describe the kind of "way" He is. Jesus would then be saying something like, "I am the true way that leads to life," or even, "I am the true and living way [to the Father]."

However, Jesus is being quite specific here, and is most probably using the words as three distinct nouns, saying: "I am the way *and* the truth *and* the life." Clearly, therefore, while He is stressing that He is the *way* to God, He is also stressing that He is more than a route—more, even, than the only route, more than an interim stage or figure in the spiritual life. Jesus is so uniquely "the way" that believers find the destination as soon as they find *Him.* They "arrive" at God as soon as they step on to the Way of God. They do not find Jesus and then, at a later stage, find the Father and His eternal, life, even if they have to wait before arriving at the Father's house (v. 2).

Jesus *has* that life in Himself (John 5:26; 10:28; 1 John 5:12) and immediately communicates it to those who come to Him and commit themselves to Him. He leads to the Father precisely because He is "in the Father" and the Father is "in" Him (vv. 9–10). We reach the Father as soon as Jesus reaches us (v. 7). Jesus is then not only the way *to* life, He is the way *and* the life.

But how can anyone be sure of all this in a world of conflicting claims? In John's gospel the word *truth* is very prominent. Anthony Thiselton notes that nearly half of the 109 occurrences of *truth* in the New Testament are in John's gospel and in His epistles, where the word regularly has the sense of "reality in contrast to falsehood or mere appearance"[17] (For examples, see John 4:23–24; 6:55; 8:32, 45; and 17:3). However, what is in view is not merely an intellectual grasp of reality. As Scripture so often emphasizes, in both the Old and the New Testaments, God's truth is not only truth to be intellectually recognized, but truth to be trusted.

This emphasis, so prominent in the psalms, for instance (e.g., Psalm 25:10; 57:3, 108:4), that God's truth is His faithfulness, His firmness, His reliability, must not be lost. God's realities are reliable because God Himself is dependable: He is there to be trusted, and His promises are given for men to build their lives on them (John 1:14, 17; 17:17).

Precisely in harmony with this, notice that Jesus does not point away from Himself to some higher or later stage of truth, but says that He Himself *is* truth. As Thiselton notes, "truth is not abstract or supra-historical but revealed in the actual personal life of the Word made flesh."[18]

Moreover, Jesus is telling us that He Himself is the final and absolute validation of all His words (John 8:14). "Christ," says Thiselton, "is also the truth because He is the revelation of God, and therefore His own witness is valid."[19] He does not wait for anything or anyone else to validate His words. Therefore men can come to Him and trust Him as soon as they hear His call.

To one's own age, where men and women are desperate for reality, for truth, for spiritual certainties, this same Jesus speaks and tells us to believe what He says on His own authority. He understands our panic and our fear, especially in the face of death, and speaks to it with great patience and authority and reassurance. There is a lovely example of this a few verses earlier in this chapter (John 14:1–3), when Jesus says, assuring His disciples of life after death, "If it were not so, *I* would have told you." (emphasis added). The idea is that it is as unthinkable and impossible for Jesus to mislead as it is for God to lie: "Trust in God; trust also in me" (v. 1).

### "I am the True Vine" (John 15:1)

An important clue to Jesus' meaning in calling Himself the true vine is found in the adjective *true*. Clearly Jesus is contrasting Himself with something specific, and that is found most obviously in the many Old Testament references to Israel as a vine of God's planting (e.g., Psalm 80:8–10; Jeremiah 2:21; Ezekiel 15:1–5; 17:1–21; 19:10–15; Hosea 10:1–2), or even a vineyard (Isaiah 5:1–7). It is striking that, as Beasley-Murray notes, "In every instance when Israel in its historical life is depicted in the OT as a vine or vineyard, the nation is set under the judgment of God for its corruption, sometimes explicitly for its failure to produce good fruit."[20]

God said to Israel by Jeremiah, "I planted you like a choice vine, of solid and reliable stock. How then did you turn against me and become a corrupt, wild vine?" (Jeremiah 2:21). In contrast to the false vine that Israel had become, Jesus appears as the true vine. He is all that Israel was not, and only in Him can the new people of God bring forth the fruit God requires. Carson makes the observation:

> Just as Jesus' body is the true temple (John 2), and He is the true bread from heaven (John 6), the water that truly quenches thirst (John 4), the good shepherd (John 10), and the life which resurrects men from dead (John 11), so as He the true vine. All of the shadows of the Old Testament disappear in the light of His substance.[21]

What follows in John 15 brings out in various ways the importance and the implications of being closely related to Christ, as branches are to their vine, as He is to His Father. This theme, union with Christ, is fully worked out, after the events of the cross, the resurrection and Pentecost, in Paul's term "in Christ," and in the concept of the church as the body of Christ.

It is clear that throughout John 15 we should keep together the two metaphors "I am the true vine" (v. 1) and "you are the branches" (v.5), since Jesus is telling us something not only about Himself, but about the relationship between Himself and us. The relationship that exists between Jesus and His people reveals His unique place and absolute significance in God's kingdom. He is crucial for our lives, for our success, and indeed for our very identity as the people of God. He is saying, in effect: "I define you and I condition you by what I am to you. I am God's true vine, and as you belong to me you are the branches. My life lies at the foundation of your life, and my power is the source of your fruitfulness. Without me you can be nothing and do nothing, but in me you have life, the life of God, and by me you can bear fruit for God in abundance."

## A CRISIS OF IDENTITY

Our Western society has seen a crisis of identity emerge from the suffering of two world wars, the dizzying growth of knowledge about the universe and our physical place in it, and the absence of a philosophy that can offer a satisfying explanation of mankind and its world. Historically, over the past two hundred and fifty years or so the pride of the early eighteenth-century Enlightenment and the confidence of nineteenth-century humanism gave way to the disillusionment and anxiety of twentieth-century existentialism. We had begun as the only ones who could make sense of anything; we ended by being unable to make sense of ourselves. We moved from nineteenth-century confidence to twentieth-century despair in a generation. The great question, "Who am I?" became the unanswerable question of a society which had long ago stopped asking the even greater question, "Who is God?"

We are doomed to lose our identity when we deprive our Creator of His. Conversely, it is when we rediscover God that we rediscover mankind. And when God tells us who He is, we begin to learn who we are. Israel learned this in a new and unforgettable way when God sent Moses with the message that "I am" had chosen them and would redeem them, giving them a place and a destiny with Him forever. We, who are not Israelites, and whose only "qualification" is that we are the exiled in darkness, the lost and hungry and the dying, only recover hope and meaning in our lives when we meet Him who said, "I am the bread of life . . . the light of the world . . . the door for the sheep . . . the good shepherd . . . the resurrection and the life . . . the way and the truth and the life . . . the true vine."

# PART 2

## THE DIVINE EXPLANATION

# 7

# GOD IS WITH US

In the beginning was the Word, and the Word was with God, and the Word was God. He was with God in the beginning.

Through him all things were made; without him nothing was made that has been made. In him was life, and that life was the light of men. The light shines in the darkness, but the darkness has not understood it.

The true light that gives light to every man was coming into the world.

The Word became flesh and made his dwelling among us. We have seen his glory, the glory of the One and Only, who came from the Father, full of grace and truth.

No one has ever seen God, but God the One and Only, who is at the Father's side, has made him known. (John 1:1–5, 9, 14, 18)

There is a title given to Jesus Christ in the New Testament that sounds strange to the modern ear and which, at first, may mean very little. Nevertheless, in the world of the first century, in religious debate and philosophical thinking, this term was repeatedly used. The term is "the Logos of God," or as we translate it, "the Word of God." Sometimes it meant the divine Reason, sometimes the divine Wisdom, sometimes the creative or sustaining power of God, and sometimes His self-revelation.

Even if, as D. A. Carson persuasively argues, John is writing his gospel as an apologetic work addressed in the first place to

Jews,[1] the apostle is writing to Jews of the dispersion who live in the Hellenistic world of Greek vocabulary and thought, as well as to others. Hence we cannot ignore either the Greek or the Old Testament background to his vocabulary in these opening verses.

## THE MEANING OF *LOGOS*

The term *logos* was used in a wide variety of contexts and with various meanings in first-century Greek thought. For centuries it had a central if imperfectly defined significance in speculative thought, and was adopted and used in a host of ways from the fifth century B.C. onward in the developing sciences of psychology and metaphysics, theology and mathematics, logic, rhetoric and grammar. More significantly for our understanding here, the use the Stoics made of the term *logos* was especially familiar to thinkers of John's day and world. On Stoic philosophy G. Fries writes:

> A fundamentally new orientation of thought, namely the thesis that ethics is the basic problem for man, was provided by the Stoics, who confronted the Gk. starting-point of knowledge with the formulation of their question: How must I live in order to be able to be happy![2]

They answered this in terms of a universal *logos* principle which was sometimes equated with God, sometimes combined with God, and which was, as Fries puts it, "the constitutive principle of the cosmos, which extends right through matter" and thus "the expression for the ordered and harmonious purposiveness of the world,"[3] permeating the world around with order and growth and bestowing on mankind the power of knowledge and thence of moral behavior.

The difference between John's "Logos" and this is vast. This, observes B. Klappert, is an idea of *logos* as the "world-reason" that sustains the cosmos like a fine spiritual substance, while "the personal character of the Logos (John 1:1f.) and the thought of the world resisting the Logos (John 1:10f.) are both absent."[4]

Much closer to the mind (and heart) of John's Jewish readers would be the use and significance of the *logos* concept in the Jewish Scriptures and in Jewish philosophy. The Hebrew equivalent for *logos* is predominantly *dabar* and the term *word of Yahweh* (*debar YHWH*) is found 241 times in the Old Testament. Klappert says that in 93 percent of these occurrences it denotes "a prophetic word of God" virtually representing "a technical term for the prophetic revelation of the word."[5] However, he notes also its use as a powerful word, creating and ordering nature, shaping history and bringing men and women into covenant with Yahweh.[6] God's Word is a power, though not a magical power (as in ancient oriental nations); it is a moral power, and ultimately a *saving* power.

Closely connected with Jewish concepts of the divine Word was the Jewish concept of the divine wisdom that was with God in the beginning (Proverbs 8:22–27), with which He created the world (Proverbs 8:31), and which offered them the wisdom and truth of God (Proverbs 8:32–36), though it was often and tragically rejected (Proverbs 1:20–33; 8:1–21; 9:1–6). The use of the wisdom concept abounds in intertestamental literature, but once again, though often personified, it is not truly a person, and falls far short of John's thought here.

The Jewish philosopher Philo (ca. 20 B.C.–ca. A.D. 50) combined elements from both his Jewish and Greek backgrounds. Writes Klappert:

> In Philo not only is the Jewish Wisdom identified with the Logos, the Logos understood as a mediating power between God and the Creation and ascribed divine predicates, but Philo . . . also simultaneously combines OT statements of creation by the word, Stoic statements of the Logos as the world soul and Platonic elements (the Logos as the archetype of the created world) with one another.[7]

However, John's use of the term is again profoundly different from Philo's. Philo's Logos is not a person at all, only a force, a power: John's Logos is a person. Philo's Logos embraces the world: John's Logos became a baby in a manger, a boy in a carpenter's shop, a man among men, and the one who bears the sin of the world. Many Jews could say, "In the begin-

ning was the Word . . ." and would have affirmed that the Logos
was "with God" and was "the true light," and perhaps John
intends to capture their interest with his opening words. But
only believers in his gospel could say, "And the Word became
flesh and made his dwelling among us"; and that is the challenge and good news he brings to his intended readers.

## UNDERSTANDING "THE WORD" IN JOHN 1

Much more detail could be given about the various ways in
which the term *logos* was used in the philosophies of the Gentiles, the religions of the Orient, or even the theology of the
Jews, but what really matters here is the way the author of the
fourth gospel uses it. Therefore let us in this chapter look
briefly at what is one of the most exalted passages in the entire
Scriptures, and one that uniquely uncovers the life, in eternity
and in the Godhead, of the one whom we know as Jesus of
Nazareth.

*"In the beginning was the Word . . ." (v. 1).* The words "In the
beginning" clearly recall the opening words of Genesis: "In the
beginning God created the heavens and the earth." However,
John does not want us to concentrate on the creation yet. (He
will do that in v. 3.) Here he wants us to stand at the dawn of
time and to discover Someone there already. So he begins his
gospel (if we may translate his words): "In the beginning the
Word already was."

J. H. Bernard says that the imperfect tense of the verb "to
be," used in all three clauses of the verse, is "expressive in each
case of continuous timeless existence."[8] The threefold "was"
contrasts with later verbs in these verses. Creation came into
being (v. 3), John the Baptist came onto the scene (v. 6), even
the Incarnation occurred at a point in time when the Word
became flesh (v. 14), but the Word did not at any point come
into existence: "There never was when the Word was not."

John clearly means to proclaim the preexistence of Jesus as
the Word of God in eternity (vv. 14, 16, 18). He is telling us that
He who was at the beginning of everything Himself had no
beginning. Jesus Himself conveys this in various ways (e.g.,
John 8:58; 17:5), as do Paul (e.g., Colossians 1:17) and other

New Testament writers (Hebrews 1:10), as we shall see in chapter 13. Still, John is uncovering Jesus' eternal identity and life in a very studied and special way. He is taking us into the inner life of the Godhead itself, and to its eternal existence in which more than one person subsists in the one Godhead.

". . . and the Word was with God . . ." (v. 1). In the phrase "and the Word was with God" are found several supremely important principles for all truly Christian faith: that the Word was a distinct person; that the Word was uniquely related to God; that the Word was Himself God.

First, we learn that "the Word" was not simply another name for the Deity. *The Word* is all that God is; yet, although part of the Godhead, He is in some way distinct from God. Later in John's gospel we shall learn from Jesus Himself the much easier concept of a Father-and-Son relationship within the Godhead.

Second, in the phrase "was *with* God," John does not use the more obvious Greek construction for *with* (i.e., the preposition *para* plus the dative case of the noun following). Instead, he uses a different preposition, *pros,* plus the accusative of the noun. This has the basic thrust of "motion toward." The suggestion is of movement and orientation, of a dynamic rather than a static relationship. The Word eternally existed in a personal, face-to-face relationship with God.

". . . and the Word was God" (v. 1). We must try to appreciate the full significance of the phrase "and the Word was God," and it is worth attempting to understand something of the original Greek here.

John says in the Greek, *"theos ēn ho logos":* "the Word was God," literally "God was the Word." In the Greek "God" does not have the definite article "the," although the word *Logos* does. It is not "and the Word was *the* God," but simply "and the Word was God." Much is made of this fact by those who reject the traditional Christian understanding of the divinity of our Lord. The Jehovah's Witnesses' "New World" version, for instance, translates the phrase "and the word was a god." However, this is a quite unacceptable translation, for a number of reasons.

First, in a pagan world that acknowledged many gods any such statement would have been unthinkable to the New Testament writers. It was a fundamental tenet of Old Testament faith that Yahweh alone was God: "Before me no god was formed, nor will there be one after me. I, even I, am the Lord, and apart from me there is no savior" (Isaiah 43:10–11). If in His preexistent heavenly life Jesus had not been God in the truest sense, then John would not have dreamed of writing such a statement as this.

Second, its uncompromising and far-reaching nature is also seen in John's avoidance of the word *divine* (*theios*) in favor of the straightforward word *God* (*theos*). He is making it clear that the Word, the Logos, is not divine in some lower sense than God's uttermost deity.

Third, as Ed Miller argues, in the three consecutive statements "In the beginning was the Word . . . the Word was with God . . . the Word was God" it is "unthinkable from a stylistic standpoint,"[9] that "*theos* means 'God' in the first and third while the adjective 'divine' intrudes in the second." Moreover, "such an adjectival interpretation would destroy the suggested climax: He was with God and He *was* God."[10]

Fourth, there is a grammatical reason for the absence of the definite article: in the Greek New Testament definite nouns that precede the verb in a construction like this commonly lose the article, as for instance in John 19:21, where it is literally "King I am of the Jews" and where it means "I am *the* King of the Jews."

There also may be a good theological reason why John used this particular sentence construction. He may have wanted to avoid the idea that the Word was all there was in God—that there was nothing besides the Word. Of course, this would not be true, for as he has said, the Word was with—in communion with, in dynamic relationship to—God. The Son dwelt with the Father and with the Spirit in the triune Godhead. As C. K. Barrett puts it: "The absence of the article indicates that the Word is God, but is not the only being of whom this is true; if [*the* God] had been written it would imply that no divine being existed outside the second person of the Trinity."[11]

It is quite true that such a direct statement concerning the deity of Jesus Christ is rare in the New Testament (though note

John 1:18; 20:28; Romans 9:5; Colossians 2:2; Titus 2:13; Hebrews 1:8–9; and 2 Peter 1:1), and the New Testament writers usually avoid saying starkly, "Jesus is God." But in the circumstances in which they wrote there were good reasons for this reticence. R. E. Brown writes:

> The reluctance to apply this designation to Jesus is understandable as part of the New Testament heritage from Judaism. For the Jews "God" meant the heavenly Father; and until a wider understanding of the term was reached, it could not be readily applied to Jesus. . . . (The way that the New Testament approached the question of the divinity of Jesus was not through the title "God" but by describing his activities in the same way as it described the Father's activities; see John 5:17, 21; 10:28–29.)[12]

However, John has made his message about the person of Jesus Christ as clear at the beginning of his gospel as he will towards its end, when Thomas confesses the risen Christ as "My Lord and my God!" (John 20:28).

"Here then," observes Carson, "are some of the crucial constituents of a full-blown doctrine of the Trinity." Quoting Barrett, he continues, "John intends that the whole of his gospel shall be read in the light of this verse. The deeds and words of Jesus are the deeds and words of God; if this be not true the book is blasphemous."[13]

*"Through him all things were made" (v. 3).* Here John takes us from the fact of the Word in eternity to the place of the Word in time and His function at the beginning of the creation (v. 3). Notice, however, that he has already precluded the idea that the Word simply functions as God in some way without actually possessing the divine nature in the fullest measure. Once again in verse 3 we are reminded of the Genesis account of creation: "And God said, 'Let there be . . .,' and there was" (Genesis 1:3, 6, 9, 14, 20, 24). There, and throughout the Old Testament, the "word" of God was not empty sound, but a dynamic action, a mighty and creative (or destroying) power. God's speech was His activity.

In Genesis the Word of God is not explicitly a distinct person; in John it is. "The Logos is asserted to be the Mediator of creation," G. R. Beasley-Murray writes.[14] He is God's agent through whom it actually comes into being. However, Beasley-Murray is swift to make the point that, in view of the crucial words "and the Word was God" that "the concept of the Logos as *Mediator* must be distinguished from that of an *intermediary* between God and creation."[15] There were many philosophical and religious notions of the relationship between God and creation that either viewed matter as evil, or God as far too elevated above the created universe to be in any sort of direct contact with it. They therefore positioned intermediary beings and powers, including the Logos (however conceived), in creation and government.

John is making the point here that God created the world and that the creative activity of the Logos is the activity of God, not of some deputy or intermediary. The Word is the divine and personal agent in creation. He is not less than God, whatever His relation to the world may be. Leon Morris makes a further point: "He does not say that all was made 'by' Him but 'through' Him. This way of putting it safeguards the truth that the Father is the source of all that is."[16]

Paul similarly distinguishes the roles played by the Father and the Son: "for us there is but one God, the Father, from whom all things came and for whom we live; and there is but one Lord, Jesus Christ, through whom all things came and through whom we live" (1 Corinthians 8:6). Creation was not the solitary work of either. Both were at work (and still are, cf. John 5:17, 19). For Paul in 1 Corinthians 8:6, however, God and the *Word* has become God and the *Lord* Jesus Christ.

In the past two hundred years Western man, especially, has attempted to understand and explain his world in terms of an impersonal physics. Consequently he has left himself in a cold, mechanistic universe in which humanity has no ultimate or objective meaning or purpose. John here gives us the key we threw away. He tells us that the ultimate explanation of the creation, the supreme fact of all created reality, is not a formula but a person: "Through him all things were made; without him nothing was made that has been made" (v. 3).

*"In him was life, and that life was the light of men. The light shines in the darkness, but the darkness has not understood it. . . . The true light that gives light to every man was coming into the world" (vv. 4–5, 9).* Throughout John's gospel words that occur in the prologue are developed, including: *Word, glory, grace, truth, revelation, life,* and *light.* It may be that *life* and *light* in these early verses refer to the sustaining power and goodness of the Word at work in the world since creation, in spite of the subsequent fall. However, as Morris points out, the metaphors of life and light are later developed by John to show "that Jesus is *the* life-bringer and light-bearer."[17] The significance of the Logos arches over from His sustaining work as Creator to His saving work as Redeemer and Reconciler.

Carson calls verse 5 "a masterpiece of planned ambiguity."[18] Reading the words "The light shines in the darkness," a reader who was not (yet) a Christian, whether Jew or Gentile, might see here simply a reference to creation, in quite familiar and unchallenging terms. However, on reading further in this gospel he would soon be faced with more profound and challenging possibilities. As Carson observes: "The 'darkness' in John is not only absence of light, but positive evil (cf. 3:19; 8:12; 12:35, 46; 1 John 1:5, 6; 2:8, 9, 11); the light is not only revelation bound up with creation, but with salvation."[19]

One could translate the last clause of verse 5, "and the darkness has not understood it." The Greek verb used here, *katalambano,* can mean "grasp" in the sense of "understand," or it can mean, less commonly, "overcome." Morris, however, argues for the latter meaning, observing that "Darkness is not usually conceived as trying to understand light." He notes that the tense involved in the clause "has not overcome it" (the aorist tense pointing back to a particular moment) indicates that Calvary is meant, the place where "light and darkness came into bitter and decisive conflict and the darkness could not prevail."[20]

John's further statement in verse 9, "The true light that enlightens every man was coming into the world" (RSV), increases the ambiguity. Is it "the light" that is viewed as coming into the world (as most modern translations) or is it "every man" (as translated in the Authorized Version)? John's evident concerns here strongly support the first. A question remains, however, which can be argued both ways. When John speaks of "the true light that enlightens every man," does he refer to the Logos of God as the light that *reveals* or as the light that *exposes?* If it is the first, then we must ask: Is the reference to a general revelation of God given to everyone without exception, leaving none with an excuse for his rebellion (as perhaps in vv. 4–5 and in Colossians 3:11)?

If on the other hand John's word is taken in its primary lexical sense, he is telling us that the Logos "makes visible," "brings to light" and so "exposes" everyone on whom it shines. John may therefore be referring to the effect of Jesus in the world. He is light in a world of darkness where people hate the true light of God. Consequently He divides them even as they react to Him (John 1:10–13). Carson observes: "In John's Gospel it is repeatedly the case that the light shines on all, and forces a distinction (e.g. 3:19–21; 8:12; 9:39–41)."[21]

The statement that "the true light . . . was coming into the world" prepares us for the dramatic announcement which follows soon after, in verse 14.

*"The Word became flesh . . ." (v. 14).* To read verses 1–3, and then, immediately after, verse 14, is to get the full impact of John's great prologue, with its astonishing climax. What no Gentile philosopher would have believed, what no Jewish theologian had conceived, God had done. The Word became flesh: the highest being became a lowly creature; the source of life became a dying man; the ultimate fact became a commonplace feature.

It may be that in putting it in this strong, almost crude way, John is confronting religious opponents who want to "spiritualize" the Incarnation because they are reluctant to admit that God, who is pure spirit, could taint Himself with coarse and fallen flesh. He counters such early "docetism" (as in 1 John 1:1–3) with an unambiguous claim, that God has come among us as one of us (cf. Hebrews 2:14). "Therefore," reflects Brown, "instead of supplying the liberation from the material world that the Greek world yearned for, the Word of God was inextricably bound to human history."[22]

*". . . and made his dwelling among us. We have seen his glory, the glory of the One and Only, who came from the Father, full of grace and truth" (v. 14).* Here John uses a word for "dwelling" that recalls the old tabernacle of Moses' day (Exodus 25:8–9). He writes literally: "The Word became flesh and 'tabernacled,' or 'tented,' among us." The ensuing reference to "glory" further recalls the cloud of divine glory that filled the tabernacle (Exodus 24:16; 40:34–38). Less obviously, but more particularly, the "glory" is described in terms of "grace and truth," giving a *covenantal* flavor to the statement, for in Exodus 34:5–7, which is probably in view here, God shows His glory to Moses, accompanying the manifestation with the words: "The Lord, the Lord, the compassionate and gracious God, slow to anger, abounding in love and faithfulness . . ." (Exodus 34:6). In the Old Testament the idea of "truth" has the sense of faithfulness or reliability, as well as reality. "Here," says Anthony Thiselton, John means "that truly to 'see' God is to see nothing other than his glory in Christ,"[23] and this is true whether one thinks of God's reality or His reliability.

What the law witnesses to in Moses' writings one actually encounters in Jesus Christ (John 1:17). This is because in Jesus we encounter "the glory of the One and Only, who came from the Father" (v. 14). He is not only a servant like Moses, He is a son like no other: the only Son of the Father (Gk. *monogenēs*, "only begotten"; "the only one of its kind"). Jesus is not only the dwelling-place of God, He is God dwelling among us; He is tabernacle *and* glory; the form and the substance of God with us, and hence the revealer and the revelation of God (v. 18). His flesh is where God is, and His person is who God is: God the eternal Word (v. 14).

"Up to this point," observes Carson,

> a reader might be excused for thinking that the glory manifest in the incarnate Word was openly visible. . . . But as John proceeds with his Gospel, it becomes clearer and clearer that the glory Christ displayed was not perceived by everyone. When He performed a miracle, a "sign," He "revealed his glory" (2:11), but only His disciples put their faith in Him. The miraculous sign was not itself unshielded

glory: the eyes of faith were necessary to "see" the glory that was revealed by the sign.[24]

John has shown us the Word in eternity, the Word in creation, and the Word made flesh. He ends the prologue to his gospel by telling us of the Word in revelation, the revealing Word.

*"No one has ever seen God, but God the One and Only, who is at the Father's side, has made him known" (v. 18).* Here the function of the Word as the revealer of God is in view. We all know the place and the power of words. By our words we make known our inner attitudes and private thoughts. By them we can express and even project our personalities. The property of speech is very much an essential property, as well as a notable feature, of our humanity, and it marks us off from the animals. Wherever there is personality there will be communication: even in the Godhead this holds true as divine person communicates with divine person, "face to face."

Jesus is the unique, supreme, and, in an ultimate sense, the only revealer of God. No other can reveal God as Jesus reveals God: His revelation is personal, underived, and absolute. Jesus is not simply a word *about* God, nor even only a word *from* God; He Himself *is* the Word of God, and He Himself is God the Word. As the Word, He is and always has been all that God has to say about Himself. In Himself He is God's self-revelation, and in His work He is God's saving revelation. He is God's speaking and acting Word.

When John says, "No one has ever seen God, but God the One and Only . . . has made him known," he is not saying that we cannot know the first person of the triune Godhead, but only the second. He is recalling God's word to Moses, who had requested to see God's glory: "you cannot see my face; for man shall not see me and live" (Exodus 33:20, RSV). Moses, after all, "saw God" only in a diminished sense; he saw the afterglow of God's glory (Exodus 33:20–23), just as Isaiah saw only the hem of God's glorious garment in the temple (Isaiah. 6:1, 5.) Moses was in danger (Exodus 33:20–22), and Isaiah overcome with fear and shame (Isaiah 6:5). Sinful men and women cannot live in the blaze of God's holy being. John is saying here that God in His glory can only be known in and through the Son, the Word, whose unique work it is to reveal the otherwise unknowable and unapproachable Godhead.

As the creating Word, the Son has revealed much of God's eternal power and deity in creation; as the inspiring and prophetic Word, He has revealed more of God's love and saving purposes in the Old Testament revelation; but, as Jesus, the incarnate Word, God with us (Hebrews 1:1–3), He has revealed most of God in His saving work. He who has seen Jesus has seen the Father in the glory of His love and grace (John 14:9–11).

After the prologue, the title "Logos" is not used again in John's gospel. There is a very good reason for this. He is to be know as Jesus of Nazareth now. The enfleshed Word becomes, in the words of C. F. D. Moule, "the brilliant focal point" of God's activity, and the eternal Logos is totally and forever identified with Jesus Christ the Lord. From now on the Word can never be understood and must never be described in abstraction from His identity as Jesus, the Son of God.

Carson makes the point that in the Christological confessions of Philippians 2:5–11 and Colossians 1:15–20, we have close conceptual parallels to John's prologue.[25] And Beasley-Murray, together with many others, sees the form of a hymn in at least part of John's prologue.[26] Both writers draw the same conclusion from this: here we have a fundamental tenet of the early Christian churches who knew Jesus as the Logos incarnate and worshipped Him as Lord and God.

# 8

# GOD HAS SPOKEN

The first four verses of Hebrews sound out like a fanfare of trumpets in praise of Jesus Christ, and His supremacy and all-sufficiency is the master-theme of the letter. That supremacy towers above all who ever came before Him, whether prophets or priests or patriarchs. Indeed His supremacy literally reaches to the highest heaven, and He is acknowledged, in this first chapter, to be as far above angels as men in this respect. He is the Son of God. The writer begins:

> In the past God spoke to our forefathers through the prophets at many times and in various ways, but in these last days he has spoken to us by his Son, whom he appointed heir of all things, and through whom he made the universe. The Son is the radiance of God's glory and the exact representation of his being, sustaining all things by his powerful word. After he had provided purification for sins, he sat down at the right hand of the Majesty in heaven. So he became as much superior to the angels as the name he has inherited is superior to theirs.(vv. 1–4)

Oscar Cullmann has said that the divinity of Jesus is "more powerfully asserted in Hebrews than in any other New Testament writing, with the exception of the Gospel of John,"[1] and, we might add, nowhere is it asserted in Hebrews more powerfully than in these opening verses.

## JESUS, THE DIVINE DECLARATION

*"In the past God spoke to our forefathers through the prophets at many times and in various ways, but in these last days he has spoken to us by his Son" (vv. 1–2).* The writer begins by making three contrasts, each of which displays not only the superiority but the incomparableness and finality of Jesus Christ. First, he contrasts the many prophets with the one Son. Second, he contrasts the fragmentary and incomplete character of ancient prophecy, divinely given though it was, with the full and final revelation of God in Jesus Christ. And third, he contrasts the days of old with "these last days," made so by the critical entrance into the world of the long-promised Messiah.

The history of Israel, we are told, witnessed not merely the evolution of a religion, but the unfolding of a revelation. "God spoke" in vision and in dream, in word and in writing and in historical event; calling out and to Himself a people; guiding them, blessing them, warning them, and even chastising them; but never ceasing to be their God. Throughout a long historical process God added truth to truth, unfolding more and more of His nature and His purposes, and increasingly pointing forward to a time when He would come as He had never come before, and would do what He had never done before. That future time would be decisive for Israel—and for the world.

In Jesus, says the writer of Hebrews, that time has come. The prophets *spoke* God's early words; Jesus *is* God's definitive word (John 1:14–18); for Jesus Christ is not a prophet, but "a Son." Here, and at several other points in Hebrews, *Son* stands by itself without the definite article (cf. 3:6; 5:8), intensifying the contrast between the category of "the prophets" and the unique category and absolute relationship of "Son" to God.

What kind of "Son," then, is this whose coming ended one era (days "of old") and began another ("these last days"), and who will never be superseded? The title "Son" is applied to Christ thirteen times in Hebrews. The first reference to the sonship of Christ (1:1–3) demonstrates Cullmann's contention that "Hebrews understands 'son of God' to mean 'one with God,' so that Son of God means 'complete participation in the Father's deity.'"[2] This is the key to the Old Testament citations that follow, and especially to verse 10, where an Old Testament address to Yahweh is transferred to "the Son."

## JESUS, THE DIVINE CREATOR AND RADIANCE

"... *whom he appointed heir of all things, and through whom he made the universe" (v. 2).* The writer of Hebrews first connects this *Son* with a messianic prophecy. His words "whom he appointed heir of all things" recall the words of Psalm 2, where Yahweh says to His *anointed,* His *king,* His *Son:* "Ask of me, and I will make the nations your heritage, and the ends of the earth your possession" (Psalm 2:8, RSV). The references to *appointment* and *inheritance* clearly show this to be a reward set within the context of His forthcoming earthly work of redemption, reconciliation, and mediatorial rule. This Son will inherit the nations.

However, the writer adds a dimension that raises this Son above any created messiah or merely human king, "through whom he made the universe" (lit. "worlds" or "ages"). As F. F. Bruce writes: "The whole created universe of space and time is meant" (cf. John 1:3).[3] The point will later be made that He who redeemed the world is He who made the world; He who had the power to create it in its original goodness (Genesis 1:31) earned the right to save it in its fallenness and to become, as Mediator, the heir of a restored creation and a new humanity. The apostle Paul explores much the same theme in Colossians 1:15–20.

"*The Son is the radiance of God's glory and the exact representation of his being . . ." (v. 3).* The image recalls the Shekinah of Old Testament times, and the bright glory of God that is so often recorded.[4] The picture is of the radiance that streams from a brilliant light, and the central idea is of an essential likeness to God, a participation in the divine nature. He is, as the Nicene Creed says, "Light of Light." The essential being of the Son is the essential glory of God. He is the essence and overflow of God.

The writer continues: "and the exact representation of his being." *Representation* (Gk. *charaktēr*) occurs only here in the Greek New Testament, and the picture is of the impression made by a seal on wax (the *Revised Standard Version* renders this *stamp*). The meaning is that there is an exact correspondence between the Son and the Father. It expresses that truth, observes Bruce, "even more emphatically than *eikōn* [*image*], which is used elsewhere to denote Christ as the image of God (2 Corinthians 4:4; Colossians 1:15)."[5] This is integral to the Son's unique revealing work. The Son is able to reveal God perfectly because He is one with God essentially: the very "*stamp* of his being." The Greek word translated *being* here (*hypostasis*), comments P. E. Hughes, "denotes the very essence of God."[6] When Jesus reveals God, He does not reveal something other than Himself. The persons are distinct, but the same divine nature is common to both.

"*. . . sustaining all things by his powerful word*" (v. 3). This statement is scarcely less far-reaching than the earlier one "through whom he made the universe" (v. 2). Indeed the two ideas are linked, for He who made all things sustains them in being by His ongoing power. He who was at the beginning of creation is at the foundation of creation also; His is the word of power that throbs through its subatomic life and holds in being its elemental energies.

Many writers on this passage emphasize that the Son's work in "sustaining all things" ("upholding the universe," RSV) is a dynamic, not a static thing. It is, as we shall see elsewhere, one of the great doctrines of the New Testament that all power has been given to Jesus to lead the entire creation on to the goal of God, which is reconciliation and perfection in the Son He has given.

William L. Lane draws attention to the writer's use throughout these verses of well-known ideas and vocabulary from the wisdom tradition of diaspora Judaism:

Reflection on the Wisdom of God in Alexandrian theology provided him with categories and vocabulary with which to interpret the person and work of Christ. Although Jesus is introduced as the divine Son (v. 2a), the functions attributed to him are those of the Wisdom of God: He is the mediator of revelation, the agent and sustainer of creation, and the reconciler of others to God. Each of these christological affirmations echoes declarations concerning the role of divine Wisdom in the Wisdom of Solomon (cf. Wis 7:21–27).[7]

However, while using familiar words and concepts to teach the significance of Christ, the writer of Hebrews also goes well beyond anything said of the wisdom of God in the biblical (e.g., Proverbs 8:22–31) or extra-biblical writings (e.g., Wisdom 7:22; 9:2, 9), as we can see both from a closer examination of his use of terms and from the climax of his statement in verse 3b.

The Greek word "radiance" (*apaugasma*) is a rare word, found only here in the New Testament and only twice in the Septuagint translation of the apocryphal Wisdom of Solomon. There the divine Wisdom is praised in similar terms to here: Wisdom is "the radiance (*apaugasma*) from everlasting light . . . and the image (*eikōn*) of God's goodness" (Wisdom 7:26). The writer of Hebrews, says Lane, out of pastoral concern took a familiar concept to gain a hearing for what he had to say.[8]

Similarly, he uses the Greek word *charaktēr* against a known background, but lifts it far above and beyond that background. Though the term *charaktēr* appears only here in the New Testament, it was a much-used word in the writings of the Jewish philosopher Philo, who, says Lane, applied it frequently to man, whose soul bears the "imprint" (*charaktēr*) of God. However, Lane warns against exaggerating the importance of such alleged "parallels" to the expression in verse 3.[9] Here the Son is said to be the exact representation of God's *nature*, an idea far above anything predicated of mankind in Philo, or elsewhere in such writings.

## JESUS, THE DIVINE PURIFIER

*"After he had provided purification for sins, he sat down at the right hand of the Majesty in heaven" (v. 3).* It is in these words that the author of Hebrews, Christian preacher that he is, most completely leaves behind anything hitherto conceived of the divine Wisdom, which after all was never a distinct person, but a term for the divine activity, creating, upholding, and reconciling.

In these words we have not a divine influence reconciling the world by educating men and women in it but a divine person making "purification for sins." Lane comments:

> Although His pre-existence has been described in categories borrowed from the wisdom tradition, that tradition is sharply modified by the introduction of this participial clause. The reconciling activity of divine Wisdom was fundamentally educative (Wis 7:27; 9:9). There is no association of divine Wisdom with sacrifice in order to procure cleansing from sins. . . .
>      . . . This brief, unadorned reference to Jesus' achievement is slanted in the direction of the later discussion of His priesthood and sacrifice. The effect of Christ's death is cleansing . . . from sins. Here sin is viewed as defilement which must be purged.[10]

He points out that in chapters 9 and 10 "the categories of defilement and purgation are foundational to the argumentation."[11]

Martin Hengel stresses the similarity between the opening verses of Hebrews and the Christological hymn of Philippians 2:6–11, and in particular the fact that in the latter Christ's substantial preexistence and equality with God are given more precise definition.

We might even put the similarities in table form:

| Philippians 2:6–11 | Hebrews 1:1–4 |
| --- | --- |
| "in very nature God" (v. 6) | "the Son" (v. 3) |
| "obedient to death . . . on a cross" (v. 8) | "After he had provided purification for sins" (v. 3) |
| "exalted . . . to the highest place"(v. 9) | "he sat down at the right hand of the Majesty in heaven" (v. 3) |
| "every knee should bow, in heaven" (v. 10) | "superior to the angels" (v. 4) |

| **Philippians 2:6–11** | **Hebrews 1:1–4** |
|---|---|
| "God . . . gave him the name . . . above every name" (v. 9) | "as much superior to the angels as the name he has inherited is superior to theirs" (v. 4) |

However, Hengel notes, "the basic theme of the Epistle to the Hebrews, on which there are many variations, is the representative atoning suffering of the Son"; consequently, "it is remarkable that at the very point where the divine sonship and preexistence of the exalted Christ are stressed, the shame of His passion also stands in the centre."[12] He notes that for the writer of Hebrews, no less than for the author of the fourth gospel, the glory of the Son of God "cannot be separated from the shame of His cross" (cf. John 3:14; 8:28; 19:5).

Hebrews constantly elaborates, as one of its principal themes, that Christ Jesus, and He alone, by His sinless death, made a once-for-all sacrifice for sins that forever cleanses His people for the worship and service of God (e.g., Hebrews 9:15–10:25). This note is sounded as early in the epistle as this verse, and sounded rather dramatically too. For to sit down signifies a completed work, and in the Old Testament economy, with its endless line of sacrifices and repeated oblations and ceremonies, no priest was allowed to sit down (Hebrews 10:11), for no priestly work was final and complete: it only typified and foreshadowed the work of another. Perhaps that is why there was no chair among the tabernacle furniture. The idea of a seated priest was virtually a contradiction in terms.

Furthermore, the writer takes the kingly prophecy of Psalm 110:1 ("The Lord says to my Lord: 'Sit at my right hand . . .'") and unites it with the once-for-all purification for sins that Christ made as God's high priest, declaring Him seated "at the right hand" of God, having accomplished forever His priestly work. This position, writes Hughes, "indicates that His is the place of highest honor, that He is not merely on a seat but on a throne, and that He is not just 'sitting' but ruling."[13]

The two figures of king and high priest taken together against the background of His divine nature remind us that Christ's present position is conditioned not simply by His intrinsic Godhead, but by His past work, His earthly atonement for sin. His crowning, as the epistle later tells us, is "because he suffered death," it is because He obediently and fully tasted death "for everyone" (Hebrews 2:9). His kingship now is a mediatorial kingship: it exists for Himself and for the people He represents until He gives it up to God at the end (1 Corinthians 15:24–28). As He died for His people, so now He is able to reign for them (Hebrews 6:19, 20; 7:23, 25), preparing also to return for them in a final act of judgment and vindication (Hebrews 9:27–28; 10:23–29; 12:25–29). He is a priest-king in the courts of heaven.

## JESUS, SUPERIOR TO ANGELS

*"So he became as much superior to the angels as the name he has inherited is superior to theirs" (v. 4).* In the Old Testament, angels are members of Yahweh's heavenly court who exist to serve and praise Him (Job 1:6; cf. Isaiah 6:2–3). They witnessed the creation of the world (Job 38:7), act for God in it when commissioned, sometimes bringing judgment (Exodus 12:23; Psalm 78:49), sometimes bringing revelation (Ezekiel 40:3; Zechariah 1:9, 11–12; 2:2–5). Special kinds of angels include the cherubim and the seraphim. In Daniel they appear more clearly as powerful archangels, watchers, and angels of the nations; even personal names are given in some cases, and their numbers involve many millions (Daniel 4:13, 17; 7:10; 8:16; 9:21; 12:1).

One angel-like figure, however, must be distinguished from all of these. The "angel of the Lord" is a heavenly being who comes to help either Israel or an individual. H. Bietenhard writes:

He is virtually a hypostatic appearance of Yahweh, the personified help of God for Israel (Exod. 14:19; Num. 22:22; Jdg. 6:11–24; 2 Ki. 1:3f.). Only in 2 Sam. 24:16f. do we find Him in opposition to Israel. Sometimes we cannot distinguish between Yahweh and His angel. When the reference is to Yahweh without regard to man, "Yahweh" is used. Where man observes Him, the expression "the angel of Yahweh" is used. This preserves Yahweh's transcendence (e.g. Gen. 18; Exod. 23:20–23). Because Yahweh's holiness could have destroyed Israel, only His angel was to go with the people.[14]

"In later Judaism," Bietenhard informs us, "popular belief in angels greatly increased."[15] He continues:

> Angels represented Yahweh's omniscience and omnipresence, formed His court and attendants, and were his messengers. They were linked with the stars, elements, natural phenomena and powers, which they ruled as God's representatives. The individual had his guardian angel. National guardians were set over the peoples, including Michael over Israel (Dan. 10:13, 21). There were 4, 6 or 7 archangels. Other groups of angels included powers, dominions, thrones, lords, authorities, serving angels.[16]

The idea of worshipping such angels would no doubt have been repugnant to Jews. And yet there is some evidence that at the very least a preoccupation with the activity—heavenly and earthly—of angels was, in Paul's words, almost amounting to the worship of angels (Colossians 2:16–19). There, as here, a cardinal distinction is made between "God's angels" and "the Son" (Hebrews 1:6, 8). Angels have the name of messenger; He has the name of Lord (v. 4). Angels have the name of servant; He has the name of Son (v. 5). Angels exist to worship God; angels are told to worship Jesus (v. 6). Angels run to serve; He sits to rule (vv. 7–8), on the throne of God (v. 8) which is His by right (v. 9) forever (vv. 10–12). History is not determined or controlled by angels, or for them, but by Christ (v. 13) and for His church, which angels are to serve (v. 14; cf. Ephesians 1:21–23).

The angels of heaven are very exalted beings, "but none of them," observes Bruce, "has ever been invited to sit before Him, still less to sit in the place of honor at His right hand."[17] This position the Son assumed through His obedience unto death and as the seal upon His finished, sacrificial work. Here again the reference is not to the Son as the second person of the Trinity, but to the Son as incarnate Mediator, reaching His glory through suffering: He has "become" superior to the angels, having put Himself far beneath them (cf. Psalm 8:5; Hebrews 2:7–9). The phrase "he became" points to a particular, definable and datable event of history—that is, the glorification of Christ in His human nature at the Resurrection and Ascension. At that point He "obtained" in a new way the name of "Son." It was the name He had borne before (Hebrews 1:2), even in the days of His humiliation (Hebrews 5:8), but which was only fully published in respect of His incarnate state and mediatorial office after the Resurrection, when and by which God said publicly, "You are my Son; today I have become your Father" (Acts 13:33; Hebrews 5:5).

As the name of "Son" is greater than the name of angels, so the place of the Son is greater. He is in the place of God, therefore "Let all God's angels worship him" (Hebrews1:6). They serve. He rules; and His rule is the rule of God in our nature (vv. 7–9).

The writer makes his point with striking finality when he takes from the Old Testament a passage (Psalm 102:1, 12, 25–27) that is specifically addressed to Yahweh and applies it to the man seated at His right hand, the eternal Son of the eternal Father: "In the beginning, O Lord, you laid the foundations of the earth, and the heavens are the work of your hands. They will perish, but you remain . . . they will be changed. But you remain the same, and your years will never end" (Hebrews 1:10–12).

The revelation of God in Jesus Christ will never be superseded or surpassed because He will never be superseded or surpassed. Jesus Christ is the same "yesterday and today and forever" (Hebrews 13:8). His person is eternal, His place supreme, and His truth absolute.

# 9

# THE DOCTRINE
# OF THE INCARNATION

John's prologue reaches a dramatic climax with his statement "The Word became flesh" (John 1:14). The philosophically unthinkable becomes fact. While philosophers were seeking to escape the "flesh" and be free in "spirit," God who is Spirit becomes flesh. The Creator, even in a fallen world, proclaims the essential goodness of His creation and sanctifies flesh and blood (Hebrews 2:14).

## JESUS: FULLY GOD
## *AND* FULLY MAN

However, we are not to think of the Son as leaving a sort of gap in the Godhead, a vacancy in the Trinity, at His coming down to earth as a man. In His divine nature God the Son filled all things and was in all places at all times, "a Spirit, infinite, eternal and unchangeable in His being, wisdom, power, holiness, justice, goodness and truth," to quote the grand description of God (Father, Son, *and* Holy Spirit) in the Shorter Catechism.

This did not alter with the Incarnation. What was new was that this same divine being became *personally* united with human nature at its earliest stage: He took it as His own. In this way the second person of the blessed Trinity truly and personally "became" a pinpoint fetus in the body of a young Hebrew woman. But though He became what He was not, He did not cease to be what He was. He who continued to fill all things and to sustain all things, also became contained in a virgin's womb, and was sustained by a human mother, living simultaneously the massive life of Godhead and the creaturely and painful life of humanity. In the words of the fourth-century theologian Athanasius:

> The Word was not hedged in by His body, nor did His presence in the body prevent His being present elsewhere as well. . . . At one and the same time—this is the wonder—as Man He was living a human life, and as Word He was sustaining the life of the Universe, and as Son He was in constant union with the Father.[1]

This concern not to misunderstand or misuse John's *became* is reflected in Calvin's insistence that

> even if the Word in His immeasurable essence united with the nature of man into one person, we do not imagine that He was confined therein. Here is something marvelous: the Son of God descended from heaven in such a way that, without leaving heaven, He willed to be borne in the virgin's womb, to go about the earth, and to hang upon the cross; yet He continuously filled the world even as He had done from the beginning.[2]

This assertion of the Reformer has been called the *extra Calvinisticum,* the *extra* being that infinite "more" which remained even when the Word became flesh. A modern theologian, Helmut Thielicke, comments:

> The point of the Calvinistic *extra* was that Calvin . . . did not want to see the second person of the Trinity "exhausted" in the historical man Jesus. The Logos is not completely absorbed by the flesh which He assumes. For He is the subject of this assuming. He thus transcends it. Consequently He is out of the flesh (*eksarkos*) as well as in it (*ensarkos*).[3]

The mystery of the Incarnation lies precisely here: in the simultaneous fullness of John's two words *Word* and *flesh;* in the completeness of our Lord's divinity and the completeness of His humanity. "For we affirm," continues Calvin, "His divinity so joined and united with His humanity that each retains its distinctive nature unimpaired, and yet these two natures constitute one Christ."[4]

## CHRIST'S HUMANITY

Consequently, as we stress the fullness of His deity, so we must stress the fullness of Christ's humanity. Notwithstanding our need of caution, John's *became* must be taken very seriously when he says "the Word became flesh," for the eternal Logos did indeed experience and undergo a "becoming." His humanity was not only an adding, an extension, a new horizon. It was also a boundary, an entrance into an authentic human experience of finitude. Therefore, although (as Athanasius and Calvin warn us) we must not think literally of "our God contracted to a span," we are nonetheless faced with a descent into creatureliness in which God "enters" His creation in a new way and experiences it "from within," while still retaining, as inalienable, His identity and work as "God over all blessed forever."

The eternal Logos assumed a full human psychology no less than a human physiology. He was—and is—not merely God in the form of man, but God in the nature of man; not God in disguise, but God in the flesh. He did not only come among us; He *became* one of us, possessing, as His very own, a true and full human nature from its conception. In that nature He as the second person of the Trinity resided, and to Him that nature properly belonged, so that God the Son consciously and experimentally lived His life through that humanity.

In that humanity He felt pleasure and pain, as we feel pleasure and pain. In that human nature He laughed and cried, hoped and feared, knew delight and disappointment. In that human nature He received and gave, blessed and suffered, was tempted as man and perfected as Mediator. The mystery and message of the Incarnation is that in Jesus God acquired manhood and the Deity became a member of the human race.

No more celebrated or venerated attempt to enshrine the apostolic tradition in a systematic theological formula exists than the definition of the Council of Chalcedon (A.D. 451):

Therefore, following the holy Fathers, we all with one accord teach men to acknowledge one and the same Son, our Lord Jesus Christ, at once complete in Godhead and complete in manhood, truly God and truly man, consisting also of a reasonable soul and body; of one substance [*homoousios*] with the Father as regards His Godhead, and at the same time of one substance with us as regards His manhood; like us in all respects, apart from sin; as regards His Godhead, begotten of the Father before the ages, but yet as regards His manhood begotten, for us men and for our salvation, of Mary the Virgin, the God-bearer [*Theotokos*]; one and the same Christ, Son, Lord, Only- begotten, recognized IN TWO NATURES, WITHOUT CONFUSION, WITHOUT CHANGE, WITHOUT DIVISION, WITHOUT SEPARATION; the distinction of natures being in no way annulled by the union, but rather the characteristics of each nature being preserved and coming together to form one person and subsistence [*hypostasis*], not as parted or separated into two persons, but one and the same Son and Only-begotten God the Word, Lord Jesus Christ; even as the prophets from earliest times spoke of Him, and our Lord Jesus Christ himself taught us, and the creed of the Fathers has handed down to us.[5]

It is often said that this is an attempt to use the philosophy and vocabulary of the fifth century to define spiritual truth, and that it is thereby limited and dated. It is true that it is the language of Greek thought and culture, and not that of Scripture. But what is said in that language would have been as unacceptable to a devotee of ancient Greek philosophy as it would be today to many modern theologians and philosophers. However, it was necessary for the fathers of Chalcedon to reply in this way to certain questions, challenges, and uncertainties that themselves were the product of contemporary Greek thinking and that threatened both the received doctrine and the stability of the church.

In an earlier period some (the Apollinarians) had stressed the divine nature of Christ and diminished His human nature: He was not a 100 percent human. Others (the Nestorians) had so worded their Christological doctrine that Christ appeared to be two persons as well as to have two natures: Christ *bearing*

God rather than being God. Others (the Eutychians), in reaction, not only claimed one person in Christ, but one nature too: a fusion of divine and human natures into a third entity. Here the human was absorbed into the divine. It was against such various errors that the Chalcedonian definition was framed.

Writing on the famous four negatives of the Chalcedonian definition, "without confusion, without change, without division, without separation," G. C. Berkouwer says:

> The four negatives of Chalcedon are the riches—and not the poverty—of a modest believing church. Its pronouncement is comparable to a double row of light-beacons which mark off navigable water in between and warn against the dangers which threaten to the left and to the right.[6]

The statement of Chalcedon was not intended to be an explanation of the mystery of the God-man, but a confession of His divine person and of His complete and true deity and His complete and true humanity, together with warnings about the limits of reflection, calling a halt to speculation at certain points crucial for the integrity of the biblical doctrine. "Boundary lines," observes Berkouwer, "are a matter of life and death for the church of Christ."[7] Within such boundaries the church may indeed go "beyond Chalcedon" in theological inquiry and exposition, but it should always be inquiry into Scripture, an exposition of the revelation which was "once for all entrusted to the saints" (Jude 3).

What matters most is not so much the use of Greek vocabulary and forms of expression, but whether the theologians of Chalcedon were preserving the New Testament revelation at critical points. B. B. Warfield maintained that the "two natures" doctrine was the universal presupposition of the orthodox church long before Chalcedon, and accepted even by warring factions and camps in the various controversies of the early centuries, and has trenchantly argued that "The Chalcedonian Christology, indeed, in its complete development is only a very perfect synthesis of the biblical data."[8] And a contemporary scholar, Klaas Runia, writes:

It is generally acknowledged that, even though Hellenistic terms and concepts were used, the resulting Christology was very un-Hellenistic. John Marquarrie is altogether right when He says: "Christian doctrines were not conformed to the mould of already existing terminologies, but terms already available were adopted into Christian discourse and given new meanings."[9]

Of course the Gospels themselves do not give us an abstract account of the "one-person-in-two-natures" mystery. They are concerned to show it in action. They show Jesus as being fully aware of Himself in both respects. Hence, though He has only one area of self-consciousness, because He is but one person, yet He indicates two areas of consciousness. He both claims a knowledge of God that can only be divine (Matthew 11:27), and admits to an ignorance that is characteristic of man's limitedness (Matthew 13:32). He can relate to God as an eternal equal (John 17:4–5) and also as a creature should relate to His Creator (John 14:28). God is thus both His Father and His God (John 20:17).

How all this could be the case without a division in the person remains a mystery. Certainly we have no hint of schizophrenia in Jesus, only a thoroughly integrated person. At every point we have *the same Jesus*, yet there are times when He points to depths of His being and reaches of His personal history that transcend the very finitude and creatureliness from within which He speaks.

There is, of course, no adequate human analogy to this or explanation of it, for in all the world and in all the universe there is no greater mystery. Ranked only with the mystery of the Trinity, the Three-in-One, is the mystery of the Incarnation—one person in two natures "without confusion, without change, without division, without separation." Only the infinite intelligence of God can fully grasp it, as only the supreme wisdom of God can devise it and only the omnipotence of God could achieve it. Of it the apostle Paul speaks when he writes, "Great indeed, we confess, is the mystery of our religion: [God] was manifested in the flesh . . ." (1 Timothy 3:16, RSV).

## A DOCTRINE UNDER ATTACK

The doctrine of the Incarnation has been under attack from earliest times until now—from both inside and outside the Christian tradition. At the beginning of the church's life, philosophical prejudices that were then in vogue made it seem crude and unworthy that a real flesh-and-blood existence should be attributed to a God who is pure Spirit untainted by flesh. Among the Gnostics of the second century and the Manichees of the fourth, who believed strongly in the inherent evil of all matter, a full-blown "docetism" was developed, with the view that Christ's body was not real, but only the appearance of a physical body (from the Gk. *dokein,* "to seem"). An earlier form of this error appeared in the teaching of Cerinthus, the Jewish Gnostic, about A. D. 100, who maintained that the divine being "Christ" came as a Spirit upon the earthly man Jesus of Nazareth at His baptism but departed before His crucifixion.

The apostle John uncompromisingly attacks such thinking, which seems to have begun even in His day, when He writes in His first epistle: "That which was from the beginning, which we have heard, which we have seen with our eyes, which we have looked at and our hands have touched" (1 John 1:1; cf. 4:2–3). And he insists in his second letter that "many deceivers, who do not acknowledge Jesus Christ as coming in the flesh, have gone out into the world. Any such person is the deceiver and the antichrist" (2 John 7). And it is noteworthy that New Testament writers such as John and the author of Hebrews, who so clearly and emphatically teach the supreme Godhead of Christ, also teach with equal clarity and emphasis His real flesh-and-blood humanity (e.g., John 1:1, 14; Hebrews 1:3; 2:14–17).

Today, however, the fight is on a different front: it is not the humanity of Christ that is in doubt, but His deity. In some parts of the church we are presented with a more acceptably humanist alternative to traditional understanding, a view in which the Incarnation as taught in the New Testament is regarded as a myth to be reinterpreted. Jesus is regarded as a man (not more) who was so open to God, so obedient to God, so full of God that He came to have the value of God for His followers; that is, in seeing Him they saw God in man and consequently understood God as never before. The reward of His earthly life was heavenly

honor: a unique place with God, but one which opened to
mankind its own God-intended future. In Jesus, therefore, and in
Jesus as human, not divine, man discovers His destiny in God.

Here, it seems, we have a gospel of humanism, in sharp
contrast to the gospel of the New Testament. The incarnation of
God is set aside and the divinization of man put in its place. G. C.
Berkouwer, however, sees this as no new struggle confronting
the church: "Was it not the unceasing battle of the church to
witness against every form of humanism which in some way or
other still expected redemption from man or from the regener-
ating power of man?"[10] P. T. Forsyth had earlier made much the
same point, saying of Christ's atoning death: "He was God
doing the best for man and not man doing his very best before
God. The former is evangelical Christianity, the latter is humanist Christianity."[11] If the incarnation of God is set aside,
then salvation is no longer of God who stoops but of man who
climbs.

Can it be that nearly twenty centuries after the New Testament writers we are encountering in a new form an error which
they combated in their day? Traditional and even foundational
doctrines such as the incarnation of God, the virgin birth of
Jesus, His miracles and bodily resurrection are commonly held
to be negotiable or even unimportant in comparison with the
"spiritual" truths which they are meant to express. Many conservative scholars would agree with H. D. McDonald that
"modern theology, by divorcing the Christ of faith from the
Jesus of history, is in danger of initiating a new form of
docetism"[12] in which the appearance and effect of such ideas is
really independent of their literal happening in space-time history. God is kept in the world of spirit, a world eternally
removed from man's world of flesh. This may be good Greek
philosophy, but it is very bad Christian theology! It has been
well said that a savior who is not quite God is a bridge broken
at the farther end, while a savior who is not quite man is a
bridge broken at the near end.

Here again, therefore, the whole church needs to sit
humbly at the feet of its first teachers and the Spirit who led
them (John 16:12–15). Listening must precede speaking; revelation must guide reflection; we must ponder not the possibili-

ties but the data, the proclamation of a *given* truth—the word of God in Scripture.

The vigor with which the church—yesterday and today—has repudiated attempts to dilute the teaching of a full and literal incarnation of God in Jesus Christ (Colossians 1:19; 2:9) is necessary. The issue is not simply an abstract philosophical dogma. A clear statement of the Incarnation is essential to the integrity of the New Testament message and its pastoral relevance to men and women.

If Jesus of Nazareth is not God in our humanity, then God has not come to us; God has not shared our pain and borne our guilt; God has neither spoken the final word necessary for our peace nor done the final deed necessary for our justification. If Jesus of Nazareth is not God in our humanity, then neither Jesus nor God is our Savior and the hope of the world. Over against this, however, and in words which Runia says "show no trace of mythological speculation [and] contain in a nutshell the whole Christology of the New Testament,"[13] is Paul's confident assertion: "For you know the grace of our Lord Jesus Christ, that though he was rich, yet for your sake he became poor, so that by his poverty you might become rich" (2 Corinthians 8:9, RSV).

## THE NECESSITY OF THE INCARNATION

It is true that the Incarnation was a great mercy on the part of God: an infinite condescension and an astonishing stoop of grace. God was not bound to take such a step; He did it in the freedom of an unnecessitated love. For fallen man by his rebellion had forfeited the natural outflow of the divine benevolence and now called down upon himself only the divine wrath for sin. Yet once God had purposed to save men from the eternal result of their fall, the Incarnation became a necessity and not an option. It was man who outraged the justice of God by sinning, and it was man who was bound to honor the justice of God by bearing and paying sin's true penalty. It was man who needed to be holy and righteous before God if man was to live with God forever. Hence God became man that as man He might atone for sin and meet the requirements of a holy God with a perfect righteousness and a holy obedience.

Consequently our redemption, even by God, was impossible apart from the incarnation of God. How could God, who is Spirit, suffer for the sins of man, who is flesh? How could God take upon Himself all *human* suffering and the penalty for sin in human experience without entering human physiology and human psychology and human spirituality? It was a human penalty He had to bear; therefore it was a human nature He had to acquire. The sin-bearer must be a true member of the race that fell.

That is why our Lord was born of the actual substance of the Virgin Mary by the Holy Spirit. Mary was the true *mother* (not merely the "host") of our Lord according to His humanity, for it was not a replica of human nature that the Son assumed but genuine humanity, the real and original thing, only purified in the moment of its conception by the Holy Spirit (Luke 1:35). God the Son became one *of* the race as well as One *among* the race. The writer of Hebrews expresses all this perfectly when he writes: "For surely it is not angels he helps, but Abraham's descendants. For this reason he had to be made like his brothers in every way, in order that he might become a merciful and faithful high priest in service to God, and that he might make atonement for the sins of the people" (Hebrews 2:16–17).

It comes to this: for our salvation it is as necessary that the Son of God be truly and fully human as that He be truly and fully divine. If this humanity is less than full and true, then He is inadequate as a mediator, incompetent as a sympathizer, and disqualified as a redeemer. If (save for sin) He is not all that we are in our uttermost humanity, then He cannot perfectly represent us either in His life or in His death. If He does not descend to us from God, then He cannot lift us up to God.

Now it is the emphasis of much of the epistle to the Hebrews that our Lord's assumption of true and total humanity is precisely the factor that qualifies Him in all these respects (Hebrews 2:9–18; 4:14–16; 5:8–9, etc.). Moreover, because it is one and the same person—the eternal Word—who lives out His life in these two natures, everything He does as man derives unique significance from His divine identity. All that He does as man has the value of God's doing: His righteousness is the righteousness of God (Romans 1:17); His atonement is the atonement of God (Romans 8:3); His victory is the triumph of God (Romans 8:31–39).

We, as Christians, adore our Lord's divinity, but let us never neglect or relativize His humanity, for it is His great acquisition and accomplishment: with it He came alongside us as our helper, in it He embraced us as our brother, by it He died for us as our redeemer. It is now in both natures that He mediates the grace of God to us and fulfills for us the rule of God. Let us then cherish this truth, for it is in the humanity of Jesus that we encounter the nearness of God. Thus we bless Him as "Immanuel"—God with us.

## THE HUMAN LIFE OF GOD

I said earlier that the Gospels are concerned to give us not so much theology in abstract as theology in action. This is especially true of their presentation of the great doctrine of God coming among us as a man. In the Gospels we observe the effect of the Incarnation on the Lord from heaven. He takes to Himself a true and full human nature, one with our own. In this humanity of ours and His, God the Son lives as a man and runs the entire gamut of human experience and human emotions in a true human body with a full human psychology. In and through that nature He was able to see things as we see them, feel things as we feel them, and experience things as we experience them.

This does not mean that God has no emotions of His own— that was a Greek idea of God, not a Hebrew one. God knows the power of love and the force of wrath; He knows what it is to delight in the good and to revolt against the bad. Yet here, in the incarnate state, God the Son begins to experience *distinctly human* types and levels of emotion and reaction; surprise, relief, shock and horror, human love and human anger, disappointment and distress, human gusts of exuberance and human outbursts of grief.

There is perhaps no better way to uncover the extent of the Lord's true humanity than to trace in the gospel accounts the various references to His emotional life.[14]

## Compassion

Repeatedly, for instance, we read of Jesus' *compassion*. This word is attributed to Him even more than *love*, not because love was a secondary characteristic of Jesus' life and attitudes, but because His love was of a certain sort. It was a love that wrestled rather than a love that rested; a love that met men in their folly, their turbulence, and their utter unworthiness, rather than a love that calmly dwelt on men as suitable objects of the divine good pleasure.

It was a love that was active: a love that pitied the lost, that strove to overtake the sinful stupidity of men so that it might steer them from the cliffs and gather them into the safety of the fold. Thus Jesus saw the crowds as sheep without a shepherd, scattered and confused (Mark 6:34), bedraggled and torn (Matthew 9:36); and out of a great compassion for such shepherdless sheep in such hostile country, He taught them and healed them (Matthew 14:14). Similarly with individuals: "filled with compassion," He reached out and touched the lepers (Mark 1:41) and hastened to the relief of the heartbroken (Luke 7:13).

From such texts, with their authentic touches of color, we learn with what *emotion* Jesus healed men and women. We are apt to imagine His healings as rather placid affairs, at least as far as Jesus Himself is concerned—the emotion being confined largely to the crowds. But we would be wrong. There are powerful emotions at work—in the healer as well as the healed. As one writer put it: "He not only gave the required help in such cases, He gave it with an amount of sympathy which doubled its value."[15] Those who were healed were also warmed, they as well as their troubles were dealt with. Where the heart allowed it, there was a wholeness about Jesus' healings that left the sufferer more than biologically functioning as he ought. In Jesus we have the best of physicians—aware of the human being and not just the medical condition.

## Anger

A most surprising emotion, which not infrequently accompanied our Lord's healings, was that of anger in one form or another, ranging from irritation to fury. We meet this unexpected element of some of His miracles early in Mark's gospel. In the synagogue at Capernaum, He was about to heal a man on the Sabbath and, knowing the hearts of His critics, "He looked around at them with anger . . . , deeply distressed at their stubborn hearts" because they determinedly put ritual above humanity (Mark 3:5).

We meet it as irritation and annoyance in Mark 1:43, where, after healing the leper, our Lord perceived the character of the man and knew that His enthusiastic but thoughtless gossip would threaten the whole synagogue tour on which He had just embarked: "Jesus sent him away at once with a strong warning." In the Greek the force of the verbs here is such that we could perhaps venture the free translation, "He packed him off with a flea in his ear"! As Jesus foresaw, the result was indeed the end of His series of synagogue-missions at that time. Even the crowds had to look out as Jesus "strictly charged" or "forcibly ordered" them not to advertise Him as a wonderworker (Matthew 12:16).

We meet this anger in stronger forms still, before demons (Matthew 17:18), before nature in upheaval (Matthew 8:26), before sickness (Luke 4:39), and especially in the presence of death. At the death of Lazarus He "raged inwardly" (Gk.) at the grief death had produced (John 11:33) and wept in consequence of that (v. 35). As He approaches the tomb He "rages" with irrepressible anger at the havoc death has wrought in the creation of God (v. 38), His indignation boiling over in groans and tears. Nothing could be stronger than the Greek word used to describe His emotion in these verses, a word usually translated "deeply moved," but which in classical Greek was used among other things for the snorting of horses and the fretting men!

Recalling that last scene, and the vivid Greek word used to depict Jesus' emotion, Os Guinness's comment reminds us of the full perspective of horror which Jesus must have had upon the world around Him: "Entering His Father's world as the Son of God, He found not order, beauty, harmony and fulfillment, but fractured disorder, raw ugliness, compete disarray—everywhere the abortion of God's original plan. Standing at the graveside, He came face to face with a death that symbolised and summarised the accumulation of evil, pain, sorrow, suffering, injustice, cruelty and despair."[16] When we consider that perspective, we are perhaps less surprised that anger so frequently accompanied Jesus' compassion, and indeed was an integral part of it.

Here, then, were no placid healings, but healings by a *man*, a deep-souled, red-blooded man whose healing ministry was carried out in strong reaction and conflict and warfare with sin and Satan. Moreover, and apart from His healings, we meet with Jesus' anger in naked and judgmental force in the cleansing of the temple, where He wrecks the market and drives out the stall-holders (Mark 11:15–17; John 2:13–17), and we see it too in His violent denunciation of the Pharisees as "hypocrites," "whited sepulchers," a "brood of vipers," and in the terrible woes of Matthew 23. How vividly all of this stresses the totality of that humanity which He assumed.

## Joy and Sorrow

From the Gospels we also discover something about the joys and sorrows of our Lord in His humanity. We see Him enjoying the feasting and the merriment of life—so much so that His enemies slandered Him as a drunkard and a glutton (Matthew 11:19). And we see Him filled with spiritual joy as He "rejoiced in the Holy Spirit" (Luke 10:21, RSV) in contemplation of His Father's conquering mercy and triumphant grace. We see Him too, and most memorably, as the "man of sorrows": not, to be sure, permanently morbid and depressed, but profoundly aware of human sin and misery, and deeply conscious that He must bear the burden of it alone and to the full. In prospect of His suffering He is agitated with grief and foreboding (John 12:27), filled with turmoil at the thought of being separated from the Father in His human consciousness. He felt the chill of Calvary's shadow long before He opened His submissive soul to its darkness.

Nowhere do compassion and sorrow appear more dramatically human in the life of Jesus than in Luke's account of His approach to the city of Jerusalem shortly before His passion: "As he approached Jerusalem and saw the city, he wept over it and said, 'If you, even you, had only known on this day what would bring you peace . . .'" (Luke 19:41). Here the key Greek

word in the original is much stronger than our English rendering, and refers to a loud, demonstrative expression of grief. It
says not that our Lord "wept" over Jerusalem, but that He
"wailed" over it.

Think of it: here we are on the first Palm Sunday; Jesus is
making His famous entry into Jerusalem surrounded by cheer-
ing crowds, His way strewn with palm branches. The air is
filled with joyful Hosannas as they round the bend in the road
and see before them the ancient city in its glory, when suddenly
Jesus Himself breaks forth in a flood of tears, and wails loudly
over the terrible rejection that is about to take place there. He
wails over a rejection that will bring such catastrophe and
wrath upon the people. Over the doomed city God is wailing
like a first-century Jewish peasant.

Finally, at the end of His ministry and in the Garden of
Gethsemane we are given an unforgettable sight of the Son of
Man as the "man of sorrows," almost buried in the desolation
of the hour. Remember, in Gethsemane Jesus is standing on the
brink of the abyss, on the borders of hell itself! He has been the
sin-bearer from the moment He came "in the likeness of sinful
flesh," but now He is to bear to the full the wrath of God for sin
so that the children might go free.

In their account of His feelings at this point, the gospel
writers seem to compete with each other in the vividness of the
Greek words they use. Before the cross of Golgotha Jesus feels
grief and loathing (Matthew 26:37), alarm and agitation (Mark
14:33), a profound agony of fear (Luke 22:44). Yet running
through all His emotions like a wind blowing a fire to greater
and greater strength, there is His determination to go where
the Father is leading Him and to do the work He has. In Jesus
at Gethsemane "the horror of death and the ardour of obedience meet."[17] Here the perfect man is ready to become the perfect sacrifice for sin.

## THE INCARNATION: AN ETERNAL FACT

However, we are not to leave the incarnation of the Son of
God behind as a past event, something to be consigned to history. There is a sort of eternal postscript to the record of His
human life on earth that we must understand. Having become

man, God the Son will never cease to be man. Even in heaven
and through all eternity He will be God-in-the-flesh, albeit glorified flesh. The humanity that He assumed on earth He has
taken to heaven. There, it is no longer a penalized, suffering
humanity, but a human body irradiated with the glory of God
and a human mind filled with the joy of God. The eternal Logos
will forever know in Himself the joy of the redeemed as well as
the triumph of the redeemer. He will forever live in and through
His two natures.

The implications of this for our planet and its people are
enormous. It means that there is a *human being* on the throne
of the universe! In the place of supreme and central significance for all creation there is a man, a member of and the head
of the human race.

Science has taught us something of the vastness of the created universe. But because of its alienation from God and its
consequent deficient understanding of humankind as it should
be, our society has felt shrunken and lost and insignificant in a
vast cosmos. But it is in the teaching and life and redeeming
work of Jesus Christ that we discover reconciled man's true significance and real destiny. It was not into an angelic race that
God was born, but into the people of this "inconspicuous" planet. It is not an angelic nature that He now inhabits and lives
through at the Father's right hand, but a human one.

Go to the spiritual heart of this created universe, and you
will find a man. Go to the place where angels bow who never
fell, and you will find a man. Go to the very center of the manifested glory of the invisible God, and you will find a man: true
human nature, one of our own race, mediating the glory of
God.

# 10

# THE SIGNIFICANCE
# OF THE VIRGIN BIRTH

L uke begins his gospel with two miraculous births, one
from a woman long past child-bearing age, the other from
a young virgin who had never had sexual relations (Luke
1:18, 31). Both of these women, Elizabeth and Mary, are in-
formed of the divine purposes for them by an angel of the Lord,
Gabriel (Luke 1:19, 26). The child of the first—John—is destined
to become the herald and forerunner of the child of the second.
John, a prophet and reformer (Luke 1:15–17), would prepare
the way for one who will be far greater and who would be
called "the Son of the Most High" (Luke 1:32).

The heavenly origin of the second child—Jesus—is
announced in unmistakable terms and demonstrated in an
unmistakable way: "The Holy Spirit will come upon you, and
the power of the Most High will overshadow you. So the holy
one to be born will be called the Son of God" (Luke 1:35).

Throughout the annunciation the divine identity of the
child is the primary truth about Him. He is "the Son of the
Most High" before He is the son of "his father David" (Luke
1:32). Even David's throne is a step down for Him. He does not
derive dignity *from* David's line—He gives dignity to David's
line. I. Howard Marshall makes the statement: "In christological content vs. 32 and 35 stand close together; the concept of
divine sonship, stemming from OT royal ideology, has undergone a transformation of meaning."[1]

As Isaiah 7:14 lies behind the vocabulary and thought of
Luke 1:31 (cf. Matthew 1:21–22), so also Isaiah 9:7 lies behind
1:33. Frequently in the Old Testament David's line is said to be

forever (2 Samuel 7:13, 16; Isaiah 9:7; Psalm 89:3–4, 28–29; 132:1–2, etc.), but here it is not a line of representatives but the Messiah Himself who is to reign forever. As a response to Mary's question (Luke 1:34), it is clear that in verse 35 the angel is not referring to God superintending or assisting a merely human process, but Himself initiating a divinely originated, divinely defined, divinely partnered one: "the power of the Most High will overshadow you." Marshall notes that the verb "to overshadow" is "used of God's presence resting on the tabernacle in the cloud" (Exodus 40:35) and "metaphorically protecting His peoples" (Psalm 91:4; 140:7),[2] and concludes: "The description culminates in the phrase [Son of God], here undoubtedly in its full sense of one begotten by God."[3]

Yet throughout Luke's birth narrative, as in Matthew's, the marvelous birth is set forth not simply as a miraculous event, but as the coming of a savior. As in Matthew's account Gabriel says to Joseph, "She will give birth to a son, and you are to give him the name Jesus, because he will save his people from their sins" (Matthew 1:21), so in Luke's narrative the angels tell the shepherds, "today in the town of David a Savior has been born to you; he is Christ the Lord" (Luke 2:11). He whose name is Joshua/Jesus is Himself what the Hebrew name "Yahweh saves" points to, for He is "God with us" (cf. Isaiah 7:14).

## THE VALIDITY OF THE VIRGIN BIRTH

Few ingredients of the gospel are as commonly ridiculed outside the Christian church, or as widely disputed within it, as the virginal conception (commonly called the Virgin Birth) of Jesus. Many theologians consider it only a myth or a theological interpretation of who Jesus was, the early church's way of making a statement that needs not be taken in a "crudely literal" way today. There are several objections commonly made to the doctrine of a literal virgin birth, despite its long attestation in the ancient creeds. It is commonly pointed out that it is recorded in only two of the four Gospels and is conspicuous by its absence from Paul and the other New Testament writings.

In reply, we have to point out a number of things. Firstly, it is clearly taught in Matthew and Luke and recorded as part of historical narrative as well as theological reflection. Secondly, elsewhere there are a number of hints at the unusualness of Jesus' origins, both from enemies and followers of our Lord. For instance, it may well be that the Pharisees are referring to rumors about Jesus' birth when they say to him, "*We* were not born of fornication" (John 8:41, RSV, emphasis added). Certainly by the second century it was commonly asserted among Jews that Jesus was born out of wedlock, and Origen had to refute Celsus' taunt that the story of the Virgin Birth was invented to cover up Mary's adultery with a Roman soldier.

Thirdly, it is noticeable too that more than once, and in three separate epistles, Paul uses the Greek verb *ginomai*, which means "to come to be," when referring to Jesus' birth, instead of the more obvious and usual verb *gennaō*, which means "to generate, to produce, to beget." (See Galatians 4:4; Philippians 2:7; Romans 1:3; cf. Matthew 1:16, where Matthew brings in the former after repeatedly using the latter in his genealogy of Jesus.) That Paul knew about theVirgin Birth is all the more likely when one considers his involvement with Luke, His traveling companion. Luke had carefully researched his historical materials (see Luke 1:2). He was a physician and would be deeply interested in such information. That he should know about this while Paul did not seems very unlikely indeed.

The alternatives to the biblical testimony either cast doubt on the historical reliability of the biblical writers and their informants, reducing the whole story of the angelic announcement, Mary's astonishment, and Joseph's perplexity and reassurance to a patchwork of myths; or they raise questions about Mary's behavior—not to mention Joseph's gullibility. At the end of the day, of course, the question is a matter of belief in the biblical account as true, and of faith in it as divine revelation.

A second objection commonly brought against the traditional doctrine of the Virgin Birth is that it distances Christ from the rest of us. To this we may be forgiven for saying, "Thank heaven!" for the great message and meaning of the Virgin Birth is precisely that help has come from outside, that something new has begun *in* human history which has not already been fatally vitiated *by* human history. As A. N. S. Lane argues:

The role of Christ requires that there should be both continuity and discontinuity between him and us; that He
should be one of us (Hebrews 2:10–18) and yet also different from us. Jesus is the second Adam—one of the human
race, yet inaugurating a new redeemed humanity. The virgin birth points to this combination of continuity and discontinuity.[4]

Other factors in the Gospels besides this set Jesus apart
even while they bring Him near. After all, the account of His
earthly beginning does not stand in isolation from the rest of
His life as portrayed in the Gospels. He entered this world as no
man has ever entered it, He continued in this world as no man
has ever continued in it, and He left this world as no man has
ever left it. Millard J. Erickson replies to the objection that
Jesus could not be fully human if He had only one human par-
ent by saying: "This confuses the essence of humanity with the
process which transfers it from one generation to another."[5]
Humanity is what the Word assumed (took up into union with
Himself) at the Incarnation: He did not emerge from it, He
entered into it; He came, and unlike us He chose to come (John
6:38, 51; 1 Timothy 1:15; Hebrews 10:7). The biblical writers do
not feel Him to be less close because of this (Hebrews 2:14–18),
or to be less of a comfort to us because of the distinctions that
remained (Hebrews 4:15). They do say, however, "Beyond all
question, the mystery of godliness is great" (1 Timothy 3:16).
A third objection is that God simply does not do this kind of
thing: He does not interfere with "natural laws," He does not
further His purposes by impossible biology—whether virginal
conceptions or bodily resurrections. Readers of the Gospels,
these critics argue, should think less literally and materially
and more spiritually in all this. This objection entirely misses
the uniqueness and the relevance of Christian faith. For the
religion of the Bible makes two things very clear: God acts in
history and God cares for man and His world. The biblical revelation does not leave God in a distant heaven or keep Him on
the sidelines of eventful human history. The God of Abraham,
of Moses, and of the prophets *acts;* not only in the general way
of superintendent but in the specific and marvelous way of Sav-

ior, rescuing His people Israel and leading them to His destiny. The God of the New Testament acts, and in the mightiest of His mighty acts, in the fullness of time, into the world of Caesar and Herod, He sent His Son so that there might be peace on earth and thereby "glory to God" (Luke 2:14).

Everything that Christ does thereafter belongs to the world of things, not just ideas: His healings, His ethics, and His promises. He has come to men and women in His bodily existence to save them in their bodily existence, to be a dying man's "resurrection" as well as his "life" (John 11:25). He shows this in His incarnation into human, concrete—yes, brutish—human existence: a baby with dirty diapers, an adolescent with sexual drives, a man weary and in pain, and finally a dying man *among* dying men, but also a man dying *for* dying men; and, on the ground of His atoning death, rising in His body; raised in His material (yet precious, Psalm 139:14) existence; raised not as a spiritual memory, but as a concrete fact by a Father who loves Him in His whole divine-human existence, and who in Him loves us and will raise us in "[our] mortal bodies also" (Romans 8:11, RSV; cf. 1 Corinthians 15:42–44).

The more sophisticated and philosophical and "spiritual" we become, in some ways the less biblical and even Christian we become in our thinking. For the Christian gospel is in crucial ways more materialistic than any alternative! Whether in the doctrine of the Virgin Birth or the doctrine of the bodily resurrection of Jesus; whether in its accounts of the miraculous or its encouragement of the merciful; whether in the Genesis account of creation or the Revelation description of a new (renewed) heaven and earth, the religion of the Bible shows that God is not divorced from the material world but dedicated to it, not separated but involved, not the prisoner of His laws but the king of His kingdom. As the teaching of the Virgin Birth reflects this, it must never be lost to the church or the church will be lost to the world.

## AVOIDING A FATAL ERROR

A proper knowledge of the miraculous and virginal conception of our Lord will protect us from a fatal error which has, unhappily, been common from the earliest days of the church in one form or another. In the early centuries the error was abroad that Jesus Himself was a good but otherwise ordinary man who was "adopted" into God at some later date, having been possessed by the eternal Logos at His baptism. Today it is frequently maintained by theologians that Jesus was a man (no more) who acquired "the significance of deity" at His resurrection and ascension. In either case we are left with a deified man (and a corresponding idolatry in the church that worships Him!), whereas Scripture and the manner of His birth assert His unique and divine identity *at the start* of His earthly life.

However, Jesus' uniqueness from the start of His earthly life is not due simply to the fact of a virginal conception. It is the product of a unique and direct work of the divine Logos operating with and by the Holy Spirit in that event. In other words, we must not think of the conception of Jesus, even as a miraculous event, in biological terms alone. It is not merely a freak parthenogenesis (which would anyway invariably produce a girl, the male Y chromosomes being absent in the female). It is a deliberate and utterly special work of the Holy Spirit who *Himself* achieves by a fresh creative act the fertilization of Mary's ovum and the beginning of a human life with which the eternal Logos unites from the earliest moment of its creation.

## A FOUNDATIONAL DOCTRINE

However, the question remains: Why is this fact of virgin birth so important in regard to a doctrinal understanding of Christ's person and work, especially His incarnation and His atonement considered as an unbreakable unity? Is the doctrine of the Virgin Birth at that point debatable, negotiable, or dispensable, or is it foundational, both as a historical fact and as a theological truth? Karl Barth recognized that this doctrine is as vital for Christology as for salvation as a whole, and stressed that the virginal conception of Jesus means that "God Himself—acting directly in His own and not in human fashion—stands at the beginning of this human existence and is its direct author." It is, he says, "the first attestation of the divine Sonship of the man Jesus of Nazareth, comparable with the miracle of the empty tomb." And, challenging those critics who regarded it as dispensable, he insists: "The question is pertinent whether

His divine Sonship and the mystery of His incarnation are
known in any real seriousness and depth when these attesta-
tions of it are unrecognised or overlooked or denied or explained away."[6]

But why, precisely, is the doctrine so crucial? After all, Jesus
did not become the Son of God by the Virgin Birth. Nor is the
virginal conception itself the Incarnation, but rather a circum-
stance of the Incarnation. The Incarnation itself is the Logos
assuming flesh; the virginal conception is the means and method
by which He chose to do it.

By His virgin birth Christ, the last Adam, enters the world
guiltless of the sin of the first Adam. This is the key to Joseph's
exclusion. God has constituted the first man, Adam, as the head
of the race and the representative of all others. All men are
involved in the primal rebellion of the Fall, in the guilt that follows from it as well as the depravity (sinfulness) that flows
from it (Romans 5:12; cf. Hebrews 7:10; Psalm 51:5). Like all
others, any child of Joseph and Mary would have been involved
in the guilt of that first, racial, transgression. That is why help
from the outside is necessary. Christ the last Adam must be
such as can begin and *be* a new beginning for humanity. He is
born of Mary so that His humanity can be true; He is born of
God so that His humanity might be new. He is connected with
the race ("Behold, you will conceive in your womb," Luke 1:31,
RSV), but He is unconnected with the racial sin ("What is conceived in her is from the Holy Spirit," Matthew 1:20; "therefore
the child to be born will be called holy, the Son of God," Luke
1:35, RSV). It is an understanding of guilt that is decisive for our
understanding of the Virgin Birth.

It is not that Jesus will avoid guilt. Not at all! Rather He will
not share in the world's guilt as a sinner, but will bear the
world's sin as a savior (Matthew 1:21). And He will do so volun-
tarily; not passively in His birth, but actively in His death. As
G. C. Berkouwer says:

He, the man from heaven, does not originate in this world.
He is not by virtue of His birth subject to the judgment
which rests on mankind, but He will vicariously take it
upon him. . . . The guilt, the alien guilt comes into this life

only when He, the Son, God's holy child Jesus, takes it upon Himself, and only thus He enters into judgement, foresakenness and condemnation.[7]

The line between Christ's conception and His atonement is unbreakable. In the one we have God in the person of the Son breaking into human history; one golden link entering the iron chain of human descent. What no evolution could throw up God sent down. What man was helpless to do (Romans 5:6), God did. And in the other we see Him carry that work through to a final conclusion, for "when the time had fully come, God sent his Son, born of a woman, born under law, to redeem those under law, that we might receive the full rights of sons" (Galatians 4:4–5).

## MATTHEW'S USE OF
## ISAIAH'S IMMANUEL PROPHECY

On Matthew's use of Isaiah's famous Immanuel prophecy a great deal has been written and claimed. The disciple wrote: "All this took place to fulfill what the Lord had said through the prophet: 'The virgin will be with child and will give birth to a son, and they will call him Immanuel'—which means, 'God with us'" (Matthew 1:22–23).

Because of the remoteness of any such "sign" from Isaiah's day (Isaiah 7:14), and because of the ambiguity of the Hebrew word *almāh*, which may mean simply "a young woman of marriageable age," two different understandings of Matthew's use of the prophecy call for attention here.

One view is summarized by T. M. Dorman. Matthew recorded his birth narratives, says Dorman, "as a sign of God's grace in His history of salvation." In harmony with this he cited Isaiah's prophecy of Israel's imminent deliverance from Syria not as a one-to-one fulfillment of the Immanuel saying, but rather as "a foreshadowing or type, of an even greater even (anti-type): the coming of the true 'Immanuel' and Israel's deliverance from the bondage of sin" (Matthew 1:21). "Thus," he concludes, "Matthew cited Isaiah 7:14 not to provide a proof text for the claim that Jesus was virgin-born, but to interpret the meaning of the Virgin Birth as a sign of God's salvation within the frame-work of Israel's history as God's covenant people."[8]

John N. Oswalt recognizes a historic and decisive moment in the history of David's house in Ahaz's apostasy (Isaiah 7:1-17; cf. 2 Kings 16:10-16). In the king's refusal of a sign from Yahweh, Oswalt sees "an abandonment of God by the dynasty" that "opened the door for its eventual destruction" as a reigning house. He continues, "Although Ahaz, through his distrust of God, has brought the strictly human dynasty to an end, God is still with David and Judah, as finally evidenced in the divine Messiah, Immanuel."[9]

However, Oswalt insists that the sign eventually given in spite of Ahaz's refusal must bear upon his situation, and "to suppose that the sign did not occur in any sense until 725 years after the fact flies in the face of the plain sense of the text."[10] What would be a sign to Ahaz is that a child shortly to be born would not exceed a certain age (Isaiah 7:15) before the present crisis would be over and Ahaz's panic shown to be unnecessary and faithless. Oswalt himself sees two levels of fulfillment at work in regard to this prophecy. He finds it "perhaps the most attractive option" to suppose that Immanuel and Maher-shalal-hash-baz (Isaiah 8:1-4) "were one and the same,"[11] pointing however to the ultimate Immanuel.

D. A. Carson takes a different view.[12] Citing work by J. A. Motyer and J. Jensen, he sees the Isaiah passage as predicting a long period of tribulation, not only for Ahaz but for the whole "house of David" because of its unfaithfulness to Yahweh (Isaiah 7:2, 13). The curds and honey Immanuel will eat (Isaiah 7:15) represent the only food left in the land on the day of wrath (Isaiah 7:18-22). Motyer shows the close parallels between the prophetic word to Judah (Isaiah 7:1-9:7) and the prophetic word to Ephraim (Isaiah 9:8-11:6). Both are chal-lenged with a moment of decision as a future of both wrath and rescue is prophetically unfolded:

If this is correct, Isaiah 7:1-9:7 must read as unit—i.e., 7:14 must not be treated in isolation. The promised Immanuel (7:14) will possess the land (8:8), thwart all opponents (8:10), appear in Galilee of the Gentiles (9:1) as a great light to

those in the land of the shadow of death (9:2). He is the
Child and Son called "Wonderful Counselor, Mighty God,
Everlasting Father, Prince of Peace" in 9:6, whose government and peace will never end as He reigns on David's
throne forever (9:7).[13]

## THE GENEALOGIES OF MATTHEW AND LUKE

The two genealogies of Matthew and Luke are strikingly
different, and the problem of harmonization is impossible to
solve with certainty. However, as F. F. Bruce writes:

> The main purpose of the two lists is to establish Jesus'
> claim to be the Son of David, and more generally to empha-
> size His solidarity with mankind and His close relation with
> all that had gone before. Christ and the new covenant are
> securely linked to the age of the old covenant.[14]

The New Testament gives frequent and united witness to
Jesus' place in David's line, as Joachim Jeremias shows. He
holds with others that "Matthew traces the genealogy of Jesus
back to David through the reigning line (i.e. Solomon), but
Luke traces it through a non-reigning branch (Nathan)."[15] Thus
Matthew gives the legal line of descent from David, stating who
was the heir to the throne in each case, but Luke gives the actual descendants of David in the branch of the family to which
Joseph belonged. "At the same time," comments Marshall of
Luke's genealogy, "we may be sure that the carrying back of the
genealogy to Adam is meant to stress the universal significance
of Jesus for the whole of the human race, and not merely for
the seed of Abraham."[16]

The question may be asked: Why, if Jesus is the child of
Mary and not Joseph, are the genealogies of Matthew and Luke
necessary, since they are Joseph's pedigrees and not the physical family tree of Jesus at all? Furthermore, how can Jesus be of
the line of David and "great David's greater son" if He is not
physically related to Joseph, David's descendant?

First, it is not necessary, as some have done, to take the
genealogy in Luke as relating to Mary in order to make at least
one of the genealogies relevant by our standards and to harmo-

nize their differences. This line of argument has a very old pedigree, but J. G. Machen thinks it "very doubtful."[17] It is, to say the least, rather forced, since there is no real evidence for it in Luke's account, and one would certainly have expected Luke to make clear something so relevant to his main purpose in tracing the genealogy. Indeed, nowhere in the New Testament is Mary said to have been of the Davidic line, nor was it necessary that she should have been. Moreover, among the Jews women did not have such genealogies, since ancestry was traced on the paternal side.

How, then, do we relate Jesus to these genealogies? The answer lies in the ancient laws of adoption, where an adopted child was legally and in the fullest sense regarded as the true and proper child of his adoptive parents. Hence Joseph, in taking Mary as his wife (Matthew 1:24), and in himself naming the child Jesus (Matthew 1:25), as the angel had directed, takes the child as his own, investing Him with all the inherent rights of sonship, including pedigree and inheritance. Jesus is the son of David because Joseph is the son of David. This does not in the least "reduce" Jesus' relationship to the house of David, a relationship that was common knowledge in His life (Matthew 15:22; 21:9; Mark 10:47) and carefully asserted by His apostles after His resurrection (Romans 1:3, etc.). Nevertheless David's son is also David's Lord (Mark 12:35-37); and while on earth, and even in heaven, His human connection with the house of David remains, to fulfill all the ancient promises. Yet He is not "contained" in David's household, but is far greater in His heavenly person than in His official earthly lineage. He takes His place *over* rather than simply within David's house. This is precisely the point Jesus makes to the Pharisees in Mark 12:35-39.

Even "great David" is not the explanation of his "greater Son." "The doctrine of the Virgin Birth," concludes Erickson, "is a reminder that our salvation is supernatural." It "points to the helplessness of man to initiate even the first step in the process. Not only is man unable to secure his own salvation, but he could not even introduce the Saviour into human society."[18] However, "with God all things are possible" (Matthew 19:26; cf. Luke 1:37).

# PART 3

## JESUS CONFESSED
## AND ADORED

# 11

# "YOU ARE THE MESSIAH"

In this part we are going to examine five great titles of Christ and two outstanding confessions by which the New Testament churches and their leaders acknowledged His uniqueness as the Savior whom God sent into the world for its salvation.

Oscar Cullmann developed *The Christology of the New Testament* largely by means of the titles given to Jesus in the New Testament, titles such as Lord, Son of God, Mediator, etc.[1] There is enormous value in considering those titles in depth. However, it is wise to note David Wells's caution that "The titles are part of the overall affirmation" of the New Testament concerning Jesus "and should not be considered apart from it."[2] C. F. D. Moule wonders if the concentration on titles has missed the "even more significant" Pauline insight of Christ as "more than individual."[3] This, for lack of a better term, he calls "an understanding and experience of Christ as corporate,"[4] implied when all Christians are described as "in Christ," or the church is described as "his body" and "temple."

Nonetheless, it is obvious and universally agreed that the various titles given to Christ in the New Testament are supremely important, and we turn now to look more closely at some of the most prominent.

## "MESSIAH" IN THE OLD TESTAMENT

Most of us are not Jewish. But it is to the Jewish people that we owe the knowledge of the true God, His character and His purposes. They kept burning the lonely flame of true religion when all the world was dark in ignorance, superstition, and pagan religion. They did so because God had chosen them as a nation for this task and sent to them His prophets with His message concerning His character, His will, and His future purposes.

Our New Testament writings build on this and record the fulfillment of much that had been prophesied centuries before. They too are written largely by Jews and refer back to the ways in which God had taught His chosen people and prepared the world for what He planned to do, and of course center on Jesus, the Jew who claimed to be God's Savior-Son for all men.

We cannot fully understand the New Testament unless we understand something of the Old Testament writings: their prophecies, their concepts, and their hope. And nowhere is this more obviously true than in connection with Jesus as the Messiah of the Jews and, more specifically, the Messiah of God.

The term *Messiah* means "anointed." It is, in its origin, a Hebrew word, and its Greek equivalent is *Christos*, hence our word "Christ." In the Old Testament both the king of Israel and the nation's high priest were formally anointed with oil when they were inaugurated into their offices and functions. Their anointing was the point at which God publicly appointed them and by His Spirit empowered them for their work. They were in different ways God's "messiahs" or "anointed ones" although the term *Messiah* is not often used. While certain priests and certain prophets were also anointed in this way, it is notably the king of Israel who is called "The Lord's anointed." However, as the sacred writings of Israel unfolded, hints began to appear that someone would come, in connection with the promised kingdom of God, who would be more than one of Israel's many kings—greater even than Israel's model king, David—and who would function as more besides: Yahweh's King and Priest and Servant.

It is a mistake to look for large blocks of worked-out, finished teaching in the Old Testament. A unique feature of Hebrew religion is that Yahweh is the sovereign Lord of history and revealing Himself step by step as they progressed historically stage by stage. God's revelation in word accompanied His revelation in deed.

Consequently, when we look into the Old Testament writings we should not be surprised to find the truth concerning the Messiah in a growing but fragmentary and diversified form. Indeed there are few explicit references to the Messiah as such in the Old Testament: only a series of varied prophecies and oracles that find in Jesus and His historical work (His ministry, cross, resurrection, and second coming) their unifying point and complete fulfillment. That is one reason why Jesus waited until His work was achieved before interpreting "what was said in all the Scriptures concerning himself" (Luke 24:27). It is only His fulfillment that makes sense of hidden types and cryptic prophecies that appear in Israelite history, temple ritual, and prophecy.

Central to the Old Testament hope is the coming of Yahweh Himself to establish His kingship in the world He has made. The various Old Testament theophanies are His appearances on earth for the deliverance of His people; the "day of the Lord" is His coming to earth in judgment and salvation; and the hope of the kingdom of God is the expectation of His advent to establish His sovereignty and salvation. "There could never have been a stage in Israel's history," writes G. R. Beasley-Murray, "when the kingdom of God was looked for apart from the coming of Yahweh."[5]

The Old Testament has much to say about the future kingdom of peace that God will bring to the world. In fact, in the Old Testament revelation the future kingdom receives much more attention than the future Messiah.[6] The reason for this may well be the long-emphasized expectation that the future era of peace will come about by the personal intervention of Yahweh, who would come in justice and mercy to establish His kingdom in the world. Out of this prior and primary hope grew the expectation that a messianic figure would appear as the representative of Yahweh in His kingdom. Only the event itself would show how completely the two would be one.

As we read the Old Testament there appears at crucial points a figure who is closely connected with the future kingdom of God on earth: a figure who is at one time prophetic (Deuteronomy 18:15–19), at another time priestly (Psalm 110:4; Zechariah 6:12–13), and often kingly (2 Samuel 7:12–13;

Psalm 2:6; Isaiah 11:1). Various "royal psalms" become messianic as their theme connects and disconnects with Israelite monarchs (Psalms 2, 18, 21, 45, 63, 72, 89, 110, 132), and the best ideal of earthly kingship acts only as a springboard from which the thought of the writer leaps to a greater destiny in the plan of God. However, the identity of such a ruler would remain obscure until He came.

Similarly, in Isaiah's series of servant songs (Isaiah 42–53) the scene keeps shifting from the servant Israel to the messianic servant of Yahweh; but more and more an individual appears whose life of mysterious contrasts will only be illumined by the person and work of Jesus Christ (e.g., Isaiah 42:1, 6, 7; 49:5–6; 50:4–8; 52:13–53:12).

Other messianic figures appear in the Old Testament besides the Davidic king and the servant of Yahweh. There is the anointed deliverer of Isaiah 61:1–3; there is Daniel's "son of man" figure from Daniel 7:9–14; there is Jeremiah's "Righteous Branch" (Jeremiah 23:5–6; 33:14–16); and there is Micah's "Ruler from Bethlehem" (Micah 5:2–4). There are also the three figures of Zechariah 9–14: the king riding on an ass of chapter 9, the martyr of chapter 12, and the shepherd of chapter 13, all three of whom are recalled by Jesus (Mark 11:1–10; Matthew 24:30; Mark 14:27).

Even the history of Israel foreshadows His coming, as events and circumstances become types—that is, models or patterns—of what He will do. These lie embedded in the Old Testament record, to be integrated theologically by New Testament writers and preachers as well as by Jesus Himself, who is the anti-type to which they point. (See, for example, Matthew 2:15; 12:38–41; 1 Corinthians 10:1–4; Hebrews 9:8–9; 10:1.) R. T. France traces many more such types, and concludes:

> Thus Jesus saw His mission as the fulfillment of the Old Testament Scriptures; not just of those which predicted a coming redeemer, but of the whole sweep of Old Testament ideas. The patterns of God's working which the discerning eye could trace in the history and institutions of Israel were all preparing for the great climax when all would be taken up into the final and perfect act of God which the prophets

foretold. And in the coming of Jesus all this was fulfilled. That was why He could find "in *all* scriptures the things concerning Himself."[7]

## "MESSIAH" IN THE TIME OF JESUS

From the Gospels it is clear that by the time of Jesus the term *Messiah* had become the outstanding title and name of one expected person in Jewish history: a figure prophesied in the sacred writings and long promised as the final Savior of His people.

However, it would appear that contemporary ideas about the coming Messiah were very vague and confused. The people, as we see from the Gospels, generally thought of Him as a heroic national leader who would drive Israel's enemies (and especially the Romans) from the sacred territory and would lead God's chosen people to world supremacy and dominion. Their Messiah was a kingly, national, and political figure (Matthew 21:9; John 6:15).

The Jewish leaders may have had more sophisticated ideas about Him, seeing Him in more spiritual and theological terms (though still stressing His kingly victory as another David—Matthew 22:41–42; Mark 12:35). However, here is a very curious fact: close research into the rabbinic traditions of the period suggests that the religious leaders of our Lord's day spoke and thought surprisingly little about the Messiah. It may be that this was due to political compromise; it may well be that it was out of a reaction against messianic excesses in the past and present. Most likely, it was due to an excessive preoccupation with the Torah, the law of Moses. At any rate, the most recent research has failed to find outside the Gospels a single saying about the Messiah by the teachers of Israel in the time of Jesus. In contrast to this, we learn from the Dead Sea Scrolls that the monastic Jews of the desert Qumran community at this time spoke a good deal about the Messiah. In fact they envisaged two Messiahs, one a kingly and the other a priestly Messiah, and they stressed the superior role of the priestly Messiah. Neither, however, was a suffering Messiah. Only later would speculation grow in Judaism that the Messiah would suffer defeat and death before the consummation (4 Ezra 7:28–29).

The nearby Samaritans, with their own semi-Jewish theology, also expected a Messiah, whom they called "the Taheb," the Restorer, who would, in some way not clearly worked out, restore the fortunes of His people, including the despised Samaritans with their mixed descent.

One common awareness ran through all these different traditions: the sacred writings promised that Yahweh would one day vindicate His true worshippers by establishing His kingdom on the earth and over all the nations. Out of that hope the various messianic traditions and expectations grew.

## JESUS' SENSE OF MESSIANIC IDENTITY

I find it impossible not to suppose that Jesus was fully aware of His ultimate messianic significance and destiny from the start of His ministry—and before. His birth had been surrounded by such announcements (Luke 1:32–33, 43; 2:11, 26), and no doubt His "silent years" at Nazareth had included a good deal of reflection both upon Mary's account of His birth and upon the Old Testament Scriptures, which were so full of Him. His messianic self-understanding surely grew with His general self-awareness in a complex of growth and influences that are hidden from us. The first we know about it is that at twelve years of age He gave voice to an already well developed inner awareness of a unique relationship with God: "And he said to them, 'How is it that you sought me? Did you not know that I must be in my Father's house?'" (Luke 2:49).

Certainly Jesus saw Himself as the anointed speaker of Isaiah 61 (Luke 4:16–22), and He regarded His precursor and herald, John the Baptist, as the promised "Elijah" who was to prepare the way for the Messiah in "the last days" (Malachi 3:1; Matthew 11:14). John himself, it will be recalled, spoke of the Coming One (whom he later identified as Jesus [John 1:29–36]) in distinctly messianic categories of both salvation and judgment (John 1:19–27; Luke 3:15–18).

In His public speech and in His private utterances the disclosure, though often ambiguous, was present to those who had "ears to hear." Jesus demonstrated the presence of the kingdom of God as operative in His mighty acts and effective in His authoritative words. In His various parables He set forth

His unique relation to the kingdom as its champion (Mark 3:27), initiator (Matthew 11:12), instrument (Matthew 12:28), representative (Luke 17:20–21), mediator (Mark 2:18–19) and revealer (Matthew 13:16–17; cf. 11:25–26).

The conclusion is irresistible, says Beasley-Murray, that Jesus "*assumed* for Himself the function of Messiah" (emphasis added).[8] Indeed it is hard to believe that the title "Christ" should even have become a personal name for Him, if Jesus had not implicitly during His ministry, and explicitly after His resurrection, connected Himself with the messianic hope.

At least two of His public acts were self-consciously messianic: the cleansing of the temple near the beginning of His public ministry, which was surely a deliberate fulfillment of the prediction in Zechariah 14:21; and, of course, near to the close of His public ministry, the entry into Jerusalem on a donkey, in clear fulfillment of Zechariah 9:9. However, in neither case was there an attempt to add worldly resources to messianic privileges. The cleansing of the temple repudiated clearly and even violently the power base Jesus might have sought among the ruling classes. The Zechariah prophecy, though known to be messianic, linked Messiahship to peaceful and nonpolitical ideals, and Jesus only chose to make such a public "statement" when His rejection by the Jewish rulers was irreversible and His death very near.

At His trial Jesus broke His reserve on this subject because He was faced with direct questions as to His identity from the high priest who, in spite of personal unworthiness, was the highest representative of the people: "Again the high priest asked him, 'Are you the [Messiah], the Son of the Blessed One?' 'I am,' said Jesus. 'And you will see the Son of Man sitting at the right hand of the Mighty One, and coming on the clouds of heaven'" (Mark 14:61–62). And at the second trial Pilate could speak to the crowd of "Jesus who is called Christ" (Matthew 27:17, 22); and it was as a messianic pretender that Jesus was crucified, condemned out of His own admission.

In spite of Jesus' reluctance to use a title that had become debased by political and nationalistic associations, the event at Caesarea Philippi recorded in all the Synoptic Gospels puts

Jesus' messianic identity and self-awareness beyond doubt. It is for that reason worthy of close attention.

Jesus Himself precipitated Peter's confession at Caesarea Philippi, and it is clear that the incident that is recorded as a turning point in terms of Mark's gospel (Mark 8:27–30) was also a deliberately planned turning point in Jesus' self-revelation.

William Lane shows how, in recording this episode, "Mark has placed at the center of his narrative the recognition that Jesus is the Messiah."[9] Up to that point Jesus' public ministry in both word and deed had been strikingly ambiguous. His extraordinary deeds of power amazed the people (Mark 1:27), even while His association with sinners scandalized their spiritual guardians (Mark 2:16). At times He seemed to claim everything (Mark 2:7), and at others refused to claim anything (cf. Mark 6:44–45; John 6:14–15). Demons retreated in terror even as they confessed Him (Mark 1:24–26; 3:10–11; 5:7–8), but religious leaders confronted Him without terror as being in league with demons (Mark 3:20–23). The disciples themselves were in a degree of confusion and uncertainty. Lane comments:

> The disciples raised the question of Jesus' identity but found no categories by which they could understand Him (Ch. 4:41; 6:51f.), and failed to penetrate the veiledness which characterized His words and works (Ch. 8:17–21). By weaving these several strands of the tradition together in the first half of the Gospel, Mark creates a climate of tension which can be resolved only by the recognition of Jesus' dignity.[10]

At Caesarea Philippi Jesus asks His disciples the question, "Who do people say I am?" (Mark 8:27). They reply that Jesus is John the Baptist raised from the dead, or Elijah come to herald the end of time, or another of the great Old Testament prophets. To the people these may have been attributions of high honor, but they fell hopelessly short of the truth. They assigned to Jesus a role that was preparatory rather than definitive, subordinate rather than supreme. Jesus did not come to point to another, but was Himself that other to whom all the prophets pointed.

Therefore He brushes aside these suggestions and asks the question more urgently, "But who do you say that I am?" Peter answers, "You are the Christ [the Messiah]" (Mark 8:29). Matthew (16:16) fills out Peter's confession ("You are the Christ, the Son of the living God") and records more of Jesus' response. There is no reserve at this point, only further and deeper revelation about Himself as He replies, "Blessed are you, Simon son of Jonah, for this was not revealed to you by man, but by my Father in heaven" (Matthew 16:17).

Almost immediately, however, this break in the clouds closes up again and Peter, striving to mold Jesus to his own messianic expectations, urges Him to turn away from the path of suffering and the cross—and is sharply rebuked (Mark 8:31–33). In this He shares with all the disciples a persistent confusion about the nature of Jesus' messiahship (e.g., Mark 10:35–36; Acts 1:6)—confusion which could easily fuel the wrong kind of enthusiasm. Hence they are bound to silence after the Transfiguration (Mark 9:9; cf. Matthew 17:9). They will never understand Him as the Messiah until they understand Him as the suffering Son of Man; therefore they cannot preach His glory until they can also preach His passion.

The point, however, has been made and affirmed; the statement that Jesus is the long-awaited Messiah has been made no less by Jesus than by Peter; the "messianic secret" is to the disciples a secret no longer, though the full significance of it remains a mystery until after Calvary.

## JESUS' SENSE OF MESSIANIC SUFFERING

Before the Resurrection Jesus did not systematically expound the messianic theme of the Old Testament. In His three years of preaching, the kingdom is to the forefront. Only after the climactic events of Calvary and the Resurrection does He interpret to His disciples "what was said in all the Scriptures concerning himself" (Luke 24:27; cf. 24:44–45). His finished work would gather up the scattered and disparate images of the Messiah in the Old Testament. Only when His life, death, and vindication by God lifted His claims above contention could He clearly be seen to be David's Lord, Isaiah's servant of the Lord, Jeremiah's righteous Branch, and Zechariah's lowly king, martyr, and shepherd.

However, there is one aspect of prophecy concerning Himself that Jesus did begin to emphasize to His "inner circle" of disciples during the last six months of His public ministry, as well as after His resurrection. Again and again He warned them that the Son of Man (His frequently used alternative to the abused title "Messiah") must suffer and die to fulfill His ministry of redemption and salvation (e.g., Matthew 16:21; 17:9–12, 22–23; 20:17–19, 28; 21:33–42). This, though persistently misunderstood before the event, was the core of His teaching after Calvary and the Resurrection:

> "Did not the Christ have to suffer these things and then enter his glory?" . . .
> Then he opened their minds so they could understand the Scriptures. He told them, "This is what is written: The Christ will suffer and rise from the dead on the third day, and repentance and forgiveness of sins will be preached in his name to all nations, beginning at Jerusalem." (Luke 24:26, 45–47; cf. Acts 17:3; 26:23)

This revelation of the Messiah's work is repeated in other Son of Man sayings, and most clearly during the Last Supper.

There is reason to think that from the start of His ministry—and long before, in "the silent years" at Nazareth and in Galilee—Jesus had reflected long and prayerfully on the suffering servant songs of Isaiah's prophecy, and especially on the climactic chapter 53. We have, surely, a direct allusion to Isaiah 53 in Mark 10:45, "For even the Son of Man did not come to be served, but to serve, and to give his life as a ransom for many." There the term "ransom," says France, is "not far from equivalent" to "offering" in Isaiah 53:10, and the phrase "to give His life a ransom for many" is "a perfect summary of the central theme of Isaiah 53, that of vicarious and redeeming death."[11] This is confirmed by Jesus' words at the Last Supper: "This is my blood of the covenant, which is poured out for many" (Mark 14:24). This recalls the sacrificial offerings of Exodus 24:8, whose blood Moses calls "the blood of the covenant."

Here Jesus, the self-conscious anti-type of those offerings, sees His own sacrifice as the sign and seal of the new covenant that God had promised through Jeremiah (Jeremiah 31:31) and the foundation of the new community that God was about to build. However, His words also recall the closing words and central theme of Isaiah 53. Isaiah says of the servant, "He bore the sin of many," *many* being almost a technical term in the song (vv. 11–12). Correspondingly, Jesus here speaks of His blood as "poured out for many." Here He gives the theological rationale for the necessity of His death by saying that there can be no new covenant and no new community apart from His own vicarious and redemptive suffering as it is predicted in Isaiah's final servant song.

It would be strange indeed if we did not find references by the New Testament writers to the outstanding prophecy in Isaiah 53. And it is a fact that while there are few direct, explicit quotations, the echoes and recollections of Isaiah's suffering servant songs are many.

Matthew recalls the words "He took up our infirmities and carried our diseases" (Matthew 8:17) from Isaiah 53:4, although he links it more generally with Jesus' whole work rather than solely or more particularly with His work of atonement on the cross. Luke records Jesus quoting the words "And he was numbered with the transgressors" (Luke 22:37) from Isaiah 53:12. John explains the unbelief of the Jerusalem crowds in the words "Lord, who has believed our message, and to whom has the arm of the Lord been revealed?" (John 12:38) from Isaiah 53:1. In Acts we read that Philip expounded Isaiah 53:7–8 ("As a sheep led to the slaughter," etc.) to the Ethiopian treasurer in terms of "the good news about Jesus" (Acts 8:32–35). The apostle Paul in Romans (15:21) explains the rationale behind His missionary work in terms of Isaiah 52:15; and in Philippians (2:6–11) Paul uses many striking verbal echoes of Isaiah's words, such as "[he] emptied himself" in 2:7 (RSV).[12]

## "MESSIAH" IN THE
## PREACHING OF THE APOSTLES

Jesus' emphasis on His ordained sufferings and atoning death became central to the apostolic gospel. Peter preaches it on the day of Pentecost, proclaiming to the crowds that Jesus' resurrection by God was the final proof that He is in truth God's Messiah, destined to suffer (Acts 2:23) for the sins of the people. He adds that the Messiah now was enthroned as Lord by God: "Let all Israel be assured of this: God has made this Jesus, whom you crucified, both Lord and [Messiah]" (Acts 2:36).

Similarly, we learn that Paul begins his ministry in various parts of the empire by showing the local Jews in their synagogues and elsewhere that the Old Testament Messiah was *destined* to suffer as well as conquer, and that in Jesus all this has been fulfilled. For example, of his mission at Thessalonica we read:

> As his custom was, Paul went into the synagogue, and on three Sabbath days he reasoned with them from the Scriptures, explaining and proving that the Christ had to suffer and rise from the dead. "This Jesus I am proclaiming to you is the Christ," he said. (Acts 17:2–3)

This emphasis could not have been more astounding to most Jews, whose idea of their Messiah was of an irresistible conqueror rather than a suffering servant. Recent attempts to show a line of tradition in pre-Christian Judaism that did suggest a suffering Messiah are not convincing, and the consistent impression given by the New Testament is that the apostles' teaching about a suffering Messiah constituted a scandal to the Jews generally (John 12:34; 1 Corinthains 1:23). Certainly the *manner* of Jesus' death made it seem outrageous to most devout Jews that He could possibly be the Messiah, for impalement upon a stake was, in Jewish law, the sign of God's final and complete abandonment and curse (Deuteronomy 21:23; Galatians 3:13), whereas the true Messiah would be God's beloved Son and champion. The obvious meaning of Isaiah 53 was incomprehensible to them, and its message was either ignored or changed into the suffering not of Messiah, but of His enemies. Only later, perhaps as a counter to the Christian claims from the Old Testament, or because of profound experiences of national sufferings (such as the fall of Jerusalem in A.D. 70 and the disastrous revolt of Simon bar Kochba in A.D. 135) did the idea of suffering as well as conquest enter into the Jewish traditions concerning their great Messiah.

For Paul the crucified Messiah ("Christ") is central both in his theology and his preaching. Indeed he speaks of the cross of Christ rather than the death of Christ (1 Corinthians 1:17, 23; Galatians 6:12) because the Cross fills, not empties, his claim that Jesus is God's anointed Savior. Christ crucified is the end of the line of Old Testament sacrifices for sin and guilt: He is the passover lamb that redeems us from our bondage (1 Corinthians 5:7), and His blood is the ratification of God's new covenant (1 Corinthians 11:25).

For Paul, then, the term *Christ,* while it has become a personal name for Jesus (he uses it no less than 379 times), never loses its historical sense. The place of God's Messiah in Old Testament prophecy and the place of the Old Testament Scriptures themselves (2 Timothy 3:16–17) ensure that. But Paul's old Judaistic understanding of the promised Christ has been totally transformed, both by the Christ-event and by the change in Paul himself (2 Corinthians 5:16). He no longer sees the Messiah as the embodiment of nationalistic bigotry and pride, but as God's Christ for all peoples, the author and promoter of Paul's great work among the Gentiles:

> For I tell you that Christ has become a servant of the Jews on behalf of God's truth, to confirm the promises made to the patriarchs so that the Gentiles may glorify God for his mercy, as it is written: . . . "The Root of Jesse will spring up, one who will arise to rule over the nations; the Gentiles will hope in him." (Romans 15:8–9, 12)

In a word, Jesus is not merely the Jews' Messiah, He is *God's* Messiah. He is not only God's anointed Savior to Israel (Romans 11:26), but to the whole world besides (Romans 15:19–20; 2 Corinthians 1:19). He belongs not only to Israel, but to all who believe and who thereby become His people (Hebrews 2:13).

## THE SON OF DAVID

It was commonly supposed that the Messiah would be a descendant of King David, fulfilling in Himself the great prophecy of 2 Samuel 7:13, 16: "I will establish the throne of his kingdom forever. . . . Your house and your kingdom will endure forever before me; your throne will be established forever." The Old Testament writings taught that the Messiah would be a descendant of David (Isaiah 11:1, 10; Jeremiah 23:5–6; Ezekiel 34:23–24), and He is even called "David" (Jeremiah 30:9; Ezekiel 34:23; Hosea 3:5).

Matthew in particular gives attention to the title "Son of David," and it occurs more frequently in his gospel than in the whole of the rest of the New Testament. Jesus becomes "Son of David," although it is Joseph who is a descendant of David (Matthew 1:20) and who adopts Mary's child as his own (Matthew 1:20–21). "It is significant," writes C. E. B. Cranfield, "that in Matthew 1:21 Joseph is commanded to name the Child. . . . To give the name was to accept the child as one's son. Joseph's acceptance of Jesus as his son would have conferred on Him all the legal rights of legitimate sonship."[13] This is reinforced for his readers by the genealogy which Matthew provides, where "David the king" plays a key role in the structure of the genealogy (Matthew 1:6, 17). The same emphasis, however, also occurs in Luke (Luke 1:27, 32, 69; 2:4, 11).

As with the title Christ, or *Messiah,* Jesus does not use *Son of David* of Himself, but allows others to use it. It was clearly messianic language and as such both appropriate and dangerous. Those who use it in the gospel accounts are often people of no social or political or theological account, the "little children" in contrast to the "wise" (Matthew 11:25; 21:14–16), often the sick and needy, the blind, the lame, the dumb, the outcast (Matthew 9:27; 15:22; 20:30–31). From these Jesus accepts the designation. The shadow-side of this is a popular acclaim in which Jesus is seen as the focus of merely material or nationalistic hopes (Matthew 12:23; 21:9; cf. John 6:15).

Jesus Himself consistently walks away from such dangerous populism and also counters misunderstanding among the Pharisees in this respect in Matthew 22:41–45. The point of Matthew's account of Jesus' repudiation of its use, as France notes, "is not that Jesus is not Son of David, but that He is *more than* Son of David." He continues: "The explicit contrast is with being David's *Lord,* which at least implies someone superior to David rather than a mere replica of the former king of Israel."[14] Moreover, the invitation given by Yahweh to David's Lord, "Sit at my right hand," means that He does not merely occupy the throne of David, but the throne of God, and takes up a position of transcendent authority.

Jesus' Davidic origin was clearly a feature of the early Christian preaching (Acts 2:29–36; 13:22–23; Romans 1:3), but other references to it in the New Testament are very few (2 Timothy 2:8; Revelation 3:7; 5:5; 22:16). For Jews it would be seen as an important messianic qualification and as fulfilling prophecy. Further, Paul uses it in Romans 1:3 as the sign of Christ's full human nature. Just as "Son of God" for Paul involves a community of nature with the Father, so being the Son of David "according to the flesh" (RSV) shows a community of nature with the house of Israel and with the whole of mankind.

While "Messiah" is an obviously Jewish category in so much of its history and use, it is clear that it cannot be left in its Jewish past. For He who is the long-awaited Messiah of one people comes at last as God's anointed for all peoples. His mission transcends all nationalisms, as His message challenges all politics. He is Christ for the nations, who breaks down divisions, and in whom "the Gentiles are heirs together with Israel, members together of one body, and sharers together in the promise in Christ Jesus" (Ephesians 3:6). He is our Messiah too, our King of Glory and our Prince of Life.

# 12

# "JESUS IS LORD"

A gainst a general background of "many gods and many lords" in the pagan world of the first century, the apostle Paul, writing to Christians in Rome, summarized the uniqueness of their Christian hope and baptismal faith in these words: "If you confess with your mouth, 'Jesus is Lord,' and believe in your heart that God raised him from the dead, you will be saved" (Romans 10:9). At another time, against a church background of "superior" charismatics at Corinth, he showed the unity of all Christian spiritual experience and the giftedness of all Christians in the Corinthian church in these words: "No one can say, 'Jesus is Lord,' except by the Holy Spirit" (1 Corinthians 12:3). Elsewhere, against a cosmic background of alien demonic powers and rebellious human societies Paul, writing to the Philippians, can look forward to the time when every knee will bow "and every tongue confess that Jesus Christ is Lord, to the glory of God the Father" (Philippians 2:10–11).

It is clear, then, that in the initiatory rite of baptism, the ongoing life of the church, and in her creedal expressions of hope for the future, this was the mark of Christian faith: the confession that "Jesus is Lord." But what precisely does the term *Lord* mean when applied to Jesus, how is it used, and how did it come to be used in this way?

## JESUS AS LORD
## IN HIS PUBLIC MINISTRY

In the ancient world, the title *Lord* could be used in a variety of ways. In the mouth of a polite subordinate it could mean no more that "sir"; on the lips of a slave it could mean "master"; in the worship of an individual or congregation it could mean "God." Consequently, when we come across the term in the Gospels, or see it in the Epistles as a confessional statement about Jesus, we are likely to wonder precisely how far it actually takes us. It denotes dignity, certainly; but we shall find that in the way the New Testament uses the title *Lord* of Jesus, it carries us beyond creaturely dignity right up to divine honors and ultimately means of Jesus all that it means of God.

First of all, it is clear that in the Gospels "Lord" can be a quite elastic form of address, virtually synonymous with "Master" or "Teacher." As a polite and respectful form of address it need be no more indicative of divine honors than the schoolboy's "O Sir" confers a knighthood on his schoolmaster—to recall Moule's amusing comparison.[1] However, while we cannot attribute to all or even most of the occurrences of the word in the Gospels the theological significance that it would have later, there is still an element that we should not miss. When lepers (Matthew 8:2) and blind men (Matthew 9:28), distraught parents (Matthew 17:15; Mark 9:17, 24) and anxious friends (Matthew 8:5) kneel before Jesus and say, "Lord, help," there is already an acknowledgment of competence beyond the normal. This remains true even if titles like "Teacher" or "Master" are used.

The address "Lord" assumes precisely the dimensions of the situation, and when the situation is grave and even humanly hopeless, and yet the need of that situation is met, the word is likely to retain all those dimensions in the wondering and grateful hearts of those who have been helped. Jesus becomes to some degree, in the minds of those He cures and of those who witness the events, "Lord" over disease, over demons, even over death itself.

### The Disciples' Use of the Word "Lord"

Similarly, the disciples' use of the word "Lord" to Jesus deepens when they turn to that lordship in extreme danger (such as "Lord, save us!" in Matthew 8:25), or when they begin to share its power ("Lord, even the demons submit to us in your name" Luke 10:17); the word has deeper meaning when they anxiously invite His inspection into their deepest heart ("Is it I, Lord?" Matthew 26:22 [RSV]).

Yet even deeper and more obviously theological dimensions to the title occur early in the Gospels, indicating from the start that Jesus is Lord in a special way. The angelic announcement in Luke 2:11 ("for to you is born this day in the city of David a Savior, who is Christ the Lord" [RSV]) occurs in a context where "Lord" is used to denote God Himself no less than twenty-seven times. At that point, surely, as Donald Guthrie says, the title "must convey some connotation of divine lordship."[2] Jesus' words in Luke 6:46, "Why do you call me 'Lord, Lord,' and not do what I tell you?" (RSV), taken in conjunction with what follows, cause I. H. Marshall to conclude: "The authority of Jesus over His disciples goes beyond that of a rabbinic teacher. . . . Already, therefore, during His ministry the address of [Lord] was taking on a deeper significance than a mere honorific 'sir.'"[3]

This is vividly illustrated by the incident involving Peter and Jesus in Luke 5:1–11, where after Peter has heard Christ teach the people with unique authority and insight the deep things of God (see Matthew 7:29; John 7:46), he observes Jesus' power in the physical realm also. And the combination of the sermon he has just heard and the miraculous catch of fish he has just witnessed causes Peter, utterly overcome with awe before this person who clearly has authority in realms both heavenly and earthly, to sink to his knees at Jesus' feet. He cries out, "Go away from me, Lord; I am a sinful man!" (Luke 5:8). There is already far more than respect in that reaction of Peter: there is religious awe. Thereafter, the title is often found on Peter's lips in one form or another.

Perhaps, however, there is no instance more moving or more charged with final conviction about Jesus' unique and eternal worth than Peter's reply to Jesus' question after many other disciples had left Him. Jesus asks His twelve closest followers: "You do not want to leave too, do you?" We read: "Simon Peter answered him, 'Lord, to whom shall we go? You have the words of eternal life. We believe and know that you are the Holy One of God'" (John 6:67–69).

All this is not to make the term Peter's alone, for the others

use it too, and not only the Twelve. John records an incident in
which Jesus is addressed and perhaps even worshipped as Lord
by a man whose congenital blindness has been marvelously
cured. In him Jesus finds an unlikely defender before the Pharisees (John 9:30–33), even at great personal disgrace and cost.
In a sense, the experience of Peter at Galilee referred to earlier
is repeated here, for in the subsequent meeting with Jesus word
and miracle meet, Jesus reveals Himself as the Son of Man, and
this man responds, "Lord, I believe," and he worships Him
(John 9:38). Leon Morris comments: "There is little reason for
thinking that 'Lord' has less than the maximum content."[4] Morris later concludes, "The man has already recognised that Jesus
came from God (v. 33). Now he goes a step further. He gives to
Jesus that reverence that is appropriate to God."[5]

In John 11, with its account of the raising of Lazarus,
Martha and Mary both know Jesus as "Lord" (vv. 21, 27, 32),
and Martha learns that His lordship is not even limited or
dwarfed by death itself:

> Martha answered, "I know he will rise again in the res-
> urrection at the last day."
> Jesus said to her, "I am the resurrection and the life. He
> who believes in me will live, even though he dies; and who-
> ever lives and believes in me will never die. Do you believe
> this?"
> "Yes, Lord," she told him, "I believe that you are the
> Christ, the Son of God, who was to come into the world."
> (John 11:24–27)

It is obviously ludicrous to dismiss the title "Lord" in such
contexts as merely a polite form of address!

One disciple who receives far less attention in the Gospels
than Peter, and who is chiefly remembered as doubting the
Resurrection, is Thomas. Yet to him it is given to confess the
lordship of Jesus in the highest way of all, uniting it directly
with deity: "Thomas said to him, 'My Lord and my God!'" (John
20:28). That, however, is after the Resurrection, a time when
the title comes into its own in a new way.

### Jesus' Use of the Word "Lord"

Meanwhile, we should not fail to note how Jesus uses the title "Lord" of Himself. Here too it is raised far above any merely human lordship. He announces himself as "Lord of the Sabbath" (Matthew 12:8); "Lord of the harvest" of men and women destined for the kingdom of God (Matthew 9:38); supreme "Lord of the day of judgment," who will be acknowledged as such by saved and lost alike (Matthew 7:21–22; 24:42–51; 25:11–44).

One of the most important of Christ's sayings about His lordship, and one especially significant for the Jews of His time, is found in Matthew 22:41–45. There He asks the Pharisees, "What do you think about the Christ? Whose son is he?" They reply, "The son of David," to which Jesus responds, "How is it then that David, speaking by the Spirit, calls him 'Lord'? For he says, 'The Lord [Yahweh] said to my Lord: "Sit at my right hand until I put your enemies under your feet."' If then David calls him 'Lord,' how can he be his son?"

The point here was that the Jews, and especially the Pharisees, had effectively subordinated the lordship of the expected Messiah to that of David, by making the Messiah's lordship something that was *conditioned* by the historic model of Israel's greatest king. In response, Jesus warns them against subordinating the Christ, the Messiah, to their political and nationalistic dreams about a second David and a restored golden age of military and political supremacy.

Earlier He had said that in Him someone greater than Jonah (Matthew 12:41) and someone greater than Solomon (Matthew 12:42) was present among the Jewish people. Here He insists that someone greater than David is present in Him, and someone whose lordship is correspondingly greater: one before whom David himself bowed in the spirit of prophecy, one whose lordship transcends any human and earthly sovereignty, and who has His true origin as well as His destiny in the heavenly places. "Implicit in these words," says F. F. Bruce, "is a suggestion of the divine dignity of the Messiah."[6]

It is noteworthy that an element that appears more than once in Jesus' use of the word "Lord" is that of absolute and authoritative *ownership*. He expects those who call Him Lord to do whatever He commands: "Why do you call me 'Lord,

Lord,' and do not do what I say?" (Luke 6:46). He warns that those who do not submit to His absolute lordship will not survive His judgment (Matthew 7:21–23). The demands of His lordship transcend all other loyalties, even family ones: "Anyone who loves his father or mother more than me is not worthy of me" (Matthew 10:37–39; cf. Luke 9:59–62). Loyalty and obedience to Jesus' lordship is loyalty and obedience to God, and the one easily shades off into the other: He and the Father are one, and men must honor the one as they do the other (John 5:23).

Even in His parables this element of ownership is prominent: Jesus appears time and again as the master, the lord, the owner. In Matthew 10:25 and Luke 13:25 He calls Himself "the master of the house." (The Greek word for "master" there is *despotēs,* from which we get our word "despot.") Few words could express more forcefully the sovereignty of Christ over His kingdom and all who are in it.

## JESUS AS LORD
## AFTER THE RESURRECTION

It is, however, after the Resurrection that the New Testament preaching and teaching about Jesus is showered with references to Him as "Lord." In the last two chapters of John, for instance, the title is used again and again, and Jesus is continually referred to as "the Lord." The greatest confession comes from the greatest doubter among the Twelve—Thomas: "My Lord and my God!" On this G. R. Beasley-Murray writes:

> His statement is not simply a mode of address to Jesus, in the vocative ("O my Lord and my God!"), still less an exclamation, to the praise of God . . . ("My Lord and my God!") . . . Rather it is a confession issuing from the depths of Thomas' soul: "You are my Lord and my God." . . . His utterance does not simply acknowledge the reality of the resurrection of Jesus, but expresses its ultimate meaning, i.e., as revelation of who Jesus is.[7]

In the preaching of Acts the title becomes not only a title of honor, but an emphatic declaration, proclaiming to all men the real significance of Jesus both in His earthly character and work and in His heavenly glory and power. While most of the addresses to Jesus as "Lord" in the Gospels have a basically nontheological use and content, this changes after His resurrection, and the title regularly assumes its full significance. Nevertheless, even after the Resurrection it is not simply Jesus' essential, eternal lordship that is referred to, but most often His mediatorial lordship. Such a lordship is one decreed (Psalm 2:7–8; 89:27), earned (Hebrews 2:9; 5:8; 10:12–13), and invested (Acts 13:33; Hebrews 5:5). John Murray makes this distinction clear when commenting on Paul's words in Romans: "For this very reason, Christ died and returned to life so that he might be the Lord of both the dead and the living" (Romans 14:9). He writes:

> The lordship of Christ here dealt with did not belong to Christ by native right as the Son of God; it had to be secured. It is the lordship of redemptive relationship and such did not inhere in the sovereignty that belonged to Him in virtue of His creatorhood. It is achieved by mediatorial accomplishment and is the reward of His humiliation (cf. Acts 2:36; Romans 8:34; Philippians 2:9–11).[8]

It is worthwhile at this point to consider once more the Old Testament passage quoted by Jesus, Psalm 110:1, and to notice the further use the New Testament preachers and writers make of it. This perfectly encapsulates the two levels of lordship, essential and earned, eternal and acquired. In Mark's gospel Jesus quotes the entire verse, "The Lord said to my Lord: 'Sit at my right hand until I put your enemies under your feet'" (Mark 12:36), but concentrates on the fact that "David himself calls him 'Lord'" (Mark 12:37). Typically, Jesus makes no direct use of the enthronement spoken of in the quotation, since He has consistently avoided crude Jewish enthusiasms about the reign of the Messiah. But He does point His critics to the implied dignity of the Messiah, a dignity essential to His identity from the start, and present there and then.

The apostles, however, when they make use of the quotation, stress the reign of "David's Lord," a reign that was still future for Jesus when He first quoted the Scripture, but a reign with which He was invested at His ascension. So we read repeatedly of His place "at the right hand of God" as the promise of the ancient messianic psalm is again and again recalled.[9] The apostles use the phrase to emphasize Christ's mediatorial lordship. That lordship is not simply a passive honor; it's an active rule, a universal and a priestly rule that exists for His people, the church.

This, of course, is entirely in harmony with Jesus' point, for such a place is essentially incompatible with any mere created being, even one of the highest order: "To which of the angels did God ever say, 'Sit at my right hand until I make your enemies a footstool for your feet'?" (Hebrews 1:13).

We can see, then, that while the elements of Jesus' original lordship and His acquired lordship may be distinguished, they are not divorced from each other in the later New Testament texts.

The many references in Acts to Jesus as Lord also maintain His essential and rightful position alongside the Father, and also alongside the Holy Spirit. Thus the gospel is summarized as turning "to God in repentance and [having] faith in our Lord Jesus" (Acts 20:21), and believers are said to be baptized "into the name of the Lord Jesus" (Acts 19:5) as an appropriate shorthand for baptism into the triune name of the Deity (Matthew 28:19).

"It is characteristic of Acts," writes B. B. Warfield, "that a large number of passages occur where we cannot be sure whether *Kurios* means God or Christ,"[10] the Father or Jesus. Throughout Acts, as throughout the rest of the New Testament, the title Lord "vibrates between the two," to quote Warfield's vivid phrase. The interchange between God the Father and Jesus the Son is nowhere more strikingly brought out than in Stephen's dying words, "Lord Jesus, receive my Spirit," which recall Christ's last words on the cross, "Father, into your hands I commit my spirit" (Acts 7:59; Luke 23:46). Where Jesus commends His spirit to God, Stephen commends His spirit to the "Lord Jesus."

## JESUS' LORDSHIP
## IN THE EPISTLES OF PAUL

As we might expect, it is in the New Testament epistles that we find a more fully worked-out theology of Jesus' lordship. Here we shall confine our attention mainly to the writings of Paul, for whom "the Lord" is a favorite name for Jesus. (It occurs over 230 times in his letters.) The significance of this is that "Lord" was the name given to Yahweh in the synagogues and in the common speech of Greek-speaking Jews, and it occurs as such over six thousand times in their Greek version of the Old Testament, the Septuagint. In the Greek-speaking synagogues throughout the world it would be used in the reading out loud of the Scriptures when the sacred name "Yahweh" occurred in the text. The name of Yahweh was considered too sacred to pronounce, and it was substituted in Hebrew with the word *Adonai* and in Greek with the word *Kyrios*—that is, "Lord." *Kyrios*, "Lord," was the utterable name of the unutterable God.

Hence, in Paul's work among the Gentiles and the Jews of the dispersion, the Greek Bible's name for Yahweh becomes his name for Jesus—and in contexts just as worshipful, just as heavenly, just as cosmic as anything found in the Old Testament. As J. G. Machen observes:

> When the Christian missionaries used the word "Lord" of Jesus, their hearers knew at once what they meant. They knew at once that Jesus occupied a place which is only occupied by God. For the word "Lord" is used countless times in the Greek Scriptures as the holiest name of the covenant God of Israel, and these passages were applied freely to Jesus.[11]

The New Testament is full of instances of this last point. Time and again Paul takes from the Greek version of the Old Testament, the Septuagint, passages that refer to Yahweh as Lord and applies them directly to Jesus as Lord. An example of this is in Romans 10:13, where he applies the important text Joel 2:32 to Jesus so that it becomes no longer "everyone who calls on the name of the Lord [Yahweh] will be saved," but "everyone who calls on the name of the Lord [Jesus] will be saved." (This seems to be the thrust of Peter's argument, too, in Acts 2:21, 36, 38.) In Isaiah 45:23, the statement "To me every knee shall bow, every tongue shall swear" (RSV) is clearly spoken of Yahweh. Yet while Paul refers this text to God in Romans 14:11, he refers it to Jesus in Philippians 2:9–11, giving Him equal honor with the Father: "Therefore God exalted him to the highest place . . . that at the name of Jesus every knee should bow . . . and every tongue confess that Jesus Christ is Lord." Yahweh "gave him the name that is above every name." This, says Cranfield, "can hardly mean anything else than the peculiar name of God Himself."[12] It is given to Jesus in order that every created being in the universe might accord Him the divine honors proper to God.

So close is the connection between Jesus and God, and so complete is their essential unity, that, far from diminishing the Father's glory, the confession of Jesus as Lord is an integral part of it. God has given Him His own name of Lord, so that every knee might bow "and every tongue confess that Jesus Christ is Lord, to the glory of God the Father" (Philippians 2:11).

Among the greatest prerogatives of God, according to Old Testament teaching, is the final judgment of the world. In the New Testament this prerogative is transferred to Jesus. In Paul's teaching, as in Jesus' own teaching while on earth, the famous Old Testament "Day of the Lord," the day of judgment, has become "the day of our Lord Jesus Christ" (1 Corinthians 1:8; 1 Thessalonians 5:2, 2 Thessalonians 2:2). The judgment seat of God (Romans 14:10) and the judgment seat of Christ are one and the same (2 Corinthians 5:10). If the Aramaic cry *Maranatha* in 1 Corinthians 16:22 does not mean "Our Lord has come," but rather "Our Lord, come!" (as RSV), then it is best understood as an early eschatological prayer similar to the "Come, Lord Jesus" of Revelation 22:20, and as an invocation used in the worship of the Aramaic-speaking churches of Paul's day.

In view of this, it is not surprising to find the apostle Paul ranging Christ alongside God when he prays to Him as Lord (2 Corinthians 12:8), blesses believers in His name as Lord (1 Thessalonians 3:11–13; cf. Romans 1:7, 1 Corinthians 1:3; 2 Corinthians 1:2), and directs doxologies to Him as Lord (2 Timothy 4:18). As Old Testament believers called upon the name of Yahweh, so now New Testament believers call upon the name of Jesus (1 Corinthians 1:2) as Lord of the church (1 Corinthians 1:2) and overlord of the world (Acts 10:36). What only God has, He has: the kingdom of God is the kingdom of Christ (Ephesians 5:5), the Spirit of God is the Spirit of Christ (Romans 8:9), the gospel of God is the gospel concerning His Son (Romans 1:1, 3), without whom God himself would have had no gospel and the nations no hope (Romans 1:4–6). "Paul's entire preaching," writes Herman Ridderbos, "is characterised by the recognition of the absolute equality and unity between Christ and the Father. Everything which is ascribed to God is ascribed also to Christ."[13]

One outstanding example of this is in 1 Corinthians 8:6, ". . . for us there is but one God, the Father, from whom all things came and for whom we live; and there is but one Lord, Jesus Christ, through whom all things came and through whom we live." This statement of Paul's is remarkable, according to D. R. deLacey,[14] as a Christianizing of the famous Jewish *Shema*—a twice-daily recital of prayer of several vital passages from the early Old Testament Scriptures (Deuteronomy 6:4–9; 11:13–21; Numbers 15:37–41). This prayer begins in words that are the heartbeat of Jewish monotheism: "Hear, O Israel: The Lord our God is one Lord . . ." (Deuteronomy 6:4, RSV); words that stress to generations of Jews the uniqueness, the unity, and the absolute sovereignty of Yahweh. For Paul, who had recited the great *Shema* thousands of times, there is indeed "one Lord" who is Jesus, as there is one God who is the Father, who sent Him into the world.

In his letter the apostle has spoken of the many "gods" and "lords" of the Gentiles, contrasting with this his readers' knowledge that for them and himself there is, as the *Shema* reminded the Jews daily, only "one God" (1 Corinthians 8:5–6). But Paul is a Christian as well as a Jew, and a descendant of Abraham living in a time of fulfillment to which Abraham looked with joy (John 8:56; cf. Genesis 12:1–3). The Messiah has come who is truly the Son of God and who, by His resurrection and exaltation to the right hand of God, has been proclaimed "Lord of all." It is inevitable rather than surprising that Paul should modify the old statement, sacred and fundamental though it was: for the lordship of Jesus Christ was just as sacred and fundamental.

De Lacey concludes, quoting N. T. Wright, "It is hard to conceive of a clearer means by which Paul could indicate both that he was aligning Jesus with the *Kyrios* of the LXX [Septuagint] *and* that he was doing so within a thoroughly Jewish framework of thought."[15] God is still "one" but Christ is one with Him (John 10:30). Of 1 Corinthians 8:6, Gordon Fee notes that while Paul implies that Christ as mediator is subordinate to the Father as source, "the formula is so constructed that only the most obdurate would deny its Trinitarian implications."[16]

Two further items connected with the subject of Jesus as Lord are outstanding in Paul's letters. Firstly, "Lord" has become not only a description but a *name* for Jesus Christ. It is noteworthy that in Paul's letters Jesus is referred to as "Lord" far more often than is God the Father. So persistent is this feature in the New Testament that, according to Warfield, the title "the Lord" becomes "the Trinitarian name of Jesus,"[17] distinguishing Him from God the Father, and yet at the same time placing Him alongside the Father.

Secondly, for Paul the lordship of Jesus is the central testimony of the apostolic preaching (2 Corinthians 4:5), involving as it does not only His heavenly person but His actual work on earth, culminating in His triumphant resurrection. It is the confession of this lordship—the lordship of Him who bore the sin of the world as the crucified Lord (1 Corinthians 2:8) and offers life to dying men as the risen Lord (Romans 6:23)—that saves. As the apostle reminds his readers, "If you confess with your mouth, 'Jesus is Lord,' and believe in your heart that God raised him from the dead, you will be saved" (Romans 10:9).

We can see, therefore, that for Paul "Lord" is the incomparable name of Jesus. It reveals at once His place in the Godhead and in the divine plan of salvation. Cranfield summarizes his own examination of the use of the term "Lord" in Paul's letters thus: "We take it that, for Paul, the confession that Jesus is Lord meant the acknowledgment that Jesus shares the name and the nature, the holiness, the authority, power, majesty and eternity of the one and only true God."[18]

## JESUS' LORDSHIP
## IN THE NON-PAULINE EPISTLES

Outside Paul's letters there are a considerable number of references to Jesus as Lord, none of them insignificant, but two passages that cannot be passed over are in Hebrews and Revelation. In Hebrews 1:10 the writer takes a sublime passage in Psalm 102 in which, amid all the changes of life, some of them cruel and perplexing, Yahweh (Psalm 102:1) is extolled and trusted as the unchanging Creator (Psalm 102:25–29). The writer takes this passage and applies it to Jesus as the eternal Creator whom God addresses as an equal and whose life and power are said to be coextensive with His own:

> But about the Son he says, . . . "In the beginning, O Lord, you laid the foundations of the earth, and the heavens are the work of your hands. They will perish, but you remain; they will all wear out like a garment. You will roll them up like a robe; like a garment they will be changed. But you remain the same, and your years will never end." (Hebrews 1:8, 10–12)

In Revelation 17:14 the lordship of Christ is graphically given its divine dimensions when two of the greatest and most exclusive Old Testament titles of Yahweh are given to Jesus. In Deuteronomy 10:17 Yahweh is acknowledged as "God of gods and Lord of lords," but here this very title is made over to Christ, the Son, when it is said that the Lamb "is Lord of lords and King of kings" (Revelation 17:14; 19:16). The difference between the Old and New Testament forms of the title need not disturb us. "Lord of lords" replaces "God of gods" to preserve the distinctiveness of the Son from the Father, not to deny Him deity; and "King of kings" is synonymous with "Lord of lords" in the Deuteronomy passage, where "Lord" especially stresses Yahweh's exercise of kingly sovereignty. In this, as in all the other references we have considered, we can easily see the impossibility, indeed the blasphemy, of attributing such honors to a mere creature—however good or great—whether man or angel. Men are sinners, angels are servants, but Jesus, the Son of God, is Lord (Hebrews 1:6–8).

Throughout this study we have seen the term "Lord" oscillate between what Jesus was in Himself and what He became in His mission, between the lordship He had always had as Son and the lordship He achieved as Savior. At times it is difficult to know which is meant. However, what is of chief importance is that the one could not have come into being without the other: Jesus could never have become the Lord He became if He had not already (and eternally) been the Lord He was. Only because of His divine identity was it possible for Him to attain such divine honors as were given to Him upon His ascension and promised to Him at His second coming. Only a divine capacity made it possible, and only a divine identity made it fitting, that Jesus of Nazareth should become Lord of all. That is why the martyrs of the early church chose to die in agony than say the fatal (because they were blasphemous) words "Caesar is Lord." Together with one joyful voice they rose to acknowledge, "Jesus is Lord."

In our own day, too, Christians must make the same affirmation: unique, uncompromising, exclusive as it is. In some cultures such a confession will cost Christians not only comfort and reputation, but jobs, liberty, and even life. In those cultures other gods are Lord or God is not acknowledged as the God and Father of our Lord Jesus Christ. In our own affluent, tolerant, secularized Western culture, however, the only comparable affirmation of Jesus' lordship will be His evident lordship over our lifestyles and our involvements. In the imitation of His universal love, in His practical care and profound self-giving, Christians as individuals and in church communities are called and equipped by His Spirit to make the great confession: "Jesus Christ is Lord."

# 13

# "HE IS THE SON OF GOD"

Jesus is referred to as the Son of God about eighty times in the New Testament. Around the title there cluster many questions. Does its use here imply anything more than it does in the Old Testament, where angels are called the sons of God and where the term is used of kings of Israel and of the nation itself? Does the term place Jesus higher than believers who in the New Testament are called "children" and "sons" of God, and who learn to call God *abba*, "Father," as Jesus did? Was Jesus a different kind of Son from the start, or did He become different only in degree, by His life of perfect harmony with the Father, by His obedience even "unto death," and by the reward which was given Him in His resurrection from the dead and glorification "at the right hand of God"?

It is not surprising that such questions have been asked, since the title Son of God, and indeed the notion of sonship itself, has more than one level of meaning, especially in the Gospels. For instance, what the disciples meant by the term early on (such as John 1:49) was not all that they understood it to mean later (see Matthew 14:33; 16:16), nor was it by any means all that Jesus Himself meant by it.

Martin Hengel carefully explores ideas of divine sonship in the Hellenistic and mystery religions current around this time and (more strongly) after. He sharply corrects twentieth-century ideas that the apostle Paul and others distorted the picture of Jesus to fit in with such thinking. To have made an innocent rabbi from Nazareth into the kind of son-of-God figure which appears in these religions would have involved, within a few years of Jesus' death, "a syncretistic paganization of primitive Christianity"[1] by such early leaders as Barnabas and Paul. Hengel goes on to show how fundamentally different is the early Christian confession "of the one Son of the one God,"[2] and concludes: "There may have been many crucified righteous men in the ancient world. . . . But for Jews and Greeks the crucified God was an unheard of idea."[3]

## JESUS' SENSE OF UNIQUE SONSHIP

Fifty-one times in the first three Gospels, and more than a hundred times in John, Jesus speaks of God as "Father." This in itself is remarkable, and we should not lose sight of that through our own familiarity with the term. For instance, only twice in the Old Testament is God directly addressed as Father, and only fifteen times is the word *Father* used of Him at all— and then only of His relationship to the nation and the king rather than to individuals as such. In corporate worship Jews sometimes spoke of God as "our Father," but the general reluctance to call God "Father," much more "my Father," is reflected in the Palestinian literature around Jesus' time. Indeed, O. Hofius writes, "We have yet to find an example of an individual addressing God as 'my Father,'"[4] even if the phrase "Father in heaven" was occasionally used later.

Jesus, on the other hand, always addressed God in His prayers as "Father" (e.g., Matthew 11:25; Mark 14:36; John 11:41; 12:27; 17:1, 5), a form of address to the Deity which was, as Hofius states, "something totally new in Palestine."[5] Moreover, as D. A. Carson notes, "Jesus' usage of this expression is set in sentences, dialogues and discourses that mark it as unique."[6]

Even more outstanding is the fact that Jesus used the familiar Aramaic word *abba* when speaking to God. We see this recorded explicitly in His cry of agony in Gethsemane (Mark 14:36), where the Aramaic word is retained as well as its translation; but it underlies all such addresses to God in His prayers, as we can see from the variant Greek renderings used in His recorded prayers. The remarkable thing about this is that, although *abba* was the common domestic name for a father (used by children and adults alike, in a way similar to our term "dad"), it was unthinkable to Jews to use such a term before the sovereign God, majestic in power and holiness, father of the nation Israel though He was. Hence Hofius can write: "Nowhere in the entire wealth of devotional literature produced by ancient Judaism do we find [abba] being used as a way of addressing God,"[7] and: "it must have seemed nothing short of outrageous that Jesus should make use of the completely unceremonious Aram. word [abba]."[8] This revolutionary expression in Jesus' prayer life clearly grew out of a unique relationship to God; a relationship prominent in all four Gospels, especially Matthew and John.

## JESUS' SONSHIP IN MATTHEW

"Few," says R. T. France, "are likely to quarrel with the assertion that the presentation of Jesus as the Son of God is central to Matthew's christological enterprise."[9] Matthew, like Mark (Mark 1:1) and even Luke (Luke 1:32), prepares his readers for this revelation early on. The virgin's child will be called "Emmanuel (which means, God with us)" (Matthew 1:23, RSV), and even in His infancy He will in His own person and history prefigure the fulfillment of God's gracious plan for Israel: "Out of Egypt have I called my son" (Matthew 2:15, RSV).

The address is made publicly at His baptism when Jesus, at least, hears "a voice from heaven, saying, 'This is my beloved Son, with whom I am well pleased'" (Matthew 3:17, RSV). Donald Guthrie writes: "There is no reason to suppose from the words themselves that sonship was a new experience for Jesus. . . . The most natural interpretation of these words is to regard them as a heavenly declaration of what was already in the consciousness of Jesus."[10]

After Jesus' baptism, the temptations in the wilderness depend upon rather than dispute the sonship of Jesus for their force (Matthew 4:3, 6; Luke 4:3, 9), since Satan tempts Jesus to use His sonship in a way inconsistent with His God-ordained mission. Carson notes that the parallels between God's son Israel and His son Jesus continue, and writes: "The main point is that both 'sons' were tested by God's design (Deuteronomy 8:3, 5; cf. Exodus 4:22 . . .). . . . The one 'son' failed but pointed to the 'Son' who would never fail."[11]

The Father's declaration at Jesus' baptism is repeated in the incident of His transfiguration where He adds to the words "This is my beloved Son, with whom I am well pleased" the direction to the disciples, "listen to him" (Matthew 17:5, RSV). The synoptic accounts all place it after Peter's confession at Caesarea Philippi, where Peter gives voice to what God has revealed to him in that special moment: "You are the Christ, the Son of the living God" (Matthew 16:16). "What Peter had previously declared," Guthrie concludes, "is visually and orally attested in a supernatural way" at the transfiguration of Jesus.[12]

Jesus' words in Matthew 11:25–30 are of outstanding importance. More clearly and vividly than almost any other of His sayings in the synoptic Gospels, they show Jesus' consciousness of having a unique, exclusive, and crucial knowledge of God as the Son; a knowledge from which all other authentic and saving knowledge would flow to men.

Another significant statement about His sonship is made when, speaking of the day of the Lord—the end, when He would come in the fullness of His kingdom and glory—Jesus says of its timing: "No one knows about that day or hour, not even the angels in heaven, nor the Son, but only the Father" (Matthew 24:36). What is most striking here is not Jesus' confession of ignorance (which should not surprise us), but His sense of occupying an entirely distinct relation to the Father from that of any created being. The Son has a rank and place above men and angels, whatever constraints and limitations He may at present be under.

At His trial, when adjured in His Father's name to say if He is "the Christ, the Son of God," Jesus responds in the affirmative, "Yes, it is as you say." France comments, "Jesus' acceptance of the title 'Son of God' here is taken up as a taunt against Him at the cross, when a remarkable sequence of Christological themes and titles used ironically by the bystanders (including two further uses of 'Son of God,' 27:40, 43) serves to inform the reader of who Jesus really is"[13] And in Matthew 28:19, he notes, "The whole Son of God Christology of the gospel comes to its remarkable climax in the association of 'the Son' with the Father and the Holy Spirit as the joint object of the allegiance of those who are to be made disciples."[14]

## JESUS' SONSHIP IN MARK AND LUKE

Although I have chosen to trace the theme in Matthew, the sonship of Jesus is just as essential to Mark's portrayal and goes to the heart of his Christology. Thus the proclamation by "believing Israel" at its beginning (Mark 1:1) is echoed by a believing Gentile at its end (Mark 15:39), and as in Matthew the theme runs clear through Jesus' ministry (Mark 1:11; 3:11; 8:38; 9:7; 12:6; 13:32; 14:36, 61). Mark leaves his readers in no doubt about the supernatural character of Jesus' sonship. It cannot be "reduced" to an honorific title as in some Old Testament texts, and William Lane writes: "In the ultimate sense 'Son of God' is a mysterious term which Jesus alone can clarify. What Son means is determined by what Jesus is, by what He does, by what He says, and it is this revelation which dominates Mark's Gospel."[15]

In Luke, too, although the title is less conspicuous, it is established from early on (Luke 1:32, 35), and Luke alone has the account of a twelve-year-old Jesus lost in Jerusalem and found in the temple (Luke 2:41–51). Here Luke gives us Jesus' first recorded words, which, in the light of Luke 1:32, 35, as well as what follows, indicate that Jesus already saw Himself in a unique and all-transcending relationship with God His Father. "This event," comments I. H. Marshall, "was a temporary unveiling of Jesus' relationship with His Father; it remained a 'secret epiphany,' a momentary glimpse through a curtain into a private room."[16]

## JESUS' SONSHIP IN JOHN

In his gospel John records more than a hundred occasions when Jesus speaks of God as Father: the Father who sent Him (e.g., 3:34; 5:36, 38; 7:29; 8:42; 11:42), who loved Him (e.g., 3:35; 5:20; 10:17; 17:24), and who waits to receive Him again in glory (e.g., 8:54; 14:12, 28; 16:10, 28; 20:17).

Among Jesus' most important allusions to His sonship in John is His defense against the criticism of the Jewish leaders in John 5:17. They have charged Him with Sabbath-breaking in His healing work, and with claiming equality with God in the sense of competing with God. In response Jesus affirms *both* His equality with and submission to the Father. "The Son can do nothing by himself" (John 5:19), that is, in terms of independent, self-determined action. He works only and always in cooperation with God; and yet His equality is such that "whatever he does, that the Son does likewise." He is indeed subordinate to the Father in terms of His function as mediator and in His earthly state of dependence and lowliness, but He shares the exclusive prerogative of God in the matters of judgment and the eternal destinies of men and women (John 5:20–29).

G. R. Beasley-Murray makes an important point when he argues that although the fourth gospel is "preeminently 'the Gospel of the Father and the Son,'" even "the term 'the Son' itself needs to be complemented with all that the other titles attributed to Jesus in this Gospel signify." In particular, "the frequently reiterated obedience of the Son to the Father (e.g., 4:34; 5:19; 8:29), whom He acknowledges to be 'greater than I' (14:28), requires complementation by the statements in the prologue such as ['and the Word was God'] (1:1)," and by such statements as John 1:18 and 20:28.[17] "Such is the content which the Evangelist would have his readers import into the declaration of faith, 'Jesus is the Christ, the Son of God' (20:31)."

John's Christology is not simply functional, concerned though he is with God's action in Christ. As Beasley-Murray notes, "The unremitting concentration of the Evangelist on the person through whom God acts makes it plain that for him 'function and person are inseparable.'"[18]

God's intention in view of Jesus' matchless prerogative and unequaled relation to the Father is "that all may honor the Son just as they honor the Father" (John 5:23). Carson writes:

> This goes far beyond making Jesus a mere ambassador who acts in the name of the monarch who sent Him, an envoy plenipotentiary whose derived authority is the equivalent of His master's. That analogue breaks down precisely here, for the honour given to an envoy is never that given to the head of state.[19]

Jesus' equality with the Father is no competitive equality, but an essential oneness and inner harmony which God is always ready to affirm in the life and work of Jesus (John

5:36–37). This gives Jesus His true and proper glory without detracting from the glory of His Father.

In John 10:30, in His good shepherd discourse, Jesus says, "I and the Father are one," a statement that in its immediate context means they are "one" in that they share the same will and task, the preservation of the sheep. However, this oneness in function points to a still deeper oneness since, as Carson expresses it, "the oneness of will and task, in this context, is so transparently a *divine* will, a *divine* task (*viz.* the saving and preserving of men and women for the kingdom)."[20]

This oneness with the Father is the guarantee of Jesus' reliability as the revealer and indeed the revelation of the Father. Because He can say, "I am in the Father and the Father is in me," He can say, "Anyone who has seen me has seen the Father" (John 14:9, 10). To reject Him is to reject the Father (John 5:23; 15:22–23), since His words and works are the witness of God (John 5:30, 36; 14:10; 15:24).

No witness to the eternal, pre-temporal nature of Jesus' sonship is clearer than John's record of His "high priestly prayer" in chapter 17: "And now, Father, glorify me in your presence with the glory I had with you before the world began" (John 17:5). If, as Beasley-Murray[21] and others think, the elements of this prayer were spoken by Jesus in the Upper Room amid the profound attention of the disciples, it may be an important link in a chain of thought leading to Thomas's great confession as he sees the risen Lord, ceases to doubt, and finally worships with the famous words: "My Lord and my God!" (John 20:28). Certainly for John, who begins and ends his gospel with Jesus' divine identity (John 1:1, 20:31), the reader, like Thomas, is meant to kneel and adore.

One other feature in John's gospel that highlights the unique nature of Jesus' sonship is His teaching that others can become sons (and daughters) of God only by Him and in Him (e.g., John 1:12; 14:6; 17:22–26).

This is indeed a central principle of the New Testament teaching: "To all who received him, to those who believed in his name, he gave the right to become children of God" (John 1:12). It was commonplace in much pagan philosophy and religion that the deity was a universal father. But in New Testament Christianity, as in Old Testament religion, the fatherhood of God is seen not as something inevitable and universal, but something voluntary and gracious. God's fatherhood is to be associated not with creation, but rather with election: it is not a biological necessity but a saving relationship that God establishes with sinners only in Jesus as their mediator and head.

Hence the New Testament writings in general repeatedly maintain that it is out of God's free love (1 John 3:1) and through the adoption of grace (Galatians 4:5) that we become God's children. "He destined us in love to be his sons through Jesus Christ" (Ephesians 1:5, RSV), and has now sent "the Spirit of His Son" into our hearts so that we cry "Abba! Father!" (Galatians 3:26–27; 4:6; cf. Romans 8:16). Jesus, then, did not see Himself as one among many in this respect, but as incomparable in His sonship, possessing a relationship with God, His Father, which, while itself underived, formed the basis of every other familial relationship with God.

John's gospel in particular is written with such a connection in mind: "These are written that you may believe that Jesus is the Christ, the Son of God, and that by believing you may have life in his name" (John 20:31).

## THE DISCIPLES' GROWING AWARENESS

From early on in their relationship with Him, Jesus' closer disciples began to see something of His unique relationship with God. It is true that we ought not to make a profound theological statement out of Nathanael's enthusiastic acclamation, "Rabbi, you are the Son of God! You are the King of Israel!" (John 1:49, RSV), uttered only minutes after meeting Jesus. It has been claimed that "Son of God" was at this time in Jewish history just coming into use as a title for the Messiah (Matthew 26:63). This may be so (Psalm 2:7; 2 Samuel 7:14), and the connection between the two is made in the Gospels by a disciple (John 1:49) and a critic (Matthew 26:63). There is, however, only a very small amount of evidence (and that disputed) from the Dead Sea Scrolls to support this. For Nathanael at this point, then, "Son of God" is surely not much more than synonymous with "the Messiah."

However, as the disciples' experience of Jesus deepens, so

the terms of honor they give to Him begin to fill out and assume new dimensions. As Guthrie points out, "In view of the
numerous occasions on which Jesus called God His Father it
would have been extraordinary if none of the disciples had recognized Him in a special sense as Son of God and confessed
Him as such."[22] There are elements, in addition to His own
teaching, which would have had this effect. The disciples' awe-
struck cry after Jesus' stilling of the storm and walking on the
water, "Truly you are the Son of God" (Matthew 14:33), is
accompanied by an act of worship which, however limited and
confused in understanding (see Mark 6:51–52), forms an important background to Peter's declaration at Caesarea Philippi:
"You are the Christ, the Son of the living God" (Matthew 16:16).

Peter's words should be judged by Jesus' own response to
them. He states that Peter's insight and confession go beyond a
declaration of messiahship alone; he is, by revelation of the
Father, giving voice to the deepest truth concerning Jesus of
Nazareth: His divine sonship. Brief, and even passing, as this
intuition might have been, it marks an important stage in Jesus'
self-disclosure to His disciples (Matthew 16:21).

Furthermore, after seeing their master transfigured, and
hearing God declare from the Shekinah cloud, "This is my
beloved Son, with whom I am well pleased; listen to him"
(Matthew 17:5, RSV), it is incredible that Peter, James, and John
should not have become aware then, if never before, of a
dimension of Jesus' identity and person that was more than
earthly. They may have "kept silence" (Luke 9:36, RSV)—but
they surely didn't stop thinking!

On a number of occasions the disciples had seen their master narrowly miss death by violence because He made Himself
"equal with God" (John 5:18; 8:58–59; 10:31–33; cf. Luke 4:29),
and from the beginning they had heard demons try to get
power over Him, addressing Him as the divine Son of God in a
futile attempt to render Him harmless. "These cries of recognition," writes Lane, "were designed to control Him and strip
Him of His power, in accordance with the conception that
knowledge of the precise name or quality of a person confers
mastery over him."[23]

## SONSHIP AND PREEXISTENCE

Jesus saw His sonship not only as an earthly reality, but as an eternal fact. It is in the fourth Gospel that sonship and preexistence most frequently and clearly come together. In John's gospel Jesus speaks of Himself nearly forty times as one whom the Father has "sent" into the world. Furthermore, He makes it quite clear that He has not been "sent" in any general or comparable sense. He was sent down to the world before He was sent out into the world: "For I have come down from heaven not to do my will but to do the will of him who sent me" (John 6:38; cf. 8:42; 10:36; 17:18). While others are born in the world, He "came" into the world: from above (John 8:23) and from God (John 8:42). And the place to which He is going is the place from which He came: "Even if I testify on my own behalf, my testimony is valid, for I know where I came from and where I am going" (John 8:14; cf. 16:28; 17:5). What loomed largest in His mind before His passion and death was the knowledge that He was returning to the Father and His preexistent glory: "I have brought you glory on earth by completing the work you gave me to do. And now, Father, glorify me in your presence with the glory I had with you before the world began" (John 17:4–5).

To Jesus, His past was as important as His future. Indeed past and future were vitally joined, for He brought with Him the resources of His eternal Godhead to light man up to something of the quality and duration of the life which He had always had and which He came to share with men—the life of God. Because He is "the true bread from heaven" (John 6:32) He is able to give "life to the world" (v. 33). He has "come down from heaven" (v. 38) to "raise up" (vv. 39–40) all who believe in Him to share in the life of the age to come, the life of the kingdom, "eternal life" (v. 40). The manna of Moses' day, though given from heaven (v. 31), offered only temporary help (v. 58). Jesus, by contrast, is the true bread, of ultimate significance because He shares in the imperishable life of God (v. 57). To believe in Him as sent from God (vv. 28–29), and to receive Him in His full character and work and thus to eat His flesh and drink His blood (vv. 53–54), is to live forever (v. 58) and hunger no more (v. 35).

Thus Jesus links His person and His work, His preexistent life and His resurrection life; He who alone had the first has come to share the second.

If it true that Christ's work is the key to His person, it is equally true that His person is the foundation of His work. P. T. Forsyth writes of Christ's earthly life:

> That life of His was itself but the obverse of a heavenly eternal deed, and the result of a timeless decision before it all began. His emergence on earth was as it were the swelling in of heaven. His sacrifice began before He came into the world and His cross was that of a lamb slain before the world's foundation. There was a Calvary above which was the mother of it all. . . . Unlike us, He *chose* the oblivion of birth and the humiliation of life. He consented not only to die but to be born.[24]

John reflects profoundly on this truth in the early part of His gospel (John 1:1–3; 3:31–32). "Indeed," says Guthrie, "John's whole approach demands that his portrait of the historical Jesus should be viewed from the standpoint of His preexistence."[25]

However, John is not alone in this. This truth was the property of the early church as a whole, and Paul's doctrine of Christ too is firmly rooted in the eternal preexistence of the Son of God. It is the confessional cornerstone of his Christology, as the great passages Philippians 2:6–11 and Colossians 1:15–20 show. If these are indeed early Christian hymns or creeds, as many scholar now agree, it indicates that the preexistence of Christ was a major element in Christian thought and worship from the start.

Paul's doctrine of the preexistence can be found directly in Philippians 2:6–11 and Colossians 1:15–20 and indirectly implicit elsewhere. In Galatians 4:4 and Romans 8:3 we should notice that Christ is said to be a Son *before* His earthly work and heavenly session: "When the time had fully come, God sent his Son, born of woman," and again, ". . . sending his own Son in the likeness of sinful man." And in 2 Corinthians 8:9 Paul urges his readers to generosity by reminding them, "For you know the grace of our Lord Jesus Christ, that though he was rich, yet for your sake he became poor, so that by his poverty you might become rich."

"This pre-existence of Christ with the Father so emphatically declared by Paul," writes Herman Ridderbos, "underlies his whole Christology and makes it impossible to conceive of all the divine attributes and power that he ascribes to Christ exclusively as the consequence of His exaltation."[26]

## SONSHIP AND EXALTATION

A very clear connection is made in the New Testament between Christ's sonship and His exaltation after the resurrection appearances to the "right hand of God." It is not, as we have seen, that there and then Christ began to be the Son of God. Helmut Thielicke insists that "Christ is not made what He is by His task or work. He is not in himself a mere anybody who comes to be qualified as the Christ in virtue of His mission."[27] He was the only Son of God before His exaltation, as He was even in His lowest humiliation. Nevertheless Christ's sonship and His messianic work are so linked that we may not separate His status from His activity, His sonship from the twin considerations of His obedience and its reward.

The apostle Paul writes in the opening words of his letter to the Romans that Jesus has been "appointed" [not merely "declared,", as RSV] by the Holy Spirit "the Son of God by his resurrection from the dead" (Romans 1:4). Commentators are divided on many points here, but C. K. Barrett, John Murray, and C. E. B. Cranfield[28] all agree that "appoint," "constitute," or "install" is the meaning of the first word, not "declared" or "designated," and that it is the Holy Spirit Himself who is referred to as the divine agent in this. Murray quotes Geerhardus Vos's seminal work on this and agrees with his conclusion that the reference is to "two successive stages" in Christ's life, a stage when He was "son-of-God-in-weakness" and a stage when he became "son-of-God-in-power."[29]

The author of Hebrews also follows the same line of descent/ ascent, and everywhere sets Christ's previous standing as the Son (Hebrews 1:2–3) firmly in the context of His work of obedience, suffering, and exaltation: "Although he was a son, he learned obedience from what he suffered" and was by this process "made perfect" as the Son God sent to be the Savior of the world (Hebrews 5:8; 7:28; 1 John 4:14).

The same writer twice applies to Jesus the words of Psalm 2: "You are my son, today I have begotten you" (Psalm 2:7, RSV; Hebrews 1:5; 5:5; cf. Acts 13:33). These words are not meant by the New Testament writers to indicate that at a particular time Jesus became the Son of the Father. "The 'begetting' in the text," says Marshall, "obviously refers metaphorically to the new life in the resurrection and not to any initiation of divine sonship." The Resurrection, he argues, "was a confirmation of His existing position and status."[30] As we saw when examining the question of the preexistence of Christ, it was a basic datum of apostolic teaching that He who was "begotten" at the Resurrection as the Redeemer-Son was Himself without beginning as the eternal Son.

However, the repeated connection between Christ's exaltation and sonship that we find in the New Testament must still be taken very seriously, for it indicates that we must think of Christ always in terms of His commission. Herman Ridderbos is right when he says cautiously: "It is not the Godhead of Christ in itself but that He is God and God's son for us which is the content and foundation even of the most profound of His Christological pronouncements. . . . In a word, His sonship and His Redeemership are in Paul's preaching nowhere abstracted."[31]

## SONSHIP AND REVELATION

In the prologue to his gospel John uses the titles *Word* (John 1:1) and *Son* (John 1:18) interchangeably. While he is not concerned to make a merely philosophical statement about our Lord's essential place in the Deity (he is, after all, writing a gospel of redemption), he is nevertheless concerned to show that the truth of Jesus' eternal being is in fact the explanation of His unique revelation of God and the guarantee of its truthfulness and adequacy. Later in his prologue John speaks of Jesus revealing the glory of God the Father as only a *monogenēs*, an "only begotten" (KJV) or "one and only" (NIV) Son could do: "We have beheld his glory, glory as of the only Son from the Father" (John 1:14, RSV).

As John teaches here and everywhere, Jesus is not just *a* Son or *another* Son, but *the* Son—uniquely significant and beloved by the Father. It is out of that status and relationship that He comes to us with a true and profound revelation of the Father. No one knows the Father as He knows and is known (Matthew 11:25–27). That is why Jesus is the perfect and final revealer of the Father's being and character and will.

Having spoken of the Son as being the "only begotten" of God (John 1:14, KJV), John then uses a more familiar and even domestic picture to show the vantage point from which the Son reveals Him: "The only Son, who is in the bosom of the Father, he has made him known" (John 1:18; cf. 6:46). Scholars are generally agreed that the original statement here, which is preserved in some of the best of the ancient manuscripts, reads "the only *God* who is in the bosom of the Father, he had made him known" (emphasis added, RSV; cf. NIV, main text).

Beasley-Murray, seeing *theos* ("God") as being in apposition to *monogenēs* ("one and only") and as indicating "God by nature" and recapitulating the essence of verse 1 of John's prologue, translates the lines: "God no one has ever seen. The only Son, by nature God, who is ever close to the Father's heart, has brought knowledge of Him."[32] He also points to John's choice of words in saying that this Son who is in the bosom of the Father "has *made him known*": "The term [*exegesato*] is related to the English term 'exegesis'; in Josephus it is the technical term for the exposition of the Law by the rabbis."[33] Even Moses, the Old Testament mediator of the law, who was permitted to see something of God's glory, saw no more than His back (Exodus 33:18–20). "By contrast, however," writes Beasley-Murray, "the only Son, who shares the nature of God . . . has given an authentic exposition of God to man."[34]

Carson describes the remarkable parallels between verses 1 and 18 as "a kind of literary envelope that subtly clasps all of 1:1–18 in its embrace."[35] So, in verse 1 we read that the Word "was with God"; here we read that the only Son was "in the bosom of the Father." In verse 1 we read the Word "was God" and here that the only begotten is himself "God"; in verse 1 He is the Word of God, here "he has made him known." John's prologue is complete. Jesus is the self-disclosure of the unknown

God; He has shared the Father's nature as well as His company, and His revelation of God is not only the echo of an immediate communion (John 5:19, 30), but the outflow of an eternal experience (Matthew 11:27; John 3:13; 8:42).

It is because of this sharing of everything that makes God God, that Jesus can say in reply to Philip's cry, "Lord, show us the Father, and that will be enough for us" (John 14:8):

> "Don't you know me, Philip, even after I have been among you such a long time? Anyone who has seen me has seen the Father. How can you say, 'Show us the Father'? Don't you believe that I am in the Father, and that the Father is in me? The words I say to you are not just my own. Rather, it is the Father, living in me, who is doing his work. Believe me when I say that I am in the Father and the Father is in me; or at least believe on the evidence of the miracles themselves. (John 14:9–11)

There are two things here that are especially prominent. It is not only that the Father is "in Him," but that He is also and conversely "in the Father." There is a mutuality, a mutual interpenetration that raises the Son's condition from privilege to parity. Jesus is not an inspired servant; He is an indwelt and indwelling Son.

Secondly, Jesus does not say, as we might expect, that the Father who dwells in Him "speaks His words," but that He "does His works." Here as elsewhere in John's gospel, Jesus is the Word and revelation of God in all that He is and does as well as in what He says. As Gerhard Kittel puts it: "Jesus is not just the One who brings the Word but the One who incorporates it in His person, in the historical process of His speech and action, of His life and being."[36] When, characteristically, Jesus inserts the caution, "I do not speak on my own authority," it is not because He speaks of God at second hand, but precisely because He is not giving an independent, external testimony about God and the things of God, but is speaking from within an abiding relationship ("the Father who dwells in me"). He is speaking out of a oneness with God ("I am in the Father and the Father in me") which is so close that the Son simply *cannot* speak with an authority which is separable from that of the Father.

As the epistle to the Hebrews reminds us, there have been other revealers of God among the patriarchs, prophets, and psalmists of old, but Jesus is the *climax* of God's self-revelation (Hebrews 1:1–2) precisely because the truth about God comes to us not only through Him but in Him, and that truth becomes saving in His utterly incomparable and decisive work in the cross. The whole of the New Testament is an assertion of Jesus' uniqueness as God's Son and Savior, God *with* us, God *for* us. Its message is that God had only one Son, whom He freely gave up for us all.

## SONSHIP AND SACRIFICE

We shall consider the concept of sacrifice itself in more detail later in this book, but it is worth noting here how the truths of sonship and sacrifice are repeatedly brought together by the New Testament writers both to exhibit the extraordinary love of God and, by implication, to affirm the worth of His "sacrifice for sin." In the most well known of summaries of the Christian "good news," John writes, "For God so loved the world that he gave his one and only Son" (John 3:16), and we should realize that the "giving" here is not simply God sending His Son into the world to be born, but sending Him to die for the world. John puts this clearly in his first letter when he writes: "This is how God showed his love among us: He sent his one and only Son into the world that we might live through him. This is love: not that we loved God, but that he loved us and sent his Son as an atoning sacrifice for our sins" (1 John 4:9–10). God gave His only Son not only to be a preacher of good news, but to become a sacrifice for sin (1 John 1:7), a sacrifice which, with the triumph of the Resurrection, would be the foundation and content of the good news: that sin, guilt, and condemnation had been radically and for all time dealt with by God in Christ, and now sinful men and women could be reconciled to God forever.

John's thought is the same here as that of Paul when Paul writes that God "did not spare his own Son, but gave him up for us all" (Romans 8:32). It was only by "sending his own Son in the likeness of sinful flesh and for sin" that God could "con-demn sin" in the Son as its bearer and free from condemnation those who deserved wrath (Romans 8:1, 3). It is through the death of His Son that God has reconciled His enemies to Him-self (Romans 5:10). Ridderbos observes, as something "highly characteristic of Paul's 'Christology'" that "Christ's sonship and His redeemership are in Paul's preaching nowhere abstracted."[37] Emphatic as Ridderbos is concerning the importance of the preexistence of Christ for Paul, he adds: "It is not the Godhead of Christ in itself, but that He is God and God's Son for us which is the content and foundation even of the most profound of His Christological pronouncements."[38]

Thus two things are repeatedly kept together in New Testa-ment thought: the sacrifice God provided and the sacrifice God accepted. For Calvary was as truly the work of the Father as of the Son. If we hold together these two we shall not make the wrong kind of divisions between Father and Son at Calvary. It was not a case of Christ doing a work separately from His Father, but in perfect union and profound partnership with Him. We cannot enter into that partnership of pain, but notwithstanding the important distinctions that must be made between the Son as God who suffered in our nature and the Father who went with Him to Calvary, we may be sure of this: that Father, Son, and Spirit were united in the great atoning work, for "God was in Christ, reconciling the world unto him-self" (2 Corinthians. 5:19, KJV).

It is crucial that we understand that Christ, as the eternal and preexistent Son, performed the perfect atoning work in His sacrifice. Thus Hughes writes concerning Hebrews 9:13–14: "No finite, temporal creature could ever offer himself as a pro-pitiation of eternal efficacy for the sins of the whole world (1 John 2:2)."[39] If we do not accept Christ as the eternal Son—if we regard sonship as an honor eventually accorded to someone who was originally not more than "man"—then we shall quick-ly lose the entire New Testament witness to the atonement of "Jesus Christ crucified" as being central to the gospel and cru-cial for the forgiveness of sins. Jesus is not simply a Son because of His earthly obedience unto death; His death had its value because He was, in His own being, the Son of God "who loved me and gave himself for me" (Galatians 2:20).

At the Resurrection and Ascension He became the Son in a new way—the Son in His glorified humanity—but He had been no less the Son, the same Son, in His humiliation and earthly life: "Although he was a Son, he learned obedience from what he suffered and, once made perfect, he became the source of eternal salvation for all who obey him" (Hebrews 5:8–9). These words obviously do not refer simply to some kind of moral improvement from moral imperfection to moral soundness, since had Christ been a sinner He could never have been a savior; a sacrifice for the sins of the world had to be unblemished (1 Peter 1:18–20). Christ's suffering was not necessary for His correction but for His qualification (Hebrews 2:10). By it He was perfected as sacrifice, having perfectly resisted all temptation (Hebrews 4:15); perfected as liberator, having annulled Satan's power (Hebrews 4:14); and perfected as a sympathizing and interceding high priest, the mediator between man and God (Hebrews 2:17).

That He was the Son of God does not mean that Jesus had no reserve about this matter. He did not, after all, go about the streets crying out on every corner, "I am the Son of God!" In fact, only three times in John's gospel does Jesus explicitly refer to Himself as "the Son of God" (5:25; 10:36; 11:4; cf. also 19:7), though "the Son" is a common designation of Jesus (e.g., John 5:19–23, 26; 6:40; 8:35–36; 14:13), and "the Son of man" is Jesus' favorite self-designation even in John. (Remember, though, that this designation, lies very near to "Son of God" throughout the gospel.)

Incidentally, given John's declared aim in writing this gospel "that you may believe that Jesus is the Christ, the Son of God" (John 20:31), the sparing use of the term as a title shows that John does not manufacture evidence, putting into Jesus' mouth words He did not say or mean to say. In John, as much as in the synoptic Gospels, we have the true Jesus. As with other titles, Jesus' reserve may be accounted for, among other reasons, by His decision to wait for His finished work (and the Father's attestation and reward of it) to reveal His identity in its full dimension. The time would come, after Calvary and the

Resurrection, when His apostles would proclaim openly and in the synagogues, "Jesus is the Son of God" (Acts 9:20). This lies at the heart of the apostolic message and the apostolic joy.

# 14

# THE LAST ADAM

Besides being a significant strand of Paul's teaching in the New Testament, the idea of Jesus Christ being another Adam has passed into the popular Christian conscious- ness today largely through the celebrated English hymn of John Henry Newman:

> O loving wisdom of our God!
> When all was sin and shame,
> A *second Adam* to the fight
> And to the rescue came.[1]

The reference to the "second Adam" is, of course, a some- what inaccurate reproduction of 1 Corinthians 15:45, where Jesus is referred to as the last Adam: "So it is written: 'The first man Adam became a living being'; the last Adam a life-giving spirit."

Jesus is referred to as the last (not the second) Adam to show that He is not one of a possible series but the *only* alterna- tive to the first Adam. All men now, as we shall see, are either in the one or the other. The connection with the one is by nature, the connection with the other is by grace through the gospel.

When Paul says that Christ as the last Adam *became* "a life- giving spirit" he is referring to Him as risen, when, having become the Son-of-God-in-power (Romans 1:4), He assumed His cosmic role as mediator and life-giver to all who believe. It is not that He became the last Adam at His resurrection. He stood in that capacity from the start (Romans 5:19), but His resurrection released as well as perfected the full effect of His true, complete, and dynamic headship.

A few verses later in 1 Corinthians 15 the word *second* does indeed occur in connection with Christ. In verse 47 He is called the *second man:* "The first man was of the dust of the earth, the second man from heaven." And here second man (not last) is very appropriate, for two reasons. First, Adam in his innocence was man as God created man, man as God intended him to be, true man. When sin entered the race man ceased to be man as originally created and became something less than full and true humanity. (For sin always reduces rather than adds!) Consequently Jesus Christ in His sinless humanity was indeed the "second" man, the only figure in history since the Fall to stand as fully man in the world. Nevertheless, and secondly, the whole point of His mission as the second man "from heaven" was that He might not be the last man, but rather the beginning of a new series, the foundation of a new humanity, the "first-born among many brothers" (Romans 8:29). However, His success as "the second *man"* depends on His relation to us as "the last *Adam."*

Paul does not here develop in detail the work of Christ as the last Adam, because he is not concerned with the person and work of Christ in general, but only as it guarantees the resurrection of all believers at the Last Day, the day of His coming (1 Corinthians 15:42–57). Hence the one point he brings out is that although the first Adam was created with life for himself, a life which because of sin proved earthly and temporary, God's new Adam, Christ, through His victorious death and resurrection, has life of a spiritual and eternal kind to communicate to His people. We who once shared only the life of the first Adam have begun to share the life of the last Adam, who will raise us up to share the glory and immortality of His heavenly life: "Just as we have borne the likeness of the earthly man, so shall we bear the likeness of the man from heaven" (1 Corinthians 15:49).

What is briefly alluded to and assumed in Paul's first letter to the Corinthians is much more fully worked out in the fifth chapter of his letter to the Romans. To that we must now turn.

In the first eleven verses of Romans 5 Paul has been speaking of our justification before God because of Christ's work on the cross for us. But how is it that Christ's work can have such relevance for us? And how is it that His present life in heaven (v. 10) is so decisive for us?

Paul gives us his answer to these questions in terms of Christ and Adam, and that answer will illuminate not only much of chapters six and eight of his great epistle, but indeed much of the gospel itself.

Here in a few verses Paul summarizes the biblical doctrine of history, the Fall, and salvation. Here he sets forth the two representative men of human history who embody within themselves all their followers, and whose acts and achievements are crucial and decisive for all those whom they represent.

### "AS IN ADAM . . ."

In this hyper-individualistic age we, in the Western world anyway, like to think of ourselves as self-contained units without reference to the human race or to others before us or around us. We think it is a necessary part of our freedom that we should be entirely self-directing and self-determined in our individual lives. The teaching of Scripture and of Paul here is very different. God deals with us not only as individuals but as part of the race, the human race of which each of us is a product, by which each of us is conditioned, and in which each of us bears a share of responsibility for the state of the whole. Despite its individualism we still have some example of such "solidarity" or "corporate identity" in our own society. In times of war or in union negotiations (or strikes) the principle of solidarity comes in. However, there is a level of corporate identity much deeper and more far-reaching than any of these. Romans 5:12–19 uncovers that level, and in doing so it uncovers a principle of divine government that affects not only our condemnation but our eventual salvation also.

Romans 5:12 is one of the most crucial as well as most dramatic verses in the New Testament: "Therefore, just as sin entered the world through one man and death through sin, and in this way death came to all men, because all sinned. . . ." It explains in one seminal statement the ruin of life and the fact of death. It tells us of one decisive point at which the human race, with every advantage and every blessing, rebelled against its God and plunged itself into universal ruin; one act of rebellion that soured the nature of humankind from then onwards; one point at which sin entered the race as a reigning principle to dominate our lives and cripple our progress.

Let us be quite clear what Paul is *not* saying. He is not treating Adam as a symbol for mankind, and he is not illustrating the fact that we all inherit sinful natures and personally, in our individual lives, rebel against God's authority. He is dealing with something even more decisive than our individual transgressions, and he is dealing with Adam as a fact, not a symbol. Like Jesus (e.g., Mark 10:6), Paul believed in the origins of the race from one created man made upright and in the unspoiled image of God (Genesis 1–3).

His whole argument depends on the two concrete facts: that one man, Adam, provided the ground of our condemnation; and that one man, Jesus, provided the ground of our justification. Six times in the following verses Paul stresses the one act of the one man by which sin entered, and again and again the contrast is drawn between him and the "one man" by whom sin was dealt with and righteousness recovered.

In verse 12 Paul affirms that "sin entered the world through one man, and death through sin, and in this way death came to all men, because all sinned." In these last three words Paul is making a crucial point. He is not content to regard us as helpless victims, unfairly caught up in the act of another or in the rush of alien events. First of all notice the tense he uses: "all sinned"; not all "have sinned" or all "are sinners." The tense he uses in the Greek is a punctilio aorist, pointing backwards in time to one decisive point at which "all sinned."

In this difficult but fundamental statement Paul involves every man, woman, and child in the primal sin of the primal man and in the rebellion that brought about the downfall of the race so that we are justly condemned for his crime and fairly involved in its consequences.

In the history of theology two classic explanations have been given of this. The one teaches that God sovereignly constituted Adam the *federal head* of the race and the representative of all, so that his fortunes became our fortunes. Hence Adam's sin was legally, judicially, imputed to the whole of mankind, and its outworking was permitted to take its course in inherited depravity and environmental hardship. We ourselves see something like this being done when heads of state determine the future of whole nations; or when generals sign treaties of surrender for whole armies.

The other explanation teaches that Adam was by nature the *seminal head* of the race, original humanity in its unindividualized form, in whom all human nature resided and from whom all individuals, in their entirety—body and soul—have flowed as streams from a fountain. Consequently, what Adam was the whole race was, and what he did the entire race did (cf. Hebrews 7:4–10). This last view is usually called the "realist" and sometimes the "Augustinian" view of the Fall. It may be that some of the common facts of heredity point not to the separate creation of each soul but to its propagation and its emergence out of the race. Metaphorically speaking, as individuals we are not pebbles on a beach, but leaves on a tree—united and issuing from a single root.

Such concepts may seem remote or unlikely to the average man or woman in our society, but we would do well to pause, for in some respects our modern view of reality is very narrow and selective, our understanding of life as a whole falling far short of our technical knowledge of some of its parts. Here in Romans 5—however we explain the mechanics of it—we are given the Christian explanation of man's painful history and crippled process and the Christian justification of God in the face of life's cruel disorder, injustice, and failure. Here we have the Bible's plain and principal answer to the common complaint, "Why does God allow such evil, such injustice, such cruel sufferings as we meet in the world?" Humanity has been allowed to work out what it first worked up. Our entire history of malice and misfortune is the outworking of our rebellious independence of the God who made us for Himself and without whom we cannot live well in our world.

This, then, is the historic Christian doctrine of original sin—that God has imputed to the whole of the human race, including ourselves, the sin of Adam's original rebellion, and has done so justly.

Paul goes on in verses 13 and 14 to see the most vivid evidence of this in the presence and universality of death. The biblical teaching concerning death is that it is not "natural" where man is concerned, but "penal." Man was not originally created to die, he was not originally "programmed" for death—that is why he can never really come to terms with it! Even now, so many generations later, he is still outraged at its savagery, its fruitlessness, and its unfathomed possibilities. Death was decreed as man's lot when he sinned, and as a part of the total curse that lies upon sin (Genesis 2:15–18), summing up in its futility and horror the enormity of sin's crime and the catastrophe of sin's punishment. Rebellion against God led to final and eternal alienation from God, and of this death is still the most potent reminder.

Paul's point is that the universality of death is the result of the universality of guilt, and the sin of which all human beings are guilty is the original sin of the original man. This means that sin is more than each individual's violation of a known commandment. There are many who do not know the law of God as the Israelites came to know it, and many (such as infants) who do not know it in any way. They do not repeat Adam's sin, yet they suffer Adam's fate and die Adam's death (v. 14). They do so because they are guilty of the one trespass of the "one man" (v. 12).

Verses 13 and 14 amplify the statement of verse 12 that "all sinned" in Adam's transgression. The absolute and universal "reign of death" showed it to be so. Even those who in their individual lives did not repeat the Eden story, "those whose sins were not like the transgression of Adam" (v. 14, RSV), suffer Adam's fate. This assumes that whether or not men had understood God's law in their individual lives, collectively in Adam they had law, knew law, and broke the law of God. This may be the best way to approach verse 13: "For before the law was given, sin was in the world. But sin is not taken into account when there is no law. Nevertheless, death reigned . . ." In his phrase "taken into account" Paul uses a commercial term—"put in the ledger." However, C. E. B. Cranfield thinks that

Paul's words are only to be taken "in a relative sense," that is, "only in comparison with what takes place when the law is present," for "those who lived without the law were certainly not 'innocent sinners'—they were to blame for what they were and what they did."

The fact that men died before the law of Moses was given (v. 14) "shows clearly enough," he says, that "in the sense of being charged to men's account, reckoned against them, imputed . . . their sin was indeed registered." But sin "was not fully apparent, sharply defined thing which it became" in the presence of the law.[2] C. K. Barrett agrees, and says: "Law is not necessary to the existence but only for the assessment of sin,"[3] adding elsewhere, "Sin is turned into transgression, and becomes visible and assessable, only when a law is given."[4] Whichever way we understand verse 13, the consequences of having the laws of Moses were such as to point up the greater need of the Jew for a Savior.

This was Paul's earlier point against those who preferred to be adherents to the law of Moses than to God's gracious promise in Abraham that was fulfilled in Christ. But what transgression can account for the universal dominion of death between Adam and Moses, even over those whose grasp on God's standards was poor at best? Paul's one answer here is: the "one trespass" of the "one man." He does not turn aside to heredity or environment, or even a man's personal history: all die because all sinned, and all sinned in Adam's sinning, and Adam sinned against known law.

### "... SO IN CHRIST"

In Romans 5:12 Paul breaks off in mid-sentence. He does this not only to prove his point that all men were condemned as sinners on account of that first rebellion (vv. 13–14), but to qualify the comparison he is about to make between Adam and Christ. He is about to show (vv. 18–20) that as men by nature were in the first Adam and share his fall, God has put believers into Christ, the last Adam, to share His victory.

But first of all (vv. 15–17) he feels bound to emphasize that Adam and Christ are only parallel in regard to their representative positions, their relationship with those who follow them.

In every other respect they are a study in contrasts: in Adam
men get their just deserts, but in Christ they receive God's free
gift; in Adam judgment and condemnation come hard on the
heels of the first trespass, but in Christ God achieves our justification despite innumerable transgressions; on account of
Adam's fall death came with unchallengeable power, but
through Jesus Christ life comes with eternal honor and
abounding grace. On this Cranfield writes memorably: "That
one single misdeed should be answered by judgment, this is
perfectly understandable: that the accumulated sins and guilt
of all the ages should be answered by God's free gift, this is the
miracle of miracles, utterly beyond human comprehension."[5]

In verse 18 Paul at last completes the comparison he began
back in verse 12: "Consequently, just as the result of one trespass was condemnation for all men, so also the result of one act
of righteousness was justification that brings life for all men."
Here Jesus' whole life and work on earth, culminating in His
self-giving on the cross, is summed up as "one act of righteousness." In an unbroken unity of obedience, Jesus, who was "born
of a woman, born under law" (Galatians 4:4), fulfilled in love
and reverence all that the law and the prophets required, maintaining a perfect openness and obedience to God (John 8:29)
and becoming "obedient to death—even death on a cross!"
(Philippians 2:8). Where Adam failed, he succeeded; where
Adam asserted himself against the rights of God, Jesus surrendered Himself and asserted the rights of God, even in the matter of sin's utmost punishment.

But He did this in precisely the same capacity as Adam: He
did it for Himself and for those whom He represented. As effectively and disastrously as men are by nature bound up in the
disobedience and ruin of the first Adam, so effectively and
redemptively are believers bound up in the success of the last
Adam. As in Adam we passed into failure and condemnation
and death, so in Christ we have passed into (His) life and victory. Our relation to the one is exactly parallel with our relationship to the other: the mechanics of those relations may differ,
since we are "in Adam" by nature and "in Christ" by grace, yet
the parallel or relationship is exact and decisive.

Adam's sin constituted us sinners, it put us in the category of sinners. Christ's obedience by God's gracious appointment constitutes us righteous, it puts us in the category of righteous persons, it gives us a new status as justified men and women. We become persons who have been found "not guilty" of sin, persons formally acquitted from blame and pronounced righteous in the sight of God with what Luther used to call an "alien righteousness"—that is, not our own righteousness, but the righteousness of another (cf. Romans 1:16–17; 1 Corinthians 1:30–31). In the words of Paul's concluding explanation in Romans 5:19: "so also through the obedience of the one man many will be made righteous."

Before we consider that union further, by examining the phrase "in Christ," let us address ourselves to an outstanding question: If the entire race and every human being "died" in the first Adam, is Paul implying here that, correspondingly, every human being will be "made alive" in the last Adam? That would be to take the comparison much further than Paul here or elsewhere allows (see 2 Thessalonians 1:8–9). Throughout, he is explaining to Christians, to believers, the full significance of Christ for them now that they are "in Him." He does not mean, by the "all" of verse 18, that every man is justified by Christ just as every man is condemned in Adam. As John Murray points out, Paul is dealing here with the *method* of operation of God's government:

> What the apostle is interested in showing is not the numerical extent of those who are justified as identical with the numerical extent of those condemned but the parallel that obtains between the way of condemnation and the way of justification. It is the *modus operandi* that is in view. All who are condemned, and this includes the whole human race, are condemned because of the one trespass of Adam; all who are justified are justified because of the righteousness of Christ.[6]

It is all who are "in Christ" who are justified. That is the point; no more and no less!

As he approaches his climax, Paul turns from his sustained comparison and contrast of Adam and Christ and once again

shows that the coming of the law in Moses' day, far from providing salvation by law keeping, served only to increase men's
sense of sin: "The law was added so that the trespass might
increase" (v. 20). Leon Morris explains this function of the law
thus:

> It was not concerned with preventing sin (it was too late for
> that). Nor was it concerned with salvation from sin (it was
> too weak for that). The law can only condemn (4:15). It was
> concerned with showing sin for what it is, and it certainly
> showed magnificently that there was much sin (cf. 3:19–
> 20).[7]

However—and this is Paul's point—because Adam was not
the last Adam, sin was not the last word, either in its original
act or later increase: "But where sin increased, grace increased
all the more" (v. 20). Sin "reigned in death" over us (v. 21): but it
did not reign over Him who "broke the power of death," having
redeemed us from sin's penalty by His perfect atonement
(Romans 3:25). By that one justifying act of righteousness
(Romans 3:21–26) the situation has been reversed and the reign
of death has given way to the reign of grace "through Jesus
Christ our Lord" (v. 21).

Closely related to the concept of Christ found in this passage in Romans is a phrase which appears very frequently in all
of Paul's letters: "in Christ."

## THE BELIEVER'S NEW LIFE: "IN CHRIST"

In describing the new life of the believer, no phrase is more
prominent in Paul's writings than that term "in Christ." In all,
he uses it no less than 240 times. Often its use is instrumental
and means "through Christ's agency," but at times it has a local
sense in which Christ is the "place" in whom believers are, in
which salvation is, and in which all God's gracious purposes
come to fruition. From the epistle to the Ephesians alone we
can see both its breadth and depth as a term and a concept:

• In Christ God has blessed us with every spiritual blessing
  (1:3).

- In Christ He chose us before the foundation of the world (1:4).
- In Christ we have redemption through His blood (1:7).
- In Christ God planned the salvation of Jew and Gentile (1:9).
- In Christ God will unite all things in a universal reconciliation (1:10).
- In Christ we have individually been appointed to live for the praise of God's glory (1:12).
- In Christ believers are sealed with the promised Holy Spirit (1:13).
- In Christ we share the significance of Christ's historic work and are lifted up into the power and promise of His present life (2:4–7).
- In Christ we are created anew for good works (2:10).

The same idea is present in many of the "with Christ" statements of Paul, where "with" also means "in":

- We have been crucified with Christ (Galatians 2:20).
- We were raised with Him (Colossians 2:12–13).
- We have been made to sit with Him in heavenly places (Ephesians 2:6).

But what is the connection between Christ and ourselves; where is the central point of contact? *How* is it that we can be "in Christ"; and how can all these things that belong to Him come to belong to us? How are we "in Christ," and when, and in what respect?

A number of explanations have been given of this union with Christ. Some have said that the union is metaphysical, and that we are all in one essence with God, part of the divine being, one with Christ by creation. Such theories fail to distinguish between the Creator and the creature, the divine and the human in important respects. Moreover, it is not by creation but by election, redemption, and regeneration that we are one with Christ; and this is true not of all, but of "the church" which is "his body" (John 17:9; Ephesians 1:4–14, 22–23).

Others have said that this union is mystical, and have even spoken of "Pauline mysticism." But, although the term "mystical union" has traditionally been used in an orthodox sense (meaning "spiritual union"), the New Testament teaching makes it clear that union with Christ is true of believers not merely in sublime moments, but at all times. In the words of Herman Ridderbos, it is "an abiding reality determinative for the whole of the Christian life to which appeal can be made at all times and in all sorts of connections and with respect to the whole church without distinction (Colossians 2:20ff.; 3:1ff.)."[8]

Ultimately there is no explanation or analogy that fully satisfies, and it is easier to say what the union is not than what it is. As Millard J. Erickson notes:

> It is not a union of persons in one essence, as in the Trinity. It is not a union of nature in one person, as is the case with the incarnation of Jesus Christ. It is not a physical bonding, as in the welding of two pieces of metal. It is in some way a union of two spirits which does not extinguish either of them.[9]

The union is helpfully illustrated in several ways in the New Testament writings. For example: by the union of husband and wife in marriage (Ephesians 5:32); by the union between vine and branches (John 15:1–7); and by the union of stones in a temple (Ephesians 2:20–22). But while these illustrate the union, they do not explain its nature, which remains mysterious, ineffable, and even cosmic (Ephesians 5:32; Colossians 1:26–27). Similarly the sacraments of baptism and of the Lord's Supper illustrate it in visible signs, but it remains true that, as Calvin says, "This mystery of Christ's secret union with the devout is by nature incomprehensible."[10]

One line of thought that does help us to understand this reality better is the concept of Adam and Christ as the respective heads of two groups of people. As we saw earlier, God sovereignly constituted Adam as the incorporative head of the human race, with the result that what he did as such is imputed to all his descendants. So also God has constituted His Son, Jesus Christ, as the incorporative head of a new humanity. It is here we may find a key to the "how" of our being "in Christ" as it appears in at least some of the "in Christ" statements (e.g., Romans 8:1; Philippians 3:9). Ridderbos writes:

> The Adam-Christ parallel not only casts a clear light on the significance that Paul ascribes to Christ Himself, but also on the way in which he [Christ] sees His own [people] as involved in Him and with Him in His redemptive work. This is very clear, for example, from the words of I Corinthians 15:22 ". . . for as in Adam all die, so also in Christ shall all be made alive." . . . Here "in Christ" is parallel with "in Adam." Herewith the character of this "in" becomes plain. As the decision has fallen in Adam with respect to the "all" who pertain to him, that they should die, so in Christ that they shall live.
>
> Adam and Christ here stand over against each other as the two great figures at the entrance of two worlds, two aeons, two "creations," the old and the new; and in their actions and fate lies the decision for all who belong to them, because these are comprehended in them and thus are reckoned either to death or to life. This is now expressed by "in Adam" and "in Christ." And it is therefore in this sense that Adam can be called a type of Him who was to come.[11]

However, the parallel between Christ and Adam still does not give us a full explanation of the union between Christ and believers. Christ Himself in His risen glory had become more than an individual outside of us and above us. He has in some way already taken every believer (e.g., 2 Corinthians 5:17) and entire churches (Galatians 1:22) up into Himself. In Ephesians 2:6 believers are said to have been raised with Christ and seated with Him "in the heavenly realms" precisely by being "in Him"; and in Ephesians 1:10 Christ is the cosmic Lord who will "unite" or "sum up" all things in Himself.

Scholars have sought various ways in which to express this cosmic dimension of Christ's heavenly existence *vis-à-vis* His church, attributing to Him "universal personality," "inclusive personality," "corporate personality." While some or even all of these terms can be misleading, they all attempt to show that Paul's Jesus can be described in supra-individual terms.

That Jesus Christ should have such far-reaching significance, that His life, death, and resurrection should so incorporate us in another, and a higher, Adam, is surely the greatest demonstration of His more-than-human capacity. As C. F. D. Moule puts it:

> A person who had recently been crucified, but is found to be alive, with "absolute" life, the life of the age to come, and is found, moreover, to be an inclusive, all-embracing presence—such a person is beginning to be described in terms appropriate to nothing less than God Himself. . . .
>
> Paul was led to conceive of Christ as any theist conceives of God: personal, indeed, but transcending the individual category. Christ is like the omnipresent deity "in whom we live and move and have our being."[12]

## THE ROLE OF THE SPIRIT
## IN OUR UNION IN CHRIST

Donald Guthrie brings another important phrase to bear on this, one which he calls a "kindred phrase" and which he suggests throws light on the term "in Christ." It is Paul's phrase "in the Spirit," and of it Guthrie writes:

> It has been shown that Paul regards the Christian life as dominated by the Spirit. Christians are "not in the flesh" but "in the Spirit" (Romans 8:9). Since Paul in the same context speaks of the Spirit as the Spirit of Christ, the conclusion is inescapable that "in the Spirit" and "in Christ" must mean the same thing. All that has been said above about the radical change which has been effected in Christ could come about only through the activity of the Spirit.[13]

He further points out that the reference to believers being "in the Spirit" finds its counterpart in the indwelling Spirit being "in" them, just as "in Christ" is a concept complemented by Paul's "Christ in us" concept (Romans 8:9; 2 Corinthians 13:5; Galatians 2:20; Colossians 1:27).

Calvin long ago made the connection between union with Christ as the last Adam and the work of the Spirit. He states that "the Holy Spirit is the bond by which Christ effectually unites us to Himself,"[14] and explains further:

> we ought to know that he is called the "Spirit of Christ" not only because Christ, as the eternal Word of God, is joined in the same Spirit with the Father, but also from his character as the Mediator. For he would have come to us in vain if he had not been furnished with this power. In this sense he is called the "Second Adam," given from heaven as "a life-giving spirit" [I Corinthians 15:45].[15]

It is the Spirit in His total action who makes the union of the believer with Christ *vital* and not only *legal*. Both kinds of connection are involved, and both are given their place in Scripture in elucidating the great "in Christ" reality. When individuals become men and women "in Christ," the past and the present meet. Christ's history becomes their history, His past achievement becomes the foundation of their present endowment, His right becomes their claim. But in addition to that, what was done *for* them becomes operative *in* them; an historic event becomes an abiding reality, the impetus of all their actions and the motivation behind all their decisions: "In the same way, count yourselves dead to sin but alive to God in Christ Jesus" (Romans 6:11; cf. 13:14).

This being "alive to God" is no fiction, but a vital reality in our union with Christ by the Spirit. The concept of being made a new spiritual creation, "created in Christ Jesus" (Ephesians 2:10), writes Anthony A. Hoekema, "describes an entirely new kind of life—a life filled with good works, sparkling with love and devoted to God's glory."[16] Union with Christ, says James Stewart, is "not only . . . the mainstay of Paul's religion but the sheet-anchor of His ethics," a relationship to Christ which constrains us to live accordingly: "It is a fact but it is also a duty. It is a present reality, but also a beckoning ideal. . . . 'Are you in

Christ?' says Paul to the believer. 'Then *be* a man in Christ indeed!'"[17]

## THE CORPORATE CHRIST

Being "in Christ" is, however, a concept larger and wider than the individual's status or experience. It involves the whole church, the body of Christ (Romans 12:4–5; 1 Corinthians 12:13, 27), the fullness of Him who fills all in all (Ephesians 1:23). Hence Paul writes "To all the saints in Christ Jesus at Philippi" (Philippians 1:1), and speaks of "the churches of God in Christ Jesus which are in Judea" (1 Thessalonians 2:14, RSV). All the people *of* Christ Jesus are people *in* Christ Jesus, individually and corporately considered. Paul expands this thought even more widely and dramatically in 2 Corinthians 5:17, when he writes: "Therefore, if anyone is in Christ, he is a new creation." The words read literally: "Therefore, if anyone is in Christ—a new creation!"

On this Ridderbos comments: "When he speaks of 'a new creation,' this is not meant merely in an individual sense ('a new creature'), but one is to think of the new world of the re-creation that God has made to dawn in Christ and in which everyone who is in Christ is included."[18] It is perhaps as if Paul had said: "In Christ there is a new world—and you (believers) are now part of it!" Therefore a term which points first to our election in Christ before the foundation of the world (Ephesians 1:4) points finally to our eternal future and God's everlasting kingdom in the same Son, Jesus Christ our Lord (Colossians 3:4).

The concept of union with Christ is perhaps the largest of all the theological categories relating to salvation, containing within itself all the others such as election, redemption, regeneration, justification, sanctification, and glorification. It is, says John Murray, "the central truth of the whole doctrine of salvation"[19] and "it underlies every aspect of redemption both in its accomplishment and its application."[20]

There are many metaphors of nearness, of involvement, of relation between God and His people in Scripture. We are children of a Father, chicks of a mother-bird, branches of a vine, etc. "In Christ," however, surpasses all of them in revealing the divine commitment to us and our closeness to God. We have been taken into the very heart of God, into the center of the divine life. We "who once were far off have been brought near through the blood of Christ" (Ephesians 2:13). Our lives, which were once lived far from God in pride and folly, are now, to translate Paul by means of a modern idiom, "wrapped up with Christ in God" (Colossians 3:3). This is the first truth about us, and is our eternal security. There can be no greater or more final revelation of our place in the universe than this.

# 15

# THERE IS ONE MEDIATOR

The Bible never allows us to take God's grace for granted. Always grace is displayed as a miracle and salvation as a triumph of wisdom, love, and power that leaves us lost in wonder, love, and praise. God in Scripture continually warns us that good and loving though He is, He is against us on account of sin. He tells us that sin in man has made man (sinfully) hostile to God and God (righteously) wrathful towards man. There is thus a double alienation. The gospel is the story of how God (not man) bridges this gulf and achieves reconciliation by means of a perfect and adequate Mediator whom He appoints and sends.

A mediator is a middleman, one who stands between two parties, representing the intentions of both and protecting the interests of both. Hence he must be equally related to the persons between whom he comes. God's eternal Son and equal became man in order that in two natures, human and divine, He might be all that we needed for our help and all that God required for His vindication.

While the word *mediator* does not itself often occur in Scripture, the idea contained within the word is everywhere present. It pervades the Old Testament and it dominates the New Testament. Indeed where Christianity is concerned, the place of Jesus Christ as the one mediator between man and God is absolutely fundamental and is its chief distinguishing feature. To be a Christian is to know God in the Mediator, to be right with God by the Mediator, and to live for God through the Mediator.

## THE MEDIATORS OF THE OLD TESTAMENT

"Though the word is not used," writes Albrecht Oepke, "mediatorship is at the heart of Old Testament religion. The theologically significant point is that God cannot be approached at our pleasure, but only when he offers himself for fellowship."[1]

From the beginning God taught Israel the real nature of the distance between Himself and fallen man. The distance was infinite not only in terms of power, but in terms of purity also. God revealed Himself in His utter "otherness" as holy, and in His undeviating righteousness as just. Thus from the start He gave His people a lesson in sin and the need for forgiveness that dominated their worship and their religious life until Christ came. Only then were they taken on from such necessary tutelage into the freedom of the sons of God, at their New Testament "coming of age," the lesson learned, God's holy grace valued (see Galatians 3:23–4:7).

Recall, for instance, the unforgettable "giving of the law" at Mount Sinai, when Yahweh descended among His people (Exodus 19:16–25). The process of ritual purification over three days (including the solemn washing of garments and abstention from normal sexual relations), by which the people were to be consecrated, impressed upon them from the start their natural unworthiness to meet with God. And the manner of His approach dramatically sealed the lesson. In the midst of the thunder and the lightning and the smoke, the strange darkness and the stranger fires, while the mountain trembled and an unearthly trumpet-sound grew louder and louder, Yahweh spoke from the midst of His angelic hosts (Deuteronomy 33:2; Psalm 68:17; Galatians 3:19; Hebrews 2:3). The mighty God had come with His heavenly court, the king of kings to meet His chosen people Israel.

### The Cry for a Mediator

But the people, overwhelmed with this display of God's true nature and character, cried out to Moses, "Speak to us yourself, and we will listen. But do not have God speak to us or we will die" (Exodus 20:19). There is the cry for a mediator, and it is born out of a sense of holiness and sin, distance and ill-desert.

The result was that Moses did indeed become the intermediary
between God and the people, the mediator of the old covenant
(Exodus 24:4–8; 33:7–11; cf. Galatians 3:19; Hebrews 3:2–5). As
such he is found pleading with God for the people (Exodus
32:31–32) and speaking to the people on behalf of God (Numbers 12:6–8).

### Priests and Prophets and Kings as Mediators

The sacrifices of the Mosaic system reminded the worshippers that if God was accessible in His grace He was also dangerous in His purity. To approach Him in sin was to bring the
unclean into contact with the holy. Only disaster could result
from that, for Yahweh is a jealous God who maintains His
righteousness above everything. Consequently God provided
sacrifices that substitute for the sinner under the death-dealing
wrath of God, the holy Judge; and He made a way of access into
His presence by the work of the *priests,* who alone could apply
the blood to His altar and pronounce the sinner clean and
restored into fellowship with Yahweh.

Thus the priests represented men to God and God to men
(Deuteronomy 10:8). Most vividly of all, the high priest acted as
mediator for God and the whole people of Israel, both on the
day of atonement when he took the blood into the holy of holies
(Leviticus 16:1) and when the names of the twelve tribes were
engraved (Exodus 39:6–14).

Besides the priests of the cultus, the *prophets* acted as mediators. The prophets' task was to stand "in the council of the
Lord" to hear and deliver His word (Jeremiah 23:18, 22). They
received the message of God in words and visions (Isaiah 55:11;
Hosea 12:10) and understood the significance of historical
events (Amos 3:7).

In a unique way the *king,* who in his office represented the
kingly rule of God, also acted as a mediator. He frequently
pleaded for the people before God. (For example, see 2 Samuel
24:17; 1 Chronicles 21:16; 2 Chronicles 6:21, 42; 14:11; 20:5–12;
Isaiah 37:14–20.) He became a focal point for God's dealing
with the nation and made with him "an everlasting covenant,
arranged and secured in every part" (2 Samuel 23:5; 7:5–17;
Psalm 89:19–37; 132:11–18).

Yet we must note that all these were mediators only in their office and delegated functions, not in their persons. They were intermediaries who were themselves never allowed to forget that they too needed a more perfect mediator (Leviticus 16:6; Deuteronomy 17:20; Isaiah 6:5).

## Hints of a Higher Mediator

Even alongside Old Testament kings and prophets and priests we glimpse vivid indications that a higher mediation between God and man exists. There is, for example, that most mysterious of Old Testament figures, "the angel of the Lord," who in spite of the title is no mere angel and who speaks as God (Genesis 16:10; 22:11–12; 31:11, 13; Exodus 3:2–6) while also being distinguished from God in some way.

There is also "the servant of the Lord." The "servant" passages in Isaiah 40–53 hint of one who will mediate more profoundly and more finally than Moses or Aaron or any other has ever done. He is to be a covenant to the people and a light to the nations (Isaiah 42:6), called in righteousness to open the eyes of the blind and free the prisoners (Isaiah 42:7). He is the ideal Israel, prepared by God for a mission as wide as the world (Isaiah 49:2–3, 6–7), and to which he will be faithful in spite of discouragements (Isaiah 50:4–7).

In Isaiah 52:13–53:12 the concept of the mediator reaches what Oepke describes as "its final metaphysical and soteriological profundity prior to Christ."[2] Beloved servant though He is (Isaiah 42:1; 52:13), He bears the sin of the people and the wrath of God which was due to them, so that they may be healed and reconciled to God (Isaiah 53:4–6). He Himself becomes "an offering for sin," but it is so that "the will of the Lord will prosper in his hand" (Isaiah 53:10). His sacrificial mediation is acceptable, His intercession is effective, He Himself is exalted (Isaiah 53:10–12). Therefore, says God, "he will see the light of life and . . . my servant will justify many righteous" (Isaiah 53:11). Other Old Testament mediating figures and symbols include the increasingly personified concept of the Wisdom of God (Proverbs 1:20; 8:22–23; 9:1–2) and the divine-human king of the royal psalms (e.g., Psalm 2:6–8; 45:6; 110:1, 4).

In this way the Old Testament stressed both the nearness and the distance of God. The fact that He approached His people and became available to them displayed His love and His grace. The way He became available to them—always through mediators—displayed His holiness and justice.

## THE MEDIATOR OF THE NEW TESTAMENT

Let us now turn to the New Testament revelation of the mediatorship of Jesus Christ. In Jesus, every Old Testament mediatorial concept or figure comes to a head. He is supremely and in Himself Prophet, Priest, and King; He is Sacrifice and Offerer; He is Servant and Son; "For there is one God and one mediator between God and men, the man Christ Jesus, who gave himself as a ransom for all" (1 Timothy 2:5–6). In these words of Paul, observes Oepke, "The mediator concept is Christianised. . . . The new thing as compared with all previous conceptions is that the function of the *mesitēs* [mediator] is related exclusively to Christ."[3]

### Jesus: Our Attorney and Negotiator

The aspects of Christ's work brought out by the Greek word *mesitēs* are those of attorney and negotiator. The thought in Paul's mind, however, is not far from that of the writer to the Hebrews, who uses the term in the sense of arbiter of the covenant (Hebrews 8:6; 9:15; 12:24). Paul too grounds the mediator's work in His priestly act of atonement at the cross, the "exchange price" or "ransom" that He gave "for all" (1 Timothy 2:5–6; cf. Isaiah 53:12). This was His central mediatorial work. But how could God take upon Himself the penalty due to man for sin without a true and full human nature? It was a human penalty He had to bear, the penalty for sin in human experience. Therefore it was a human nature He had to acquire. The righteousness of God for man (Romans 1:17–18) could only be achieved in one who was both God and man. God condemned sin in the flesh of His own Son, says Paul (Romans 8:3), and on those words John Murray comments: "The battle was joined and the triumph secured in that same flesh which in us is the seat and agent of sin."[4]

It is in His two natures that the divine person of the Logos becomes for us "wisdom from God—that is, our righteousness, holiness and redemption" (1 Corinthians 1:30). All that He does as man has the value of *God's* doing: His righteousness is the righteousness of God for us (Romans 1:17), His atonement is the achievement of God for us (Romans 8:3; 2 Corinthians 5:21), and His victory is the triumph of God for us (Romans 8:31–39).

The part of God the Father in all this is crucial. Although Christ came as the Mediator, as "the man in the middle," it was no independent act that He performed, as though He had come to reconcile a reluctant God to a hostile world. Nothing, in fact, is more constantly emphasized than that the Mediator is of God's appointment—in His coming into the world (1 John 4:9), in His priestly act in it at Calvary (Hebrews 5:4–6), and in his continuing priesthood in heaven (Hebrews 7:20–22). Christ mediates for a holy God, but not for a reluctant God. If He stands between, it is because the Father has placed Him between. The perfection of the Mediator proceeds from the wisdom of the Father (1 Corinthians 1:24).

Calvin sums this up:

> Our most merciful Father decreed what was best for us. Since our iniquities, like a cloud cast between us and him, had completely estranged us from the Kingdom of Heaven, no man, unless he belonged to God, could serve as the intermediary to restore peace. But who might reach to him? Any one of Adam's children? No, like their father, all of them were terrified at the sight of God. One of the angels? They also had need of a head, through whose bond they might cleave firmly and undividedly to their God [cf. Eph. 1:22; Col. 2:10]. What then? The situation would surely have been hopeless had the very majesty of God not descended to us, since it was not in our power to ascend to him. Hence, it was necessary for the Son of God to become for us "Emmanuel, that is, God with us," and in such a way that his divinity and our human nature might by mutual connection grow together.[5]

Later he writes:

His task was so to restore us to God's grace as to make of
the children of men, children of God; of the heirs of Gehenna, heirs of the Heavenly Kingdom. Who could have done
this had not the self-same Son of God become the Son of
man, and had not so taken what was ours as to impart what
was his to us, and to make what was his by nature ours by
grace?[6]

Since Calvin, the classical Protestant way of expounding
our Lord's full mediatorial work has been in terms of his offices
as prophet, priest, and king. However, as other parts of this
book deal in more detail with Christ's work in these respects, I
can confine my remarks here to a brief statement about each of
them.

## Jesus: The Supreme Prophet

Firstly, *Jesus is the supreme Mediator in His prophetic office.*
Even before His actual coming as the God-man, the Son acted
as Mediator. Carl Henry states that "The Logos of God—prein-
carnate, incarnate and now glorified—is the mediating agent of
all divine disclosure."[7] Consequently: "To expound the revelation of God, it is impossible to go beyond or around or behind
God's revelation . . . we can neither transcend nor supplement
what God says about himself in his free disclosure through
Jesus Christ."[8] Arguing from John 1:1–3, Colossians 1:13–16,
and Hebrews 1:2–3, Henry concludes: "Christ is not merely a
special feature within a larger panorama of revelation of God
from eternity past or eternity future but, as mediating agent,
encompasses the whole revelation of God from eternity past to
eternity future."[9]

Touching the earthly work of our Lord, he writes:

In depicting the role of the Logos as God's revelatory agent,
the Bible avoids two costly exaggerations: first, it avoids the
notion that divine revelation is given only in Jesus of
Nazareth (the nature of revelation being here made exclusively salvific); second, it avoids the notion that the revelation given outside Jesus of Nazareth occurs independently
of the Logos. Instead, the Logos-doctrine of Scripture pre-

serves the existence both of a universal and of a particular revelation. In its delineation of the Logos, it maintains a crucial link between the general revelation of the eternal Christ in the cosmos and human history, and the special redemptive revelation in Jesus Christ and Scripture.[10]

Of that special and saving revelation the author of Hebrews writes in his opening statement: "In the past God spoke to our forefathers through the prophets at many times and in various ways, but in these last days he has spoken to us by his Son" (Hebrews 1:1–2). Here he establishes at the start that Jesus in His person, words, and work is the supreme, full, and final revelation of the God who saves: that in Himself He gathers up and transcends every previous display of God's character and will. Jesus is the prophet *par excellence*.

As God's unique prophet He was predicted (Isaiah 61:1–3) and anointed (Luke 4:18–21) and confirmed (Mark 9:7). Yet He is also greater than the prophets (Matthew 12:41; Mark 8:27–36). He fills and overflows every office and every prediction (Acts 3:22). He not only *speaks* God's word, He *is* God's word; not God's partial or provisional word, but God's full and final word, whether of judgment or salvation (John 3:34–36; 12:47–50).

In Jesus God has spoken to us, not more truly than in Old Testament times, but more clearly, more immediately and in a unique way. No mode of revelation could equal the Word made flesh. As man, our Lord could come close to man to show him God; as God, He could show man perfectly and adequately who and what God is. In His familiar humanity He brought the Deity within our narrow horizons, preempting our terror and calming our dread. Yet in His perfect divinity He spoke of God with unparalleled authority: an authority born of immense dignity and issuing out of an eternal experience (Matthew 11:27; John 1:18).

Thomas F. Torrance pays particular attention to Jesus' words recorded in Matthew 11:27: "All things have been delivered to me by my Father; and no one knows the Son except the Father, and no one knows the Father except the Son and any one to whom the Son chooses to reveal him" (RSV), and to the fact that "the Father/Son or Son/Father relationship falls *within the very Being of God*" (emphasis added).[11] "Our being children of God," he points out, "falls outside the Being of God. . . . But Jesus Christ . . . is Son of God within God, so that what He is and does as Son of the Father falls within the eternal Being of the Godhead."[12]

This is the doctrine of the mediator to which Torrance draws attention in two respects: (1) in Jesus' revelation of God and (2) in Jesus' atoning and reconciling work for God. As to the first, so much is the Father/Son relationship "within the very Being of God" that "knowledge of God the Father and knowledge of Jesus Christ the incarnate Son of the Father arise in us together, not one without the other."[13] Consequently, "We come to know the Son and the Father, the Father and Son, in one indivisible movement of knowing" in which "in a profound sense we are given to share in the knowledge that God has of himself within himself as Father and Son or Son and Father." This, Torrance continues, "is part of what is meant by our knowing God through the Spirit of God who is in Him and whom He sends to us through the Son." In this way "Jesus constitutes in His own incarnate Person the mediating centre of that revelation whereby all our knowledge of God is controlled."[14]

## Jesus: The Supreme Priest

Secondly, *Jesus is the supreme Mediator in His priestly office.* The book of Hebrews has much to say about Christ's priesthood, His priestly activity as the mediator. But it begins with His person as sent by God and proceeding from God: His divinity that makes Him one with God (Hebrews 1:1–3). Torrance stresses the importance of this in the work of reconciliation as well as that of revelation: "All that Jesus Christ was and is, all that He said and did while on earth, His whole work of atoning reconciliation, are not without but are within the Being of God."[15] Later he says: "I believe it is important for us to ask ourselves today whether we intend to regard atonement for sin as some external transaction between God and man worked out by Jesus, or whether we think of it as having taken place within the Being of the Mediator."[16] This is the theology of Hebrews no less than it is of Paul (compare Hebrews 1:3 with 2 Corinthians 5:19).

After establishing Jesus' share in the divine nature that identifies Him with God, the writer of Hebrews affirms in the second chapter His share in our humanity, by means of the expressions "flesh and blood" and "made like his brothers in every way" (Hebrews 2:14, 17). It is this quality that makes Him a sympathizing high priest (Hebrews 4:15) who was equipped and perfected as mediator and savior by His human experience (Hebrews 5:7-9). He became one of us in order that He might be both priest and sacrifice (Hebrews 10:5-14) and thus become the mediator of a new covenant (Hebrews 8:3; 9:12, 15).

It is not so much with the priests of the Mosaic covenant in general as with the high priest that Jesus is compared and contrasted, and in particular with the high priest in his work on the annual day of atonement when he made a sacrifice for the sin of the whole people of God and took the blood into the holy of holies (Hebrews 8:1-3; 9:1-10). Hebrews repeatedly makes it clear that this priesthood belonged to an old covenant, which was interim and preparatory, only a "shadow" of what was to come (Hebrews 10:1). Its provisions for sin reminded men of their sin but failed to cleanse and ease their consciences (Hebrews 10:2-4).

Now, however, God has provided in Christ a new priesthood as the center and substance of a new covenant (Hebrews 7:11-22). And His priesthood is grounded not on symbolic and inadequate sacrifices, but by the once-for-all sacrifice of Himself (Hebrews 7:27; 9:12, 26-28; 10:10-14). This is the basis of His saving mediatorship (Hebrews 9:15). It is what enables this covenant to be a covenant of grace and forgiveness and peace with God (Hebrews 12:22-24). And it is itself the purpose and goal of His incarnation: "Since the children have flesh and blood, he too shared in their humanity . . . that he might make atonement for the sins of the people" (Hebrews 2:14, 17).

This finished work stands forever (Hebrews 7:16, 23-25) and is effective in the immediate presence of God (Hebrews 8:1-2; 9:24). Its eternal validity has been sealed by God's oath (Hebrews 9:20-22). It gives us access to a throne of grace and confidence to draw near to God with full assurance, having our hearts sprinkled with the atoning blood of God's heavenly high priest (Hebrews 4:14–16; 10:19–23). By it our worship is welcome and our service is acceptable (Hebrews 9:14).

The superiority of Christ's priesthood over that of Aaron (Hebrews 5:1–10), and its finality, is notably illustrated in Hebrews by a shadowy Old Testament figure, Melchizedek. He was priest-king of Salem (later Jerusalem) long before Moses and the time of Aaron. He appears quite suddenly in the Genesis account (14:18–20), and afterwards nothing further is recorded of him or any successors to him. In this brief account, F. F. Bruce observes, the author of Hebrews "finds as much significance in what is not said about Melchizedek as he does in what is said about him:"[17] "Without father or mother, without genealogy, without beginning of days or end of life, like the Son of God he remains a priest forever" (Hebrews 7:3).

It is not, of course, that Melchizedek was literally *sui generis* or eternal, only that in terms of the Genesis account he aptly illustrates what is true of Jesus; he is a fitting model of God's true high priest (Hebrews 5:6, 10; 7:1–21; cf. Psalm 110:4), whose priesthood continues "forever." Furthermore, since Abraham had dealings with God through this "mediator," "one might even say that Levi," the ancestor of Israel's priestly tribe and Aaron's family in particular, "paid the tenth [tithes]" through Abraham and consequently acknowledged as a superior priesthood that priesthood which typified Christ's (Hebrews 7:9).

Repeated reference is made to Psalm 110:4: "The Lord has sworn and will not change his mind, 'You are a priest forever in the order of Melchizedek.'" This is used by the writer of Hebrews to substantiate several crucial facts about Christ's priesthood: that Jesus did not "[take] this honor upon himself" (Hebrews 5:4), intruding into a priesthood to which He had no claim (Hebrews 5:5); that His priestly work had been successfully accomplished—however painfully (Hebrews 5:8–10); that it depends not upon bodily descent from others, but upon its own intrinsic character and achievement (Hebrews 7:16–17); and that it has perpetual validity for God (Hebrews 7:21) and consequently enables Him "for all time to save those who draw near to God through him" (Hebrews 7:25, RSV).

## Jesus: The Supreme King

Thirdly, *Jesus is the supreme mediator in His kingly office.*
While Jesus Christ stands in the place of mediator and representative of the people of God throughout all the stages of His
saving work from the covenant of redemption in eternity (John
6:37; 17:4, 6) onward, only at His enthronement does His mediatorial function operate fully (Matthew 28:18). Only as the
exalted Lord at the right hand of the Majesty on high could He
be fulfilled as the mediator. For God has made Him "head over
everything for the church" (Ephesians 1:22). His exaltation is
our encouragement (2 Timothy 2:8, 10–12; Hebrews 13:8).

The kingship of Christ is a kind that could never be rightly
claimed or really exercised except by one who was both God
and man, divine and human. It stretches through the entire
cosmos and it reaches into the hearts and minds of men. Where
God alone rules, there Christ the Lord is King. In perfect
knowledge of the thoughts and hearts, the feelings and the
fears of millions of souls, Christ presides over His church,
knowing every one of His subjects as only God could do, but
knowing them too as only a fellow human could do; that is,
knowing them not only from within the divine omniscience,
but also from within the human condition. In this capacity He
rules as man for God (Philippians 1:11; 1 Corinthians
15:24–28) even while He rules as God over all, "blessed for
ever" (Romans 9:5, RSV; cf. Hebrews 7:26).

The full doctrine of the mediatorship of Jesus Christ as
both God and man is central and crucial to biblical Christianity. It is crucial to the Christian doctrines of atonement and justification, and it is crucial to Christian experience of hope and
peace. If Jesus Christ is not God, then to know Him is not necessarily to know God; to find in Him a would-be Savior is not to
find a sure redemption. Further, to believe in His resurrection
is no longer to know with certainty that where *He* is, one day *we*
will be. On the other hand, if Christ's humanity is less than full
and true, then again He is inadequate as a mediator, incompetent as a sympathizer, and disqualified as a redeemer. If He is
not all that we are (save for sin) in our uttermost humanity,
then He cannot perfectly represent us either in His life or in His
death. If He is not all that God is in His uttermost deity, then He

cannot bear "the sins of the whole world" (1 John 2:2). Only as God "manifested in the flesh" (1 Timothy 3:16, RSV) could He purchase the church "with his own blood" (Acts 20:28). If Christ did not descend to us from God He can never lift us up to God.

Torrance has stated this powerfully:

> To claim that Jesus Christ is not God himself become man for us and our salvation, is equivalent to saying that God does not love us to the uttermost, that he does not love us to the extent of committing himself to becoming man and uniting himself with us in the Incarnation. . . . If there is no unbreakable bond of being between Jesus Christ and God, then we are left with a dark inscrutable Deity behind the back of Jesus Christ of whom we can only be terrified.[18]

This is not a merely abstract problem:

> Here we have to do with a theological principle which is of immense importance in pastoral care. How often people have said to me: "Will God really turn out to be what we believe Him to be in Jesus Christ?" That is the question I have been asked on the battle field by a young man who had barely half an hour to live: "Is God really like Jesus?"[19]

He warns: "Questions like that, which gnaw at the back of people's minds but which they suppress and which come to the surface only in moments of sharp crisis and hurt, tell us of the insidious damage done to people's faith by dualist habits of thought which drive a wedge between Jesus and God." Torrance concludes:

> It is quite different when the face of Jesus is identical with the face of God, when His forgiveness of sin is forgiveness indeed for its promise is made good through the atoning sacrifice of God in Jesus Christ, and when the perfect love of God embodied in Him casts out all fear. But all that depends upon the identity between Christ's mediation of divine revelation and reconciliation and His own Personal Being as Mediator. [20]

# 16

# THE CONDESCENSION
# OF CHRIST

Philippians 2:5–11 describes the profound condescension of Christ in coming to earth, and we shall study it in this chapter. The language and style suggest that this passage was an early Christian hymn (or part of one) written either by Paul or another. It celebrates the whole life of Jesus Christ, confessing first His preexistence in the mysterious Godhead and tracing the course of His redeeming work as one marvelous act of obedience that God has honored and that one day the entire universe will acknowledge.

## THE IMITATION OF CHRIST

*"Your attitude should be the same as that of Christ Jesus" (v. 5).* We often tend to idealize the first-century churches. The New Testament, however, shows them to have been in many ways as flawed as our own. Here in Philippi, for example, there are divisions and quarrels within the church (Philippians 4:2–3), and our passage is embedded in a series of exhortations to the Christians to live out their common life in Christ in the spirit of humility, love, and service (Philippians 2:1–4, 12–15). They belong to one another in the body of Christ; therefore, they must live for one another in the spirit of Christ.

Many older writers see in the famous verses that follow a call to the imitation of Jesus. For instance, B. B. Warfield, the nineteenth-century Princeton theologian, has a sermon entitled "Imitating the Incarnation" in which he says: "Next to our longing to be *in* Christ is our corresponding longing to be *like* Christ,"[1] and quotes the words of Augustine, "Thou wouldst perhaps be ashamed to imitate a lowly man; then at least imitate the lowly God."[2] In this way the apostle Paul elsewhere urges the Corinthian Christians to imitate the Incarnation in their care for the Jerusalem Christians in their poverty and need: "For you know the grace of our Lord Jesus Christ, that though he was rich, yet for your sakes he became poor, so that you through his poverty might become rich" (2 Corinthians 8:9).

However, as R. P. Martin and others stress, what we have here is really far more than a call to imitation. It is a call to the Philippian Christians to realize what they, and all Christians, are already a part of.[3] The work of Christ portrayed in the hymn/Bible passage is not so much an example to be imitated as an achievement that we already share, which has revolutionized our destinies and therefore should revolutionize our lives.

In verse 5 the Philippians are reminded that they are now "in Christ Jesus," and all things have become new, including their relationships to others who are also "in Him." Consequently, they have a new mentality, new attitudes, and a new judgment, "the mind of the Lord" (1 Corinthians 2:16), which they must apply to their church relationships. "Have this mind among yourselves," Paul writes, "which is yours [already] in [your union with] Christ Jesus" (RSV). He is saying, in effect: "Work out what God has worked in; live out the new life which flows into you from Christ; be *like* Him because you are part *of* Him." The Christian life should be natural in the best sense: an outward life in conformity with an inward principle. It should be imitation, yes (e.g., Ephesians 5:1); but an imitation that is more than mere mimicry. It should be the imitation of a child exhibiting family traits.

## THE HUMILIATION OF CHRIST

*"Who, being in very nature God, did not consider equality with God something to be grasped" (v. 6).* These lines have been the subject of very long and complex debates between scholars. The differences of opinion and argument cannot be summarized in a paragraph or a page. What follows, therefore, is one line of interpretation, utilizing some recent research of particular importance and fruitfulness.

The phrase "in very nature God" is almost immediately explained by the phrase "equality with God." It therefore seems inadequate simply to equate "in very nature God" here with "image of God" in Genesis 1:27, as some have done. Peter T. O'Brien surveys a number of recent positions for and against this point,[4] and concludes: "It is very doubtful . . . whether the apostle intended to draw the Adam-Christ parallel at all, and the view has been subjected to linguistic, exegetical, and theological criticisms that have not been satisfactorily answered."[5] In the Genesis passage "equality with God" is something beyond anything Adam possesses, and is held out to Adam (via Eve) by the serpent as a temptation (Genesis 3:5). Here, though, equality with God is seen as something already possessed.

The most natural reading of these words suggests that before He was born "in the likeness of men," our Lord sustained a mode of existence that is described in the *Revised Standard Version* as being "in the form of God" and as enjoying "equality with God." O'Brien agrees with those who understand "the form of God" as a reference to His "glory," "that shining light in which, according to the OT and intertestamental literature, God was pictured."[6] The "form" therefore "does not refer to external appearance alone since possession of the form implied participation in its nature or character." [7]

We are not told precisely in what His "equality" consisted. Against the wider background of other New Testament confessions, however, the equality needs no qualification and is confession of the Son's true and full divinity and substantial oneness with the Father. He was God with God (John 1:1)— who came from above (John 8:23), where He had glory with God (John 17:5); who alone knows the Father and alone can adequately reveal Him (Matthew 11:27); who is His perfect image (Colossians 1:15) and His Agent in creation (v. 16), preservation (v. 17), and redemption (v. 20; cf. Hebrews 1:3-4). As such, Jesus has to be His equal in the highest sense: "the only-begotten Son of God, Begotten of the Father before all the ages, Light of Light, true God of true God, begotten not made, of one substance with the Father . . ."[8]

However, our passage tells us that Christ did not consider

this supreme advantage "something to be grasped." Here Paul uses a word which should be translated other than "grasped." It is a word so obscure that scholars have found great difficulty in coming to agreement about it. Literally the line reads " [He] did not consider [or regard] equality with God a *harpagmos*." Now, no one is sure what a *harpagmos* is, because the word occurs nowhere else in the New Testament or in the Septuagint, and is obscure in Greek literature generally. There is a closely related and common verb *harpazo*, which means "to seize" or "to snatch at" (though never "to hold on to," as some versions indicate), and there is also a closely related word *harpagma*, which on its own can mean "booty" or "spoil" that has been seized. These two facts have until very recently tended to color almost all modern renderings of this passage.

In an attempt to be true to the verse as a whole and to its stress on Christ's preexistence, some older theologians attempted the rendering "He did not count equality with God a thing to be held on to." But practically all modern scholars reject that explanation of *harpagmos* because its related verb never has such a meaning as "to hold on to." Many of them therefore go on to suggest that the statement means that Christ did not consider equal glory with God as something to be snatched at or seized (in the way that Adam and Eve did in the Garden when told they would be "like God," Genesis 3:5). In stark contrast, they say, He took the path of lowly obedience and received that glory as a reward.

However, there is a serious weakness here; for the previous phrase, "being in very nature God," has told us that Christ was already equal with God. How then could equality be a temptation held out to Him, a prize to be unlawfully snatched at or seized? This has always been a major objection to the current renderings, and the replies to it seem forced and unlikely. Moreover, as Moises Silva points out, "The notion of Christ's aspiring (or being tempted to aspire) for equality with God is completely foreign to the New Testament; conversely, the notion that Christ set aside His 'advantageous' position for the sake of others is at the very heart of the New Testament message."[9] Second Corinthians 8:9 is a clear statement of this.

In recent years a very important and exhaustive piece of

research into the use of *harpagmos* and *harpagma* has been published by Roy W. Hoover. Entitled "The Harpagma Enigma," it has opened up a new and arresting solution to the old problem of the meaning of *harpagmos* in Philippians 2:6.

Hoover made a very thorough survey of Greek literature, not only studying occurrences of the word *harpagmos* on its own, but, more crucially, of the entire phrase "*to count something* as a *harpagmos.*" He says: "In every instance which I have examined, this idiomatic expression refers to something already present and at one's disposal." He continues: "The question in such instances is not whether or not one possesses something but whether or not one chooses to exploit something."[10]

He concludes, therefore, that the translation of Philippians 2:6 which best fits both the clear context of Christ's preexistence and the comparable use of the word *harpagmos* in other literature is: "He did not regard being equal with God as something to use for His own advantage."

Therefore the statement does not tell us how Christ *refused* equality with God (as a temptation), or how He *achieved* equality with God (as a reward), or even how He *let go* of equality with God (as a possession), but *how He used it.*

It may be a somewhat unsuitable comparison, but our common English idiom "to have an ace up one's sleeve" might illuminate the point. Often we mean we have something in our grasp which we will use to our advantage, to win the game, to clinch the deal, or to avoid a threat. The point here would be that Christ used His advantage for us, not for Himself; to save us in our trouble, not just to keep Himself out of trouble.

In his survey of the interpretations of this passage, N. T. Wright offers a better illustration:

> Over against the standard picture of oriental despots, who understood their position as something to be used for their own advantage, Jesus understood His position to mean self-negation, the vocation described in vv. 7–8. . . . The pre-existent son regarded equality with God not as excusing Him from the task of (redemptive) suffering and death, but actually as uniquely qualifying Him for that vocation.[11]

In the words of C. F. D. Moule, "Instead of imagining that equality with God meant *getting,* Jesus on the contrary *gave.*"[12] This "giving" is then described in the next verse.

"... *but made himself nothing, taking the very nature of a servant, being made in human likeness*" (v. 7). The phrase "made himself nothing" is translated "emptied himself" in New American Standard and Revised Standard translations—a vivid way of describing Christ's self-humbling. It is as if Paul had said, "He made himself nothing at all" or "He beggared himself," or as the King James Version finely puts it: "[He] made himself of no reputation."

We must be very careful here not to imagine, as some have done, that at the Incarnation our Lord "left behind" something of His Godhead or of its attributes. God exists in the perfection of His attributes. Take away any of His perfections and you no longer have God. You cannot have a reduced Godhead. There is God and there is not-God: but there is nothing in between! We have seen in our study of John 1:1–3 and Jesus' divine nature that our Lord continued even during His incarnate life to fill the heavens and the earth with His power and presence.

Moreover, had the eternal Logos ceased in any way to be fully divine, His earthly work could not have taken on its cosmic dimensions. His righteousness could not have been the righteousness of God for us (Romans 1:17; 3:2–12; 10:3–4), and His atoning death could not have been of infinite value and timeless effect (Hebrews 9:12, 26–27; 10:13–14). Only because "God was pleased to have all his fullness dwell in him" was God able through Christ "to reconcile to himself all things, whether things on earth or things in heaven, by making peace through his blood, shed on the cross" (Colossians 1:19–20).

From the beginning the church has safeguarded the integrity of both the divine nature and the human nature in Christ, who united them in His one person and never ceased in all His saving work on earth to be fully God and fully man. Hence Augustine makes the point, referring to these verses, that "He emptied Himself not by losing what He was but by taking to Him what He was not."[13] And elsewhere he puts it like this: "Thus He emptied himself, taking the form of a servant, not losing the form of God. The form of a servant was added; the form of God did not pass away."[14]

Augustine's point is that our Lord did not and could not abandon the form (nature) of God, but hid the form of God under the form of a servant, veiling His glory beneath a humble, creaturely life. He did not exchange one mode of being for another but, on earth, hid one mode of being in another. He did not cease to be what He had always been, but became what He had never been. God, in a great act of self-humbling, became a man, but He did not cease to be God. It was an emptying by addition rather than by subtraction!

Some, notably Joachim Jeremias, who finds many verbal echoes of Isaiah 52:13–53:12 in this whole passage, see here a direct reference to the servant of Isaiah 53:12.[15] However, O'Brien believes the evidence for this last point to be "insufficient," and argues that "it seems best on balance to understand the expression ['taking the form of a servant'] against the background of slavery in contemporary society. Slavery pointed to the extreme deprivation of one's rights, even those relating to one's own life and person."[16] Jesus' washing of the disciples' feet and His drying of them with a towel He had tied around His waist (John 13:3–5) is a "particularly telling" illustration of this.

*"And being found in appearance as a man, he humbled himself and became obedient to death—even death on a cross!" (v. 8).* There is more to Jesus Christ than meets the eye, as the words "being found in *appearance* as a man" suggest. Of course, what does meet the eye is demonstrably flesh-and-blood humanity. "Man" is indeed what He was, but not *all* that He was; He was truly man but not merely man.

We are reminded too that though He remained sinless Himself, yet as Paul puts it elsewhere, He came "in the likeness of sinful man" (Romans 8:3), being subject to pain and weakness and transience, frail, and liable to suffering. He was no Superman but the Lord of men in common clay. Those around Him found Jesus clearly, obviously, demonstrably human (cf. Luke 2:52; John 1:14; Romans 8:3; Galatians 4:4; Hebrews 2:17; 4:15; 5:7–8; 1 John 4:2–3).

We might have expected the phrase "he humbled himself" to occur earlier in the poem, as indeed in its original form it might have done. But the cross was a place of such self-abasement, such disgrace, such pain and loss, that the phrase is kept until this point in the hymn. From any perspective it was the lowest point in our Lord's humiliation. John Stott writes:

> Crucifixion seems to have been invented by "barbarians" on the edge of the known world, and taken over from them by both Greeks and Romans. It is probably the most cruel method of execution ever practised, for it deliberately delayed death until maximum torture had been inflicted. The victim could suffer for days before dying.[17]

In one of his speeches the Roman orator Cicero referred to crucifixion as "a most cruel and disgusting punishment," and it was so degrading a form of death that Roman citizens were exempt from that method of execution except in extreme cases of treason. Martin Hengel shows how common and cruel this method of execution was, including the fact that while already nailed to the cross the crucified criminal could be tortured in unspeakable ways.[18] From Hengel's accounts it is little wonder that in polite Roman society the word *cross* was an obscenity, not to be uttered in conversation. It is understandable, therefore, that the style of the hymn becomes abrupt at this point, the additional phrase "even death on a cross" being inserted like an exclamation mark to signal emphasis or astonishment.

Paul saw Christ's death on the cross as the ultimate act of obedience and the lowest point of humiliation in a more-than-earthly sense. It took Christ as far beneath His original incarnation as the Incarnation was beneath His heavenly glory. In His coming He made Himself a beggar; in His dying He made Himself a curse. In the one He descended to earth; in the other He descended to hell. For on the cross He became "sin for us" (2 Corinthians 5:21), He suffered the curse that is due to sin and became "a curse for us" (Galatians 3:13). He chose to become a mortal man and carried His free act of obedience to the end-point of death, the darkness of a cosmic desolation expressed by death on a cross (Matthew 27:46). And so the exclamation deepens for all who sing this hymn with Paul's theology "obedient unto death—even death on a cross!"

## THE EXALTATION OF CHRIST

*"Therefore God exalted him to the highest place and gave him the name that is above every name, that at the name of Jesus every knee should bow, in heaven and on earth and under the earth, and every tongue confess that Jesus Christ is Lord, to the glory of God the Father" (vv. 9–11).* At verse 9 the hymn takes a sharp upward turn. There is no lower point than Calvary, where the suffering servant tasted death for everyone. His cry, "It is finished" (John 19:30), marks the completion of His voluntary obedience "unto death." After Good Friday, Easter Sunday is inevitable, for it was not possible for death to keep its hold on Him (Acts 2:24). After the finished work, the full reward; a humiliation that plumbs the depths is answered by an exaltation that scales the heights.

The phrase "exalted him to the highest place" contains a compound verb (translated "highly exalted" in the NASB and RSV versions) that might be rendered "super-exalted." Jesus has been exalted to the highest place above everything in the universe. Here is the response of the Father to Jesus' prayer in John 17:4–5. The Son has glorified the Father in His obedience unto death; God will now glorify His Son in restoring Him to His eternal glory and in giving "him the name that is above every name."

What name is that? Commentators differ. Some say "Jesus" is the name that will be exalted above every other name (as Acts 4:12). Others that the name is "King of kings and Lord of lords" (as Revelation 19:16). And others that it is "Immanuel" (as Isaiah 7:14). Many, perhaps most, scholars believe that the answer is given in the passage: all will confess that "Jesus Christ is *Lord*" (emphasis mine). In the phrase "the name of Jesus," "Jesus" is in the possessive genitive case. As O'Brien says, "It is not the name Jesus but the name which belongs to Jesus that is meant."[19]

Throughout the Greek version of the Old Testament *Kurios*, "Lord," is used to translate the Hebrew *Yahweh*. It occurs more than six thousand times in this sense. Its attribution here to one who has been described as "being in the form of God" and having "equality with God" as His right and possession, is unmistakable. Jesus is given the Name. He is *Yahweh-Jesus,* He is *the Lord Jesus.* God has given Him not *a* name, but *the* Name; the Name that is His own Name, the one Name which is above every name; the Name that was once uttered by one of the least of His disciples and is now proclaimed from heaven; the name that says, "My Lord and my God!" (John 20:28).

This is supported—decisively, I think—by words that follow in the hymn, "every knee should bow," which are a quotation from Isaiah 45:23, and that show us that the one Name has been given to Christ Jesus that could not be given to any other person in the universe of men and angels. God alone can bear it.

In the Isaiah prophecy Yahweh states uncompromisingly His incommunicable honor as God: "I am the Lord, that is my name; my glory I give to no other" (Isaiah 42:8, RSV). Thereafter His uniqueness is repeatedly stressed, until in Isaiah 45 it is said: "There is no God apart from me, a righteous God and a Savior; there is none but me. Turn to me and be saved, all you ends of the earth; for I am God, and there is no other" (Isaiah 45:21–22). It is in consequence of that uniqueness that He decrees: "Before me every knee will bow; by me every tongue will swear" (Isaiah 45:23). It could not be more dramatically revealing, therefore, that honors jealously guarded by the God of the Old Testament are given to Jesus in the New Testament because they both are one "God over all, forever praised!" (Romans 9:5).

In regard to His eternal deity the Son had shared this name with the Father in the eternal Godhead. But He had become the Son-in-weakness, becoming the God-man. In this respect, what honors He had possessed from eternity could now be publicly and newly given to Him in this capacity. Jesus did not begin to be Lord at the Ascension, but He began to be Lord in a new way. To Paul, Jesus did not become the Lord of glory after He was crucified, for it was precisely the Lord of glory who was crucified (1 Corinthians 2:8). But for the first time He was in heaven in our nature, and at the right hand of God as the God-man.

The hymn ends with an implied call to worship and an announcement that at the end of this present age, willingly or unwillingly, *every* knee will bow in submission to Christ Jesus and in acknowledgment of His supremacy. In His heavenly, mediatorial lordship as God's King, Jesus Christ now rules over everything and everyone; He rules over the entire universe of created beings: angels, men, and demons. None is free of His sovereign rule, however one may dispute it and seek to avoid it.

He is Lord now, and will be seen to be Lord then. None shall be able to deny His lordship in the great day, the day of judgment, the day of Yahweh, the day of Jesus (cf. Isaiah 45:23; Romans 15:11). The pacification of the universe will be complete, and all will acknowledge that "Jesus Christ is Lord, to the glory of God the Father" (Philippians 2:11).

Thus the hymn quoted by Paul ends with its great climax. And yet, as elsewhere in Paul, there is to be another climax: one that takes place in the lives of those who sing it, and one that must take place in their present lives.

It is remarkable that some of the greatest doctrinal passages in the New Testament are embedded in pastoral and ethical exhortation. Doctrine never stands alone and must never be divorced from life. On the other hand, Christian living is founded squarely on Christian truth and is never "mere morality." The Philippians are encouraged to put one another's interests first because this is indeed Godlike. Wright puts it like this:

The real humiliation of the incarnation and the cross is that one who was himself God, and who never during the whole process stopped being God, could embrace such a vocation. The real theological emphasis of the hymn, therefore, is not simply a new view of Jesus. It is a new understanding of God. Against the age-old attempts of human beings to make God in their own (arrogant, self-glorifying) image, Calvary reveals the truth about what it meant to be God.[20]

Which of us can "stand on our rights" when we are joined to such a Lord as this? We can stand before God only because the Son of God did *not* stand upon His rights. He had everything to live for, yet He died; He had every reason to assert His rights, yet He surrendered them. Let us live out His life together, for we are *in Him* to be *like* Him.

# 17

# THE COSMIC CHRIST

With Colossians 1:15–20 we come to one of the most majestic and profound Christological passages in the New Testament. In a burst of confessional praise it arches from the dawn of creation to the restoration of all things, and Jesus as the Son of God is dominant throughout.

It is commonly held that here, as in Philippians 2:5–11, we have the elevated style and rhythmic lilt of a poem or even a hymn, and a glance at the Old Testament will show us how often in Scripture the Spirit of God moves men to the highest reaches of prophecy in poetic form and sung praise. If this is the sort of thing first-century congregations sang, what a depth of meaning and what a height of rapture must have characterized their gatherings. However, Peter T. O'Brien reminds us that the term "hymn" is not to be understood in the modern sense, for "The category is used broadly, similar to that of 'creed.'"[1] We should not begrudge a great passage like this some close study and hard thinking. But when our study is ended, our work is only half done: we should then rise up and sing the hymn of Colossians chapter 1 to the risen Christ and the Father who sent Him.

## THE JEWISH INFLUENCE: WISDOM LITERATURE

Scholars have conjectured various backgrounds to the hymn as a whole or in part. J. D. G. Dunn, for instance, argues at length that the background to the whole passage is to be found in the wisdom literature of Judaism,[2] while Herman Ridderbos maintains that the passage "very definitely cannot be understood as a Christological interpretation of Wisdom [literature],"[3] and that the terminology contains only "vague reminiscences" of the wisdom literature, speaking as it does of a divine eternal person and not a poetic abstraction or creation. In the Jewish wisdom literature, wisdom is called "the image of God's goodness" (Wis. 7:25), "the master-builder of all things" (Sap. 7:21) and "of all things the first created" (Sir. 1:4). In the book of Proverbs it is called "the first of [God's] acts of old" (Proverbs 8:22, RSV).

O'Brien cautiously acknowledges that New Testament Christology is indebted to a general "Wisdom" background in Hellenistic Judaism, but he also notes the differences between this passage in Paul and anything in Jewish wisdom literature or the rest of the extant Jewish materials.[4] For instance, he points to the statement "all things were created by him and for him" as being far removed from anything predicated of wisdom in Jewish literature. There (as in Proverbs 8:22–31), wisdom is a personification but not a person; a means but not an end.

John F. Balchin sees the Jewish wisdom motif as providing a conceptual background to our passage: "Faced with a cosmological heresy at Colossae, Paul was prepared to exploit wisdom terminology to establish the supremacy of Christ."[5] However, he argues, "the text already identifies Christ as the agent of creation, revelation and providence, for although Paul is using wisdom language here, he is not talking about an abstract principle as his forbears were."[6] The wisdom category provided the quarry from which many of the New Testament writers took Christological motifs. But always they saw that "Christ has both fulfilled it and gone beyond it."[7] Balchin concludes:

> Christ is not only the one who expresses or imparts God's wisdom, although He does both of these things, He is God's wisdom. This is what Paul and the others said about Him, and when they did it they were attributing, possibly against every inbred instinct to the contrary, the prerogative of deity to a man who had been their contemporary.[8]

Ridderbos, on the other hand, sets the language of the

hymn firmly against the background of the Adam story in Genesis,[9] a background familiar elsewhere in Paul's writings (e.g., Romans 5:12–21; 1 Corinthians 15:45–50). He shows, however, that here Paul takes language appropriate to Adam at his creation (e.g., "image" and "firstborn," Genesis 1:26), and applies it to Christ in such a way that Christ is not modeled on Adam (as in "the last Adam"); rather Adam is modeled on Christ, who precedes him and exceeds him in every way.

In the end, it seems best to understand the hymn against the background of New Testament teaching in general rather than in terms of particular Jewish traditions or of Gentile philosophies. Even the famous "Colossian heresy" (referred to in Colossians 2:8–10, 16–19, 20–23) is best kept firmly in its place when understanding a hymn which may have been sung long before such a heresy began.

## THE COSMIC CHRIST OF COLOSSIANS 1

*"He is the image of the invisible God . . ." (v. 15).* The first description of the cosmic Christ appears in the word *image.* When we speak of an image today, we generally refer to something quite different from the original in its essence, but like the original in its form or appearance. For us, an image is either a copy of the original or a representation of it that reminds us in some way of the thing it points to.

In Greek thought, however, and in the world of the New Testament, the word *eikōn* ("image") pointed to a real counterpart of the original. The image participated in the substance of the thing it pointed to. It was not an imitation of reality, but shared the reality of the thing it "imaged." As Gerhard Kittel observes: "When Christ is called the image of God in 2 Corinthians 4:4 [and] Colossians 1:15, all the emphasis is on the equality of the image with the original."[10]

In our passage, then, the "Son he loves" of verse 13 is said to be the visible counterpart in the world of men of the invisible God. He is not merely a "reminder" of God, and He is not merely "like" God in some way. He is in His great person the *image* of God's innermost essence, and hence must partake of that same *essential* deity (cf. Hebrews 1:3). What He images He must also possess; He images God's real being precisely because He shares that real being. As the image of God, Jesus Christ is God's equivalent in the world of men (John 14:9).

In 2 Corinthians 4:4 Paul has already used this in close connection with the "glory" of God (2 Corinthians 3:7, 13, 18; 4:4, 6). Now, in Colossians 1, the Old Testament "glory" of Yahweh is once again implied in the word. In the Old Testament the glory of God is inseparable from God Himself (Exodus 33:22; Leviticus 9:4, 6, 23) and is the one way in which His transcendent and holy being can be directly manifested. No human and created form could display the true God, but in this unique way He could and did manifest His real presence; divine glory revealing divine essence; the hidden God revealing Himself from within Himself. Now, in Colossians, Christ is said to *be* that glory in our midst—though strangely veiled; the image of the invisible God.

Hence we ought not to think of the Son as being simply the image of God in the way that Adam was in his innocence, when created in the image and likeness of God (Genesis 1:26–28). Adam was the created and relative image; Christ was and is the uncreated and perfect image. Verse 16 distances Christ from such a comparison and makes it altogether inadequate.

Moreover, Jesus is the image of the invisible God not only in what He is, but also in what He *does*. Is God the creator? So is the Son (Colossians 1:16). Is God the power that sustains and guides and provides for His creation? So is the Son (Colossians 1:17). Is God the Savior of His people? He is so by the Son (Colossians 1:18–20). Is God the judge of all the earth? The Father has given all judgments to the Son (Colossians 1:20). In His earthly activity as well as in His heavenly identity, what the eternal God is, the beloved Son is.

The Colossian hymn is therefore not simply a piece of information about the eternal Godhead of the Son, but is a dynamic confession about God revealed in Jesus, God discovered in Jesus, God encountered in Jesus. When all was darkness, Jesus came: not as a light on the road to God, but as the radiance of God in a world which had left the road long ago.

"... *the firstborn over all creation. For by him all things were created: things in heaven and on earth, visible and invisible, whether thrones or powers or rulers or authorities; all things were created by him and for him" (vv. 15–16).* The title *firstborn* here should certainly not be taken to imply that there was a time when God created the Son, and that the Son, for all His eminence, is but the first in a long series of created things. This would be to miss the whole point of the title, as we shall see. Besides, verse 16 puts this out of court by saying not that "the rest" of created things were made by Him, or "all other" created things were made by Him, but *"all* things" were created in Him and for Him.

Some of these are immediately singled out. "Thrones . . . powers . . . rulers . . . authorities" are probably various ranks of supernatural beings, whether good or bad, fallen or unfallen. They stand for what F. F. Bruce calls "the invisible forces of the spirit-world," none of whom rivals or equals Christ, and all of whom are subject to Him as their "original creator" and "final disposer."[11] He created them, He overrules them, and He will judge them. To a church like that at Colossae, troubled by heretical teaching that stressed angelic powers and the worship of angels, there could be no greater comfort than this. And in our own age, too, when the occult is again becoming for so many first a fascinating and then a threatening power, it is crucial for the church of Jesus Christ to proclaim boldly that the spirit world as much as the material world is under the ultimate dominion of God's Son, who is as much exalted above angels and demons as He is above men and beasts (Colossians 2:9, 15).

Here Christ is given the same place in relation to creation that He receives in the prologue of John's gospel, where we read: "Through him all things were made; without him nothing was made that has been made" (John 1:3). The Son is differentiated from every created thing in a crucial and ultimate manner. The Son is the uncreated Creator, the Father's agent in all creation and the one in whom all things begin and continue their existence. If He has chosen to be alongside creation by human birth, He must also be worshipped and adored as above all creation by eternal existence.

The importance of the title *firstborn* here is that it is a title of honor and supremacy. In the ancient world in general, and in

Israel also, the firstborn son had a place of special primacy and
inheritance in the family (e.g., Deuteronomy 21:17; 2 Chronicles 21:3). From that early custom the term "firstborn" came to
denote honor and rank irrespective of an actual family situation. For instance, in Exodus 4:22 Israel is called God's "firstborn son" even though none of the other nations are "other
sons." It has in fact become a title expressing the special love
which God has for Israel. Similarly, in Psalm 89:27 God's king
in Israel is called "my firstborn, the most exalted of the kings of
the earth." But none of the other kings were in Yahweh's family
at all. Hence the title "firstborn" is not meant to suggest other
"later-born" sons: as in the Exodus quotation, it has lost its
original, literal sense and again simply highlights the unique
place the king has as the beloved of Yahweh.

When in the New Testament the word *firstborn* is applied to
Christ, it is not used to stress the birth aspect of the word
(except in Luke 2:7), but either the supreme rank Christ holds
in relation to the creation (Colossians 1:15–16), or the special
*relationship* that He has with the Father (Hebrews 1:6), or the
*precedence* that He has in the redeemed family of God by virtue
of His victorious work for them (Romans 8:29; Colossians
1:18). Thus the word "firstborn" in our passage does not imply
that He too is a created being, but is used as a figure of speech
to display Christ's primacy and lordship in His created universe.

Paul adds in verse 16 that all things were created "for him"
as well as through Him. Everything has been given being and
existence "with a view to" the Son, with Him as its "goal" and
its perfecter (cf. Ephesians 1:10). The idea of the entire cosmic
order existing for a first-century Jewish carpenter would be
incomprehensible and absurd if it were not spoken against the
background of the incarnation of God in Jesus. But it is against
precisely such a background that the hymn, and Paul, and the
Colossian Christians, and ourselves, can reach such heights of
confidence and devotion.

This is not merely a matter of philosophical interest to
believers, for the breathtaking "good news" of the New Testament is that God has further decreed that what is Christ's by
creation should become ours by redemption. That is why Paul

can assure the Corinthian Christians, "all things are yours" including "life" and "death," "the present" and "the future" (1 Corinthians 3:22, RSV). That is why He can tell the Roman Christians that they are "co-heirs with Christ"—who may have to "share in his sufferings" now, but who will "share in his glory" soon (Romans 8:17). And that is why he can write to the Ephesians (and to us) that God has "placed all things under his feet and appointed him to be head over everything *for the church*" (Ephesians 1:22, emphasis added).

*"He is before all things, and in him all things hold together"* *(v. 17).* The words "before all things" may be taken in either of two ways. They may mean that Christ pre-dated all creation, that when nothing at all existed except God, the Son already was. Or they may mean that the Son has pride of place in this universe He has made, that He is before all things in importance. There are reasons, both contextual and grammatical, why either meaning might be argued. Certainly both things are true of Him, and in fact both are stated in the preceding lines.

What is most striking, however, is the remarkable clause "and in him all things hold together." Again there is the suggestion of two things here, neither of which is unrelated and both of which are of tremendous significance. First, Christ is said to be not only the explanation of the origins of all existence outside of God, but also the full and ultimate explanation of its continuance. He is "the innermost, animating, cohesive principle of power, of the entire cosmos."[12] Such a claim, colossal as it is, is found also in Hebrews, where the Son is said to uphold the universe by His word of power (Hebrews 1:3). In such a revelation we are given a glimpse, beyond science, of the ultimate explanation of life in all its forms. We split a single atom and produce a chain reaction of devastating force through the energies that are released. He is the power that keeps the *entire* atomic universe in check.

However, we must think merely in terms of the origin and support of creation. There is something *even higher.* What we have here is the doctrine of providence in its most personal and purposeful form. He who keeps all things in being is leading all things towards their goal in Him. The Christian doctrine of providence is a world removed from the philosophical doctrine of iron necessity or the pagan doctrine of blind fate. Essentially, God's providence is His support, government, and guidance of the universe in general, and of our world in particular, fallen and rebellious though it is. Most importantly, however, Scripture consistently teaches us that God's providence exists as part of His great plan of *salvation,* that He is overruling all things and working deep within all things with a view to the spread of His gospel and "the kingdom of his beloved Son" (Colossians 1:13, RSV).

God's providence is both personal and purposeful, and in this passage we see Christ as the person and His reconciling work as the purpose. C. K. Barrett points out that the Greek word translated "hold together" can imply the re-joining of sundered fragments, and suggests that it points to the reconciliation and restoration celebrated at the end of the hymn.[13] Certainly, He who began all things and who continually sustains in being all things is the one in whom the fractured and fragmented parts of a fallen creation will one day be perfectly put together and healed. He is leading all things to that end. Christ will be the perfecter of the new heaven and the new earth no less than He was the originator of the creation in its first form (Ephesians 1:10; Colossians 1:20).

*"And he is the head of the body, the church; he is the beginning, and the firstborn from among the dead, so that in everything he might have the supremacy" (v. 18).* Leaving the creation and proceeding to the church is, for Paul, not a step downward but rather a step upward. Christ's lordship is more glorious here than anywhere. He could produce the world with a word, but it needed His own incarnation and death to produce a church of ransomed sinners. His care for His church corresponds to the cost of its salvation (Colossians 1:20; Acts 20:28).

Paul often speaks of the church as the body of Christ and of Christ as the head of the church, but it may be correct to keep these two distinct metaphors separate.[14] Paul is not saying that the body that is the church is a headless trunk and limbs apart from Christ. Indeed he expressly pictures the church as a complete body, head and all, when, for example, he describes some members of the Corinthian church as ears and eyes (1 Corinthians 12:14–26). Moreover, it would make no sense at all, if Christ were indeed the head of the body in this sense, to speak of the body "growing up" into its head (Ephesians 4:15–16).

In fact, when Paul speaks of Christ as "the head of the body, [which is] the church," he is using not a physiological metaphor, but a social one. The philosophers of the ancient world did not for the most part trace the motor-action of the body to the brain, but to the heart. The metaphor is therefore very unlikely to be medical. We must look elsewhere for Paul's meaning. Edmund Clowney writes: "Paul uses the term 'head' . . . to describe the supremacy of Christ over all things and all ages (Eph. 1:22; Col. 2:10). . . . The 'head' has primacy, origination, honour, authority, summation."[15] Clowney adds that this involves a headship over all powers in heaven and on earth, but that they are not His "body." The church, on the other hand, is brought into unique closeness to her Lord, her husband, and her head (Ephesians 5:23), and He is uniquely her "head" and she is uniquely His "bride" and His "body."

Paul goes on to refer to Christ as "the beginning." Here we must not think that he is going back in his thought to the beginning of creation (Colossians 1:16). "This is the moment," observes N. T. Wright, "when, according to the careful structure of the poem, the thought moves from creation to new creation."[16] Paul is developing his statement and taking a further step forward. Here "beginning" means a new beginning in the world of men. This is clear not only from the preceding reference to the church, but also from the succeeding reference to the resurrection of the dead. Christ is a new beginning in our fallen, dying world: the head of a new race, the initiator of a new order, the king of a new kingdom.

Earlier we examined the concept of Christ as the last Adam. As such He was a new beginning for us all, the head of a new humanity, a restored mankind. Where the first Adam failed and fell, the second Adam succeeded and, obedient even unto death, became our righteousness and our redemption (Romans 5:12–19). Now, as the risen Lord, His heavenly status taken up, He becomes "a life-giving spirit" (1 Corinthians 15:45) for all who are in Him. As such He is "the firstborn from among the dead" (Colossians 1:18), the head of a great and growing family (Romans 8:29), the firstfruits of a glorious harvest (1 Corinthians 15:20). Our resurrections shall issue from the power of His original and definitive resurrection. Our lives from the dead will be the outflow of His risen life as the Son of God in power. Our eternal places will be alongside our elder brother who is the author of the life we share (John 14:19; Romans 1:4; Acts 3:15; Revelation 1:18).

The place of Christ in both creation and redemption is therefore unique. He initiates both, and sustains and carries through both, until both find their end and goal and highest point in Him, "that in everything He might have the supremacy."

*"For God was pleased to have all his fullness dwell in him," (v. 19).* This is a far-reaching statement indeed. However, I do not think we should take it merely as an abstract statement about our Lord's deity. It is here for a further purpose. Notice the verb "was pleased." Most scholars prefer to render the Greek more clearly as, "God was pleased to have all his fullness dwell in him," as does the NIV translation above. Yet clearly the equal place in the divine essence that the Son has with the Father is not a matter of God's "pleasure," as though it were optional and freely given. The phrase would therefore be quite out of place in a description of our Lord's essential and eternal Godhead. The *Revised Standard Version* has better translated this, "For in him all the fullness of God was pleased to dwell." Notably, the verb "was pleased" is in a tense and mood which, in Greek, denotes a point at which this became true, whereas Christ's place in the Trinity as the Son was from all eternity.

O'Brien detects strong Old Testament echoes here. Firstly, the word *plerōma* ("fullness") is employed in the Greek Bible in such expressions as "the world and all its fullness," "the earth and everything it it," and "the world and all that it contains." Secondly, in language close to this, God is said to "fill heaven and earth" (Jeremiah 23:24), and the psalmist prays, "may the whole earth be filled with his glory" (Psalm 72:19). And thirdly, "to be pleased" often occurs in connection with the divine election, and God is said to be "pleased to dwell" in Zion (e.g., in

the Greek version of Psalms 68:16; 132:13–14; Isaiah 8:18).
O'Brien writes:

> These three lines converge at Colossians 1:19 in the person
> of Christ. . . . He is the "place" (note the emphatic position
> of [in Him]) in whom God in all His fullness was pleased to
> take up His residence. . . . All the attributes and activities of
> God—His spirit, word, wisdom and glory—are perfectly
> displayed in Christ. . . . This is no temporary indwelling as
> the verb [*katoikeō*] (in contrast to [*paroikeō*], "sojourn")
> with its present tense at chapter 2:9 makes plain: "in Him
> all the fullness of deity dwells [*katoikei*] bodily."[17]

It becomes clear, then, especially in view of the word *bodily*
in Colossians 2:9, and the reference to the cross in Colossians
1:20 (surely prospective?), that the passage is pointing to the
coming to earth of the Son *as the God-man*. Paul is saying here
that in Jesus Christ all the resources of God for man's salvation
are brought to a point: and that point is the human flesh of
Jesus.

Let me comment further on the word "fullness" in Colossians 1:19 and in 2:9. Most writers agree that at Colossae a
peculiar heresy was threatening the spiritual life of the church.
More recent scholars are much less confident about the details
of the heresy than earlier writers were. It is possible to understand the term "fullness" without reference to the heresy at all.
However, it does appear likely from such passages as Colossians 2:3–4, 8–10, 16–23 that Paul is countering false teaching.
Chapter 2:18, for instance, may reflect an early form of teaching that became a virulent heresy a few generations later. This
taught that between fallen man and the high God there were
various ranks of celestial beings, sharing among them the
divine "fullness," and that Jesus was but one of these. These
beings, it was said, dominate human life and need to be placat-
ed and "won over" by ascetic worship (e.g., Colossians 2:20–23).

If Paul is opposing such teaching at Colossae, then it is
indeed possible that in Colossians 1:19 and 2:9 he is insisting
that Jesus is not one of many celestial beings, but is unique in
himself and in His sufficiency as Redeemer. In Him not a frag-

ment of the divine fullness, but "all the fullness of the deity"
dwells bodily, and, in the words of one writer, He fills the whole
space between God and man. Here in the Greek "deity" (*theos*)
is a much stronger word than "divine" (*theios*), and it leaves
Paul's contention in no doubt: Jesus is the Most High God in
human flesh. He in His flesh-and-blood existence was and is
forever the decisive work of God for the salvation of lost
mankind. By faith in Him, and in Him alone, men are freed
from superstition as well as from sin (Colossians 2:8, 16, 20–23).

"*. . . and through him to reconcile to himself all things,
whether things on earth or things in heaven, by making peace
through his blood, shed on the cross*" (*v. 20*). This is the triumphant high point of the hymn: cosmic reconciliation. In the
New Testament reconciliation is always God's work. The
offended, not the offenders, initiates the work of reconciliation
and carries it through to a triumphant conclusion (Romans
5:1–2, 10–11). Man is a fallen being in a fractured world. He
needs reconciliation and his world needs renewal. Sin has
somehow affected creation itself. Man's world has been "subjected to frustration" and is in "bondage to decay" (Romans
8:20, 21). It needs healing and restoration by God. By His atoning work Christ is man's peace (Ephesians 2:14–17) and creation's hope (Romans 8:20).

This language of universal reconciliation is not to be
pressed to mean the ultimate salvation of every human being,
since it is only made effective "in Christ" (2 Corinthians 5:17),
and those who refuse Him have before them only "a fearful
prospect of judgment" (Hebrews 10:27, RSV). But in Christ there
will be a new heaven and "a new earth" in which peace and harmony will reign and only the righteous will dwell (Revelation
21:1, 4, 8, 27).

However, it is not only man who has fallen. Angelic powers
and rulers (principalities, RSV) are at work, in hostility against
God and all He has made, and they too need to be subjugated to
God. Bruce writes: "It is contrary to the analogy of Scripture to
apply the idea of reconciliation in the ordinary sense to fallen
angels; and as for Paul, he thinks rather of hostile powers as
emptied of all vitality by the work of Christ and the faith of His

people."[18] These powers oppose the ongoing work of reconciliation; they are barriers to the spread of the kingdom of peace. They need to be subjugated to God.

A similar statement is found in Ephesians 1:9–10, which speaks of God's "purpose which he set forth in Christ as a plan for the fulness of time, to unite all things in him, things in heaven and things on earth" (RSV). Bruce comments: "in Christ . . . [God] has planned to 'gather up' [the sense of 'unite' here] the fragmented and alienated universe." The reconciliation of Jew and Gentile that is celebrated in Ephesians 2 is "a stage in the unification of a divided universe."[19]

If at this point in the hymn Paul has in mind the fallen angelic powers of which he later speaks (Colossians 2:8, 15, 18, 20), R. P. Martin's words concerning Colossians 1:20 and Ephesians 1:10 are apt:

> Both passages are directed against the contrary heretical idea that human destiny lies at the mercy of the astral gods . . . no part of the universe lies beyond Christ's control and lordship . . . no fate can tyrannise over human life and strike fear into the human heart.[20]

It is interesting to note John Calvin's comment on Colossians 1:20. He sees the "all things" of our text as referring to "all creatures who have any connection at all with God" (i.e., who serve Him and belong to Him), including the angels of heaven. True, there was no revolt of these angels, and consequently no separation from God. "It was however necessary for two reasons for angels also to be set at peace with God: for, being creatures they were not beyond the risk of falling, had they not been confirmed by the grace of Christ." The grace of Christ provides them with "a fixed standing in righteousness, so as no longer to fear fall or revolt." Moreover, "In that very obedience which they render to God, there is not such absolute perfection as to satisfy God in every respect and without pardon . . . there is not in the angels so much righteousness as would suffice for full union with God." Calvin concludes: "They have, therefore, need of a peacemaker, through whose grace they may wholly cleave to God. Hence Paul rightly declares that the grace of Christ does not reside in men alone but is common also to the angels."[21]

The making of peace is said to be "through his blood shed on the cross" (Colossians 1:20). It was by His sacrificial and atoning death that Christ removed the barrier of sin and enables the most holy God to embrace a fallen world and repair its brokenness. It was, as Paul puts it later, "in his body of flesh" (Colossians 1:22, RSV) that the explosive meeting of sin and holiness, guilt and judgment, rejection and reconciliation took place. It was similarly by the cross of His Son that God "canceled the written code, with its regulations, that was against us and that stood opposed to us" (Colossians 2:14)—"a reference," argues Wright, to the Mosaic law that "shut *up* the Jews under sin and shut *out* the Gentiles from the hope and promise of membership in God's people."[22]

Here it is, then: the Cross forms the foundation of the eternal and cosmic peace of the new heavens and the new earth, of men and angels. The final affirmation of the great hymn of Colossians 1 is that there will be no part of God's renewed universe that will be unaffected by the cross—no place where Calvary is irrelevant.

# PART 4

## JESUS THE
## DIVINE REDEEMER

# 18

# THE SHADOW OF THE CROSS: THE CROSS IN THE OLD TESTAMENT

Nothing is more precious to the Christian believer than a personal awareness of the love of God. Without His love His holiness would terrify us, His power would crush us, and His eternity (and ours) would be our greatest nightmare. But knowing that in Christ God has in love committed Himself to saving us from our sin and reconciling us to Himself forevermore brings us both peace and joy. In Christ, God's power is our protection, His justice is our justification, and His eternity our glorious destiny. Indeed, in Christ the eternal God is our dwelling place, and underneath are the everlasting arms (Deuteronomy 33:27).

However, the distortion of one feature can turn the greatest beauty into something ugly and unattractive. And it is a sad truth that the biblical doctrine of the divine love is commonly distorted into something bereft of holiness, shorn of power and robbed of grace. Divorced from the person and work of Christ, the idea of God's love frequently becomes a religious commonplace, to be taken for granted rather than to be urgently sought and astonishingly found at Calvary. If we are to sing

> Ransomed, healed, restored, forgiven,
> Who like me His praise should sing?[1]

we must understand who it is that loved us and at what cost and with what consequence.

## THE HOLY LOVE OF GOD
## IN OLD TESTAMENT TEACHING

Anyone who imagines that the Old Testament presents a God of wrath and that it was left to the New Testament to discover God's love shows a pretty woeful ignorance of both. From the start of the Old Testament, and increasingly throughout its books of law and prophecy, psalms and history, we are constantly shown that love is essential to God. Carl Henry writes: "Love is not accidental or incidental to God; it is an essential revelation of the divine nature, a fundamental and eternal perfection" and "it is the shaping principle of His creative and redeeming work."[2] If holy is *what* God is, love is *how* He is.

The Hebrew Old Testament has a cluster of terms for love in general and for the divine love in particular, including *aheb*, often stressing the free, spontaneous character of love (well over 200 times); *chen*, in most cases with the sense of grace and favor (68 times); and *chesed*, mainly with the sense of kindness or loving-kindness (about 250 times).

The Old Testament begins with God in His overflowing goodness and wisdom creating a wonderful world which He approves and enjoys (Genesis 1:31), and creating man, the greatest work of all, with whom He shares that enjoyment (Genesis 1:26–28). His relationship to man as a unique creature is itself unique, and the Genesis account shows God taking man into fellowship with Himself in a personal relationship of mutual interest and affection. Adam and Eve hear, as a familiar thing, "the sound of the Lord God . . . walking in the garden in the cool of the day" (Genesis 3:8).

### An Undeserved Love

Perhaps surprisingly, it is after Adam and Eve's rebellion and fall, and the terrible alienation and divorce which they brought ("and they hid from the Lord God," Genesis 3:8), that God's relationship is shown more specifically in terms of *love*. God's immediate response is not only a holy indignation and wrath expressed in the curse of Genesis 3:14–24, but an unexpected and totally undeserved demonstration of grace given in the promise of Genesis 3:15—that the seed of the woman would one day bruise the head of the serpent, that Satan would eventually be defeated and man saved.

After that, a persistent note of mercy and grace recurs as God begins to distinguish between men, gathering a people to Himself through the centuries and generations; from the martyred Abel, and the continuation of "the godly line" in Seth (Genesis 4:26), to Enoch who "walked with God" (Genesis 5:22), and the faithful Noah whose lonely piety believed and obeyed God in a world that was almost universally wicked (Genesis 6:1–9).

Yet although Israel was taught from the start that God had destined blessing for "all peoples on earth" (Genesis 12:3; 18:18; 22:18; 26:4; 28:14), they were nevertheless left in no doubt that this was no automatic thing, no inevitable reflex of God's essential goodness. His love, utterly forfeited by sin, was free and undeserved, gracious and sovereign. The story of God's love towards Israel's revered father and earthly founder, Abraham, was the story of God's gracious initiative breaking into the heart and life of a Mesopotamian idolater and calling him to a promised land and the eternal rest that it prefigured (Genesis 12:13; cf. Hebrews 4:8–10). It is the story of God, choosing this idolater to found a nation that would keep the flame of the only true and saving religion burning bright, when the rest of the world was cold and dark. Such love would one day cause the whole world of men to bless themselves in Abraham's God (Genesis 12:3; cf. Galatians 3:16).

The free and undeserved nature of that love was emphasized from the early days of Israel's privilege. Moses reminded them:

> For you are a people holy to the Lord your God. The Lord your God has chosen you out of all the peoples on the face of the earth to be his people, his treasured possession. The Lord did not set his affection on you and choose you because you were more numerous than other peoples, for you were the fewest of all peoples. But it was because the Lord loved you and kept the oath he swore to your forefathers (Deuteronomy 7:6–8)

## A Specific Love

Geerhardus Vos points out that the Old Testament is consistently cautious in using the actual term *love* outside of God's covenant relationship with His own people.[3] The reason, Vos suggests, "lies in the absolute character the Old Testament ascribes to the divine love. In His general goodness God bestows various gifts upon the creature; in His love He gives Himself and holds nothing back."[4] In God there is indiscriminate goodness, but not undiscriminating love; God's love is universal but not indiscriminate.

Ethelbert Stauffer very clearly contrasts the heathen view of divine love with the biblical view when he states that the distinctive characteristic of love in the Old Testament "is of course its tendency to exclusivism." He explains: "Greek *eros* is from the outset a universal love, generous, unbound and *non*-selective. The love extolled in the Old Testament is a jealous love which chooses one among thousands, holds Him with all the force of passion and will, and will allow no breach of loyalty."[5] It is not only attitude but action; not sentiment in God but salvation from God; it is saving love.

This does not mean that God does not love all people. But it does mean that God does not love all people in the same way. This is a problem for some at first, but a moment's thought will show us that if love is to be meaningful it will be discriminating and varied. What mother loves the other children in the street as much as her own? What husband loves all (or any!) other woman as much as he loves his wife? The higher a love becomes, the more distinguishing and specific it is. And Scripture gives a special place for God's love to His people (Amos 3:2), for Christ's love for His church (John 17:9; Ephesians 5:25).

If we fail to make biblical distinctions here, we can in fact *reduce* the love of God to a bland impartial benevolence, blind to wrong and unexcited towards good: unemotional and mechanical. Such a love is as sub–Old Testament as it is sub-Christian. It ceases to be truly personal, and it is certainly not holy. The New Testament, particularly in the words of Jesus, has many dire warnings for those who reject the offer of God's love and who thus doom themselves to His wrath (Mark

9:42–48; John 5:25–29; 1 Thessalonians 1:7–10; Hebrews 10:26–31).

Time and again Israel is reminded that Yahweh has loved them in a special way. They are His chosen people (Deuteronomy 4:19–20, 34–35, 37–44; Amos 3:2; cf. Isaiah 43:4–5; Malachi 1:2–3). His relationship with them is unique: Israel is His bride (Isaiah 54:5), His child (Exodus 4:22–3; Deuteronomy 32:18), the apple of His eye (Deuteronomy 32:10; Zechariah 2:8).

## A Faithful Love

When the Israelites were tempted to forget the gracious nature of God's love to them, the prophets were at hand to remind them sharply that their history was a sorry reminder that apart from God they were no better than any other nation. There had been nothing in them to attract God at the start (Ezekiel 16:1–6), and their repeated backslidings and treachery (Ezekiel 16:15–34) had forfeited His love a thousand times. Yet He had remained true to His decision and oath to love the unworthy and to redeem His people in the end (Ezekiel 16:59–63; cf. Psalm 89:19–37). His love is free but not fickle, spontaneous in its rise but steadfast in its continuance.

In the book of Hosea the great God Yahweh compares Himself as the Savior of Israel to a husband who is constantly deserted by a loose, immoral, hopelessly flighty wife (Hosea. 1:1–3; 2; 3:1; 4; 5:3–4), yet who is still faithful to his marriage vows (2:14–23; 14:1–8). Like a husband, Yahweh maintains, against all provocation, the love He has decreed (11:1) and they have betrayed: "How can I give you up, Ephraim? How can I hand you over, Israel? . . . For I am God, and not man—the Holy One among you" (11:8–9). Hosea's prophecy displays the essence of God's covenant-love, and Jeremiah reveals this quality of God's love very powerfully when he cries out in a dark hour of Israel's history: "The steadfast love of the Lord never ceases, his mercies never come to an end; they are new every morning; great is thy faithfulness" (Lamentations 3:22, RSV).

However, the Old Testament teaching of the love of God must be seen in its wider context of God's self-revelation. His love is never isolated from His other perfections or given a primacy over His other essential attributes, such as righteousness and justice. This is to say that in the Old Testament God's love exists in harmony with His holiness (Hosea 11:9).

## THE HOLINESS OF GOD
## IN OLD TESTAMENT TEACHING

It is true that men and women are the objects of God's goodness and love, even before they hear His word about Himself (or are capable of hearing it). Nevertheless, when God Himself approaches any of His creatures to revealHimself to them, the first and chief thing He wants them to know about Himself is that He is holy. This is the most profound word about God in the Old Testament, and it is certainly the biggest.

### Holiness and God

It is difficult to give the term *holy* any one meaning, as it is a description of what God is in Himself in His infinite perfection. It is not one thing about God, but everything about God. It is the most fundamental feature of the divine being and it is the total glory of all He is. Holiness underlies and characterizes every attribute, and it is the sum of all His attributes. Out of His holy being all His deeds and decisions proceed: His speech is the announcement of His holiness, His glory is the display of His holiness, His wrath is the revulsion of His holiness against sin, and His love is the embrace by His holiness of all that is good and true. Hence God wants His people to know, as of first importance, that He is the holy God. Twenty-nine times in Isaiah He is acknowledged as "the Holy One of Israel."

The Hebrew word for holy (*qadosh*) probably comes from a root meaning "cut off," "separated," "set apart," and in the first place points not so much to His moral character as to God's fundamental "apartness" from everything in His creation. Even though He is in the midst of all He has made, upholding it with His power and filling it with His goodness, yet in His own unique, infinite, and uncreated nature He is utterly distinct from it. God's holiness therefore points us first to His transcendence, to His majesty, to His essential and infinite "otherness" from everything created and finite.

Hence the angels in Isaiah's vision who cover their faces in dread before Yahweh's holiness (Isaiah 6:2) do so not because they are sinners, but because they are creatures. In spite of all their superhuman power and knowledge, they are awed by the infinite reaches of Yahweh's eternal being, and it is in praise of this that they cry repeatedly: "Holy, holy, holy is the Lord Almighty; the whole earth is full of his glory" (Isaiah 6:3).

The history of the word *holy* is interesting. Originally it simply denoted the "godness" of a god: the difference between the deity and everything else. In that sense it was a little like our contemporary use of terms like *divine, divinity,* etc.; hence even the Baals were 'holy'. What was different about the Old Testament concept of holiness was the ethical element. Yahweh's holiness was ethical as well as extraordinary, moral as well as majestic. What was "different" about the God of Abraham, Isaac and Jacob was that He was "ethically pure, absolutely upright, utterly true," hating unrighteousness, challenging corruption, and judging sin and uncleanness of heart and life. This was His character (Exodus 34:6–7) and these were His demands (e.g., Exodus 20; Leviticus 19). As John Oswalt concludes, "'You shall be holy as I am holy' (Leviticus 19:1) does not refer to ritual purity but rather to ethical behavior. Thus for the Hebrew, holiness came to have a very particular ethical cast."[6]

This is Isaiah's message—and it was his experience when confronted by the Holy One of Israel. As we can see from the prophet's responses to the presence of such a God ("Woe is me! For I am lost," Isaiah 6:5, RSV), God's holiness exists not only in immense contrast with creatureliness and finitude, but in even more dramatic contrast with sin. Sin disqualifies anyone from living in the presence of God in a way that mere creatureliness does not. God is *above* His creation, but He is not *against* it as such (Genesis 1:31). Yet He is against whatever is sinful, unrighteous, or distorted in His universe, against whatever has deviated from His perfect will and left its appointed course. And that includes man as a sinner and a rebel; man, fallen and unclean, before a holy God. Hence Isaiah does not simply join with the angels' cry, but adds in counterpoint to their solemn awe his own desperate cry: "Woe is me! For I am lost; for I am a man of unclean lips, and I dwell in the midst of a people of unclean lips; for my eyes have seen the King, the Lord of hosts!" (Isaiah 6:5, RSV). Oswalt comments:

> Before the presence of this moral and ethical perfection the prophet knew that the whole issue of his life and that of his people were defiled and corrupt. Their problem was not that they were finite before the Infinite or mortal before the Immortal or partial before the Complete. Their problem was that they were morally filthy before the Morally Pure.[7]

God's holiness is thus seen to involve His moral character also. God is moral in His majesty (Isaiah 5:16). His glory is not the glare of naked power, but the beauty and perfection of a righteous being who always and in all situations acts in harmony with His innermost nature. Nothing is done at the expense of any part of the divine character, and in every aspect of His character—His power and His justice, His mercy and His love, His patience and His wrath—He is the one holy God: "righteous in all his ways and loving toward all he has made" (Psalm 145:17); and yet also has eyes "too pure to look on evil" and unable to "tolerate wrong" (Habakkuk 1:13).

## Holiness and Wrath

God's holiness is His total, unchanging, and dynamic personality out of which He expresses Himself consistently and zealously. It includes what Otto Procksch calls "the death-dealing element."[8] When confronted with purity, righteousness, and obedience, it expresses itself in blessing; when confronted with impurity, rebellion, or sin in any of its forms, it expresses itself in wrath. Edmond Jacob notes that the Old Testament references to divine wrath outnumber those to human anger almost five to one—"a fact," concludes Carl Henry, "that strongly counters the theory that human emotions were projected latterly upon the God of the Bible."[9]

God's wrath is a necessary as well as a personal response to sin. It is the reaction of His truth and righteousness to what would invalidate them (Isaiah 5:16). It is the revulsion of His holy being to what challenges its very existence and threatens to disintegrate His entire creation at every level.

The wonder that grows from all this is that the holy God can "sanctify" or consecrate to Himself and His special use people who are by nature "unclean" and at the polar opposite of holiness (Psalm 78:37–41). It is at this point that the biblical teaching concerning sacrifice comes into its own.

## Holiness and Sacrifice

It is a basic principle in the Old Testament Levitical laws that, as Gordon Wenham puts it, "The unclean and the holy are two states which must never come into contact with each other."[10] Contact between these ultimate opposites in God's universe is "disastrous" and "results in death."[11] However, "sacrifice, by cleansing the unclean, makes such contact possible. The holy God can meet with sinful man."[12] Sacrifice enables God without compromise to elevate man to the level of the "holy," to consecrate to Himself what has been purged of sin and rescued from corruption. By sacrifice a holy God can live with sinful man and can make a chosen nation a kingdom of priests, holy unto Him. Essentially, sacrifice is primarily God's work for God's sake. Only sacrifice can undo the effects of sin— on man as guilty, and in God as just. "Peace with God," writes Wenham, "is the goal of sacrifice."[13]

Repeatedly in the Old Testament we are told that sacrifice "atones" for sin and uncleanness. What "atonement" (Hebrew, *kippur*) actually means is the subject of much scholarly debate. Wenham argues that it is closely related to the Hebrew word *kōpher*, which means "ransom price."[14] In Exodus 21:30, for instance, a man whose ox has killed a man or woman is allowed to escape execution by the payment of a *kōpher*, or ransom price (cf. Exodus 30:15; Numbers 31:50; Proverbs 6:35). The idea of atonement being a *payment* for sin certainly seems more consistent with the general Old Testament attitude than the idea, now widely questioned, that it was a "covering" for sin —since in the Old Testament such "covering" is usually regarded as itself sinful (see e.g., Job 31:33; Psalm 32:5; Proverbs 28:13).

The other main possibility is that the Hebrew word *kippur* comes from the Akkadian verb *kuppuru*, "to cleanse" or "to wipe," a concept that Derek Kidner thinks "lies close to the heart of what atonement signified."[15] Kidner believes that the mechanics of "how" sacrifice deals with sin remain elusive and cannot be restricted even to the important "ransom" model:

> The reality is richly expressed in terms of ransom, of covering, of blotting out, of removing, of not imputing (Psalm 32:2), of remitting, of forgiving, of accepting; and we have still not exhausted the list. . . . What single formula could cover such a universe of divine action in terms of a single mechanism?[16]

One thing is certain: that in the provision of sacrifice Yahweh gave His ancient people a complex lesson that taught them His holiness and His love, their need and His provision, their danger and His salvation from that danger. In the sacrifices which prefigured His own Son's self-giving on Calvary, He could say, without compromise to His holiness and in entire self-justification, "I . . . sanctify you" (Leviticus 20:8, RSV; 21:8, 15, 23; 22:9, 16, 32).

## GOD'S MESSAGE OF SALVATION
## IN OLD TESTAMENT TEACHING

The system of offerings under the Mosaic covenant was quite complex. For instance, there were whole burnt offerings, peace offerings of several types, sin offerings, and guilt offerings. In these and their rituals, elements of penitence, consecration, and joy are variously emphasized. However, we should not fail to note that in spite of the different names given (and in spite of the fact that only one kind is actually called a sin offering), *all* the animal sacrifices of Leviticus were in fact sin offerings, and the crucial features of substitution, atonement, and reconciliation were present in each of them.

### Substitution
R. K. Harrison writes:

> Leviticus teaches that atonement for sin must be by substitution. The sinner must bring an offering which he has acquired at some cost as a substitute for his own life. The formal identification with it is followed by the presentation

of the offering to God and a declaration by the priest that atonement has been made. The book thus makes it evident that no person can be his own saviour or mediator.[17]

The worshipper was to present his offering in the appointed way: at the door of the tabernacle and with the laying on of hands by the offerer: "He shall lay his hand upon the head of the burnt offering" (Leviticus 1:4, RSV). That this symbolized both the worshipper's identification with the animal and the substitution of the animal in his place to become, by sacrifice, an atonement for his sin is implied in the immediate context. Thus we read, "and it shall be accepted for [i.e., instead of] him to make atonement for [i.e., instead of] him" (Leviticus 1:4, RSV). Later, however, it is made quite explicit, for we read of an identical act in regard to the "scapegoat" of Leviticus 16 that tells us explicitly the nature and purpose of this substitution: "[Aaron] is to lay both hands on the head of the live goat and confess over it all the wickedness and rebellion of the Israelites—all their sins. . . . The goat will carry on itself all their sins . . ." (Leviticus 16:21–22).

Although it is true that the symbolism of sacrifice contained devotional as well as penal elements, by which the worshipper expressed the giving up to Yahweh of his whole being in adoration and consecration, it is quite wrong to suppose, as some have, that the blood-shedding simply represents the "release of life" to God. Leon Morris argues strongly against this misunderstanding and points out that over two hundred times in the Old Testament "blood" is connected with death, not just life, and with violent death at that.[18] Beyond reasonable doubt the death of the sacrifice symbolizes the stroke of judgment due to sin and due to every sinner on account of his sin. The devotion of the worshipper is clear in the act and its consequences, but its acceptability is grounded on a penal substitution in which payment is made for his sin in order that the sacrifice of a willing heart might be acceptable to a holy God. Probably on the one hand the killing of the substitute represented the death-dealing aspect of the divine wrath, while the burning of the sacrifice represented the consecration of the

offerer as well as the giving of a costly gift to Yahweh in thanksgiving or penitence.

The crucial point in substitutionary, atoning sacrifice is
that it is *God* who makes this provision. It is He, not the worshipper, who ordains that the animal shall go proxy for the man
as a sacrificial substitute. It is He who accepts it as such from
the hands of the priests. It is He who pronounces it an atonement for sin: "I have given it to you to make atonement for
yourselves on the altar" (Leviticus 17:11). He is foremost in reconciliation, He provides the means of reparation. He is ready to
be merciful, He waits to be gracious.

### Atonement/Propitiation

We saw earlier that the word for atonement goes beyond an
indication that the sin has in some way been wiped away, and
suggests a real payment for sins. So, for example, Wenham and
Harrison agree that to make atonement literally means to pay a
ransom.[19] Yet even this is not in itself an entirely clear and specific explanation, and consequently we need to go beyond the
derivation of the word and look at the whole context of its use.
If we do so carefully, we are very likely to agree with Morris and
Wenham that the essential element of propitiation is the most
revealing factor.[20]

In the ancient world to *propitiate* meant "to placate," "to
appease," and thus to turn away wrath by persuading the gods
to be merciful. However, it had all sorts of connotations, most
of them utterly unworthy of Israel's God. It is therefore a dangerous word if wrongly used, but it is a vital and helpful word if
properly understood. Among the heathen, to propitiate the
gods meant to persuade them to change their mind and attitude by bribing them and appeasing their capricious anger: this
was usually done by means of sacrifices, animal or human. In
ancient Israel, however, the idea of propitiation was cleansed of
these impurities. True, God was wrathful towards sinful man:
but His wrath was the outgoing of His holiness, not the expression of bad temper or arbitrary dignity.

The ancient Greek version of the Old Testament, the Septuagint, so widely used before and during New Testament times,
translates the Hebrew *kippur* ("atonement") by the Greek word

*hilasmos* ("propitiation"), usually in the context of averting or turning away God's wrath. The Septuagint uses the verb *hilaskomai* ("to propitiate") more than a hundred times and the noun *propitiation* well over a hundred times more—never in a crude, pagan sense, and always with God as the merciful and gracious propitiator who Himself provides for the satisfaction of His holy wrath. In this way God is both the object of propitiation and its subject: the sacrifice is given *by* Him before it is given *to* Him; His love provides what His holiness demands.

This outstanding fact differentiates the scriptural concept of propitiation from unworthy heathen notions of celestial bribery and demonstrates that in Scripture propitiation means not "to make gracious" but "to enable to be gracious." God is *already* gracious in intention, and is making a way for His mercy to operate without prejudice to His justice and truth. Sin is the cause and sinners are the objects of His wrath, and in substitutionary atonement God turns away His wrath by expressing upon the substitute, as a sacrifice for sin, all His holy indignation against sin, visiting upon it the full penalty due from the divine justice. Thus God Himself provides the atonement for sin—both symbolically in the institution of the Old Testament sacrifices and actually (as we shall see in the next chapter) in the delivering up to sacrificial death of His own Son.

Some trends in modern theology have opposed propitiation as crude and unworthy; and some modern Bible translations, such as the *Revised Standard Version* and the *New English Bible,* outlaw *propitiation* and replace it with *expiation.* The word *expiation,* which simply means "removal," is in itself valid enough, but it is limited since it does not tell us *how* God removes sin, whereas both the Old Testament and the New are perfectly clear that God removes sin and guilt not by passing it over, but by visiting His holy wrath upon a sin-bearing substitute and satisfying the demands of His justice.

The personal character of this wrath has been questioned in modern times. Many scholars, following C. H. Dodd's seminal work in the 1930s,[21] have insisted that in relation to God wrath is an impersonal and automatic process in which the sinner willfully places himself outside the circle of God's influence and accordingly suffers deprivation and loss, and that by New Testament times, and in Paul's writings, it had acquired this meaning. The idea of God's active and personal wrath is firmly denied. Dodd's thesis, once vastly influential, has received some searching and damaging criticisms in recent years, notably by the conservative scholar Leon Morris.[22]

Such views as Dodd's, with its impersonal concept of wrath and its use of the imprecise word *expiation* instead of *propitiation* (or, as in the NIV, "atoning sacrifice"), fail to bring into the area of personal relationships the concepts of holiness and sin. But all of Scripture is clear and emphatic that God Himself is holy, God Himself is wrathful against sin and sinful creatures. His wrath is not a mechanical law of retribution, the inevitable but impersonal effect of departing from God. His wrath is "fierce" and disastrous (Exodus 32:11–12, 14). As the Old Testament theologian Walther Eichrodt writes, wrath "signifies, when applied to God, the emphatically personal character of the Deity."[23] Wrath is an action that is grounded in His own eternal, holy, and unchanging nature.

Herman Ridderbos is certainly right when he says, in a New Testament context, "'Wrath of God' not only says something about what God does, but also about what He is in doing it."[24] F. F. Bruce combines and relates the two concepts of expiation and propitiation nicely when he writes, "If sins require to be expiated, it is because they are sins committed against someone who ought to be propitiated."[25]

### Reconciliation

God's intention in providing the way of sacrifice in the Old Testament was not only to demonstrate something but to achieve something. The goal of the whole process of sacrifice was the achievement of a restored relationship between the sinner and his God. Propitiation is the means, reconciliation is the end. To play on our English word: atonement leads to at-one-ment.

There were three ways in which Yahweh's acceptance of the sacrificial substitute and His goodwill towards the worshipper were expressed. Each of them, in a dramatic and personal way, exhibited different aspects of the reconciliation that had been achieved. The ascending smoke of the whole burnt offering, rising as "an aroma pleasing to the Lord" (Leviticus 1:9), showed not only His acceptance of the worshipper but the real pleasure God had in the act of reconciliation. The symbolism is neither crude nor unworthy. The God who "delights in mercy" (cf. Micah 7:18, KJV) *savors* the moment of triumphant love. On the human side, the joyful feasting off the peace offering by the offerer and his family and friends (Leviticus 7:15) expressed in the clearest and most familiar manner possible that God and sinners were now reconciled: Yahweh and His people were table companions.

The priests, meanwhile, assisted in the reconciliation, as dramatically demonstrated on the annual day of atonement. Only on this day was the high priest—and only the high priest—allowed to enter the holy of holies, that supremely sacred and mysterious cube within the temple (veiled off even from "the holy place"), in which rested the ark of the covenant with its mercy seat. On the first of his three entrances, the high priest had to burn incense (Leviticus 16:13), designed to be a screen hiding from him the glory of God on the mercy seat. In this preliminary act, as in the subsequent entrance with the blood of a bull for the atonement of the priesthood's uncleanness before God, the lesson is brought home that entering into the holy of holies is fraught with danger. Wenham says of the day's rituals: "The purpose of these laws is to prevent Aaron, in theory the holiest man in Israel, suffering sudden death when he enters the tabernacle."[26]

The high priest was then to perform the most unusual rite of all. At one point in the day's ritual two goats were to be taken. One was to be killed in the usual way, as a sin offering for the people, and its blood presented at the mercy seat in the holy of holies and sprinkled on the altar (Leviticus 16:15–19). But the other goat was to be taken, the sins of the nation symbolically laid on it (Leviticus 16:21), and then it was to be freed and sent alive into the wilderness. These two goats were, however, not two separate sacrifices, but each was part of the one sacrifice, and this second goat, the "scapegoat," would have had no efficacy without its slain counterpart ("without the shedding of blood there is no forgiveness," Hebrews 9:22).

In this way the message was illustrated, that by atoning sacrifice the sins of the nation had been effectively removed: "The goat will carry on itself all their sins to a solitary place" (Leviticus 16:22). The sin of the nation had been borne by an ordained substitute, and borne away forever. Israel was clean, her priests were clean, her altars were clean. Yahweh had made her so.

One outstanding question remains, however, even at the center of that high point of religious confidence. Were these Old Testament Israelites taught to rest content with the animal sacrifices which they had, and did they imagine that their sacrificial system and priesthood was the whole of God's provision for sin? The writer of the New Testament book of Hebrews seems to suggest that they did not; that a certain residual dissatisfaction, a feeling that there were as yet unrealized depths both to man's sin and to God's forgiveness, compelled the thoughtful worshipper to look beyond the prescribed rites of his religion for the ultimate truth concerning atonement and reconciliation. The final and full provision must surely be *in* God as well as *from* God. The very repetition of the sacrifices showed their insufficiency as mere animal substitutes (Hebrews 10:1–4), nor could they deal with the greater sins that smote the conscience of the fallen believer (Psalm 51:14, 16; Hebrews 10:2).

It is from within the new covenant dispensation that the writer of Hebrews, after a careful examination of the old covenant's lessons and its limits, shows the utter superiority and all-sufficiency of Jesus Christ in His divine person and His atoning work. His priesthood is superior to that of Aaron since He is qualified to be a high priest not by physical descent from Aaron, but by direct appointment by God. Moreover, His appointment is not for a short lifetime, but forever, by the "power of an indestructible life" (Hebrews 7:16). In the words of an Old Testament prophecy: "The Lord has sworn and will not change his mind: 'You are a priest forever'" (Hebrews 7:21).

Jesus' priesthood is linked with God's promised new covenant in Hebrews 8:6–13. The Levitical high priests entered an earthly sanctuary to ratify the old covenant, but Jesus has entered the heavenly sanctuary as mediator of the new. W. L. Lane writes of this passage:

The writer presupposes that the new covenant required a new mediator. By means of His death on the cross as the covenant sacrifice, Jesus inaugurated the new covenant of Jeremiah 31:31–34. His entrance into the heavenly sanctuary guarantees God's acceptance of His sacrifice and the actualisation of the provisions of the superior covenant He mediated.[27]

Hebrews speaks of a new priesthood and a new covenant, but crucial to both is the new sacrifice which has been made in the blood of Jesus Christ (Hebrews 9:11–28). The ineffective sacrifices of the old covenant have been superseded by the sufficient sacrifice of Jesus (Hebrews 10:11–14). The offering that *this* high priest brought is incomparable and unrepeatable because He "offered himself" (Hebrews 7:27) as an "appointed" sacrifice (Hebrews 7:28), fully acceptable and wholly accepted (Hebrews 7:26). A word which the writer repeatedly uses of the sacrificial death of Christ is the unusual *ephapax* (a strengthened form of *hapax*), meaning "once-for-all" (Hebrews 7:27; 9:12, 10:10; cf. Romans 6:10). It underlines the finality and unrepeatability of the historic acts of salvation in contrast with the oft-repeated and insufficient sacrifices of the old covenant and its high priesthood (Hebrews 9:6–12; 10:11–12). Nothing can equal this, nothing can perfect it, nothing can supersede it.

To us, living at "the end of the age," at "the climax of history" (NEB), He has come "to do away with sin by the sacrifice of himself" (Hebrews 9:26; cf. I Corinthians 10:11; Hebrews 2:14). How that was done, and with what final and complete success, is the message of the New Testament.

# 19

# THE LIGHT OF THE CROSS: THE CROSS IN THE NEW TESTAMENT

E nglish hymn writer T. Kelly describes well the power of the cross to evoke praise among those who know the Savior who once lay upon it:

> We sing the praise of Him who died,
> Of Him who died upon the Cross.[1]

We Christians have been singing such praise for nearly two thousand years. We have been singing, teaching, trusting, glorying in the cross of Christ. Or rather glorying *in Him*, as John Bunyan's pilgrim did:

> Blest Cross! Blest Sepulchre! Blest rather be
> The man that there was put to shame for me.[2]

Martin Luther, with an eye to the ancient philosophies and their futile attempt to rise to the true knowledge of God, used to warn his hearers against "a theology of glory" that sought to climb to the knowledge of God by great thoughts on great things. Instead, he insisted, we find God in "a theology of the cross" which discovers Him in the humanity of Christ, the willing suffering of the Savior, and the triumph of His costly redemption.[3]

We could not make sense of the New Testament in particular, or of Christianity in general, without its central figure— Jesus Christ. Christianity is not a philosophy or an ethic, but a person: Christianity is Christ. But neither can we make sense of

Christ Himself without His cross. Jesus did not come simply as a healer or a teacher, but as a Savior who would give His life as a ransom for many (Mark 10:45) and as the inaugurator of a new covenant which would be ratified in His blood (Luke 22:20).

Consequently, His apostles and the first Christian teachers did not preach Him apart from His atoning death for sin. The Gospels themselves are written not as biographies but as passion narratives in which everything leads up to the death of Jesus and His triumphant resurrection. The apostolic teachers, like Peter, preached the cross of Christ as issuing from God's "set purpose and foreknowledge" (Acts 2:23) and saw the crucified one as the foreordained end and anti-type of the Old Testament sacrifices. The apostle Peter wrote, "You know that it was not with perishable things such as silver or gold that you were redeemed from the empty way of life handed down to you from your forefathers, but with the precious blood of Christ, a lamb without blemish or defect" (1 Peter 1:18–19).

Paul summed up and distinguished his ministry in the statement "we preach Christ crucified" (1 Corinthians 1:23), and reminded the Corinthian Christians: "When I came to you, brothers . . . I resolved to know nothing while I was with you except Jesus Christ and him crucified" (1 Corinthians 2:1–2).

## WHO CRUCIFIED JESUS?

To the question, Who crucified Jesus? the New Testament gives us four distinct answers: the Jews, the Romans, the human race—and God. The first answer tells the tragedy of a people who, despite their long preparation in providence and grace, failed to recognize their true Messiah and rejected Him. The second reminds us that the contempt against Christ was the calculated response of the Gentile world to the King of Love, not just a Jewish response (Acts 4:24–27). The third answer summons us all to the bar of God and, refusing to let the world's greatest crime lie conveniently buried in history, insists that we *all* bear a real and full responsibility for the crucifying of the Son of God, since we all by nature willingly share in the God-resenting depravity that hated and slew Him (Romans 8:7–8).

## The Hand of God

However, it is the fourth reply that provides the ultimate answer to the question, Who crucified Jesus? For the cross is not simply or even primarily the result of the malice of men, but it is the work of God. Secretly, unsearchably, but nonetheless certainly, God's mastering love moved behind the malice of men. They did their worst—but in their worst God did His best. Out of different motives, all of them bad, Judas, Caiaphas, Pilate, and the soldiers all united to accomplish God's unutterably good will.

It is a fundamental and repeated doctrine of the New Testament that we have in the death of Christ not merely the hand of men, but principally the hand of God. Christ's death was neither an accident, nor even a martyrdom, but a sacrifice.

Paul often speaks of the death of Christ as the only atonement for sin, of faith in His blood (Romans 3:25), of being justified by His blood (Romans 5:9), of redemption through His blood (Ephesians 1:7), and of peace with God by the blood of His cross (Colossians 1:20)—so often, in fact, that there is abundant support for Markus Barth's statement that the New Testament in general, and Paul's thought in particular, is "saturated with the concept of sacrifice."[4] At one point Paul speaks of Christ as "our Passover lamb" who "has been sacrificed" for our redemption (1 Corinthians 5:7–8). Later, the words that he quotes as Christ's when instituting the sacrament of the Lord's Supper, "This cup is the new covenant in my blood" (1 Corinthians 11:25), show as clearly as anything in the book of Hebrews that as the blood of animal sacrifices sealed the old covenant (Hebrews 9:18–20; cf. Exodus 24:5–8) so the blood of Jesus, the Lamb of God, sealed the new covenant.

For many today, such talk of "blood" and "sacrifice" is mystifying and even repugnant, and it is important to distinguish it from pagan or occult or merely superstitious practices and beliefs. However, we cannot "sanitize" the New Testament testimony to the death of Christ by eliminating such vocabulary. This is because, as John Stott says, quoting Thomas J. Crawford, "The interpretation of Christ's death as a sacrifice is embedded in every important type of the New Testament teaching"; and as he himself insists, "sacrificial vocabulary and idiom are widespread."[5]

This divine act of sacrifice was not only the climax of our Lord's earthly life; it was also the goal of His heavenly preexistence with the Father. In his Pentecost sermon the apostle Peter preaches this truth as crucially important for a true understanding of Christ's death: "This [Jesus] was handed over to you by God's set purpose and foreknowledge; and you, with the help of wicked men, put him to death by nailing him to the cross" (Acts 2:23). And we hear it given voice in one of the earliest prayer meetings of the New Testament era (Acts 4:27–28). The cross had been divinely planned, eternally settled in the eternal Trinity. "He was born," writes P. T. Forsyth, "as a result of a death He died in heavenly places before the foundation of the world";[6] and, "There was a Calvary above—the mother of it all!"[7]

God's determination that His own Son should die for the salvation of men was the heavenly rationale behind Jesus' birth. Ultimately He did not come to teach, to preach, to heal— but to die and so redeem us. The writer to the Hebrews leaves us in no doubt that Calvary was the motive behind Bethlehem and that the Incarnation was never an end in itself but the means to an act—the act of redemption. In this redemption God assumed human form and died our death so that we might share His endless life: "Since the children have flesh and blood, he too shared in their humanity so that by his death he might destroy him who holds the power of death—that is, the devil— and free those who all their lives were held in slavery by their fear of death" (Hebrews 2:14–15).

What was planned from all eternity and was supremely the purpose of the Incarnation was also the driving force of Christ's ministry. His saving death for lost mankind was both the cloud that overshadowed Him and the zeal that consumed Him in three years of unremitting ministry (Mark 8:31; 9:12; John 9:4). His whole life was lived under the "must" of prophecy (Luke 22:37; 24:25–26), and His death was to be the unfailing climax of an eternal destiny: "Now my heart is troubled, and what shall I say? 'Father, save me from this hour'? No, it was for this very reason I came to this hour. Father, glorify your name!" (John 12:27–28).

## The Great Sacrifice of God

Throughout the New Testament the emphasis is repeated again and again that God "gave," "sent," and "delivered up" His Son—and not merely to be born into the world or to preach to the world, but to die for the world. "This is love," says John in his first epistle, "not that we loved God, but that he loved us and sent his Son as an atoning sacrifice for our sins" (1 John 4:10). In Paul's letter to the Romans he speaks of Christ, "whom God put forward" as a propitiation by His blood (Romans 3:25, RSV). From the Greek verb Paul uses there we can understand the words "put forward" as meaning "proposed" (i.e., purposed) or "exhibited"; that is, we can see the cross as proposed by God in His eternal decrees or as displayed to the world to demonstrate His uncompromised holiness and justice in the salvation of sinners. Whichever interpretation we follow, the thought is equally prominent and primary: that God the Father took the initiative in our salvation, that "God was reconciling the world to himself in Christ" (2 Corinthians 5:19), that in the cross the love of the Father is as evident as the love of the Son.

It was the Father who led Him through Caiaphas's court to Pilate's scourging, who led Him to the cross and nailed Him on that cross and poured out upon His sinless but sin-bearing soul the wrath which was due to sinners from Father, Son, and Holy Spirit alike, inseparable in essence and inviolable in holiness. Terrible as all this sounds, it is the key to Calvary's mystery.

"For God so loved the world that he gave his one and only Son, that whoever believes in him shall not perish but have eternal life" (John 3:16). In this familiar verse, the apostle John does not mean simply that God "gave" His Son to be born (we are not saved by believing on Him as born), or that God gave Him to live and preach among us ("a good example is not mighty to save," as Forsyth once put it), but that God gave Him up even to Calvary and an atoning death. The thought is basically the same as that of Paul in Romans 8:32: "He who did not spare his own Son, but gave him up for us all—how will he not also, along with him, graciously give us all things?"

We see, then, that there is no blackmail at the cross, no coercion of God by God, no wresting of forgiveness from the Father by the Son. In all the Scriptures, the Father is the chief architect of the way of atonement. Jesus Christ did not die to persuade His Father to be merciful; He died because His Father is merciful—and that there might be no barrier between God's mercy and our need of mercy. It is that which gives Calvary its ultimate meaning, and it is that which makes the crucified Christ a Savior forever.

## GOD'S HOLINESS AND
## THE ATONEMENT OF CHRIST

The Old Testament is full of references to the holiness of God. In fact there is more teaching about God's holiness in the Old Testament than in the New. However, while the Old Testament teaches us about the essential holiness of God as a basic lesson, the New Testament sets forth the outgoing holiness of God as an eternal fact.

### Holiness and Sin

In Romans 1 Paul has much to say about God asserting His holiness since man first rebelled against Him. He tells us (Romans 1:18–19) that the wrath of God is continually, daily, and in every generation, "going out" into a world of rebellion and crime, "giving up" men and women to greater depravity and its inevitable judgment (Romans 1:28–2:11). In the words he uses and the dramatic picture he paints, Paul shows the wrath of God as something personal, active, and moral in the Godhead. God is holy, and He asserts this holiness in all sorts of ways, expressing and demonstrating His entire and unchangeable revulsion against sin.

The writer to the Hebrews, in a passage that Karl Barth has called "perhaps the most emphatic in the whole Bible on the theme of God's holiness,"[8] warns very clearly (Hebrews 10:26–31) about the finality as well as the certainty of God's holy judgment; and even while speaking of "a fearful expectation of judgment and of raging fire" for the impenitent and the apostate, he personalizes the whole thing in the climax of the passage: "For we know him who said, 'It is mine to avenge; I will repay,'" and again, "'The Lord will judge his people.' It is a dreadful thing to fall into the hands of the living God."

God is holy. He is holy not simply by choice, but by nature.

His law is the expression of that holiness, not only in its bene-
diction upon all that is good but also in its malediction upon all
that is corrupt. Only the compromised morality of fallen man
finds the curses of the law unacceptable. It is out of a necessity
arising from His own nature that God, who is most holy, blesses
*and* curses, accepts *and* rejects, embraces *and* thrusts away. It is
as necessary for God to assert His holiness as it is for Him to be
holy; it is as necessary for Him to punish sin as it is for Him to
hate sin.

Forsyth is right when he insists on the primacy of holiness
in God as the meaning of everything done by God or connected
with Him:

> Neither love, grace, faith, nor sin have any but a passing
> meaning except as they rest on the holiness of God, except
> as they arise from it, and return to it, except as they satisfy
> it, show it forth, set it up, and secure it everywhere and for-
> ever. Love is but its outgoing; sin is but its defiance; grace is
> but its action on sin; the cross is but its victory; faith is but
> its worship.[9]

## Holiness and Judgment

Here we discover that Christ's atonement is essential if sinners are to be saved from God's eternal wrath. Forsyth stresses
the relationship between the death of Christ and the holiness of
God. Christ's death as atonement, he states, "has a prime
regard to God's holiness,"[10] and, "The cross . . . is the central act
of God's holiness."[11] He sharply criticizes the sentimentalizing
liberalism of his day that did not give enough weight to the
holiness of God either in confessing the divine judgment or in
understanding the cross:

> Holiness and judgement are for ever inseparable. To ignore
> them or to sever them is the central failure of theological
> liberalism. . . . God must either punish sin or expiate it, for
> the sake of His infrangibly holy nature. . . . He must either
> inflict punishment or assume it. And He chose the latter
> course as honouring the law while saving the guilty. He
> took His own judgement.[12]

God did not have to save us, but having freely loved and chosen to save us in our sin, atonement became a necessity arising out of His holy nature and sin's unholiness. At Calvary we see what sin deserves and what God requires. Calvary was too terrible to be optional, the sufferings involved too enormous to be unnecessary, and the Sufferer too precious to His Father to have been given over needlessly to such pain.

## Holiness and Satisfaction

"To be sure," Stott writes,

> neither "satisfaction" nor "substitution" is a biblical word, and therefore we need to proceed with great caution. But each is a biblical concept. There is, in fact, a biblical revelation of "satisfaction through substitution," which is uniquely honouring to God, and which should therefore lie at the very heart of the church's worship and witness.[13]

The good news of the gospel is that God in holy love has sent His Son to do for us what we as sinners could never do for ourselves and to be "our righteousness, holiness and redemption" (1 Corinthians 1:30).

As we have seen in earlier chapters, God sent His Son into the world not as a private but as a public person, as the head of a people, the second and final Adam in whom a new race finds their beginning, their life, and their righteousness before God (Romans 5:18–19). He lived in our world as the representative saint ("born of a woman, born under law," Galatians 4:4), and He died in our world as the representative sinner for His people ("to redeem those under law," Galatians 4:5).

## THE MEANING OF HIS DEATH

Here we are mainly concerned with the value of His death, but precisely here we must also recall the value of His life, for it was by His representative life as well as His atoning death that He achieved "the righteousness of God" that is offered as a gift to sinners (Philippians 3:9; cf. Romans 1:16–17). However, the cross of Calvary remains the central focus of attention in this matter, for it was there that God in Christ removed the barrier to reconciliation and the provisions of grace. We can best get a clear understanding of what is involved in the death of Jesus Christ if we focus on three great New Testament passages and statements: Romans 3:19–26, 2 Corinthians 5:21, and Galatians 3:13.

## Romans 3:19–26

In Romans 3:19–26 Paul shows that in Christ, and only in Christ, can men and women be righteous before God.

Paul's entire doctrine of salvation appears in these eight verses; the passage forms the very center of his Christology. In one historical, definitive act, the apostle explains, God has made His righteousness available to sinners. He has found a righteous way of justifying the ungodly (Romans 4:5)—of "righteoussing the unrighteous," to use Stott's phrase[14]—a means by which a righteous status before God and from God could be bestowed on those who had no righteousness of their own.

Themselves guilty and condemned and worthy of the eternal displeasure of God (vv. 19–20), through faith in Jesus Christ (v. 22) they can now receive as a gift (v. 24) what they owed as a debt (vv. 19, 31). God Himself has vindicated His own holy justice, now showing His once-postponed judgment and utter opposition to sin by making His Son a full and sufficient sacrifice for sin (vv. 25–26).

Verse 26 takes up the point made at the beginning of verse 25, namely that at Calvary God put forward His Son as an atoning sacrifice in order to demonstrate His righteousness and justice in justifying sinners who had faith in Jesus. For Paul, it is vital that we should know that a holy God has not contradicted or compromised Himself by freeing sinners from their just deserts, but has found a way to justify them justly in His Son. He has maintained Himself in holiness even while He has saved us in our sinfulness. Christ is our perfect righteousness (v. 21) because He is our full redemption (v. 24). God has made Him our righteousness by making Him our wrath-bearer (v. 25). Christ, and Christ alone, is our righteousness (cf. Philippians 3:9) because Christ and only Christ, bore our sins (cf. 2 Corinthians 5:21).

The nucleus of this great passage is the statement: "For all have sinned and fall short of the glory of God, and are justified freely by his grace through the redemption that came by Christ Jesus. God presented him as a sacrifice of atonement, through faith in his blood" (vv. 23–25). Having exposed the total religious importance of humanity, Paul has made room for the entrance of grace in Christ Jesus in its essential character as a free gift, undeserved and unmerited.

This statement is as vivid pictorially as it is profound theologically; and the pictorial models are meant to help us understand the doctrinal truths. Here we have three pictures. The first, present in the words "and are justified," is taken from the world of the law courts: the picture is that of an accused prisoner acquitted of all charges against him and pronounced righteous in the sight of the law, "justified." *To justify* is a forensic term meaning "to declare righteous." Douglas Moo observes that the term *justification* is used here for the first time in Romans of justification in the Christian sense. He continues:

> [To justify] means not "to make righteous" (in an ethical sense) nor simply "to treat as righteous" (though one is not really righteous), but "to declare righteous." No legal fiction, but a legal *reality* of the utmost significance, "to be justified" means to be acquitted by God from all charges that could be brought against a person because of his sins.[15]

As Leon Morris notes, the second picture, present in the words "the redemption that came through Christ Jesus," "had its origin in the release of prisoners of war on payment of a price (the 'ransom'). It was extended to include the freeing of slaves, again by the payment of a price. Among the Hebrews it could be used for release of a prisoner under sentence of death (Exodus 21:29–30), once more by the payment of a price."[16] We shall look more closely at this idea in the next chapter.

The third picture is drawn from the Old Testament ritual of sacrifice. The sacrificial nature of Christ's death is clearly indicated by the phrase "a sacrifice of atonement . . . in his blood," as so many other New Testament references to the blood of Christ show.[17] The link with Leviticus 17:11 and the whole theology of the Old Testament sacrifices ought to be beyond dispute. Moo indicates the closeness of thought and the sharing of identical terms (e.g., *hilasterion*, "mercy seat") between Romans 3:24–26 and Hebrews 9:1–10:18, and sees the Day of Atonement ritual in Leviticus 16 as in the background of both passages. He writes:

> Hebrews makes much of the inadequacy of the Old Covenant ritual. . . . This inadequacy according to Hebrews is met in the *ephapax* [once for all] sacrifice of Christ. . . . In the same way, according to Paul, God has set forth Christ "at the present time" as a sacrifice that satisfies the demands of God's justice in His "passing over sins in the past."[18]

Paul is clearly instructing us that God is propitiated, and sin consequently expiated, or atoned for, by the sacrificial substitute who turns away the wrath of God from the guilty one (cf. 1 John 2:2; 4:19; Hebrews 2:17).

We have examined this concept of propitiation more closely in the previous chapter. It is interesting to note here that in Romans 3:25 Paul may well be using the Greek word *hilasterion* (propitiation) in the more specific sense of Hebrews 9:5. As we read there, the "hilasterion" was literally the slab of gold, the "atonement cover" (or "mercy seat" in KJV and RSV), on the top of the ark of covenant. This was the very place in the "holy of holies" where in glory and grace God was enthroned in the midst of Israel. It was also, on the Day of Atonement, the meeting place between God and man where the impossible was made possible—sinful man found peace with the holy God through the blood of sacrifice, which had been accepted as an atonement for sin. Moo, accepting this to be Paul's allusion, writes: "Christ, Paul implies, now has the place that the hilasterion had in the Old Covenant: the centre and focal point of God's provision of atonement for His people."[19] However, like Leon Morris and John Murray, C. E. B. Cranfield takes the reference in the more general sense of "a propitiating sacrifice" by which "God . . . purposed to direct against His own very Self in the person of His Son the full weight of that righteous wrath which they deserved."[20] Paul has already spoken vividly and uncompromisingly of the holy wrath of God (see Romans 1:18; 2:5, 8; 3:5), and it is clearly this same wrath which is seen as visited on Christ the sin-bearer in Romans 3:25.

Here, then, two things about Christ's death are highlighted: its substitutionary character and its sacrificial nature. In other words, and in the language of later theology, here the concept of penal substitution is plainly attached to the death of our Lord Jesus Christ. The doctrine of substitution is, says J. I. Packer, "the basic category" in the New Testament view of the cross, and "penal substitution" in particular is, he says, the heart of the matter. He writes:

> The notion which the phrase "penal substitution" expresses is that Jesus Christ our Lord, moved by a love that was determined to do everything necessary to save us, endured and exhausted the destructive divine judgment for which we were otherwise inescapably destined and so won us forgiveness, adoption and glory. To affirm penal substitution is to say that believers are in debt to Christ specifically for this and that this is the mainspring of all their joy, peace and praise both now and for eternity.[21]

This is the clear message of such statements as: "He himself bore our sins in his body on the tree" (1 Peter 2:24) and, "Christ, having been offered once to bear the sins of many, will appear a second time, not to deal with sin but to save those who are eagerly waiting for him" (Hebrews 9:28, RSV).

Nowhere is the extent and outcome of this substitution clearer than in Paul's two outstanding statements in 2 Corinthians 5:21 and Galatians 3:13, and to these we now turn.

### 2 Corinthians 5:21

Paul begins this verse with the declaration "God made him [Christ] who had no sin to be sin for us." In his day James Denney complained that it was commonplace to hear this verse paraphrased as "He became sin" whereas it says *God* "made Him to be sin." As Morris says, "The verb is active and the subject is God." In the atonement, he states, "the persons of both the Father and the Son are exceedingly active."[22] Philip

Edgcumbe Hughes says of this statement of Paul's: "There is no sentence more profound in the whole of Scripture, for this verse embraces the whole ground of the sinner's reconciliation to God."[23] Here we see the double transfer of our sin to Christ and of His righteousness to us. The second half of the verse tells us: "in him we might become the righteousness of God."

However, lest we fall prey to crude and extravagant ideas here, it is worth noting the words of C. K. Barrett: "It is important to observe that the words Paul uses are words describing relationships." When Christ became sin, what is meant, says Barrett, is that "He came to stand in that relationship with God which normally is the result of sin, estranged from God and the object of His wrath." Correspondingly, and here Barrett quotes Calvin, "Here righteousness means not a quality or habit [i.e., something in us] but something imputed to us, since we are said to have received the righteousness of Christ. What then is meant by sin? It is the guilt on account of which we are accused before the judgement of God."[24]

The concept of imputation (as distinct from literal transfer) is crucial here, and Paul clearly has this in mind, for he writes earlier that "God was reconciling the world to himself in Christ, not counting men's sins against them" (2 Corinthians 5:19). Instead, as he goes on to reason, God counted their sins against Christ as their substitute, and visited upon Him sin's penalty. This "transfer," though not literal, is, however, no less real. So complete was the identification of the sinless Son with the sinners for whom He died that Paul does not simply say (as some marginal renderings of the Greek have it) that Christ was made a "sin-offering," but that He was "made sin" for us. Christ suffered for our sins as though they were His own so that we might enjoy the reward of His righteousness as though that had been our own. By imputation we receive His perfect obedience in life even as He took our transgressions in death.

John Owen, a seventeenth-century theologian, considered one possible objection to imputing sin to Jesus: "But it will be said that if our sins, as to the guilt of them were imputed unto Christ, then God must *hate* Christ." Owen answers that it is only "inherent sin" (not imputed sin) which renders the soul hateful to God. But Christ, being "perfectly innocent, holy, harmless, undefiled in himself," was "glorious and lovely" in the sight of God. Indeed: "It is certain that the Lord Christ's taking upon Him the guilt of our sins was a high act of obedience unto God, Hebrews 10:5,6; and for which the 'Father loved him,' John 10:17, 18."[25]

A right understanding of this both preserves Paul's emphasis in 2 Corinthians 5:21 and protects us from erroneous notions, such as that Christ had personally become a sinner repugnant to God, or that God was personally angry with His Son. Stott makes a helpful distinction when he writes:

> What was transferred to Christ was not moral qualities but legal consequences: he voluntarily accepted liability for our sins. That is what the expressions "made sin" and "made a curse" mean. Similarly, "the righteousness of God" which we become when we are "in Christ" is not here righteousness of character and conduct (although that grows within us by the working of the Holy Spirit), but rather a righteous standing before God.[26]

### Galatians 3:13

In ancient Israel there were various penalties under the law, penalties of disgrace, of loss, and of physical punishments; there was banishment for a longer or shorter period, and there were fines which were carefully regulated according to the crime. There were also harsher penalties of whipping. A reasonable and proper proportion between crime and punishment was commanded, symbolized in the much-misunderstood *lex talionis*, the "law of retaliation" mentioned in Exodus 21:24 and other verses. The penalty was fitted to the offense. Of course the ultimate penalty for great crimes was death, by strangling or by stoning.

However, the law of Israel, even in its greatest penalties, could never fully express the real nature of sin or the full wrath of God towards sin. Not even capital punishment could do that! The only judge who could fully express God's wrath and inflict God's penalty against sin was God Himself; and the only penalty that could express sin's full desert and God's holy wrath was the ultimate penalty, which would be called in the book of Revelation "the second death": eternal loss and anguish, so terrifyingly symbolized in the New Testament references as eternal darkness and eternal fire.

Clearly no earthly or Israelite court could inflict this. Yet there was one thing which they could do, they could announce it. They could proclaim that a man had died under the curse of Yahweh. They expressed this by hanging his executed corpse on a wooden stake until sundown, according to God's explicit direction. This was not primitive sadism or brutality. It had a terrible and unforgettable purpose. It expressed the momentous fact that this man had died as an accursed thing and was thenceforth finally and forever subject to the wrath of Yahweh.

All this has a profound and truly awful bearing upon Paul's statement that "Christ redeemed us from the curse of the law by becoming a curse for us, for it is written: 'Cursed is everyone who is hung on a tree.'" In the clear vision of the New Testament perspective upon eternity, life after death and eternal punishment, such a text as Galatians 3:13 assumes even more terrible dimensions than the Old Testament revelation uncovered. In the light of Jesus' terrifying and urgent warnings about a place "where their worm does not die, and the fire is not quenched" (Mark 9:48); in the light of Paul's warnings of "wrath and anger" (Romans 2:8) and the punishment of "everlasting destruction and [exclusion] from the presence of the Lord" (2 Thessalonians 1:9); in the light of John's uncompromising and final statements about "the second death" and the torment which is "day and night for ever and ever" (Revelation 20:7–15), the Christian is forced to accept that sin is by far a greater evil than we had ever realized and that Christ's payment of its uttermost penalty under the just wrath of God involved a depth of suffering that we shall never fathom.

On Calvary, as nowhere else in the world, we see what sin deserved, what Christ endured and what God was willing to do to save us guilty sinners. There Jesus, the Son of God, "bore our sins in his body" (1 Peter 2:24); there He made His soul "an offering for sin" (RSV), a "guilt offering" appointed by God (Isaiah 53:10); there He "died"—the first and the second death— "for sins once for all, the righteous for the unrighteous, that he might bring us to God" (1 Peter 3:18). He stood in our place at the bar of a holy God, as the representative of sinners. He stood there, not merely alongside us but instead of us, not only sharing our punishment in solidarity but bearing our punishment in substitution and atonement. The stroke that would have fallen upon us fell upon Him.

At the cross of Calvary God asserted His holiness and expressed all His wrath against sin on the representative sinner, thrusting Him away till He cried out from the depths of hell itself, "My God, my God, why have you forsaken me?" (Matthew 27:46). In treatment, though not in affection, God cut Him off and cast Him away. He bore our sins as though they were His own, and our sins separated Him from all sense of the Father's pleasure and presence, just as they would have separated us from the Father for all eternity.

The frequent references to Christ dying "for" us, whatever else they may mean, Karl Barth insists,

> speak of a place which ought to be ours, that we ought to have taken this place, that we have been taken from it, that it is occupied by another, that this other acts in this place as only He can, in our cause and interest. [We] cannot add to anything that He does there because the place where we might do so is occupied by Him, . . .[27]

The effect of this upon human pretensions before God is catastrophic for our pride and moral presumption. "In its root and origin," says Barth, "sin is the arrogance in which man wants to be his own and his neighbor's judge . . . to be able and competent to pronounce ourselves free and righteous and others more or less guilty."[28] At Calvary, however, we see all judgments taken from us and pronounced and dispensed and endured by the only one to whom the Father has given all judgment (John 5:22). There our sin is judged by the one who becomes sin for us (2 Corinthians 5:21). There, "for us," God condemns sin in the flesh of His own Son. And for us this means, in Barth's words, "an immeasurable liberation and hope."[29]

# 20

# THE GREAT ACHIEVEMENT: REDEMPTION AND RECONCILIATION

In light of all we have learned about the sufferings of Christ, it should not seem strange that we call the anniversary of the cross *Good* Friday. For while the New Testament speaks of Jesus' death in terms of suffering and sacrifice and rejection, it also speaks of it in terms of achievement and victory. He bore our sins, but He also bore them away; He burdened Himself with our debt, but He also canceled the bill; He bowed His head to the storm, but He also disarmed the principalities and power (Colossians 2:14–15).

By many words and phrases and in various ways the New Testament proclaims this ultimate element of triumph; but there are two words that stand out particularly in their scope and significance: *redemption* and *reconciliation*.

## REDEMPTION

We can use the concept of redemption in a wide or a narrow sense. In its widest use *redemption* can span the whole work of Christ in salvation, from His first to His second coming, and can reach to the believer's "full redemption" at the resurrection (Romans 8:23; Ephesians 4:30). Often the New Testament uses the term *redemption* in connection with deliverance from sin's power as well as its penalty (Galatians 1:4; Titus 2:14), and we shall examine this in connection with the believer's sanctification in chapter 22. Here, however, we shall examine its more immediate connection with the death of our Lord and what He accomplished at Calvary, where He "gave himself as a ransom

for all" (1 Timothy 2:6). All further and future redemption is
but the outworking of this.

## Paying the Ransom Price

The idea of redemption would have been perfectly familiar
in the ancient world, to both Jew and Gentile. "To redeem" (Gk.
*lutroo*) was a process of deliverance by payment, and the price
paid was called a "ransom" (Gk. *lutron*). In the Gentile world
these terms would be used for the buying out of captivity of
prisoners of war and, more commonly, of the purchasing of
freedom for slaves (called manumission). Leon Morris writes:

> It is quite obvious that manumission in its various forms
> was widely known throughout the world of the first century,
> and that *lutron* (a ransom) was in common use to describe
> the price paid for freeing a slave, and this would be the
> most familiar usage of the term to Gentiles to whom much
> of the New Testament was written.[1]

But the idea of redemption by the payment of a ransom
price was also deeply embedded in the Hebrew tradition. There
are three main Hebrew words used in the Old Testament for
"ransom": *kōpher, padah,* and *ga'al.* In Exodus 21:30 a man who
under the law had forfeited his life through committing an
accidental homicide was allowed to "redeem" it by the payment
of a *kōpher.* The fine was the ransom money that saved his life,
releasing the guilty man from the situation that threatened his
life because of his crime. "The idea," writes Otto Procksch, "is
not that of simple freeing from a fault, but of its recognition
and expiation in the substitutionary offering." This use of *ransom,* he says, "always denotes a vicarious gift whose value covers a fault, so that the debt is not just cancelled."[2] In Exodus
30:11–16 the population as a whole is ritually redeemed in the
census, each giving "a ransom for himself to the Lord . . . to
make atonement for yourselves" (RSV).

The second Hebrew word for ransom, *padah,* also emphasizes payment. Every firstborn Israelite male was to be spared
(Numbers 18:15–17), for before the holy judgments of Yahweh
the firstborn of the Israelites were no more safe than the first-

born of the Egyptians (cf. Exodus 12:13; 13:13–16). Without a ransom their lives were forfeited also. In other connections property (Leviticus 25:15–18, 25–28), animals (Exodus 34:20), slaves (Leviticus 25:47–55), and indeed the whole nation of Israel (Exodus 30:11–16), were all "redeemed" from death by the payment of a price. Yahweh himself had redeemed Israel from its plight in Egypt "with an outstretched arm" (Exodus 6:6), but only His Christ, the Passover lamb of God (1 Corinthians 5:7), would show the price He was willing to pay.

The idea of ransom is also associated at a more intimate level with the *go'el* or "kinsman redeemer" in ancient Israel. This was a relative whose duty it was to buy back land alienated from the family (Leviticus 25:25–28) or a relation sold into slavery (Leviticus 25:48). Jeremiah and Boaz provide Old Testament examples of these (Jeremiah 32:7; Ruth 2:20; 3:9; 4:3–4). The prophet Isaiah in particular frequently uses this term to describe Yahweh's redemption of His elect people (e.g., Isaiah 49:7; 54:5–8). In such cases a ransom price, this time called a *ga'al*, was again necessary.

It is clear, then, that in both secular and sacred literature in the ancient world this concept of redemption was well known. It commonly meant quite simply deliverance by payment, not deliverance only but a *purchased* freedom. Morris concludes from his examination of these and corresponding terms in the Greek version of the Old Testament, that "the basic price-paying conception" remains "as a stubborn substratum in every case"[3] and concludes his detailed survey, "We see then, that in Greek writings generally, in the Old Testament, and in Rabbinic writers, the basic idea in redemption is the paying of a ransom price to secure a liberation."[4]

## Redemption in the New Testament

The New Testament makes significant use of this concept in explaining Christ's work for us as a redemption (e.g., Romans 3:24; 1 Corinthians 1:30; Galatians 3:13; Ephesians 1:7; Colossians 1:14; Titus 2:14). We too were prisoners. In our case the captivity was to "the law of sin and death" (Romans 8:2), under which we were the helpless slaves of our own rebellious passions and the doomed objects of the divine retribution (Ro-

mans 6:17, 23). We were both slaves in chains, "sold under sin"
(Romans 7:14, RSV), and prisoners of war, rebels under just sentence of execution (Galatians 3:13). From this hopeless situation we have been redeemed; but it took nothing less than the
death of Christ to do it.

Jesus Himself began the New Testament use of the idea
when He solemnly told His disciples: "For even the Son of Man
did not come to be served, but to serve, and to give his life as a
ransom for many" (Mark 10:45; cf. Matthew 20:28; Titus 2:14).
The word *for* (Gk. *anti*, "in place of" or "in exchange for") corresponds perfectly with the Old Testament ransom idea: the price
is an equivalent substitute for what is ransomed or "bought
out." If our Lord here has in mind the suffering servant of Isaiah 53, as many scholars think, then the whole thought of substitutionary suffering becomes even clearer.

Certainly redemption by the substitutionary sacrifice of
Christ for sinners became a major category of apostolic thought.
Peter places this beyond any doubt when he writes: "You know
that you were ransomed from the futile ways inherited from
your fathers, not with perishable things such as silver or gold,
but with the precious blood of Christ, like that of a lamb without blemish or spot" (1 Peter 1:18–19). The writer to the Hebrews also emphasizes the cost of our redemption, as well as its
worth and effect, by linking it with the Old Testament sacrifices: "He did not enter by means of the blood of goats and
calves; but he entered the Most Holy Place once for all by his
own blood, having obtained eternal redemption" (Hebrews
9:12). And Paul pinpoints the act and character of Christ's payment in terms of His blood-offering at Calvary: "In him we have
redemption through his blood, the forgiveness of sins" (Ephesians 1:7).

## Redemption and the Blood of Christ

In these texts redemption is repeatedly brought into connection with Christ's blood. But what precise aspect of the
death of Christ is stressed by the word *blood*? The emphasis on
blood in the Old Testament teaching on sacrifice is as unique as
it is frequent. T. R. Schreiner writes: "Nearly everyone agrees
that the blood ritual in Israelite sacrifice is unique. There has

been nothing found to date that parallels, in any significant way, the treatment of blood in Israel, neither in the ancient Near East nor elsewhere."[5]

It is made clear in Leviticus 17:11 and 14 that "atonement is made by blood to the extent that 'life' is in it or because 'life' is in it." "This idea," says Schreiner, "is not found outside Israel."[6] But why is this emphasis and equation made, and what does it signify in terms of sacrifice in general and Christ's sacrificial death in particular? Of course no one reasonably suggests that blood—any blood, even Christ's—atones for sin because of some magical quality inherent in it. The blood of sacrifice under the old Mosaic covenant makes atonement because God ordains that it should do so. As Schreiner states: "Blood does not make atonement because of some magical quality in it. The *divine will* itself made the blood the means of expiation."[7] But why does the New Testament repeatedly take up the blood language of Old Testament sacrifice?

In the last hundred years the view has developed among some theologians that the shedding of blood is essentially a reference to life released rather than punishment endured, and that the New Testament references to redemption, reconciliation, and justification "by Christ's blood" indicate no more than a sharing of His life. This theory is based on the wording of the texts in Leviticus and Deuteronomy that "the life of every creature is its blood" (Leviticus 17:11–14) and that "the blood is the life" (Deuteronomy 12:23). Bishop B. F. Westcott, who seems to have originated this idea, has been followed by such writers as Vincent Taylor, C. H. Dodd, and P. T. Forsyth. James Denney, however, referred to it as "a strange caprice," adding: "I venture to say that a more groundless fancy never haunted and troubled the interpretation of any part of Scripture."[8]

We can see the reason for Denney's strong language when we look at Morris's close survey of the biblical use of the term *blood*[9] and at his treatment of the death of Christ.[10] Morris traces over 200 examples of the connection between blood and violent death, 103 examples connecting blood and sacrifice, and only 7 examples connecting blood with life. He concludes, "The association most likely to be conjured up when the Hebrews heard the word 'blood' was that of violent death,"[11]

and quotes A. M. Stibbs: "Blood shed stands, therefore, not for
the release of life from the burden of the flesh, but for the
bringing to an end of life in the flesh. It is a witness to physical
death, not an evidence of spiritual survival."[12] It is against such
a background that Paul and the other New Testament writers
see the death of Christ as a payment for sin, a wrath-bearing act
of substitutionary atonement which redeems men from sin's
guilt and power.

In Paul's writings there are indeed other terms to denote the
meaning of Christ's death that are used more often than
*redemption,* but none are more crucial for promoting a true
understanding of the intent and achievement of that death for
sinners. In Galatians 3:13 and 4:5 (cf. 1 Corinthians 6:20; 7:23),
where an entirely different Greek word is used (*exagorazō,* "to
buy"; lit. "to buy out"), Paul's thought is more particular: He is
concerned there to make the point that our newfound freedom
is a legally based one. Christ's payment is not a fiction, but a
grim reality; it was because He "became a curse for us" that He
"redeemed us from the curse of the law." His ransom was not a
token fine or a gesture, however divine; it was *an equivalent
substitute in the eternal justice and love of God:* "For there is one
God and one mediator between God and men, the man Christ
Jesus, who gave himself as a ransom for all men—the testimony given in its proper time" (1 Timothy 2:5–6). Donald Guthrie
observes on that verse: "Christ is conceived of as an 'exchange
price' on behalf of and in the place of *all,* on the grounds of
which freedom may be granted."[13]

In a more general way, the idea of individual believers in
particular, and of the church in general, as being "bought with
a price," "purchased" and "ransomed," is a vivid and frequent
picture throughout the apostolic writings (1 Corinthians
6:19–20; Acts 20:28; Revelation 5:9–10). In a paradoxical way, it
expresses both our liberation and our obligation. We are free
from the bondage of sin and death, and yet precisely in that
real freedom "we are not our own," being freed to serve as
"bondslaves of Jesus Christ," whose service is perfect freedom.

The cry for freedom—political and economic, social and
personal—has been very frequently heard in our century. Yet
even in free and prosperous countries, and even in lives where

personal ambitions and desires have been fulfilled, wherever men and women live without God and outside of His provision in Christ, they are still shackled to their sins, prisoners of guilt. They have been sentenced and awaiting execution. The freedom that is needed most, and by all, is a spiritual freedom, the freedom only God can give, and which even God can give only in Christ: the justification that enables us to go free from sin as a capital crime and the new life that enables us to live free from sin as a reigning power (Romans 8:1–4).

## RECONCILIATION

While the concept of reconciliation between God and humankind is repeatedly found throughout the Old and New Testament writings, the terms *reconcile* and *reconciliation* are distinctively Pauline. The apostle's use of *reconciliation* makes it a technical term for the whole saving work of God in Christ. Even Paul, however, uses the idea more often than the word, which, in this large sense, occurs in only four passages (Romans 5:10–12; 2 Corinthians 5:18–20; Ephesians 2:16; and Colossians 1:20). Nevertheless, these passages are of great importance. They show the centrality of the theme of reconciliation in the Christian message, as does the vocabulary of "peace," "brought near," "access," etc. (for example, Romans 5:1; and Ephesians 2:13–14, 18).

The very word *reconciliation* conjures up a previous situation of hostility, separation, and alienation. We use it commonly of warring factions, or separated spouses and of estranged friends. The enmity on one or both sides is usually occasioned by hostility, clash of interest, betrayal, or other personal injury, real or assumed. Paul uses the term against such a background, and yet it is important to recognize unique elements in his use of the word vis-à-vis God and man.

The central feature of humanity's fallen state is its deep-seated hostility to God. By nature men and women are "haters of God" (Romans 1:30, RSV), "hostile to God" (Romans 8:7), "estranged and hostile in mind" (Colossians 1:21, RSV). As such they distort what impressions of God remain in their consciences (Romans 1:19–23; 2:1–5) and despise what truthful and adequate revelation of Himself God gives in the gospel (1 Co-

rinthians 1:18–23; 2:14). It is this profound alienation that pro-
duces all other alienations (Romans 3:10–18; Ephesians 4:17–19).

However, Paul, and Scripture generally, give much more
weight to the alienation from the divine side and to the fact
that, because of humanity's sin and corruption, God in His holiness and righteousness is inevitably at enmity with our race.
We have seen this in our study of atonement in the Old Testament, with its important concept of divine wrath as a corollary
of divine holiness, and we see it no less in the New Testament.[14]
There is thus a situation of mutual hostility in which God is as
justly hostile to us as we are wickedly hostile to God.

Reconciliation, however, implies the end of conflict and the
establishment of peace, the bringing together of opposed parties, the replacement of enmity by unity (Romans 5:10; Colossians 1:21–22). Who has achieved this? How has it been done?
And what are its ultimate effects?

### God the Reconciler

When we speak of conflicting parties being reconciled, we
usually think of a fifty-fifty arrangement in which both sides
give ground to each other, make certain concessions and sacrifices, and so gradually come closer to each other's demands or
convictions, until their estrangement is at an end. Does this
hold good in divine-human relationships? No, and it is precisely here that the uniqueness of the biblical doctrine of reconciliation becomes most apparent.

Reconciliation is never presented in Scripture as something
produced by the combined efforts of God and ourselves. It is not
even a work that is begun by God and completed by ourselves. It
is something *achieved* by God and *offered* to us as a gift.

In this Christianity is unique. In the pagan view of atonement and sacrifice, and of its whole ritual of worship, God was
the object of reconciliation, an offended deity that had to be
appeased and "won over"; human beings must somehow take
steps to restore the broken or threatened relationship, making
recompense for their trespasses and winning the favor of the
deity. (Even in Greek-speaking Judaism it was God who was
reconciled by the prayers of the people.) In Paul's doctrine of
reconciliation, however, the roles are completely reversed. God

has become the subject, the initiator, and the achiever of reconciliation in Christ Jesus His Son.

In strong contrast to the pagan view, the New Testament writers everywhere give precedence and preeminence to the undeserved love of God. Hence John writes: "This is love: not that we loved God, but that he loved us and sent his Son as an atoning sacrifice for our sins" (1 John 4:10). "These words," writes Calvin in a famous passage, "clearly demonstrate this fact: that nothing might stand in the way of his love for us, God appointed Christ as a means of reconciling us to himself. . . . For, in some ineffable way, God loved us and yet was angry toward us at the same time, until He became reconciled to us in Christ."[15] This is Paul's consistent emphasis: "When we were God's enemies, we were reconciled to him through the death of his Son" (Romans 5:10); Colossians 1:21–22; and "All this is from God, who reconciled us to himself through Christ" (2 Corinthians 5:18).

Thus reconciliation is a work that is all of God and all of grace. Biblical religion is here, as everywhere, a protest against every form of self-salvation. As P. T. Forsyth put it, "The prime doer in Christ's cross was God. Christ was God reconciling. He was God doing the very best for man and not man doing his very best before God. The former is evangelical Christianity, the latter is humanist Christianity."[16]

It is true that we never read of God being reconciled to the world, but always of the world being reconciled to God. But this is not to be taken as an all-controlling factor, as though no change on God's side was needed, and as though it were only necessary to change our minds by a display of forgiving love. This fails to take account not only of fallen humanity's profound antagonism to God, and its rebellious spirit, but also of God's own requirements in the matter of reconciliation.

## God's Way of Reconciliation

In the reconciliation of sinners to Himself, the work God does is not only a work of love but also a work of law. In that work God deals with the moral and legal basis of His rejection of man, enabling Him to call sinful men and women to Himself without compromising His inviolable holiness, justice, and truth.

It is often and rightly emphasized that reconciliation is a very personal term: more personal in fact than the other equally important term, *justification,* which lies so close to it in meaning. But the fact that in Paul's thinking the phrases "justified by his blood" and "reconciled to him through the death of his Son" overlap and almost parallel one another (Romans 5:9–10) should remind us that what was a warmly personal work of God was also a strictly righteous one.

Whereas atonement/sacrifice or atonement/propitiation is a concept drawn from the Old Testament temple ritual, and redemption/ransom is drawn from the Gentile scene of the slave market, and justification is drawn from the world of law, the concept of reconciliation is taken from the sphere of family and society. Paul's use of this last term, however, relates it closely to the others. In Romans 5:10–11 reconciliation is the result of a death, a death earlier signaled as sacrificial and expiatory (Romans 3:25). In 2 Corinthians 5:18–21 the reconciliation is the result of a double transfer and of the justification that is based on it. Paul says that instead of counting our trespasses against us (v. 19), God imputed them to Christ as our representative and penal substitute, "God made him . . . to be sin for us" (v. 21). "This vicarious operation," says G. W. Bromiley, "lies at the very heart of biblical reconciliation."[17]

Through His act of sin-bearing at the cross, Christ dealt with the barrier that sin had placed between God and humankind. By this one act Christ "canceled the written code, with its regulations, that was against us and that stood opposed to us; he took it away, nailing it to the cross" (Colossians 2:14). That is how He has "reconciled [us] by Christ's physical body through death" (Colossians 1:22)—not by His death as a moving gesture that persuades rebellious man, but by His death as a complete atonement that removes the ground of God's alienation from and condemnation of corrupt mankind. Reconciliation is not therefore in the first place a change in us at all. After all, it was done while we were "helpless," "sinners" and "enemies" (Romans 5:6, 10). In reconciliation God deals with His *own* hostility to man. It is God's work, for God's sake, so that it might be God's work for man's sake.

## Our Ministry of Reconciliation

Because of His reconciling work in His Son at Calvary, God now gives us "the ministry of reconciliation" (2 Corinthians 5:18), which offers reconciliation with God and a righteous status to helpless sinners through the vicarious work of Christ: "God made him who had no sin to be sin for us, so that in him we might become the righteousness of God" (2 Corinthians 5:21).

As all other alienations among men proceed from the greater alienation from God, so man's reconciliation with God is the fruitful source of all other reconciliations. By it Jew and Gentile come together, becoming "one new man" in Christ, who is our peace (Ephesians 2:11–22). By it men and women enter and become part of "a new creation" in Christ (2 Corinthians 5:17), where peace rules in the community (Colossians 3:15; cf. Romans 14:17) and in the heart (Philippians 4:7). And by it, and by faith in the Christ who "came and preached peace" to all (Ephesians 2:17), we who ourselves have "received reconciliation" (Romans 5:11) and who have been given "the message of reconciliation" (2 Corinthians 5:19) go forth into all the world as "Christ's ambassadors" and speak, "God . . . making his appeal through us" (2 Corinthians 5:20). Paul sums up the ministry and message in the words: "We implore you on Christ's behalf: Be reconciled to God" (2 Corinthians 5:20).

Here again we must be aware of the special character of this concept. Reconciliation has been achieved for all men, but it is not yet enjoyed by all men. If it is to be enjoyed, then it must be received. If it is never received, it will never be possessed. We could not be coworkers with God in achieving this reconciliation—in that regard, it was a work done outside of us. But we must nevertheless respond to God in receiving that reconciliation, for, as G. C. Berkouwer puts it: "God's decision does not cancel ours."[18] If Christ is rejected, there is no other way of reconciliation, and the one way God has opened at such cost remains untrodden and ineffective for a man. As the writer of Hebrews warns, outside of Christ "no sacrifice for sins is left," but only "a fearful expectation of judgment" (Hebrews 10:26–27).

So we become ambassadors from God with a message and

an experience of reconciliation. Into a world of multiple-alien-
ation God sends us with this message of universal reconciliation. It is universal in a number of ways: it is a reconciliation
between God and man, which promotes reconciliation between
man and man and between man and his world, his society, and
his environment. The character and breadth of this reconciliation in its heavenly and its human dimensions are to be illustrated in the church of the redeemed and reconciled community.
Here there "is neither Jew nor Greek, slave nor free, male nor
female, for you are all one in Christ Jesus" (Galatians 3:28). As
the communities of the reconciled, the churches are to be models of hope in their world and illustrations that only in Christ
can people achieve their longings for true peace and fulfillment.

Lastly, however, in its fullest scope reconciliation reaches
even beyond the world of men. In Colossians 1:19–20 Paul
writes triumphantly of Christ: "For God was pleased to have all
his fullness dwell in him, and through him to reconcile to himself all things, whether things on earth or things in heaven, by
making peace through his blood, shed on the cross." Calvin
thinks that in such a sweep Paul was including the very angels
of heaven who, by Christ's death, were forever confirmed in
righteousness (so that there would never be another fall among
the angelic powers) and whose creaturely imperfections where
covered by a superior obedience.[19]

It may even be that this aspect of Christ's death and the reconciliation it achieves are connected with that strange and difficult verse, Hebrews 9:23. Here, the writer says, "it was
necessary" that "the heavenly things," as well as the earthly
ones, be purified with the blood of Christ's sacrifice, as though
sin had in some way polluted the entire creation, even the heavenly places. Man's physical being is also included in this reconciliation in some way, as the doctrine of the resurrection of the
body intimates. (We shall consider the importance of this in a
later chapter.) Markus Barth justly observes that "The dignity
of being a living body and the honour to be offered to God as a
spiritual sacrifice (Romans 12:1–2) keep us as redeemed men
and women firmly within God's creation." As he puts it: "Atoms
and cells, energies and functions, as it were the hardware and

software, are not dispensable attributes of humanity. Unless Christ were the saviour of all things He could not be the saviour of human-kind."[20]

In a word, the reconciliation is cosmic in its ultimate accomplishments: the atonement of Jesus Christ washes to the four corners of the universe. By it a renewed heaven and a renewed earth have been guaranteed, and from it peace and union with God will flow forever.

It is only here, in reconciliation with God, that our human race can hope to locate and recover its own unity and its harmony. It is only in acknowledging God's Son as universal Savior and Lord that all nations can go forward together into their common destiny. It is here too that ecological suffering is healed and nature comes into its own full flowering and freedom. And it is here that broken relationships, bereaved families, and disappointed hopes will find restoration, reunion, and fulfillment in the perfection that shall be revealed one day.

# 21

# JUSTIFICATION
# IN CHRIST

What connections can there possibly be between the death of one man and the eternal salvation of others? The reply given to that question by the secular mind is, of course, "No connection at all!" The death of Jesus, like so much else in this world, is regarded as futile and without purpose, utterly wasteful and ultimately irrelevant. The life and death of Jesus, be it fiction or fact, is yet another piece of beautiful flotsam on the empty sea of life, the critics argue, a further proof that life is, in the last resort, a meaningless tragedy in which no help can be found from the outside because there is no one and nothing outside.

Bertrand Russell, the British philosopher, expressed in haunting words his own hopelessness: "We stand on the shore of an ocean, crying into the night and to the emptiness. Sometimes a voice answers out of the darkness but it is only the voice of one drowning, and in a moment the silence returns. The world seems to me quite dreadful."

Yet it is precisely here, at Calvary, that the gospel announces meaning and hope in the midst of chaos and failure. It places before us the most savage, unjust, and seemingly meaningless event in the entire history of this seemingly meaningless world, and shines a piercing light through all its layers of cruelty, futility, and loss. At its heart, Calvary illuminates not death but life, not failure but success, not desolation and abandonment but reconciliation and peace.

If life can make sense at Golgotha it can make sense anywhere, and the message of Christianity is that life *does* have meaning, even in the world of the Fall, where chaos wrecks so much and evil seems to triumph over good and God alike. Of course, there are "mysteries of providence" and times when we can make sense of nothing. But the God who redeemed meaning from the darkest, deepest reaches of chaos of Calvary can retrieve ultimate sense and purpose from our life with all its tangled threads. The Cross itself is a mystery, but it is also the solution to mystery; it is the riddle that resolves all other riddles; it is the key that unlocks the prison—from the inside!

We have already seen how Scripture makes sense of the Cross and the whole event of Christ's rejection and death. It shows us that God was there at its center, purposefully and powerfully. God did not make the best of it after the event; He made the best of things *in* and *by* the event. Calvary was planned by God and predicted by Old Testament prophets. Jesus Himself declared the event utterly necessary for His worldwide mission and saving work. For this cross He came into the world (John 12:27) and by this cross He would draw all men to Himself (John 12:31–33).

Yet, still the question we began with recurs: What connection can there be between Calvary and me, between Jesus' death and my life, His Calvary and my own destiny?

There are in the New Testament a clutch of words that, like a bank of spotlights, illuminate Christ's total achievement and our eternal gain. Words like *atonement, reconciliation, redemption, justification, sanctification,* and *adoption.* We have already examined the first three words in the previous two chapters. The remaining three more personally light up our present lives with a new significance and irradiate them with a new power.

As major New Testament concepts, *justification, sanctification,* and *adoption* relate directly to us. We can no more leave Calvary in the past than, at its rising, we can dismiss the sun as residing ninety-three million miles away. For as the rising sun reaches us with its light and warmth, so Christ's accomplished redemption reaches us personally with its power and life. Our Lord said in the days of His earthly ministry, "You will know the truth, and the truth will set you free" (John 8:32), and in the saving knowledge of "Jesus Christ and him crucified," the heart of the gospel (1 Corinthians 2:2), we experience the full flowering of this freedom: freedom from sin and death and freedom from sin's penalty, sin's guilt, and sin's power. We receive the freedom to live with God, to live holy lives, and to live those lives forever as the sons and daughters of God.

## A DEFINITION

*Justification,* or "to justify," means "to put in the right," "to regard as righteous," and "to pronounce righteous." It is closely related to the word *righteous,* and we must start with that idea, the concept of righteousness, in the Old Testament.

It is a great pity that an accident of English language has obscured the real meaning of this term. In the Greek New Testament the words for justification are *dikaiosunē, dikaioō,* and *dikei,* and these mean "righteousness," "to pronounce righteous," and "right," respectively. Unfortunately our early translators took the Latin translation *justificare* and of it made our English words "justification," "to justify," and "just." The problem here is that the link with the important Old Testament background is obscured (indeed, only in fairly recent times has it been given its full due). For in the Old Testament we read many times of the righteousness of God and His demands for righteousness, and it is here we must start if we would understand the full New Testament teaching.

## JUSTIFICATION IN THE OLD TESTAMENT

Though *justification* appears as a word primarily in the New Testament, it has its antecedents in the Old Testament terms for *righteousness.* In secular Greek the "righteousness" of God was an attribute of God conceived as an abstract, ethical quality. In Hebrew thinking, however, and in most of the biblical occurrences of the word, righteousness has a more active or relational meaning. This does not mean that righteousness, uprightness, is not conceived as an attribute within God's own being. On the contrary, the righteousness of His law reflected the righteousness of His character, and He always acted consistently with His righteous character.

J. Barton Payne traces the development of the concept of "righteousness" in the Old Testament revelation through nine stages,[1] but begins with righteousness as an absolute standard within God's own character and will, which evaluates all human actions and punishes moral violations of that will. Examples of this are found in Psalm 9:4-8, Psalm 50:4-6, and Isaiah 59:17-19 (cf. Habakkuk 1:13). Morris concludes from such considerations that if "the idea of righteousness is conformity to God's standard," then "justification will be a process in which this conformity is either attained, or declared to be attained."[2] On the cry of the psalmist: "Do not bring your servant into judgment, for no one living is righteous before you" (Psalm 143:2), Morris writes: "Here we are face to face with the ultimate question in religion, and the conclusion is that it is impossible for any man to have confidence in his standing before God on the ground of his deeds."[3]

However, most modern Old Testament scholarship has rightly noted the massive emphasis in the Old Testament texts on righteousness as the central and fundamental character of God's covenantal relationship with His people.

In the Old Testament righteousness is not generally an abstract ethical quality, but most often, as writers like Alister McGrath, Colin Brown, and R. A. Kelly show, it is behavior suitable to a relationship.[4] That relationship may be purely human, as between man and wife in a marriage, partners in business, or kings in treaties and coronation oaths. Righteousness belongs to the fair dealings one person or party should have with another in a given situation of agreed partnership. Such agreements were called *covenants,* and appropriate covenant behavior was called *righteousness.*

The central truth of Israel's life was that God entered into a unique and gracious covenant relationship with Abraham and his descendants. Unlike other, bilateral covenants between people, this was truly a unilateral covenant in which God freely, in undeserved love and grace, met Abraham when he was a Mesopotamian idolater, established with him and his descendants a covenant of grace in which He promised to be righteous (i.e., faithful to the agreement), and demanded a corresponding righteousness from Abraham, telling the cattleman to "walk before me and be blameless" (Genesis 17:1). From the start God demanded behavior suitable to the relationship He had graciously established, that is, loyalty, steadfastness, and faithfulness.

The sorry story of Abraham's descendants and of the Old Testament history of Israel is that Yahweh was faithful and Israel was not; Yahweh remained loyal and true to His covenantal promises, but His people forgot them and betrayed them again and again (Deuteronomy 32:4–5).

The covenant that God made with Abraham was renewed several hundred years later with Moses. However, at this time it was enshrined within complex legal stipulations, a subordinate but important "Mosaic covenant" that would dominate Jewish thinking for centuries, unchanged and unchallenged until the time of Christ. Within this legal dispensation of the original covenant of grace existed several elements in strong contrast and tension. The element of grace was still foundational (Exodus 20:2), and yet the demand for absolute righteousness was uncompromising (e.g., Leviticus 18:5). The provision of atoning sacrifice for sin relieved this tension to a degree, yet left unanswered deeper questions of sin, of righteousness, and of judgment to come; and anxieties continued (Job 9:2; 15:14; 25:4; Psalm 143:2; cf. 51:16–17).

Throughout this period Israel's only hope was in the righteousness of the righteous God who remained loyal to His covenant (Deuteronomy 7:6–9; Micah 7:18–20). Hence the psalmist who knows his sins were many (Psalm 19:12; 130:3) also knew his safety within the covenant relationship (Psalm 19:14; 130:7–8). His "righteousness" (Psalm 7:8; 18:20) is not a moral perfection, or even in the first place an ethical "high" (though it demands high ethics), but a right relationship with God, a standing or status within His gracious covenant (Psalm 143:1–2). This is the joyful confidence of all the people of God (Psalm 68; 89:14–18; cf. Jeremiah 9:23–24).

This faithfulness to His original promises in the covenant is called Yahweh's righteousness (Deuteronomy 32:4, etc.), and is the salvation of His people who would have had no hope without it (Isaiah 45:21). His righteousness is (surprisingly?) the sinner's refuge when it might have been his ruin, and He calls for His people to return to Him (Isaiah 45:20–24).

At such points as this, where God's righteousness and call to salvation coalesce, we see that righteousness is not only what God demands, it is also what God gives; His grace goes out to

establish a righteousness where it is needed and longed for.
When considering the Old Testament background to Paul's
thought on "the righteousness of God," Douglas Moo points to
texts which are, he notes, sometimes overlooked, where "God's
righteousness clearly includes the aspect of gift or status
enjoyed by the recipient,"[5] including Psalm 4:1 (lit., "O God of
my righteousness"); 37:6; 51:14; Isaiah 46:13; and 50:5-8 (cf.
Micah 7:9). Moo is sure that such usage must have had "considerable influence" on Paul's use and concept of "the righteousness of God." Certainly it would fit perfectly his statement in
Romans 1:17 that in the gospel, with its salvation, and divine
deliverance, "a righteousness from God is revealed." We would
tend to say, perhaps, "the love of God" is revealed in the gospel,
but against the background of such familiar Old Testament
expectation and ideas as God coming in covenantal faithfulness
to save His people, Paul insists on using the word *righteousness*. The startling thing is that for Paul the covenant now embraces "the Jew first and also . . . the Greek" (Romans 1:16, RSV).

We can see from all this that in the Old Testament righteousness before God is not in the first place an ethical condition but a religious relationship, not a subjective state but an
objective status; something which is, in the strictest sense of
the word, impossible from the side of sinful, flawed humanity,
but something which is made possible in the mercy of God,
who somehow finds a way to justify sinners (Psalm 32:1-11).
This merciful provision of an undeserved place, a legal status,
and an imputed righteousness lies at the very foundation of the
covenant, and without it the covenant could not exist.

So far we have considered mainly the righteousness that
God *shows* and maintains in His covenant relationship and
dealings with His people. However, there is a corresponding
righteousness that He *demands* in the relationship. From the
beginning He expected and demanded covenant loyalty to Himself and a suitable behavior to others in the covenant. The
prophets constantly called Israel and Judah back to their obligations within the covenant: to covenant righteousness, to loyalty and faithfulness, to justice and mercy. Willful neglect or
failure was met by God with chastisement (Ezra 9:10-14;
Psalm 89:30-33; Hosea 5:13-6:6); major apostasy brought

down on the guilty great judgment. But always a remnant was kept (Isaiah 6:11–13; cf. 11:1–9); God was faithful to His promise, and final deliverance and full salvation were sure (Isaiah 46:12–13; 51:7–8). This salvation would affect not only Israel, but also, as God had originally promised Abraham (Genesis 12:3), "the peoples" of the earth and "the coastlands" far from Israel (Isaiah 51:4–6, RSV; 19:19–25).

## JUSTIFICATION IN THE NEW TESTAMENT

While covenant membership was essentially and fundamentally an act of pure grace on God's part, it did call forth a corresponding covenant behavior. By the time of Jesus, however, many of Israel's theologians had sadly obscured the fundamental graciousness of the covenant relationship and had made righteousness before God depend on a human system of law keeping, of book balancing and graduated good deeds. Jesus Himself exposed their hypocrisy and the futility of any attempt to build up merit with God and so keep one's place within the covenant. Jesus re-emphasized the primary truth that righteousness is fundamentally a relationship with God in which the confessing sinner finds mercy and forgiveness and a new status from God Himself: the status of a righteous person, a justified child of God. This is the point of His parable about the Pharisee and the publican (Luke 18:10–14; cf. Matthew 5:20).

However, no less central than the covenantal or relational model (and even more revealing at some levels) is Paul's teaching concerning justification. In his picture of a courtroom and a judge's legal pronouncement we have the clear, forensic use of "to justify": to declare a person righteous before the law. Twenty-seven times Paul uses the verb *dikaioō* in the sense of "to declare (a person) righteous," "to justify," "to acquit," "to confer a righteous status on (someone)," fifteen of which instances are to be found in his letter to the Romans, where the concept receives its most profound treatment.

Morris writes: "The word is a forensic or legal term with the meaning 'acquit.' It is the normal word to use when the accused is declared 'Not Guilty.'"[6] "That Paul preserves the thoroughly forensic flavor of the word," says Moo, "is clear from his addition of the phrase 'before God' to the verb (Romans 2:13;

3:20)."[7] It is not simply with God as partner, but before God as
Lawgiver, that a person in Christ is justified. This sense is illustrated too in Paul's last use of the word in Romans. After saying, "Who will bring any charge [legal indictment] against
those whom God has chosen? It is God who *justifies*," Paul
rephrases his question using an opposite legal term "who is he
that *condemns?*" (Romans 8:33–34, emphasis added). C. E. B.
Cranfield says of this verse, "A judgment scene is envisaged,"[8]
and Moo points to the term "charge" as "the first of the explicit
judicial terms in this context."[9]

J. I. Packer sees this, rather than the relational model, as
being fundamental:

> The reason why the doctrine of justification is central to the
> gospel is that God's basic relationship to us as his rational
> creatures is that of Lawgiver and Judge, so that our stand-
> ing before Him is always determined by his holy law. The
> sinner's first problem, therefore, is to get right with God's
> law, for until he is right with the law he cannot be right with
> God whose law it is.[10]

Elsewhere he defines justification thus:

> Justification means to Paul God's act of remitting the sins
> of guilty men, and accounting them righteous, freely by His
> grace, through faith in Christ, on the ground, not of their
> own works, but of the representative law-keeping and
> redemptive blood-shedding of the Lord Jesus Christ on
> their behalf (Romans 3:23–26; 4:5–8; 5:18f.).[11]

Here God as Judge and Lawgiver, uncompromisingly upright in His standards of truth and righteousness, finds no adequate righteousness within sinners, fallen as they are. Salvation
by personal merit is impossible. Yet God has provided the Son,
God in our nature, as our head and representative. He, Jesus
Christ, has done all that we failed to do, and as our substitute
before the bar of God's justice and truth has made a full atonement for sin (Galatians 4:4–5).

By faith, believing sinners identify themselves with Christ:

believing His claims, adoring His person, and trusting His redeeming work. In justice no less than in mercy, God the righteous Judge sees believers as *in Christ,* with no guilt to answer for and with a perfect righteousness that delights Him (2 Corinthians 5:21). Now God justly pronounces those to be righteous who had no adequate righteousness of their own (Romans 3:19–21; 4:5; 5:6), because they have this and more in the Son He loves (1 Corinthians 1:30).

Justification, then, is the pronouncement that a person has become right with God, that he is now in a right relationship with God, that He has found a way of qualifying those whom sin had disqualified, a way of justifying the ungodly, of "righteoussing the unrighteous" with the righteousness of Another whose righteousness is the very righteousness of God.

Moo notes three respects in which Paul's use of justification differed from the normal Jewish usage:

> First, the verdict pronounced by the judge, according to the OT, was required to be in accordance with the facts (cf. especially Ex. 23:7; I Kings 8:32). It is a keystone of Paul's doctrine, however, that "God justifies the ungodly" (Romans 4:5). . . . It is not that God acts "unjustly," against the facts; but His justifying takes into account a larger set of facts, including the atoning character of Jesus' death and the righteousness He thereby acquired.[12]

Second, the Jewish view was that the verdict of "justification" would be pronounced only at the Last Judgment; "Paul, however, transfers the final verdict into the present," notes Moo. Third, "the justification offered the sinner in the gospel goes beyond 'acquittal,' by putting the sinner into a relationship with God in which *all* sins—future as well as past sins—are accounted for."[13]

## JUSTIFICATION BY FAITH, NOT WORKS

Throughout his writings, Paul has to counter tendencies within the Judaism of his day towards exclusivism and elitism and legalism. The attitude he encountered and opposed (and that he himself had once held) was that because Abraham, the father of Israel and the Jews, had received the promise of a covenantal relationship with God and because the law had been given to Moses both to protect Israel and show covenantal status and privilege, all Gentiles must become disciples of Moses if they wished to become children of Abraham and enter the covenant. They must be circumcised and take upon themselves the yoke of the law. It was impossible, they insisted, to be "right with God" by any other means, to be in covenant relationship with God except by circumcision and the law. Justification was by the law.

Paul opposed this in a number of ways, and we see his sustained arguments in his letters to the Galatians (e.g., Galatians 3:6–14, 19–26) and to the Romans (e.g., Romans 3:9–15). He reminds the Galatians, who are being seduced into a "Christ plus law" dependence, that it was because Abraham *believed* the promise of God that he was reckoned righteous (3:6), not because he kept the law of Moses. *Faith* was critical, not circumcision, which was only its sign. Moreover, the promise given to Abraham included "all nations" (v. 8), who become Abraham's children and share Abraham's privilege when they have Abraham's faith (v. 9): the faith which believes the promise concerning Christ. Most important of all, God's provision in Christ is full and final: salvation is in Him alone, not in Christ plus the law, or circumcision, or anything else.

The alternative to the way of faith is the way of works: the works of the (Mosaic) law, the works demanded by the covenant of Sinai. This, Paul insists, can lead only to ruin, to exclusion not inclusion, for both Jew and Gentile, since it is written in that selfsame law, "Cursed is everyone who does not continue to do everything written in the Book of the Law" (Galatians 3:10). But even under the old covenant and in the old dispensation no one was able to fulfill this demand and be justified before God by the law (v. 11). Like Abraham, the people of God under the old covenant of Moses *believed* the promises of God and so enjoyed their status within His larger covenant of grace, for "The righteous will live by faith" (v. 11).

In his letter to the Romans Paul develops this further. The gospel, he writes, is about the righteousness of God being made available to all men and women through faith, giving them a righteous status with God and a share in the life God has and gives to His people (Romans 1:16–17). Every attempt to gain favor and life from God on the basis of good works, secular or religious, is doomed because of sin (Romans 2:17, 23; 3:9–20). Only a righteousness superior to man's law-keeping can qualify a man for fellowship with God or sustain him in that fellowship. Such a righteousness is to be found only in God's Son, Jesus Christ, and is available to men only by faith in Him and on the ground of His atoning death (Romans 3:21–26).

This is the way of faith for Jew and Gentile alike (Romans 3:27–30). It is as old as Abraham, who entered a covenant relationship with God only by faith—before either his circumcision or Moses' law (Romans 4:1–3, 10–12; cf. Galatians 3:17). This principle of faith was not replaced by the law (Romans 3:31), but ran through it. Even after Moses and the giving of the law at Sinai, David knew that a man had a right relationship with God only by faith (Romans 4:6–8) and not by works of the law (v. 6). Indeed a main purpose of the law was to show that there was no other way to have such a relationship with God (Romans 4:13–15). Abraham's way of faith is the only hope, for both Jew and Gentile (Romans 4:16–17).

In the middle of his argument, and in what Cranfield calls "the centre and heart" of the letter to the Romans,[14] Paul focuses on the propitiatory death of Christ as the act where God revealed the seriousness of sin, the inevitability of His holy wrath against it, and the extent of His love for us. There, in Cranfield's words, He "directed upon His very Self in the person of His own dear Son the full weight of His wrath against sinners, so delivering them from it at His own cost—righteously and authentically."[15] He did this, writes Paul, so that He might justify sinners righteously (Romans 3:26), and so that without compromise to His own holiness He might take us into fellowship (Romans 6:1–4, 12–19; 8:1–3; 12:1–3).

## FAITH AND GOOD WORKS

We have been redeemed, freed from the tyranny of sin by the death of Christ for us, and now in Christ and in a life of faith in union with Him we can bring forth good works suitable to our new covenant relationship with God (Romans 6:13, 19, 22).

THE GLORY OF CHRIST

Thus there is no real contradiction between the teaching of

Paul and James in this matter. For both of them a relationship

to God "by faith" is full of good works. James's great point is

*not* that we are not justified by faith alone, as Paul states (Romans 3:28), but that such faith never stays alone but abounds in good works. This was true of Abraham, and it must be true of us (James 2:21–24). For James, faith which stays "alone" is never true faith, but a sterile, dead counterfeit (2:14–17, 26). Faith which bears fruit vindicates itself as true and living (2:18). The entry point into the covenant relationship is faith; the sustaining principle of the covenant relationship is faith; but the fruit and demonstration of the covenant relationship is a life full of good works in the Spirit and the likeness of God and His Christ: on this James and Paul, and indeed all the New Testament writers, are one.[16]

No one was clearer than John Calvin on the matter of the believer's justification "by faith *alone*," yet he constantly insists that while we are justified by faith alone, true faith does not remain alone. A balance exists: "We dream neither of a faith devoid of good works nor of a justification that stands without them. This alone is of importance: having admitted that faith and good works must cleave together, we still lodge justification in faith, not in works."[17]

In his most telling statement, Calvin writes:

> Why, then, are we justified by faith? Because by faith we grasp Christ's righteousness, by which alone we are reconciled to God. Yet you could not grasp this without at the same time grasping sanctification also. For He "is given unto us for righteousness, wisdom, sanctification, and redemption" [1 Corinthians 1:30]. Therefore Christ justifies no one whom He does not at the same time sanctify. These benefits are joined together by an everlasting and indissoluble bond, so that those whom He illumines by His wisdom, He redeems; those whom He redeems, He justifies; those whom He justifies, He sanctifies.[18]

However, it is crucial to preserve the distinction between faith and works in the matter of justification. Even faith must not be made a work or regarded as a work. Everywhere in this connection Paul contrasts faith with "works of the law" (Romans 4:1–25; Galatians 3:1–18), and as such faith is not a "work" considered as a religious or moral contribution of the soul to its salvation. True, this "faith" is not a mere opinion but, as Calvin liked to put it, a "full persuasion" of God's love to us and a personal reliance on Christ's finished work for us, convinced that He is what we need and has done everything necessary for our salvation. Paul calls this response to the gospel "the obedience of faith" (cf. Romans 1:5, KJV). It is in fact a real participation in the finished work of Christ for us.

Yet all this does not mean that faith is a work which contributes to justification. It is definitely not a "work" in this sense at all (Romans 4:2–5). It is rather the receiving of the work of Another for us. Faith is not a factor *in* justification, but only an instrument *of* justification. In that regard we may say we are justified through faith rather than by faith (as Romans 5:1).

Paul's entire argument in Romans 4, that Abraham was not justified by works, would lose its force if faith was itself a work. G. C. Berkouwer points to Paul's use of the word *reckoned* (*credited,* NIV) in "Abraham believed God, and it was reckoned to him as righteousness" (Romans 4:3, RSV), and writes: "Faith is not an independent function with even the slightest power to justify; but it is precisely *this* human position of impotency in contradistinction to which the 'reckoning according to grace' (and not according to debt or merit) is possible."[19] Indeed, here is the unique peculiarity of faith: that it has no content in and of itself, but finds its content and its character in its object—the Son of God.

That is why the apostle Paul, once so hopeless in his old self-righteousness (Romans 7:8–12), writes in triumph to the Philippians:

But whatever was to my profit I now consider loss for the sake of Christ. What is more, I consider everything a loss compared to the surpassing greatness of knowing Christ Jesus my Lord, for whose sake I have lost all things. I consider them rubbish, that I may gain Christ and be found in him, not having a righteousness of my own that comes from the law, but that which is through faith in Christ—the righteousness that comes from God and is by faith. (3:7–9)

To have received this righteousness as the gift of God is to have already heard the divine sentence which will be spoken at the Last Judgment. And it is, in consequence, to live in joy and peace with God and without fear of that day.

# 22

# SANCTIFICATION FROM CHRIST

O ur English word *sanctification* means basically "to make holy" (from the Latin *sanctus,* "holy," and *facere,* "to make"). The idea of holiness—both God's and ours—is a basic lesson in biblical teaching.

## SANCTIFICATION IN THE OLD TESTAMENT

The chief Old Testament word for holy is *qadosh.* This word probably comes from the Hebrew root "cut," and its basic concept is of something "cut off" from everything else. Applied to God it means that in His essential and mysterious being God is cut off, different from everything else. He is infinite, eternal, uncreated; all else is finite, created, dependent. Yahweh's holiness and His supreme otherness awes even the unfallen angels (Isaiah 6:2–3) and is His first and chief characteristic.

This term that is applied primarily to God comes to be applied in a secondary and derived sense to everything that is on the side of God, to everything related to God or reserved for His service in special ways. Thus in ancient Israel the priests of God are "holy," the temple is "holy," and even its vessels are "holy," set apart for God's use, cut off from common, profane, ordinary use. Most importantly, it is used repeatedly of the nation Israel, described as *set apart* from the nations, to be Yahweh's holy people, *reserved* for His worship, *consecrated* to His service, chosen for a unique destiny and task. Israel is God's holy nation; every man, woman, and child is holy, and the sign of this holiness upon every male born into the nation is circumcision. Israel is holy unto the Lord.

One thing we should not fail to note here is that Israel's holiness is an act before it is a process, and it is an act of God before it is in any sense an achievement of man. At Sinai God sanctified the tribes as a nation; there He set them apart publicly and definitively for Himself; from then on their holy status was a point of departure in their history as a nation, a basis on which they built, something which they were to live up to with love, gratitude, and obedience. Hence we read repeatedly at this time the crucial and definitive announcement: "I, the Lord, sanctify you" (Exodus 31:13; Leviticus 20:8; 21:8, RSV).

Along with the ceremonial uses of the word *holy,* its ethical sense also and inevitably developed. If Yahweh is removed from creatureliness, how much more from corruption; His is not only majesty-holiness (Isaiah 6:3), but also ethical holiness (Habakkuk 1:13): He is good, with nothing evil in Him; He is pure, and cannot tolerate wrong. This aspect of God's holiness, linked as it is with His righteousness, was developed strongly by the prophets, and they stressed the demands it made upon the "holy" people of Israel. God's primary demand of His people was that they should conform to His standards in holiness, righteousness, and truth (Micah 6:8), that those who belong to God should be like God. This was in fact God's command and purpose and was made plain from the start (Deuteronomy 26:16–19). He had said to Israel, "Be holy because I, the Lord your God, am holy" (Leviticus 19:2; cf. 11:44–45; 20:7), and they were able to live out and up to their high calling because of His act in constituting the nation as His holy people and because of His presence with them.

## SANCTIFICATION IN THE NEW TESTAMENT

In the New Testament this "set apart" position, this standing in unique relationship to God, is the foundation of the church of God. Believers in Christ have been gathered out of all nations and set apart for God in Christ to be a holy people. Thus Peter takes the Old Testament term and concept and writes to his Christian readers: "But you are a chosen people, a royal priesthood, a holy nation, a people belonging to God, that you may declare the praises of him who called you out of darkness into his wonderful light" (1 Peter 2:9). Elsewhere he stresses the ethical implications of this: "As obedient children, do not conform to the evil desires you had when you lived in ignorance. But just as he who called you is holy, so be holy in all you do; for it is written: 'Be holy, because I am holy'" (1 Peter 1:14–16).

Closely allied with the term *sanctification* is the descriptive term *saints*, which is used in the New Testament not of a few persons who are remarkably advanced in the spiritual life, but of all Christians, who are all "set apart" for God from the moment of their union with Christ at the new birth. Hence Paul writes in his various letters, "To the saints in Ephesus, the faithful in Christ Jesus" (Ephesians 1:1), "To all the saints in Christ Jesus at Philippi" (Philippians 1:1), and "To the saints and faithful brethren in Christ at Colossae" (Colossians 1:2, RSV).

When he writes, "To all in Rome who are loved by God and called to be saints" (Romans 1:7), Paul does not mean called (in the sense of invited, encouraged) to become saints at some stage in the future, but called effectively since their conversions (in the sense of constituted, denominated) to be (then and thereafter) saints, holy ones, set apart for God.

From conversion onwards the call of God in the Christian life is to live out our new identity consistently and gladly, in the freedom and dignity of the sons and daughters of God. J. I. Packer puts it nicely when he writes: "The New Testament does not say that Christians must lead holy lives in order to become saints; instead it tells Christians that because they are saints they must henceforth lead holy lives."[1] This is what Paul means when he begs the Ephesians to "live a life worthy of the calling you have received" (Ephesians 4:1), or when he says to the Philippian Christians, "conduct yourselves in a manner worthy of the gospel of Christ" (Philippians 1:27), or when he prays that the Colossian believers might "live a life worthy of the Lord" (Colossians 1:10; cf. 1 Thessalonians 2:12). As Herman Ridderbos says, the concept of "worthiness" here "has nothing to do with meritoriousness," but means "'answering to' the grace of having been appropriated to God."[2]

In Paul's theology holiness is a moral condition before it is moral activity, and the activity flows out of the condition. Holiness as an ongoing process of growth and development in the believer's life is a grateful, God-sustained reaction to a love received, a holy status gained, a promise given. This holy status, this sanctified condition, exists and begins the moment we are "in Christ," "whom God made our . . . righteousness and *sanctification* and redemption" (1 Corinthians 1:30, RSV, emphasis added), and that is our joy, our assurance, our glory (v. 31), on which we build. John Murray writes:

> It is biblical to apply the term "sanctification" to [a] process of transformation and confirmation into the more perfect image of Christ, but it is a fact too frequently overlooked that in the New Testament the most characteristic terms that refer to sanctification are used, not of a process but of a once-for-all definitive act.[3]

This act occurred at our conversion, when the Holy Spirit united us to Christ and we entered a new sphere "in Christ," when we "died" to our old relationship to sin and began to share His risen, heavenly life, a life forever free from the tyranny of sin and death.

## SANCTIFICATION AND THE DEATH OF CHRIST

Again and again in the New Testament the death of Christ is associated with the believer's sanctification. The writer to the Hebrews repeatedly speaks of this, understanding the term *sanctification* in its original sense of consecration to God. At the outset Christ is "He who sanctifies"; and it is by the Father's will that "we have been sanctified through the offering of the body of Jesus Christ once for all" (Hebrews 10:10, RSV); Christ "by a single offering" has "perfected for all time those who are sanctified" (Hebrews 10:14, RSV); this offering which sanctifies "the people" of God is "his own blood" (Hebrews 13:12), the sacrificial sign of atonement for sin. "Such teaching makes it very clear," comments Philip Edgcumbe Hughes, "that the 'sanctification' of which our author speaks is intimately connected with and flows from Christ's priestly offering of Himself on the cross. . . . Redeemed by the blood of the incarnate Son, the people of God are purified from defilement and constituted holy before their Creator."[4]

By His death Christ redeemed us not only from the penalty of sin—separation from God—but from the power of sin also, from its tyranny in our lives. In Paul's words to the Galatians, He "gave himself for our sins to rescue us from the present evil age" (Galatians 1:4). F. F. Bruce comments on these words: "Christ's self-oblation not only procures for His people the forgiveness of their past sins; it delivers them from the realm in which sin is irresistible into the realm where He Himself is Lord." While this evil age is "an age dominated by an ethically evil power," those who receive Christ in the gospel "are thereby delivered from the godless *Zeitgeist*."[5]

Similarly Paul writes to Titus: "For the grace of God that brings salvation has appeared to all men. It teaches us to say 'No' to ungodliness and worldly passions, and to live self-controlled, upright and godly lives in this present age" (Titus 2:11–12). Underpinning this is not simply the good example of Christ as an encouragement, but His redeeming death, which lets us escape evil's power and is an opposing power to the strength of corruption still remaining in the Christian. Hence Paul in the Titus passage speaks of the coming Christ "who gave himself for us to redeem us from all wickedness and to purify for himself a people that are his very own, eager to do what is good" (Titus 2:14).

Our sanctification is only possible because of the once-for-all death of Christ as an offering for sin and through the ongoing life of Christ as the source of new life in God. The death of Christ separates us unto God, and the risen life of Christ gives us power from God. The order of Romans 6:3–4 is important and unbreakable: Christ's death is the precondition of our life; it is even the precondition of *His* risen, eternal life for us (Romans 6:10). As that death becomes effective for us at our conversion, so the new life following it becomes operative in us thereafter: we become sharers of Christ's death to sin and of His new life with God. This is the great message of Romans 6.

The first significant thing about Romans 6 is its constant use of a past tense: we Christians "died to sin" (v. 2); we were "baptized into Christ Jesus" and "into his death" (v. 3); we were "buried with him through baptism into death" (v. 4); "our old self was crucified with him" (v. 6) so that the sinful body might be destroyed. In a word, "we died with Christ" (v. 8). In the Greek all these verbs are in the aorist tense and the indicative mood. The aorist tense signifies completed action, and also, when it is in the indicative mood, of complete past action, something finally and fully done at a particular moment in the past. Paul is telling us—all of us, not just the "high-fliers"— about something that became true in our lives at a particular point in our past. That is when through the action of the Spirit, we ceased to be "in Adam" and began to be "in Christ" (to recall Romans 5).

At the start of our Christian lives the Holy Spirit unites the sinner on earth with the Savior in heaven. This union with Christ is so full and complete that His work for us becomes ours; we share His death unto sin and His present freedom from sin's tyranny. For a while He came under the dominion of sin for us, submitting to the law in its rigors and its penalties, bearing our burdens and paying our debts: "The death he died, he died to sin once for all" (Romans 6:10). But He has been raised from that death which He died on account of sin; now neither sin nor death has any claim on Him: "the life he lives, he lives to God" (v. 10). He is out of the jurisdiction and power of sin and death entirely. Even so, says Paul, with spectacular reasoning, the moment we became united with Christ at the beginning of our Christian lives *we too* passed out from under the dominion and jurisdiction of sin and death and became sharers of Christ's heavenly and eternal freedom:

> Or don't you not know that all of us who were baptized into Christ Jesus were baptized into his death? We were there-fore buried with him through baptism into death in order that, just as Christ was raised from the dead through the glory of the Father, we too may live a new life. (Romans 6:3–4)

A share in Christ's death and resurrection contains promise for the future (vv. 5, 8–9) and power for the present (vv. 6–7, 11). Sin can no more have dominion over us than it can have domin-ion over Him (vv. 9, 11–12, 14). Henceforth it can only "reign" if we "yield" (vv. 12–13), for in Christ we share the power of a new life in which grace, not sin, reigns. We have been baptized into the freedom of Christ and are now to live in yieldedness to righteousness and a new standard of teaching (vv. 15–18). This is a reality to be worked out with more and more consistency (v. 19) as it is recognized and applied (vv. 11, 22).

We are, says Paul, to realize our status, our dignity, and the real possibilities of our standing:

> Therefore do not let sin reign in your mortal body so that you obey its evil desires. Do not offer the parts of your body to sin, as instruments of wickedness, but rather offer yourselves to God, as those who have been brought from death to life; and offer the parts of your body to him as instruments of righteousness. For sin shall not be your master, because you are not under law, but under grace. (Romans 6:12–14)

When we submit to sin, yielding to its imperious demands, it is not a matter of yielding to the inevitable or reverting to type. We are foolishly, perversely allowing sin to dominate us when in actual fact it has neither the right nor the power to do so. We have been taken once and for all out of its territory, out of the state where it holds men and women captive and in chains. Therefore, when we submit to sin and temptation, as if it had mastery, we are like freed slaves going back into the house of their former bondage and obeying their old owner. By Christ's redeeming act at Calvary we were brought out of the slave market of the world, ransomed from Satan, sin, and death. No one now but He who bought us has any rights over us: "the accuser of the brethren" has no ground on which to claim us; the powers of the demonic cannot pluck us from the safety of Christ's hands; the world's standards and priorities (and our own old standards and priorities) of self-centeredness and self-advancement cannot compel us since we have a new motivation, another goal, and an indwelling Spirit by which to reach it.

In his famous statement in Galatians 2:20 Paul shows how little justification and sanctification can be separated in experience, and how the former is the motivation of the latter. The apostle's union with Christ by faith is so complete that he shares Christ's freedom from the demands of the law due to sin and can walk free as one discharged from the law's arrest and sin's power (Galatians 2:19; cf. Romans 7:6). This is his justification by the death of Christ. In the new life that Paul has in Christ, self is so effectively dethroned and the risen Christ so operative in kingly power that as soon as he has said, "I have been crucified with Christ," denoting his justification by the blood of Christ (cf. Romans 5:9), Paul immediately adds, "I no longer live, but Christ lives in me. The life I live in the body, I live by faith in the Son of God, who loved me and gave himself for me" (Galatians 2:20).

It is from the cross of Christ, insists G. C. Berkouwer, that all lines radiate outward, and "We must be thoroughly aware that in shifting from justification to sanctification we are not withdrawing from the sphere of faith."[6] Faith, he writes later, is to be "the foundation of good works," and "It follows from the nature of faith which clings to divine grace that it cannot possibly be unfruitful."[7] Faith cannot be unfruitful because it cannot be ungrateful. It hears Paul's words, "You are not your own; you were bought at a price" (1 Corinthians 6:19–20), and it knows in faith that it is so. And so daily it responds in surrender to the Christ of the cross: "Love so amazing, so divine, demands my soul, my life, my all."[8]

# 23

# ADOPTION
# THROUGH CHRIST

In humankind, every child has a father. Even if the father does not live with the family, due to death or divorce, his imprint remains, and his absence is missed. But the idea that a mighty God, the creator of the universe and judge of all, can be called *father,* with all its connotations of love and approachability, may seem surprising. Yet the personal God of the Bible makes us His children, through an adoption process described by the apostle John (John 1:12) and many others in the Scripture.

## OLD TESTAMENT BACKGROUND

Interestingly, the title "Father" has been ascribed to God through much of religious history. "It is found," says G. Schrenk, "among both primitive and culturally elevated people, both around the Mediterranean and Assyria and Babylon."[1] Wherever human beings have groped for God in the dark, they have huddled for warmth against this name and its connotations of authority, safety, mercy, and care.

Sometimes the myths surrounding the divine fatherhood were crude and biological, sometimes they were ethical and refined, as in the philosophy of the Greek stories and of the Jewish philosopher Philo. A common feature was the universality of the divine parenthood. Thus, to give some examples, the God El of Ugarit in the fourteenth century B.C. is called "the father of mankind"; the Babylonian moon-god, Sin, is called "father of men and gods"; in Greece Zeus is called "father of men and gods"; and in Plato and the Stoics God is the "universal father" and "creator, father and sustainer" of all men who are His children (who should know it and live up to it).

## The Restricted Use of the Word *FATHER*

When we look for this concept in the Old Testament, therefore, we are likely to be surprised at the comparative reserve among writers who use the concept of divine fatherhood and human sonship. The concept appears in significant and also beautiful instances, but it is infrequent. The Hebrew word for father, *'ab*, occurs 1,180 times in a secular, family sense but only fifteen times in regard to God as Father. Only twice is He addressed as Father in prayer.

We will also discover, as O. Hofius points out, that "The description of God as Father refers in the Old Testament only to His relationship with the people of Israel (Deut. 32:6; Isa. 63:16 twice; 64:8; Jer. 31:9; Mal. 1:6; 2:10) or to the king of Israel (2 Sam. 7:14 par. 1 Chr. 17:13; 22:10; 28:6; Psalm 89:26; cf. 2:7)."[2] It never refers, says Hofius, to mankind in general. Indeed, he continues,

> The basic difference between this and the views of the fatherhood of God held by Israel's neighbors is that in the Old Testament God's fatherhood is not understood in a biological or mythological sense, but in a soteriological one. To be a child of God is not a natural state or quality; rather it [is] grounded in the miracle of the divine election and redemption.[3]

This restricted use of the concept of father is neither religious bigotry nor narrow-minded nationalism. The concept of divine parenthood could not be treated as something automatic anymore than it could be degraded as something physical. Hence the concept of covenant with God is introduced and elaborated more than that of divine fatherhood. This was a covenant relationship between Israel and God that was not inevitable but gracious—His free decision not to number Israel among the nations, but to enter into a unique relationship with the nation as His chosen people (e.g., Deuteronomy 7:6–8; cf. Amos 3:2). Only occasionally is this described in terms of a relationship between a father and his children. Yet this truth is nevertheless essential to a full appreciation of it. Peter C. Craigie writes:

> At the heart of the covenant is the concept of sonship; the human partner in the covenant is son of the covenant God who is father. This covenant principle is a part of the Sinai Covenant between God and Israel. The covenant God cares for Israel as a father cares for His son (Deuteronomy 1:31) and God disciplines Israel, as a father disciplines a son (Deuteronomy 8:5).[4]

Only in the New Testament, with the revelation of Christ, will fatherhood and fellowship replace covenant and partnership as the primary category.

While the Old Testament emphasis is mostly on the nation considered collectively as God's son, and nowhere do we find an example of an individual addressing God as "my Father" (but note Psalm 89:26 and Jeremiah 3:19), the knowledge of Yahweh's fatherhood could be personally appropriated and warmly comforting (Psalm 103:13), and Yahweh's Father-heart for Israel is sometimes poignantly expressed (e.g., Isaiah 1:2–3; 63:8–10; Jeremiah 3:18–20; Hosea 11:1–4). Undoubtedly the right point of comparison is the trustworthy authority that human fatherhood has always embodied at its best, and this forms the center of all the references to God as the Father of Israel in the Old Testament.

## Israel's Adoption

Adoption as a legal act was not a Jewish institution. However, we do read of Abraham's original intention to make Eliezer his heir (Genesis 15:2–3) and of the fostering of Moses by Pharaoh's daughter (Exodus 2:10) and of Mordecai's adoption of Esther (Esther 2:7). We have seen how early and often the free nature of Yahweh's choice of Israel to be His nation-child is emphasized, and Sinai might well be regarded as the place of Israel's adoption as a nation. Moreover, Ezekiel's allegory of Israel as a foundling babe taken up by Yahweh and in time becoming His wife (Ezekiel 16:1–14), even though it is taken into a different metaphor, has more than a little of the element of adoption in it.

All of this material lends ample support for C. E. B. Cranfield's statement that when Paul writes of Israel, his own race, "to them belong the sonship" (Romans 9:4, RSV), whatever contemporary associations may be made, "He must surely have had OT material very much in mind."[5]

Paul recognizes the reality and the privilege of Israel's adoption as a nation (Romans 9:3–5). Yet he also teaches that under the legal dispensation of Moses, under the administration of law, the "full rights of sons" were held back. Throughout this period before Christ's coming the people of God lived a religious life under restrictions and constraints, which was a kind of slavery, and did not enjoy the freedom of a sonship "come of age" (Galatians 4:1–7).

## THE NEW TESTAMENT TEACHING

### *ABBA:* God as "Dad"

The first—and most dramatic—glimpse of our full freedom in the gospel is given by Jesus Christ during His earthly ministry. He taught His followers not only to address God as Father constantly, but Himself prayed to God as *abba* (Mark 14:36; cf. Romans 8:15; Galatians 4:6). This form of the word began as baby language but acquired a much wider currency and was used generally as a warm, familiar term for father (rather as *Dad* is more familiar than *Father* in common English usage).

"Nowhere in the entire wealth of devotional literature produced by ancient Judaism," notes Hofius, "do we find [*abba*] being used as a way of addressing God. The pious Jew knew too much of the great gap between God and man (Ecclesiastes 5:1) to be free to address God with the familiar word used in everyday family life."[6] In contrast to the Old Testament's sparing use of *Father* with regard to God (fifteen times), the New Testament has it no less than 245 times.

It is widely agreed by New Testament scholars that *abba* lies behind the Greek *pater* (father) in all of the prayers of Jesus in the Gospels.[7] Only once does Jesus clearly refrain from using the *abba* term of intimacy and comfort, and that is when all comfort is denied Him as He takes the sinners' place under the judgment of God and cries, "My God, my God, why have you forsaken me?" (Matthew 27:46). By His consistent use of such a category as father, the way in which He personalized it, and the intimate *abba* form in which He expressed it, Jesus demonstrated a unique relationship with God. Furthermore, as the Lord's Prayer shows, He offered to all His followers a relationship of similar intimacy (e.g., Matthew 6:9; cf. John 20:17).

**Father Only of Those Who Follow Christ**

Schrenk is careful to point out here the essential and crucial link between being a follower of Jesus and knowing God as Father in this way. "The term alone," he warns, "does not carry the whole message. The right of sonship is within the limits of the [kingdom]."[8] He elaborates:

> The word "father" is for those who accept the teaching of Jesus about "your Father." . . . Even when a wider circle is suggested (Lk. 6:27; Matt. 23:1) the hearers are not given in this truth of fatherhood a universal truth. A new sense is imparted which includes discipleship, Lk. 6:35f.; Matt. 23:8f. The concern in Jesus' preaching of fatherhood is always to instruct the disciples about the [kingdom].[9]

Similarly R. A. Finlayson writes of Christ's teaching: "In no instance is He reported as assuming this relationship to exist between God and unbelievers."[10] Hofius observes: "The expression 'your Father' is found only in the words of Jesus to His disciples, . . . This means that Jesus did not teach the idea that God is the Father of all men. Rather, He linked the fatherhood of God to men's relationship to himself."[11]

The New Testament message is very clearly controlled by this. John, like Jesus, draws a sharp distinction between the world and its children (e.g., John 1:4, 11–12; cf. 8:19, 31–47; 1 John 3:1, 10; 4:4–6; 5:1–2, 19–20). At the beginning of his gospel (John 1:12–13) he makes it clear that men and women who belong to the world by nature can only belong to God's family by being born "of God." Jesus Himself calls for a second,

spiritual birth in order to enter God's kingdom in His meeting
with Nicodemus (John 3:5–8).

All the biblical writers call for a new birth, though in different ways. Whether we are said to become children of God by
faith (Galatians 3:26), by the Spirit (John 3:5–6), or "in Christ"
(Ephesians 1:3–4), what is clear is that sonship is not a right of
nature but a gift of grace, a rebirth of the spirit that is lovingly
planned, dearly bought, and supernaturally given.

It is as necessary now as ever to make this point. The idea
that God is the Father of every human being is not a biblical
one, common as it was then in much pagan religion and philosophy. It is sometimes said in Christian theology that all are
God's children by new birth, but this is confusing and perhaps
misleading. It is nearer to humanism than biblical Christianity,
and found new currency after the eighteenth-century Enlightenment when it was "read back" into the Sermon on the Mount.
It is sometimes said that all are God's children by creation but
only believers are His children by new birth. But this too is confusing and perhaps misleading. It comes too close to the common heathen view of divine fatherhood by creation, and is a
long way from the New Testament emphasis. It is true that to
make a point to the philosophers at Athens Paul quotes a secular poet who says that "we are his offspring," but only to illustrate that in God all men "live and move and have [their] being"
(Acts 17:28). Paul uses "offspring" in the sense of dependence
for life and sustenance, not biology or a shared divine life,
which would be a thought foreign to his thinking.

## Our Adoption

Most striking in Paul's concept of the divine fatherhood is
his use of the term "adoption," *huiothesia* (Romans 8:15; 9:4;
Galatians 4:5; Ephesians 1:5). As we have seen, the background
to Paul's thinking lies first of all in the Old Testament. However,
Francis Lyall argues—Leon Morris thinks "convincingly"—that
Paul's use of this term was "a deliberate, considered, and
appropriate reference to Roman law."[12] In this process

The adoptee is taken out of his previous state and is placed
in a new relationship with his new *paterfamilias* [father/

head of the family]. All his old debts are cancelled, and in effect he starts a new life. From that time the *paterfamilias* owns all the property and acquisitions of the adoptee, controls the personal relationships, and has rights of discipline. On the other hand he is involved in liability by the actions of the adoptee and owes reciprocal duties of support and maintenance.[13]

Certainly the image of adoption was well fitted to Paul's unfailing emphasis on the voluntary and gracious character of God's relationship to us. We see this worked out in all sorts of ways in the letter to the Ephesians. Our sonship is the result of the Father's choice in eternity (Ephesians 1:4–5), Christ's redemptive act in history (1:7), and the Spirit's unfailing and abundant work in our hearts, bringing regeneration, faith (2:8–10), and a spirit of adoption (1:13–14). Christ is the locus of every stage of this, past, present, and future. God has blessed us "in Christ" with every spiritual blessing (1:3). He has chosen us "in him" (v. 4), and in Him has given us a new identity as His sons (v. 5). In Him we have redemption, forgiveness, and infinite resources in God (vv. 7–8). In Him too we have been sealed with the Spirit, which is the guarantee of our inheritance to come (vv. 13–14). This Father-child relationship that God has with us involves and implies an intimacy which should enrich us (v. 17), a hope which should excite us (v. 18), and a life which should mark us (v. 15). In all this Father, Son, and Holy Spirit work together to bring us into the family privileges of the children of God (Ephesians 2:17; 3:14–19; 5:1, 8–10).

## ADOPTION DESCRIBED IN ROMANS 8

Paul gives further attention to this subject in Romans 8. According to D. M. Lloyd-Jones, the main theme of this chapter is the believers' certainty and assurance in knowing their sonship. He writes: "The Apostle's greatest concern is that we should know and realise that we are 'sons of God,' that we should be rejoicing and praising God and crying 'Abba, Father,' that we should be delivered from the 'spirit of bondage.'"[14]

First, Paul shows his readers the "absolute certainty and finality of the full and complete salvation of all who are 'in

Christ Jesus'" (vv. 1–4).[15] Then he gives us a picture of the contrast between the Christian and the non-Christian, which he applies to his readers specifically (vv. 5–11). Central to this contrast is their possession of the Spirit, who indwells and controls them, enabling them to live a life pleasing to God in spite of the pull of the flesh (vv. 12–13).

This, for all its struggle, is life indeed; the life of the sons of God who are led by the Spirit of God (vv. 13–14). The control of the Spirit, the government of the Spirit, is the basis of their life and the proof of their sonship. The Spirit did not and does not lead people back into bondage, but out into the liberty of the sons of God (v. 15). By Him we cry with full hearts to God, "Abba, Father," conscious of our claim on Him, eager in our desire for Him. Over and above that, "The Spirit himself testifies" to our status as God's children (v. 16). Lloyd-Jones argues that it is a further work of the Spirit beyond His other works, as in times of great spiritual experience, a distinct and immediate testimony assuring believers that they are "children of God" (cf. Ephesians 1:12).[16]

It is then that Paul turns to the inheritance aspect of the believer's adoption: "Now if we are children, then we are heirs —heirs of God and co-heirs with Christ . . ." (v. 17). In Roman law, a citizen without an heir could perpetuate his name and keep his estate within the family by adopting as his son a successor (nearly always an adult and not, as in our society, a baby) who would be legally instated as his heir, in every way to be treated as his son, and entitled to the full rights of inheritance at the death of his adoptive father.

Cranfield is concerned to distinguish this use of the ideas of heirship and inheritance from others in Paul's writings. Romans 4 speaks of sons of Abraham and heirs of Abraham; Galatians 3 and 4 speak of sons of God and heirs through God (Galatians 4:7). But in Romans 8 Paul speaks of heirs of God and joint heirs with Christ. This, writes Cranfield,

> points extraordinarily effectively to the facts that Christians are [people] who have great expectations, that their expectations are based upon their being sons of God, that these expectations are of sharing not just in various blessings

God is able to bestow but in that which is particularly His own, the perfect and imperishable glory of His own life.[17]

Paul's further phrase, "co-heirs with Christ," expresses the ground and the certainty of our hope as well as its nature. Christ came as the head and representative of His people: we were included with Him in the purposes of God at Calvary and His atonement for sin; with Him in the Resurrection and His new imperishable life; and with Him at His exaltation into the glory of His Father, where He has gone to prepare a place for us (John 14:2–3) and where He intercedes for us still (Hebrews 7:25), so that we may share His glory with the Father (John 17:22–24). While there is a glory that only the Son in His divine being can know and share with the Father, here we have the glory of Christ as Mediator, the God-man, which He has won for His people and which He promises to His people.

This glory includes "the redemption of our bodies" (Romans 8:23) at the resurrection, with its corollary, the restoration of the whole creation which, says Paul, waits "in eager expectation" (v. 19) for the time when it will be "liberated from its bondage to decay and brought into the glorious freedom of the children of God" (v. 21). We ourselves join in that eager longing, even groaning with a dying creation "as we wait eagerly for our adoption as sons, the redemption of our bodies" (v. 23). It is not that our present adoption is uncertain; only that it is incomplete, awaiting our full and final redemption from sin and death.

Meanwhile we live in hope, "for in this hope we were saved" (v. 24). However, this hope is not a tenuous, uncertain thing, but a sure and certain confidence, a patient expectation based on the promises of a God who cannot lie (Titus 1:2; 2 Corinthians 1:20), a Christ who cannot fail (1 Corinthians 15:25), and an indwelling Spirit whose presence (2 Corinthians 1:22; 5:5; Ephesians 1:13–14) in our hearts and lives is the guarantee of our future.

In speaking of this last matter Paul uses in the three texts indicated a very specific word, rare in classical Greek and used only here in the New Testament. This word, *arrabon*, was originally used in business and trade and, according to O. Becker, meant

> (1) an installment with which a man secures a legal claim upon a thing as yet unpaid for; (2) an earnest, an advance payment, by which a contract becomes valid in law; (3) in one passage (Gen. 38:17ff.) a pledge. In each case it is a matter of payment by which the person concerned undertakes to give further payment to the recipient.[18]

Paul uses the word to describe the gift of the Holy Spirit not only as a guarantee of life to come, or as a pledge of eternal glory, but as a deposit also, a guarantee in kind, a pledge which is a piece of the whole, a foretaste of promised glory, a first installment of what is to come. This sense is well illustrated in Romans 8:23, where Paul speaks of Christians as those who have the "firstfruits of the Spirit," an Old Testament echo (e.g., Leviticus 23:10–11) in which the firstfruits of the harvest were seen as carrying within themselves the pledge and significance of the whole. The Spirit's work in us is but the first installment of what shall be; as F. F. Bruce puts it: "The Spirit consciously received is 'the guarantee of our inheritance.'"[19] There can be no privilege more dignifying than adoption into God's family, and no understanding more life-transforming than the true knowledge of our sonship or daughterhood. Among His people God has no higher name than Father; and we have no higher privilege than fellowship with the Father in the Son and by the Holy Spirit. It is the entire new covenant in one word.

J. I. Packer makes the point that as Yahweh was the covenant name of God among the Old Testament community (Exodus 3:14–15; Habakkuk 1:12–13), so Father might be regarded as the covenant name for God in the New Testament community, which can approach Him with freedom and confidence (Ephesians 3:12; Hebrews 10:19). As mirrored in the earthly life of Christ it implies, says Packer, *authority* (John 4:34; 5:19; 6:38; 17:4), *affection* (John 5:20; 15:9), *fellowship* (John 8:29; 16:32), and *honor* (John 5:22; 17:1).[20]

Our adoption is the highest privilege that the gospel offers. It presupposes or contains within itself all the blessings of the gospel of God's grace. It is the ultimate goal of the death and resurrection of Christ: "I am returning to my Father and your Father, to my God and your God" (John 20:17; cf. 15:15). Our adoption is the basis of Christian living that naturally imitates the Father (Matthew 5:44–45, 48), of the life of prayer that naturally turns to the Father (Matthew 6:7; 7:7–11), and of the life of faith that naturally trusts the Father (Matthew 6:24–33).

The concept of adoption, says Packer, "is the nucleus and focal point of the whole New Testament teaching on the Christian life."[21] The result of a true understanding of it in the believer will enable him or her to say every day of his life, *"I am a child of God. God is my father; heaven is my home; every day is one day nearer. My Savior is my brother; every Christian is my brother too."*[22]

# PART 5

# CHRIST
# THE EXALTED LORD

# 24

# BELIEVING THE RESURRECTION

The doctrine of the bodily resurrection of Jesus Christ after His death at Calvary is not an option for Christians. It is not an appendix to the gospel. It lies at the core of Christianity. Without it Christianity would have been stillborn, for a living faith cannot survive a dead savior. Hence, responding to certain heretics who wanted to "spiritualize" the Resurrection, Paul insisted, "If Christ has not been raised, our preaching is useless and so is your faith" (1 Corinthians 15:14).

## THE IMPORTANCE OF BELIEF

But why does Paul places such significance upon the bodily resurrection of Jesus? Why does the whole of Christian truth depend on this event being a physical fact? The comprehensive answer is that the identity of Jesus is found in the reality of this event. So is the success of Jesus' saving work, and His present power to change lives. The issue of theResurrection also affects the integrity of the apostles—every word they write about the good news that mankind can receive the forgiveness of sins and life everlasting.

If Jesus has not risen from the dead, His own expectations are disappointed and His repeated promises proven false, His assurances worthless. In that case, whoever else the Nazarene might have been, He certainly was not and is not "Lord." If Jesus has not risen from the grave, His disciples are incompetent transmitters of truth, for this doctrine was the cornerstone of their apostolic teaching. Worse, they are actually false witnesses, claiming to be eyewitnesses of a miracle that never truly happened (John 21:24; Acts 2:32; 1 Corinthians 15:15). And if Jesus has not risen from the grave, if His body once lay moldering in Joseph's tomb and is now forgotten dust, then death is still victorious and final. There is no good news for the dying. If for a Savior we only have a ghost, then for a heaven we shall only have a dream.

In short, the whole theology of the New Testament stands or falls by this resurrection event. "The entire New Testament," writes Carl Henry, "was written within and from the perspective of Jesus' resurrection from the dead."[1] "Without it," says Murray J. Harris, "the New Testament loses its soul and the Christian faith its central pillar."[2] The Cross on Calvary's hill is the central focus of the New Testament, but it is never viewed apart from the Resurrection, as though it made sufficient sense (let alone a sufficient gospel!) in and of itself. As we shall see later in this chapter, the Cross is incomprehensible without the Resurrection, for the Resurrection explains and validates the Cross. Indeed, what the Cross won for us the Resurrection made available to us, and thus the Resurrection is as necessary for our salvation as the Cross.

Consequently, we can never move straight from Jesus' death to His work in our individual hearts and lives, passing directly from atonement to justification and short-circuiting or bypassing the Easter event and the empty tomb. There is no salvation in a Good Friday that has no Easter Sunday following it. As Paul goes on to tell the Corinthian Christians: "If Christ has not been raised, your faith is futile; you are still in your sins" (1 Corinthians 15:17).

Let us turn now to a closer consideration of the resurrection of Jesus. First we shall see it as a demonstrable event, a concrete historical "happening." Then we shall seek a further understanding of its profound and far-reaching significance. And finally we shall consider its impact and effect upon our own Christian position and experience.

## THE EVIDENCE FOR BELIEF

The evidences for the Resurrection are many, and they add up to a weighty body of proof. Let us deal with the known facts of the case. Here we have to examine the testimony of the writings that make up our New Testament.

One of the earliest of these documents, that probably predates the gospel accounts themselves, is Paul's first letter to the Corinthians. This was written within twenty years of the event, and in 1 Corinthians 15 Paul devotes an entire chapter to stressing the fact, the importance, and the implications of Jesus' bodily resurrection. In regard to the fact of the Resurrection, Paul says first that he had "received" (v. 3) what he was preaching, and that he had himself witnessed its truth (v. 8). Gordon Fee says that the phrase "what I received" (cf. 1 Corinthians 11:23) is "technical vocabulary from Paul's Jewish heritage for the transmission of religious instruction."[3] The latest date on which Paul could have received such information was his first post-conversion visit to Jerusalem (Acts 9:23–26; Galatians 1:17–19) about A.D. 35. Here he would have heard the testimony to the Resurrection of eyewitnesses such as Peter and James, a testimony that he must have known about even while still a persecutor.

## Eyewitnesses of the Resurrected Jesus

Even before that visit, the knowledge that Jesus had indeed been raised from the dead to divine honors had formed the basis of his own faith from the time of his own conversion experience (Acts 9:20). Hence, he enumerates various Resurrection appearances to Peter, to "the Twelve," to the five hundred, to James and to "all the apostles" (that Fee thinks refers to the commissioning of Acts 1:6–11), and then Paul adds: "Last of all, as to one untimely born, he appeared also to me" (1 Corinthians 15:8, RSV). Without the benefit of the three-year gestation period of the original Twelve, Paul had emerged from the Damascus road event as authorized a witness to the Resurrection as any of his peers. What he had been given was not merely a heavenly vision, but a Resurrection appearance. Moreover, he received with it a commission that gave him an indisputable place among the foremost apostles (Acts 9:5–6, 15; 26:16–18; 1 Corinthians 9:1; Galatians 2:6–10).

In full accord with this, the Acts of the Apostles shows that the belief in the Resurrection did not emerge gradually in the early church, but that from the very beginning (within seven weeks of Jesus' public death by crucifixion) the Resurrection event was being preached loud and clear by Peter at the feast of Pentecost as part of the central message of Christianity (Acts 2:23–24; cf. 3:15; 4:10; 5:31–32). The whole of the New Testament witness, in all its strata, its different writers and its various books, is united on the matter. The gospel accounts, passion narratives though they are, are all unequivocally clear on the matter of Jesus' resurrection as witnessed historical fact (Matthew 28:1–20; Mark 16:1–8; Luke 24:1–53; John 20:1–21).

It is important that so many of these testimonies and records were written and circulated within the lifetime of people who had been "on the spot," and were therefore subject to verification by contemporaries of Jesus. These things were "not done in a corner," as Paul once put it to King Agrippa, a shrewd observer of all things Jewish and Christian (Acts 26:3, 26). The main events of Jesus' ministry were played out in a blaze of publicity: His baptism, miracles, teaching, death—and empty tomb. Let us look now at some of the main facts presented in the Gospels and Acts that are easier to ignore than to explain away.

### The Empty Tomb

First of all there is *the fact of the empty tomb*. This is very important. Within a few weeks of the Crucifixion the disciples were going around Jerusalem claiming that Jesus of Nazareth had risen from the dead. Now, if they had been lying or hallucinating or had merely seen a vision or had merely had an "experience" of Jesus in a spiritual way, then all the Jewish leaders would have needed to do was to have gone to the tomb (well known as belonging to Joseph of Arimathea), dragged out the body, and displayed it to the startled crowds. They could have hung it in chains outside the city walls and so they could have discredited the "new religion" from the start. But they clearly could not do it: the tomb was empty and the body gone, despite the guard of soldiers. They were frustrated and utterly helpless before the preaching of the apostles, and as A. M. Fairbairn put it long ago, the silence of the Jews is as eloquent as the speech of the Christians.[4]

Harris makes the point that of *itself* the empty tomb does

not give us the gospel of the Resurrection: "If a corpse were to go missing from a mortuary, the empty mortuary would be in itself no evidence of resurrection."[5] Indeed such a "wonder" could just as easily have been denounced as demonic as claimed to be divine. However, the interpretation assigned Jesus' empty grave is unanimous in the Scriptures, both before and after the burial. As Harris notes, divine action was at work in the raising of Jesus: the angel announced the empty tomb (Mark 16:6), the Scriptures predicted it (Luke 24:22–27), and a post-Resurrection Jesus demonstrated it—as the apostles often proclaimed, calling themselves witnesses of the risen Christ (Acts 2:32; 3:15; 4:20; 10:40–41; 13:30–31).[6]

Nevertheless, the empty tomb has an ordained purpose from the beginning as an integral part of the total witness to the Resurrection. After all, the stone was rolled away not to let Jesus *out* (John 20:19, 26), but to let others *in*.

### The Changed Disciples

Then there is the other fact, also indisputable: *the changed disciples*. Look at the state they had been in: they all fled from Jesus in Gethsemane, terrified by the sinister and implacable forces of the hour; Peter had denied Him outright. On the road to Emmaus we find two disciples trudging wearily from Jerusalem, their confidence shattered, their faith buried with the corpse of their Master (Luke 24:21). After the Crucifixion the disciples were to be found huddled together in an upper room, locked in for fear of the Jews (John 20:19).

Yet within a matter of weeks these same fearful, bankrupt people are standing around the very temple precincts and before the gathering crowds, preaching that Jesus is Lord, that He is risen from the dead, that the guilt of His death lies upon leaders and people, and that only by repentance and faith in Him as crucified for sins and risen from the dead can any— even in Israel—be saved.

Their boldness now is as noticeable as their cowardice was before: they are no sooner released from beating and imprisonment than they are preaching again (Acts 5:40–42); they are turning the world upside down and nothing can stop them. Such boldness is a fact that they themselves explain only in terms of the risen Christ and His outpoured Spirit. Moreover, what changed them not only formed the impetus for their own ministries, it formed the foundation of the churches they founded and the church that lives and grows still. In Harris' words: "It was not the Church that mothered the Resurrection; it was the Resurrection that mothered the Church."[7]

Much of their boldness came because, like others, they had been witnesses of the risen Christ. They were among a growing number of people—sane, able people, neither senile nor adolescent—who testified consistently that the risen Christ had appeared before them and shown them visibly the truth of His bodily resurrection. Whether breaking bread in Emmaus or eating fish in Galilee, the Jesus who met the disciples established the elements of intimacy and familiarity, no less than authority, to make His disciples unshakable witnesses to His resurrection.

## THE ALTERNATIVES TO BELIEF

Along another line of reasoning, we also may consider the unconvincing nature of the alternatives to belief in the Resurrection that are still put forward (none of them at all new). They almost prove the case by default.

### The "Swoon" Theory

There is, for instance, the *"swoon" theory*, which tells us that Jesus did not die on the cross and was alive in the tomb. We are asked to believe that after a Roman scourging (under which weak men died and strong men went mad), and after a Roman crucifixion with its agonies of dislocation and thirst and blood loss, and after a spear thrust into the side performed as a gesture to an already dead body (John 19:34), that Jesus of Nazareth calmly "came to" in the coolness of the tomb, took off His grave clothes, rolled back the great stone at the mouth of the tomb (that several healthy, untortured women could not do [Mark 16:3]), laid out a guard of brawny soldiers, and walked off into the sunrise.

As Michael Green puts it:

Jesus was very dead on Good Friday evening. He was certified as such by the experienced execution squad and their commanding officer, the centurion. Pilate recognized He was dead, before allowing His body to be removed: political agitators were dangerous commodities with fidgety Roman emperors getting worried about competition. But just to make sure, we are told that the soldiers were noticed sticking a spear into His side. And the eye-witness who records this says "blood and water" came out (John 19:34). He could not have known that he was bearing testimony to the strongest possible indication of death: the separation of blood into clot and serum. Had Jesus still been alive, bright spurts of arterial blood would have emerged from the wound. Jesus was unquestionably dead.[8]

John's testimony that blood and water issued out of the wound in Jesus' side has been explained in various ways. The flow of blood may have been from the heart itself and the great blood vessels adjacent to it, with the flow of water pouring out from the acutely dilated stomach. Or the phenomenon may have resulted from a hemorrhage in the pleural cavity between the ribs and lungs occasioned by the scouring Jesus had undergone; or there may have been a rupture of the heart under the unique sufferings of the hour, a hemorrhage leaking into the pericardial sac, where there occurred a clotting of the blood, separating it from the serum. In any case John's testimony is important, and offers no clear support to those who say, "Jesus must have still been alive because dead bodies don't bleed."

The swoon theory also utterly fails to account for the life-long change in the disciples. Frank Morrison makes a perceptive comment:

It is impossible that a being who had stolen half–dead out of the sepulchre, who crept about weak and ill, wanting medical treatment, who required bandaging, strengthening and indulgence, and who still at last yielded to His sufferings, could have given to the disciples the impression that He was a conqueror over death and the grave, the Prince of Life: an impression that lay at the bottom of their future ministry.[9]

### The "Wrong Tomb" Theory

Then there is the *"wrong tomb" theory.* According to this the women were mistaken in the dark of the early morning and went to the wrong cave-tomb. There they were met not by an angel, but by a gardener who happened to be up early and who said to them, "He is not here," presumably meaning, "He's not in this grave, you want the one further along on the left." Such a theory conveniently omits to finish the sentence that the angel spoke to the women, "He is not here; he has risen, just as he said. Come and see the place where he lay" (Matthew 28:6)

### Theories That the Body Was Removed or Stolen

Then again there is the *"removed body" theory.* The idea here is that the authorities—Roman or Jewish—had already removed the body secretly so that there could be no tampering with it. Of course the answer to that is quite simple. If the authorities knew where it was, they would have brought it out and told the crowds at Pentecost why the tomb was empty, and would thus straightway have destroyed the false gospel that was being preached.

There is also, of course, the *"stolen body" theory.* This is the idea that the disciples stole the body as the guards slept. Indeed Matthew reports that the soldiers were bribed to say just that (Matthew 28:11–15). However, can we really believe that terrified disciples, who had fled in Gethsemane and were huddled and locked away in the hours that followed for fear of the Jews, had come bold as brass to the tomb in the middle of the night to steal the corpse—and furthermore had rolled the great stone from the cave mouth without waking the sleeping guard of soldiers?

Furthermore, it's unlikely that trained and disciplined soldiers in a notorious trouble spot, guarding the grave of the latest popular Messiah figure, were going to take it easy and settle down to sleep for the night. The illogical explanation, "His disciples came by night and stole Him away *while we were asleep*" (how on earth could they know who had done what, or what had or had not happened, if they were fast asleep?), reduces the contemporary opposition to the Resurrection announcements to the level of farce and shows the desperate state of the Jewish authorities. Similarly, as an invention of the disciples it is incredible: "How stupid," comments Wenham, "having introduced the useful apologetic idea of a closely guarded tomb, to give a handle to the opposition by even hinting that the guards did not do their job!"[10]

## The Hallucination Theory

Most common, yet most flawed, is *the hallucination theory*. Here we are asked to believe that all the witnesses had hallucinations, even though they had no hope or expectation of such a miracle as Jesus' resurrection from the dead. It had not entered their minds, and when the disciples first heard it they did not believe it. Luke records that when the women told the apostles of the Resurrection and the angels at the empty tomb, "they did not believe [them], because their words seemed . . . like nonsense" (Luke 24:11). Moreover, Jesus appeared on one occasion to five hundred people (1 Corinthians 15:6)—did they all hallucinate at once? Green ably dispatches the "hallucination" theory when he asks:

> Can any theory of hallucination cover those appearances? Hallucinations tend to happen to particular types of people —no one type here. Hallucinations tend to be allied with wish fulfillment—none of that here. Hallucinations tend to recur. These appearances ended after forty days and never came again. Hallucinations belong to the sick world—and it is hard to maintain that there was anything sick about those early missionaries as they preached the full health and salvation that their risen Messiah brought them![11]

We should notice, too, how prominently conversation and discourse appear in the accounts. Jesus does not appear shimmering in silence, but as their familiar, touchable, hearable teacher who at lengths expounds the Scriptures concerning Himself (e.g., Luke 24:44–49) and addresses the disciples both corporately and individually (e.g., John 21:15–24). Perhaps the most decisive rebuttal of the hallucination theory comes from psychiatry itself, which has long held that the same hallucination cannot happen to two or more people: each person has his or her own hallucination. There are no group hallucinations, much less mass hallucinations![12] There cannot be, since there is no objective reality to produce a common experience. But here the eyewitness testimonies are multiple and detailed, and the same experience common to groups of two, twelve, and five hundred is closely described in terms of appearances, conversations, bodily actions, etc.

## THE ULTIMATE GROUND OF BELIEF

Yet when all is said, and all these evidences set forth, the greatest proof remains—*the identity of the one who said He would raise from the dead.* At the beginning of his gospel John makes it abundantly clear who we are dealing with. He was the eternal Word who was with the Father from all eternity (John 1:1–2); the second person of the Holy Trinity, the mighty God. When we realize this, the surprising thing is not that He rose, but that He died. It is not the Resurrection that is difficult to comprehend: it is *the Cross* that leaves us "lost in wonder, love and praise." It is no wonder that He defeated death; the wonder is that He should "taste death for everyone" (Hebrews 2:9), that He "died for our sins according to the Scriptures" (1 Corinthians 15:3). It is worth noting here that while the New Testament stresses the place and role of the Father in the Resurrection— "God raised him from the dead" (Acts 2:24)—the active part played by Jesus is not absent, and is important as being part of His own victory over the forces of darkness (see Mark 8:31; 9:9; John 10:17–18; Colossians 2:14–15).

We should note, too, His *promise* that He would rise again after His sufferings. Though His disciples were astonishingly slow in comprehending it, Jesus had told them quite clearly and repeatedly that He would both die and rise again:

> They were on their way up to Jerusalem, with Jesus leading the way, and the disciples were astonished, while those who followed were afraid. Again he took the Twelve aside and told them what was going to happen to him. "We are going up to Jerusalem," he said, "and the Son of Man will be betrayed to the chief priests and teachers of the law. They will condemn him to death and will hand him over to the

Gentiles, who will mock him and spit on him, flog him and kill him. Three days later he will rise." (Mark 10:32–4; cf. 8:31–33; 9:30–32)

It is unconvincing to explain away such sayings as inventions by the gospel writers. There had been other, more veiled warnings and predictions. In John 2:19 Jesus responds to His critics' challenge to Him, their demand for a sign that He has authority from God to drive the money changers out of the temple courts. Jesus replies: "Destroy this temple, and I will raise it again in three days." John adds: "The temple he had spoken of was his body" (John 2:21). This saying comes up again, in garbled form, at His trial, and is thus substantiated as an authentic saying even by His enemies. G. R. Beasley-Murray points out that even the more critical and liberal New Testament scholars accept its force.[13]

The Jewish leaders, by their callous misuse of the temple, are already destroying everything it stood for, but though they will go on to destroy Jesus too, He will bring an end both to the old covenant represented by the temple, and their abuse of it. Beasley-Murray writes: "the 'destruction' of the temple is completed in the destruction of the body of Jesus, and the building of the new temple takes place through the resurrection of Jesus," adding, "Note that the temple of the new age is Christ, not the Church" (cf. John 7:37–38 with Ezekiel 47:1–12).[14] Jesus replaces both Torah and temple by His resurrection.

In Matthew 12:38–42 (and parallels) Jesus refuses His critics the kind of sign they want from Him to prove His authority, "except the sign of the prophet Jonah." But unlike Jonah, Jesus was delivered by God from death, and not from a metaphorical death "in the belly of a huge fish," but from real and complete death "in the heart of the earth" (v. 40). "Grant the authenticity of v. 40," writes D. A. Carson, "and the only legitimate conclusion is that Jesus knew long in advance about His death, burial, and resurrection, and saw His life moving toward that climax; and the Christological implications must not be avoided."[15]

At this period Jesus' disciples neither understood the true meaning of His predictions nor realized the full, divine identity of the person who was uttering them. The Resurrection itself, and Jesus' post-Resurrection appearances to them, would change all that forever. However, there remains even before that event the question of the authority of these claims in *His* mouth. He could not lie (John 8:46; 18:37), and the Father would bring to pass all that He promised (John 10:14–18).

The only right and adequate response to all this is to believe the Christ of the Resurrection—and to worship Him in His risen glory, power, and significance. The early church did this. They met in His name, to sing His praise on "the first day of the week," setting aside that most sacred of Old Testament institutions, the Sabbath day, in favor of "the Lord's Day," the day when He who died for our sins rose for our justification. God in Christ Jesus His Son had done a new thing—greater by far than His acts of creation—He had met the problem of sin and overthrown the tyranny of death. Now His risen Son would be at the center of all Christian thanksgiving, the foundation of all Christian assurance.

## THE PRESENT CHALLENGE TO BELIEF

However, this glad assurance does not go unchallenged even in the church. The Christian is used to his or her faith coming under attack from the world. Many nonbelievers accept the idea of a "closed universe," where God is either irrelevant or nonexistent, though they often leave the evidence for the Resurrection unexamined. However, most harm is done and most hurt experienced when the faith of the Resurrection is attacked from within the church by its appointed teachers and leaders, or from within believers themselves by the doubts and fears that cluster so menacingly around the fact of death itself.

On the one hand, we face repeated attempts, sometimes by distinguished theologians, to "reinterpret" what are regarded as merely traditional, rather than clearly *revealed*, doctrines, leaving us with something evidently different from that good news in which the church leaders of the first century gloried. On the other hand, we ourselves face a daily encounter with doubt in a world where death seems absolute and life beyond death the merest dream.

We are often told today that Jesus can be alive to us in various ways quite apart from a "crude" material metamorphosis of His corpse; that His Easter influence and even His personality can be alive in the faith of Christians and in the world at large without the primitive magic of an empty tomb; that we really do not need the traditional understanding of a bodily resurrection. In different ways Easter faith is offered as a substitute for Easter fact.

Many people imagine that it is sophisticated and "modern" to spiritualize the Resurrection. But in fact the ancient world—both Greek and Oriental, philosophical and religious—was very adept at this. T. F. Torrance points out that the Hebrew culture was alone among the great cultures of the ancient world in resisting the sophisticated but fatal dualism that divided and distanced the spiritual realm from the realms of material, day-to-day reality. He shrewdly observes that "St. Paul would not have been mocked in Athens (Acts 17:32), nor have been thought mad by Festus (Acts 26:25) when he spoke about the resurrection of Jesus, had he not meant the resurrection of the whole man leaving behind an empty grave."[16]

From the beginning the Christian church set its face firmly against such an attempt to keep God in the world of religious "ideas" only. The two great Christian doctrines of the Virgin Birth and the bodily resurrection unite to show that God is not only not distant from His creation, but that He does not disdain to *act* upon His creation, engaging the natural with the supernatural, encountering it at every level, and more than encountering it—*assuming* it (the Incarnation) and *redeeming* it (the Resurrection) forever by union with Himself.

The philosophers of the heathen would scorn such a proclamation. For them redemption was definitely *from* the body, not *in* the body. The heathen world had learned to dismiss the body from its ideas about the dignity of man, and such "spirituality" often led to some surprisingly unspiritual behavior: flesh and the lusts of the flesh and the destiny of the flesh no longer mattered; sin and death had lost their real significance. In contrast to this, the Christian doctrine of man is that a man's body is part of his total personality, an integral feature of his personal being in its fullness; that to abuse or to despise the body God made is to dishonor the God who made it; and that the body has both significance for God and a destiny within God.

It was in conscious resistance to so much heathen "spirituality" that the early Christian leaders insisted on the material,
physical fact of Jesus' resurrection. Their whole doctrine of the
resurrection of the body (both Christ's and ours), like their doctrines of creation, the virgin birth of Jesus, the body as the temple of the Holy Spirit, the call for compassion to the sick, the
poor and the maimed, showed the pagan world that God was
concerned with man in his entirety, in the concrete form of his
bodily existence as well as in his spiritual aspect, and had a destiny for him in this regard. Paul wrote 1 Corinthians 15 precisely in order to combat and destroy a sophisticated but false
version of the Christian doctrine of resurrection, one that did
not *need* a miraculous transformation of the body and was content to leave it moldering in the grave, with no place or part in
God's redemptive plan and Christ's redemptive work.

Paul saw clearly enough, even if some modern theologians
have not, that latent in his and his peers' witness to the bodily
and historical fact of Christ's resurrection "lay embedded the
argument that," as Torrance puts it, "if the resurrection of Jesus
is not actual and historical reality, then the powers of sin and
death and non-being remain unconquered and unbroken and
we are still in the bondage of death."[17] The gospel of the empty
tomb, however, proclaims "that Jesus arose in body, arose as
very man in the fullness and integrity of His human nature, but
human nature that through the Spirit of holiness had been
stripped of corroding forces of corruption and clad in the
incorruptible garment of deathlessness."[18] And this is gospel
(good news) to us because

> Christ has indeed been raised from the dead, the firstfruits
> of those who have fallen asleep. For since death came
> through a man, the resurrection of the dead comes also
> through a man. For as in Adam all die, so in Christ all will
> be made alive. But each in his own turn: Christ, the first-
> fruits; then, when he comes, those who belong to him. (1 Co-
> rinthians 15:20–23)

# 25

# UNDERSTANDING THE RESURRECTION

The bodily resurrection of Jesus Christ from the dead altered everything—both for Him and for us. Jesus' resurrection from the dead was "not merely a great event upon the plane of history, but an act that breaks into history with the powers of another world. It is akin to the creation in the beginning; and the Gospel is the good news that God is creating a new world."[1]

## A NEW, GLORIFIED BODY

The Resurrection does not simply mean that Jesus is alive, but that He is alive in a certain way, a way that has particular implications for us all. He is alive not in spirit only, but in His glorified body; alive in the fullness of His humanity. His bodily resurrection meant the end of a long era during which death reigned over all, the reversal of a process that had been inexorable since the Fall. Christ's resurrection signifies now and for all time the redemption of man in the body, from sickness, pain, and death. On this T. F. Torrance writes:

Resurrection as redemption means the restoration of man in all the fullness of his humanity, for it is redemption out of corruption and the lapse toward annihilation into the new being and new life of the new creation. That is why the early Church laid such emphasis upon the resurrection of the flesh, for it meant the redemption of man's perishable form of existence.[2]

We are to be redeemed precisely in that area of our lives that is dear to us and yet brings our greatest grief and trial: the body. Here lie our indwelling lusts, the source of much pain and weakness and the scene of our final failure—a death it cannot escape. Over our entire earthly and physical struggle and apparent defeat the gospel of the Resurrection enables Paul to cry defiantly: "we know that if the earthly tent we live in is destroyed, we have a building from God, an eternal house in heaven, not built by human hands" (2 Corinthians 5:1).

## FOUR IMPLICATIONS OF THE RESURRECTION

As we come to look more closely at the effects and implications of the Resurrection we must begin with its effect upon Jesus Himself, not only how it rewarded Him personally for His obedience unto death (Philippians 2:8), but also how it enabled Him to exercise His blood-bought right and to save men and women for whom He died (Matthew 28:18–20).

First, we must understand that *the Resurrection transformed the incarnate state of Jesus Himself.* The Resurrection profoundly altered our Lord's existence as the Mediator, the God-man. In the days of His flesh He had lived in an "emptied," beggared condition (Philippians 2:7, RSV), "in the likeness of sinful man" (Romans 8:3), sharing with us the weakness, pain, and mortality of our present fallen state "in the flesh." At the Resurrection, however, all that came to an end. There and then He who was "a descendant of David" was "appointed" or "constituted" ("declared" in NIV; or "designated" in RSV), for the first time and forevermore, the "Son of God in power" (Romans 1:3–4, RSV). The sonship spoken of here is not, of course, our Lord's deity simply considered, but His incarnate state which, at the Resurrection, passed from a state of weakness to one of power; from a fleshly, dependent, frail existence to a new mode of being, one free from old limitations and vulnerability.

It is precisely here that the story of Jesus is a gospel for us all (Romans 1:1), since He now lives as the Mediator to share with us His new life, a new life that He has won for us by His sufferings and death. Christ's resurrection therefore marked what John Murray calls "a new phase of His messianic lordship."[3] He came to be Lord at His resurrection in a way in which He had not been before. His entire humanity became conditioned by spiritual powers, He was constituted Son of God in power "through the Spirit" (Romans 1:4). It is precisely because He Himself, in His risen humanity, is so pervasively conditioned by the Spirit of God that He can effectively convey to us the saving power, the grace of God that He has won for us.

Paul indicates both Christ's work and His way of working when he says to the Corinthians of the risen Jesus, "the last Adam became a life-giving spirit" (1 Corinthians 15:45, RSV). R. B. Gaffin argues that "spirit" here refers to the activity of the Holy Spirit and should be written with a capital S, and that it is clear from the context that the title "the last Adam" refers particularly to Christ in His risen state.[4] Both of these conclusions are supported by Paul's words in 2 Corinthians 3:17: "Now the Lord is the Spirit, and where the Spirit of the Lord is, there is freedom." This, argues Gaffin, refers to the risen Christ working by His outpoured Spirit, changing His church and its people "from one degree of glory to another" (v. 18, RSV). For Paul the connection between the ascended Christ and the commissioned Spirit is so close that he can say, this "comes from the Lord, who is the Spirit" (v. 18). By His Spirit the risen Christ becomes the life-giving Head ("the last Adam") of a people, He and the Holy Spirit working so closely together that there is what Gaffin calls "a functional, dynamic identity"[5] between the two.

Secondly, we must understand that *the Resurrection vindicated all the claims Jesus made for Himself*. We saw earlier how much Jesus said and how much He claimed: words came from His lips that would have been blasphemous from anyone else's; He made claims for Himself that suggested either a divine being, a callous cynic, or a hopeless lunatic. He spoke and acted with a dignity unborrowed, forgave sins in His own name, presented Himself as the center of His own gospel, announced that He would give His flesh for the life of the world, His life a ransom for many. Finally, He predicted that on the third day He would rise from the dead to take His place at the right hand of God.

It had seemed that He was indeed accredited by God through His miracles, wonders, and signs (Acts 2:22), but that

accreditation had appeared to have been reversed by the hor-
rors of the Cross, for a person "hanged on a tree" was the object
of a divine curse (Deuteronomy 21:22–23). "But the Resurrection," writes Murray Harris, "was the great divine reversal. The
same one who had once declared 'a hanged man is accursed'
(Deut. 21:23) now declared 'this hanged man is accepted' (cf.
Acts 3:14–15). He whom man rejected, God accepted and
installed as His Messiah."[6]

Similarly, in His ministry Jesus had claimed a unique relationship with God in which God was His Father in an utterly
unique way (Matthew 11:27) and He Himself was the Son as no
other could ever be (Mark 12:6; 13:32; John 5:17–27). The Cross
had seemed to be God's disowning of Him—and in truth He
had suffered the desertion of the disowned (Matthew
27:43–46)—but the Resurrection was God's owning of Him
before heaven, earth, and hell. More than at the baptism in the
Jordan, more than on the mount of transfiguration, it was on
the first Easter Sunday morning that the Father finally and
fully proclaimed: "This is my Son whom I love; with him I am
well pleased." In that great event He, as it were, said publicly to
the Christ: "You are my Son; today I have become your Father"
(Acts 13:33).

This is a major emphasis of the apostolic preaching. "God
raised Him up" is the constant cry of the apostles (Acts 2:24, 32,
36; 3:13, 15; Romans 10:9; 1 Corinthians 6:14; 15:15; Galatians
1:1; 1 Peter 1:21). It was a necessary emphasis also. For while it
is true that the resurrection of Christ is the work of the whole
Godhead, Father, Son, and Holy Spirit (John 10:17, 18; Romans
1:4; 8:9–11), it was very necessary for Peter and the apostles to
stress that the Resurrection was not an independent, unilateral
act of Jesus, a wonder He performed merely out of His own
remarkable powers. If that had been so, it could have been
slandered as simply "demonic" (cf. Matthew 12:24). But as it
was the Father Himself who was the chief worker of the Resurrection, all criticism was silenced. God Himself had set His seal
to it all.

If Jesus had been a well-meaning fanatic, or a callous fraud,
the silence of the Father would have buried Him in oblivion.
But, as Harris puts it, "What Jesus had always been, although

in hidden form, the Resurrection openly declared Him to be, viz. the Son of God."[7] He who had been Son-of-God-in-weakness had now become Son-of-God-in-power (Romans 1:3–4; Matthew 28:18) by His resurrection from the dead. One final witness of that risen state, surrounded by a light from heaven on the Damascus road, saw the glory of God in the face of the risen Christ and became the adoring servant of the one whom he had despised (Acts 9:3; 1 Corinthians 15:8; 2 Corinthians 4:6; 1 Timothy 1:12–17).

Thirdly, *the Resurrection signified Jesus' complete success.* The Father raised the Son from the dead not only because He was the Son, but also because He had fulfilled His mission, completed His work and finished His sacrifice of atonement. It was not simply as the Son that He was raised, but as Mediator. The whole point of the Son's coming was to be the representative of His people. As their representative He did everything in a public capacity—as a public person and not merely a private one. He was truly "the last Adam," "the second man" (1 Corinthians 15:45, 47). Hence in His death on the cross for sinners He was treated by His Father as the representative for every one of the people of God in all ages. In that capacity the punishment due to all our sins and all our sinfulness was poured out upon Him; He in His own self "bore our sins in his body on the tree" (1 Peter 2:24).

That work was done not for some of our sins, but for all of them. God is able to forgive any sins because all sin has been paid for. Can we be sure of that? It is precisely the resurrection of Christ that assures us of such confidence. As the one who stood in our place, assuming personal responsibility for our sin, Jesus must have remained under the power of death if anything of the claims of justice had not been met then. However, His freedom from death, sin's penalty (Genesis 2:17; Romans 6:23), proclaims that the price has been paid, sin borne and borne away (Leviticus 16:15, 20–22), a complete atonement for sin offered and accepted. Torrance writes:

> If the death of Jesus on the Cross is to be regarded as the sentence of divine judgment inflicted on Him for our sakes, and on us in Him, the resurrection is to be regarded as the

obverse of that, itself the sentence and judgment of God . . .
the justification of Christ following His condemnation in
our place. . . . Hence, on the one hand, the resurrection of
Christ attests God's own approbation of what He had done
. . . and, on the other hand, the resurrection attests the fact
that through the sacrifice of Christ sin has been blotted out
and man's life has been placed on a new basis (Romans
4:25). . . . The resurrection is God's great act of *Amen* to the
Cross . . . the Father's *Amen* to Christ's high priestly self-
offering in obedience and sacrifice for sin.[8]

This gives us further insight into Peter's words on the day of
Pentecost, "But God raised him from the dead, freeing him
from the agony of death, because it was impossible for death to
keep its hold on him" (Acts 2:24). While it would have been
impossible for a just God to release Him if a full atonement for
sin had not been made, it was equally impossible for a just God
*not* to release Him after God's demands had been fully met. It
was "not possible," not because of Christ's own power or even
God's power simply considered, but because of God's justice. It
was not possible that He should be held under death, the penalty for sin, when He had borne all sins away and fully atoned for
sin. It was not possible that the Resurrection should *not* take
place. His resurrection was inevitable given the justice of God.
The atonement ensured the Resurrection quite as much as the
Resurrection validated the atonement.

The epistle to the Hebrews, which has so much to say about
the atoning death of Christ and its continuing significance and
power, indicates this when it speaks of Christ being "crowned
with glory and honor *because* he suffered death" and when it
speaks of the God of peace who "through the blood of the eternal covenant brought back from the dead our Lord Jesus"
(Hebrews 2:9, emphasis added; 13:20). Thus, the Hebrews
author concludes: "when Christ had offered for all time a single
sacrifice for sins, he sat down at the right hand of God. . . . For
by a single offering he has perfected for all time those who are
sanctified" (Hebrews 10:12, 14, RSV). We can see from such
texts the importance of A. M. Ramsey's words:

The Crucifixion is not a defeat needing Resurrection to reverse it, but a victory which the Resurrection quickly follows and seals. . . . So it is that the centre of Apostolic Christianity is Crucifixion-Resurrection; not Crucifixion alone nor Resurrection alone, nor even Crucifixion and Resurrection as the finale, but the blending of the two in a way that is as real to the Gospel as it is defiant to the world.[9]

Fourthly, *Jesus' resurrection is the pledge and power of our own resurrection.* Christ's resurrection is both the promise and the beginning of our own. In 1 Corinthians 15 Paul illustrates this by recalling the Old Testament ceremony of the firstfruits at harvest time, and further illumines the concept by use of two titles, "the firstborn from the dead" and "the last Adam." Christ's resurrection is not simply the *promise* of our own, it is actually and in itself the *beginning* of our own! G. C. Berkouwer observes:

The very fact that Christ is the "first–fruits" signifies what His resurrection implies. It is not just an isolated remarkable event, but a beginning, a foundation, a pledge, and a guarantee. It could be preached and had to be preached in order to bring out its implications so that it would provide a solid foundation for the hope and expectation of a blessed future.[10]

This is precisely where Christian joy and confidence have their source. When Paul describes Christ in His resurrection as "the firstfruits of those who have fallen asleep" (1 Corinthians 15:20), he means us to understand that firstfruits are actually part of the ensuing harvest, and Paul's point is that there is an organic connection and unity between the firstfruits and the rest of the harvest; the one is inseparable from the other. So with our Lord's resurrection and our own, His is not only prior to ours but ours is part of His. As Gaffin puts it:

His resurrection is the representative beginning of the resurrection of believers. In other words, the term "first–fruits" seems deliberately chosen to make evident the organic con-

nection between the two resurrections. . . . On the basis of
this verse (I Corinthians 15:20) it can be said that Paul
views the two resurrections not so much as two events but
as two episodes of the same event.[11]

The same truth is expressed in two of the titles given to
Jesus in the New Testament. Herman Ridderbos connects the
titles "the firstborn from the dead" and "the last Adam," and
sees them as providing what he terms one of the "fundamental
structures" of New Testament Christology.[12] He reasons that
the significance of Christ's own resurrection and its future outworking derives from the special character of His death. Because His death was uniquely redemptive His resurrection will
be cosmically effective, a new beginning in Him for the whole
people of God: In Christ's resurrection "the time of salvation
promised in him . . . dawns in an overwhelming manner as a
decisive transition from the old to the new world (2 Corinthians 5:17; cf. v. 15)."[13] Ridderbos concludes that Jesus, as firstborn from the dead "ushers in the world of the resurrection."
As "the last Adam" Jesus becomes "the Inaugurator of the new
humanity."[14]

Involved in this is the limitless power of God in Christ: a
power bought in weakness but endowed without limitation
(Matthew 28:18). The power that will raise our bodies immortal at the Last Day is variously called the power of Christ Himself, the Spirit's power, the Father's power. Of the first Paul
speaks when he writes to the Philippians of "the Lord Jesus
Christ, who, by the power that enables him to bring everything
under his control, will transform our lowly bodies so that they
will be like his glorious body" (Philippians 3:20–21). Of the second he writes to the Romans: "If the Spirit of him who raised
Jesus from the dead is living in you, he who raised Christ from
the dead will also give life to your mortal bodies through his
Spirit, who lives in you" (Romans 8:11). Of the third, he writes
to the Corinthians: "By his power God raised the Lord from the
dead, and he will raise us also" (1 Corinthians 6:14), and: "the
one who raised the Lord Jesus from the dead will also raise us
with Jesus and present us with you into his presence" (2 Corinthians 4:14).

What is common to all these statements is that the power of the bodily resurrection of all believers is closely connected with the power of Christ's own resurrection. Christ's resurrection and that of His people form an unbreakable unity—indeed are really two parts of the same crucial and definitive event (as Gaffin notes above). That is why our resurrection is a sure and certain hope.

Paul's words in 1 Corinthians 15:25–26 give us a very particular insight into this. In the context of Christ's bodily resurrection from the dead as "the firstfruits of those who have fallen asleep" (v. 20), he writes that Christ must reign over fallen world history—with all its chaos and cruelty, futility and failure —"until he has put all his enemies under his feet" (v. 25). He then states that "The last enemy to be destroyed is death" (v. 26). It is clear that he is not talking about life after death in general, since death is already "brought to nought" (to use C. K. Barrett's translation of the word *destroyed*)[15] for those who "depart and are with Christ." Rather the apostle is describing one future, decisive hour in which death will finally be neutralized for the people of Christ. It is clear from verses 20–23 that he has in mind a general resurrection of bodies, the outflow from and consequence of Christ's own resurrection: "For since death came through a man, the resurrection of the dead comes also through a man" (v. 21).

When therefore Paul says that Christ will "put all his enemies under his feet" and that "the last enemy to be destroyed is death," he clearly means to tell us that death is not so much our enemy as *His* enemy. Inasmuch as He has paid for our sins, death now has no more rights over us; rather *He* has rights now over death. In the final dispute between Christ and death it is Christ who must emerge victorious, for He has both power and right on His side. He will not allow His work at Calvary to be bypassed or to go for nought. Rather, death itself will go for nought in His appointed time. The risen Christ lives to affirm the full worth of His atonement for sin and to bring us to a full and glorious reconciliation. Death is the contradiction of all this and so must be destroyed—in our life as it was in His. And He will do it for each of us, for God "has put everything under his feet" (1 Corinthians 15:27) and has given Him power to "bring everything under his control" (Philippians 3:21).

The resurrection of Jesus is for us all the historical, public, and unbreakable guarantee given by God the Father of our own destiny and future glory (1 Corinthians 15:20–23). Our share in that great event, which has already begun, will continue until we "put on immortality" (v. 53, RSV), bearing the image of Christ, "the man from heaven" (v. 48). What He was in His own resurrection we shall be in ours: His resurrection body is the pattern of our own. He was not subject to the limitations of time and space (Luke 24:31, 36; John 20:19), neither shall we be (1 Corinthians 15:40–44). His glorified body, though real and no mere phantom (Luke 24:39–43), will never again know weakness, suffering, or death (Acts 13:34), and neither shall ours (Revelation 21:4; 1 Corinthians 15:53–56). His body was glorious (though the glory was at first veiled; cf. Luke 24:15–16 with Revelation 1:12–16), and so will our resurrection bodies be glorious—breathtakingly so (1 Corinthians 15:35–42). That is why John says in his first epistle: "Dear friends, now we are children of God, and what we will be has not yet been made known. But we know that when he appears, we shall be like him, for we shall see him as he is" (1 John 3:2).

In the bodily resurrection of Jesus Christ from the dead on the first Easter Sunday, therefore, we have in principle the resurrection of the entire church of God. The tremendous power that opens the graves on the Last Day and raises up from sea and land countless glorified bodies will be solely the power of His resurrection. The massed array of all the saints who will stand ranged alongside Christ at His judgment, complete and fully redeemed in their risen glorified bodies, will be but the consummated effect of that decisive event.

# 26

# ENTERING
# THE RESURRECTION

Christianity is an experimental faith. This does not mean that it is to be tentatively tried, like an experiment in the chemistry lab, but that it is to be personally experienced as understanding, encounter, and commitment to a person who has already committed Himself to us. Jesus Christ, the living, loving Lord, is to be met in the gospel, encountered in its preaching, and experienced in the life of faith.

This is the beating heart of Christian faith, without which we have only a creed, formal and cold in our mouths. One of the old "experimental" Puritans, Thomas Jacomb, once wrote:

> Take heed of looking no farther than merely a Christ sent. . . . Everyone knows there is a two-fold sending of Him . . . the first was Christ's sending to be man . . . the second is Christ's sending *into* man. . . . A Christ in our flesh must be accompanied with a Christ in our hearts; there must be not only a Christ sent to us but also a Christ sent into us or He will not profit us.[1]

Here we have echoes of a passage by John Calvin:

> We must understand that as long as Christ remains outside of us, and we are separated from Him, all that He has suffered and done for the salvation of the human race remains useless and of no value for us . . . all that He possesses is nothing to us until we grow into one body with Him.[2]

And this Christ Himself achieves: "But He unites Himself to us by the Spirit alone,"[3] who in turn works in us the gift of faith.[4]

It is this which makes Christian belief a living experience and not a dead loyalty. Jesus is not only the central figure in the history of the gospel, nor is He only central to any understanding of the gospel, He is also central in any *experience* of its saving, liberating, changing power. Indeed He *is* the gospel, since it is good news *about* Him (Mark 1:1), the call of God *to* Him (2 Corinthians 5:18–20), and the experience of God's love, grace, and power *in* Him (1 Peter 1:3–9). He gathers up into Himself every Old and New Testament promise about knowing God and sharing in His blessings: in Him all the promises of God find their fulfillment and touch us with their eternal blessing (2 Corinthians 1:20) as He works in us by His Spirit (2 Corinthians 1:21–22).

Three ways in which this is expressed in the New Testament are John's phrase "born of God" and Paul's phrases "raised with Christ" and "[to] attain the resurrection from the dead." In fact these become one and the same thing in the New Testament economy. (A fourth is Paul's seminal term "in Christ," but we have already examined this, together with the title "the last Adam.")

## "BORN AGAIN,"
## "BORN FROM ABOVE," "BORN OF GOD"

Jesus met the tentative inquiry of a distinguished Jewish leader and teacher named Nicodemus with the uncompromising announcement: "I tell you the truth, no one can see the kingdom of God unless he is born again" (John 3:3).

The growing Old Testament hope concerning the coming kingdom of God involved the expectation of a joyful participation in it by His people. This grew into focus as a share in the Resurrection at "the end of the . . . days" (Daniel 12:13), when "those who are wise will shine like the brightness of the heavens, and those who lead many to righteousness, like the stars for ever and ever" (Daniel 12:3).

Jews such as Nicodemus therefore looked forward to participating in the kingdom of God at the end of the age, in the resurrection. Elsewhere this is called "the renewal of all things" (Matthew 19:28). However, Jesus' startling message is that the kingdom of God has already been inaugurated in His own person, works, and message, and that "what is required is the regeneration of the individual *before* the end of the world and *in order to enter* the kingdom."[5]

Jesus puts this to Nicodemus in both new and old ways. His famous words, "You must be born again" (John 3:7, cf. 3, 5, 6), as many commentators agree, are better translated, "You must be born *from above*." This is what the Greek word *anōthen* means elsewhere in John (e.g., 3:31; 19:11, 23). Moreover, when John in his writings speaks of spiritual birth it is always in terms of its divine origin, i.e. from God (John 1:13; 1 John 2:29; 3:9; 4:7; 5:18). His emphasis is on direction ("from above"), not repetition ("born over again"). A man's earthly birth disqualifies him from the start ("That which is born of the flesh is flesh," John 3:6, RSV), and he needs a different life, from God, from above ("that which is born of the Spirit," v. 6, RSV). Man, fallen and fragile as he is, needs the Spirit of God to give him a radical new nature, a new identity, and thus a definitive new beginning.

The Spirit's work, says Jesus, is essential if a man is to see or enter the kingdom of God (vv. 3, 5). Yet the Spirit, in His activity and His effects is, like the wind, beyond the control or understanding of man (v. 8), so that man is revealed in his helplessness (vv. 4, 7, 10–12) and God is revealed in His grace (vv. 5, 8, 11–13; 6:63). As a teacher of Israel (v. 10), Nicodemus should have known this from Old Testament prophecy concerning the kingdom and its basic theology of grace. Jesus' reference to being born of water and the Spirit (v. 5) is probably an allusion to Ezekiel 36:25–27, where God promises:

> "I will sprinkle clean water on you, and you will be clean . . . from all your impurities. . . . I will give you a new heart and put a new spirit in you; I will remove from you your heart of stone and give you a heart of flesh. And I will put my Spirit in you . . ."

D. A. Carson responds to an obvious difficulty here. There are those who have argued that John is putting into the mouth of Jesus statements that are "hopelessly anachronistic," since John himself is aware that as yet "the Spirit had not been given" in His full New Testament measure "since Jesus was not yet glorified" (John 7:39). It is as the Spirit of the risen Lord, the glorified Son of God, that He will effect this new birth. Carson argues, however, that the tension here in John "is no different from the corresponding Synoptic tension as to when the kingdom dawns," and observes:

> That is why *all* discipleship in all four Gospels is inevitably transitional. The coming-to-faith of the first followers of Jesus was in certain respects unique; they *could not* instantly become "Christians" in the full-orbed sense, and experience the full sweep of the new birth, until *after* the resurrection and glorification of Jesus.[6]

John himself will make the connection between the glorification of the risen Jesus and the pouring out of the Spirit abundantly clear in the later chapters of his gospel (e.g., John 14–16).

The Spirit whom Christ pours out comes from Him, from within His unique and crucial mediatorial work. It is His Spirit, and the Spirit communicates His life in its risen and heavenly and eternal character. This is the link between John's "born from above" and "born of God," and Paul's "risen with Christ," and the apostle Peter brings the two together when he writes: "Praise be to the God and Father of our Lord Jesus Christ! In his great mercy he has given us new birth into a living hope through the resurrection of Jesus Christ from the dead" (1 Peter 1:3).

## RISEN WITH CHRIST

In the apostle Paul's writings, the entire doctrine of the Christian life is conditioned by this central and fundamental truth: Salvation consists of being united with the risen Lord Jesus Christ. The whole of the Christian life, from its first beginnings to its full and final glory, can be defined in this way. Paul urges the Colossian Christians to see themselves and their present lives in this perspective:

Since, then, you have been raised with Christ, set your hearts on things above. . . . Set your minds on things above, not on earthly things. For you died, and your life is now hidden with Christ in God. When Christ, who is your life, appears, then you also will appear with him in glory. (Colossians 3:1–3)

Similarly he reminds his Ephesian readers: "And you he made alive, when you were dead through the trespasses and sins in which you once walked," and he describes their (and his) new life as being vitally linked with the risen Christ: "But God . . . made us alive together with Christ . . . and raised us up with him" (Ephesians 2:1, 4–6, RSV).

Andrew T. Lincoln considers this concept as it occurs in Ephesians and elsewhere, and emphasizes its crucial objective basis: "When Paul used the language of dying and rising with Christ in Romans 6 and Colossians 2 and 3, he had in view not primarily some subjective religious experience on the part of believers but rather thought of believers as having been Christ's partners in the events of past redemptive history."[7] What God accomplished for Christ at the Resurrection He accomplished for Him as the representative, the head of a new humanity; believers are seen "as included in Christ" so that "What God did for Christ He did at the same time for believers."[8]

This, however, is not a concept which operates only in the world of ideas, but is a fact in space-time history which radically affects the believer's life in the present. For Paul, Lincoln writes:

Christ's death was a death to the old order, to the powers of this age including sin, and His resurrection was a coming alive to a new order in which He functioned as Lord with the power of God. Christ's death and resurrection changed the power structures in history. For believers to have died and been raised with Christ was the equivalent of having been transferred from the old dominion to the new, because in God's sight they had been included in what had happened in Christ . . . they have been assigned to the new reality introduced by Christ's resurrection.[9]

Paul is well aware that although under new ownership and enjoying new life and power in a new existence, the Christian believer still has to live and work in a fallen world, pressured and tempted by the old order. There is conflict on earth even for those who are seated in the heavenly places in Christ Jesus, who are called to "lead a life worthy" of their high calling (Ephesians 4:1); to "be imitators of God, as dearly loved children" (Ephesians 5:1); to renounce their old ways of life (Ephesians 5:3–14); and in fact to assert their new existence and identity even in the midst of the old order: "Put off your old self ... and ... put on the new self, created to be like God in true righteousness and holiness" (Ephesians 4:22, 24). It is true that the definitive work has already been done, but, as Lincoln puts it, believers must "continue to live out its significance by giving up on that old person that they no longer are. They are new people who must become in practice what God has already made them, and that involves the resolve to put off the old way of life as it attempts to impinge."[10]

Moreover, all this is not only formally true of us, but is vitally true in us. Our connection with the risen Christ is real not only in the mind of God, but in the lives of believers. And it is so from the beginning of the spiritual life; there the Holy Spirit unites the sinner on earth to the Savior in heaven. The life of the new birth is no independent life created by the Spirit, but the life of the risen Christ, destined to develop into His risen glory. It is this life which is at work within us now, the shared life of Christ, a life which is not simply a good example, but a mighty power (Ephesians 1:19–20). According to the Pauline ethic, it is out of such a vital connection with the risen Christ that lives of good works, reconciliation, and godliness flow.

This is explained more comprehensively in Paul's letter to the Romans. In Romans 6 Paul defends his doctrine of unmerited grace against abuse by reminding his readers that they have been crucially, definitively united with the risen Christ, sharing the victory of His death and His freedom from the powers of darkness and the grip of sin:

Don't you know that all of us who were baptized into Christ Jesus were baptized into his death? We were therefore

buried with him through baptism into death in order that,
just as Christ was raised from the dead through the glory of
the Father, we too may live a new life. (Romans 6:3–4)

Christian baptism signifies a remarkable union, achieved
by the Holy Spirit, between believers and their Lord. It is remarkable most of all for its closeness. Christ and His people are
said to be so much one that they share His past, His present,
and His future: His victory at the cross, His present life, and
His future glory.

A crucial statement for our understanding of this is made
by Paul in verse 10: "The death he died, *he died to sin* once for
all; but the life he lives, he lives to God" (emphasis added).
Here, says Herman Ridderbos, the thought is not that Christ
died "for the sake of" or "for the atonement of" sin (in the sense
of justification or reconciliation), but that He died to sin "considered as an authority that exercises power, asserts its claims."[11]

On the cross Jesus represented us, submitted to the law of
God against sin, paid its penalties, suffered its sanctions, and
took upon Himself the full weight of sin. But having done so
once for all, He has now, by His resurrection, entered into freedom from the law of sin and death. And this is the freedom we
enter by the new birth signified in baptism: the freedom to "live
a new life" (Romans 6:4).

This is the freedom we enter into when we are united to
Christ. We are free from the rule and power of sin as *He* is free
from the rule and power of sin (vv. 6–7). Sin cannot have dominion over *us* any more than it can have dominion over Him
(v. 14). We share His freedom from the powers that once over-
took Him and held Him as the representative sinner, but which
failed to hang on to their prize who "put away sin by the sacrifice of himself" (Hebrews 9:26, RSV). Henceforth, says Paul, we
are free from sin as a slave-owner who possesses us (Romans
6:16–22) and as a law which compels us (Romans 8:2–3). Henceforth our lives are to be conditioned by Christ, who is our life
and who lives in us as we live in Him (Galatians 2:20).

## THE SOURCE OF A TRUE CHRISTIAN ETHIC

All this has social as well as personal implications; implications for the Christian in his or her society, even in its present state. Oliver O'Donovan argues that a true Christian ethic stems directly from the bodily resurrection of Christ.[12] Through that event we now can see the divinely ordered significance of creation, its place in redemption, and the unity of a natural ethic and one revealed in the gospel. The Christian's participation in Christ does not mean a complete divorce from this world and its institutions. We who are seated with Christ in the heavenly places are also to be salt and light in the earthly places—which most truly belong to God, even now. There we are to uncover and foster the good that remains in the world of the Fall. Our ethics should make sense in the world on weekdays as well as in church on Sundays. There is a correspondence and overlap between much of what is recognized as "good" by the natural man in his conscience and what is recognized as good by the Christian from within his or her spiritual understanding. To that too we can appeal as we confront the consciences of those around us.

Properly understood, heaven and earth are *one* creation: Christ's atonement sanctifies both (Colossians 1:20) and the power of His resurrection will renew both. O'Donovan writes:

> We are driven to concentrate on the resurrection as our starting-point because it tells us of God's vindication of His creation, and so of our created life. Just so does 1 Peter, the most consistently theological New Testament treatise on ethics, begin by proclaiming the reality of the new life upon which the very possibility of ethics depends: "By His great mercy we have been born anew to a living hope through the resurrection of Jesus Christ from the dead" (1:3).[13]

It is in the power of that event, of our present as well as future share in Christ's Easter life, that we can live in moral understanding and obedience, no longer "under law" as children, but "in law" to Christ: morally aware, ethically mature, having "the mind of Christ," able to discern what is good and what is evil. At the Cross God "condemned sin in sinful man" (Romans 8:3), judging fully the negative elements that had corrupted the old order. Yet He did not condemn the old order itself, but laid the basis for its redemption and transformation in the death and resurrection of Jesus. O'Donovan concludes from this fact:

> So it is that Christian ethics, too, looks both backwards and forwards, to the origin and to the end of the created order. It respects the natural structures of life in the world, while looking forward to their transformation. This can be seen, for example, in the First Epistle of Peter, which starts with a general characterization of the Christian life in terms of "hope" which is set "fully upon the grace that is coming to you at the revelation of Jesus Christ," and then elaborates a special ethics in terms of respectful submission "for the Lord's sake" to every institution of human life, especially the institutions of government, labour and marriage (1 Peter 1:13; 2:13 ff.).[14]

In such societies as Peter's readers lived in, and as we now live in twenty centuries later, we see much that challenges us to protest, to denunciation and to corrective action. But our attitude is not to degenerate into a hatred of the world and its necessary structures, any more than it is to evaporate into a weary conformity to its distortions. O'Donovan shows a middle way:

> Man's life on earth is important to God; he has given it its order; it matters that it should conform to the order he has given it. Once we have grasped that, we can understand too how this order requires of us both a denial of all that threatens to become disordered and a progress towards a life which goes beyond this order without negating it.[15]

Perhaps this means that we can have the theology of a John Calvin *and* the social concern of a Mother Teresa.

There is a third phrase which demands particular attention here: Paul's phrase "[to] attain to the resurrection from the dead" (Philippians 3:11).

## ATTAINING THE
## RESURRECTION FROM THE DEAD

While we share in the life and power of Christ's resurrection now, this participation has not yet reached its fullness. It is partial and provisional. We share a resurrected life, yet we still die; we are free from sin and death as law, yet not from either sin or death as realities; we boast in the power of the risen Christ but also in the earthly weakness, which is its counterpoint and setting (2 Corinthians 12:9). Because of this our experience of the power of His resurrection is dynamic, not static; an ongoing thing, and one which is going on to a glorious and God-given goal: the resurrection of the dead in the full and final glory of Christ's second coming.

Paul repeatedly links our present and future participation in Christ's resurrection in this way. He encourages the Roman believers:

> But if Christ is in you, your body is dead [destined to die] because of sin, yet your spirit is alive because of righteousness. And if the Spirit of him who raised Jesus from the dead is living in you, he who raised Christ from the dead will also give life to your mortal bodies through his Spirit, who lives in you. (Romans 8:10–11)

He expresses his own longing for this final phase of participation in the resurrection glories of Christ, telling the Corinthians:

> Meanwhile we groan, longing to be clothed with our heavenly dwelling. . . . For while we are in this tent, we groan and are burdened, because we do not wish to be unclothed [disembodied] but to be clothed with our heavenly dwelling, so that what is mortal may be swallowed up by life. Now it is God who has made us for this very purpose and has given us the Spirit as a deposit, guaranteeing what is to come. (2 Corinthians 5:2–5)

It is notable that in both of these passages the Holy Spirit is specifically mentioned. The Spirit who first united us to Christ and acted as the channel for Him to reach us with His eternal, heavenly life is the Spirit who will bring His life to our mortal bodies, glorifying that aspect of our humanity too (Romans

8:11), and it is the presence and work of this same Spirit which acts as the deposit and first installment of that future glory (2 Corinthians 5:5; cf. Ephesians 1:14).

Paul's doctrine here is so far from escapist that he not only recognizes present and very *in*glorious sufferings (e.g., 1 Corinthians 4:8–13; 2 Corinthians 6:4–10; 11:24–29) but sees them also as a participation in the total story of Christ; Paul even welcomes them as such as a preparation for sharing Christ's glory: "For whose sake I have lost all things . . . I want to know Christ and the power of his resurrection and the fellowship of sharing in his sufferings, becoming like him in his death, and so, somehow, to attain to the resurrection from the dead" (Philippians 3:8, 10; cf. Romans 8:17).

In chapter 30 we shall examine in some detail the doctrine of the resurrection of the dead. It is neither crude nor unimportant as an article of belief, for it will be the final and ultimate sharing of the redeemed in the glory and likeness of the Redeemer. At that moment, those who in their perishable humanity have borne the image of the first Adam yet who definitively belong to the second Adam, will be lifted into His likeness as into His light: "Just as we have borne the likeness of the earthly man, so we shall bear the likeness of the man from heaven" (1 Corinthians 15:49). At that point man, who has been made to bear the image and likeness of God, will at last perfectly reflect His beauty and glory, being fully conformed to the image of His Son (Romans 8:29).

Once again, however, we are left not only with a forward look, but are encouraged to make a present application in our lives. There are good reasons why we should read 1 Corinthians 15:49 as saying not "we shall bear . . ." (RSV), but "let us bear the image of the man of heaven."[16] This reading adopts the grammar of the best Greek manuscripts (and the majority), and it is typical of Paul to call his people to prepare now for the future that awaits them. We should therefore read the text (paraphrasing the NIV translation): "And just as we have borne the likeness of the earthly man [conforming to the life of Adam in his corruption], so let us bear the likeness of the heavenly man [conforming to the life of Christ in the power of His risen, glorified state]."

The apostle Peter similarly draws pressing implications for the present from the believer's future:

> Therefore, prepare your minds for action; be self-controlled; set your hope fully on the grace to be given you when Jesus Christ is revealed. As obedient children, do not conform to the evil desires you had when you lived in ignorance. But just as he who called you is holy, so be holy in all you do; for it is written: "Be holy, because I am holy." (1 Peter 1:13–16)

So we are given a resurrection life *now* that shall be brought into full resurrection glory *then:* we are the "Easter people" who are called to make our pilgrimage in steadfast hope, firm faith, and lives of growing Christlikeness.

# 27

# THE ASCENDED LORD

Some years ago I was invited to preach at the opening of a new church in Doncaster. Because of the large number of well-wishers from other churches, the celebration was held in Doncaster Museum, which houses a very fine collection of items from the days when the Roman occupation of Britain made Doncaster one of the main bases and colonies.

While the congregation was singing the pre-sermon hymn, I walked to the lectern, ready to preach. Then I looked around at the scene and the full significance of what was happening struck me. I noticed there, near the museum walls, were the rusted emblems of Rome's military supremacy and the faded glories of her Caesars—in glass cases! And *here*, in this grand assembly, were the Christians: living celebrants of a living Lord whose kingdom would outlast every other kingdom. Caesar was dead; Jesus was alive. The Roman Empire was no more; Christ would reign for ever and ever. The spiritual descendants of those early Christians who had been so despised and perse-cuted and thrown to the lions were singing Christ's praises on earth even while their once-martyred forebears were singing His praises in heaven.

It was a scene fit to inspire a preacher—and a writer too. For it illustrated powerfully the subject of these final chapters of Part 5. The Christ of past history is the Christ of present real-ity; and He is exalted "far above all rule and authority, power and dominion . . . not only in the present age but also in the one to come" (Ephesians 1:21). It illustrated that the greatest story of history is the spread of His kingdom, the gathering of His people and the conquest of contrary powers—human and demonic—for "God placed all things under his feet and appointed him to be head over everything for the church, which is his body, the fullness of him who fills everything in every way" (Ephesians 1:22–23).

## CALVARY: THE BASIS
## FOR CHRIST'S EXALTATION

The three stages of our Lord's exaltation have traditionally been distinguished as His resurrection, His ascension into heaven, and His enthronement at the right hand of God the Father. At no point, however, is Calvary "left behind," for the very basis of our Lord's exaltation is His once-for-all work of sacrificial atonement. Indeed the author of the fourth gospel perceives that it is just there, on the Cross, that the exaltation of Christ begins. John uses the words "lifted up" again and again with regard to the cross and our Lord's death for sinners (John 3:14; 8:28; 12:32). It may at first seem a strange confusion that Christ's deepest humiliation should be called an exaltation of any kind. We are, however, reminded in this way that there is a unity between the death and the exaltation of Jesus Christ, a victory at the Cross which is itself the basis of the victory-shout of the ascension into heaven. In His death, the Man of Sorrows lays a foundation upon which is set His throne as the mediatorial Son of God in power and the Savior of the world.

Paul too seems to have such a connection in mind when, speaking of the ascension of Christ, he writes, "In saying, 'He ascended,' what does it mean but that he had also descended into the lower parts of the earth?" (Ephesians 4:9, RSV). Here Paul is doing something more than correlating Jesus' ascension with His burial, or even with His incarnation: He is contrasting it with His deepest humiliation at Calvary, when He "became a curse for us," and he is doing so in order to show that His present glory as Savior of sinners is vitally connected with His past achievement as a sacrifice for sin.

The connection between Christ's glory in heaven and His suffering on earth is most clearly brought out in Hebrews, from the start: "After he had provided purification for sins, he sat down at the right hand of the Majesty in heaven" (Hebrews

1:3). In the second chapter too we are told that it is "because he suffered death" that He is "crowned with glory and honor" (Hebrews 2:9). And later in the epistle we are bidden to look, in all our trials, to Jesus, "who for the joy set before him endured the cross, scorning its shame, and [has] sat down at the right hand of the throne of God" (Hebrews 12:2). We are never allowed to isolate His present glory from His past sacrifice. That is why, even in His indescribable glory (Revelation 1:12–16), He is still "a Lamb, looking as if it had been slain, standing. . ." (Revelation 5:6), whose wounds are an eternal memorial of His achievement at the cross and an abiding justification for His exercise of authority in saving men and ruling world history for the sake of the church (Revelation 5:9).

## HOW THE ASCENSION
## COMPLETES THE RESURRECTION

The church of Christ has always made much of His triumphant resurrection, but has often neglected the associated article of faith, namely, His ascension to the right hand of God. This is quite wrong, for the Christian message of the resurrection of Christ needs the proclamation of the exaltation of Christ to complete it. Brian K. Donne makes precisely this point, showing that Christ's resurrection demands the Ascension "not only to indicate that the post-resurrection appearances were being terminated but, even more importantly, to demonstrate that His going away would be no fading out but His entry into glory." The Ascension "remains the essential link between the Resurrection and the Exaltation, between the seen and the unseen, between earth and heaven."[1]

Just as, looking backwards, the Ascension completes the Resurrection, so looking forward it leads us into His enthronement. The Ascension, says Donne, "inaugurated the unseen life of Christ on earth until the Parousia."[2] He indicates how full that ongoing life and work would be by quoting the words of an earlier scholar, H. B. Swete:

How much remains of His work at which the gospels hardly hint? His mediation and intercession, His high-priestly life of perpetual self-presentation, His reign, His exercise of universal authority, His certainty of complete victory, His gift of the Spirit, His headship of the Church, His office of universal Judge. When all this is left out of sight can we wonder that men do not get beyond a humanitarian view of His Person and an equally defective conception of His mission?[3]

## WHAT HIS ASCENSION
## MEANS FOR CHRIST HIMSELF

The Old Testament verse that is cited and recalled more than any other in the New Testament writings is the opening sentence of Psalm 110: "The Lord says to my Lord: 'Sit at my right hand until I make your enemies a footstool for your feet.'" It is recalled explicitly no less than nineteen times. It is clear that this prophecy played a very large part in Jesus' own consciousness of His relationship to God, His mission, and His destiny. By it He established in debate with the Pharisees the transcendent superiority of God's Messiah over their conceptions of Him as a political deliver (Mark 12:36–37). In it He saw His own destiny: sharing the throne and the rule of God (Mark 14:61–62). And it forms part of the background to His commission to His disciples to invade the world with His gospel (John 14:12–14; 16:5–11, 23–28), as well as the basis of their final reward and vindication (Luke 22:29).

The major significance of Psalm 110:1 was clearly something of which the preachers and leaders of the early church were aware. Besides being repeated seven times in the Gospels, it is prominent in the early chapters of Acts (2:34; 5:31; 7:55) and, according to F. F. Bruce, is "the key text" of the epistle to the Hebrews (see Hebrews 1:3, 13; 8:1; 10:12–13).[4]

Its profound meaning for believing Jews can scarcely be overestimated. It means that Jesus had a higher place than any other, whether men or angels, prophets or kings, followers or opponents. "'The right hand of God' [is] metaphorical language for divine omnipotence and omnipresence,"[5] says Donne, and it affirms that Christ is reigning everywhere as King and Lord, wielding the power of divine authority.

Used less by Paul,[6] the apostle to the Gentiles, the phrase "the right hand of God" refers to that supreme authority that

Paul expresses in other ways. For instance, in Philippians 2:9–11, the apostle writes, "God exalted him to the highest place and gave him the name that is above every name, that . . . every knee should bow . . . and every tongue confess that Jesus Christ is Lord." The place of God ("enthroned at the right hand of God") and the name of God ("Lord") are really two ways of saying the same thing: in His ascension Jesus received divine honors, and He resumed power that God alone has.

The "enemies" spoken of in the psalm—enemies that must be put under Christ's feet in due time—are, says Paul, not "flesh and blood" but "principalities" and "powers" (Ephesians 6:12, RSV). "These," explains Bruce, are "forces in the universe which work against the purpose of God and the well-being of man."[7] While these are in themselves personal, demonic beings, they utilize human agents and foster human greed, superstition, and fear. Bruce adds:

> They are largely those elemental forces that dominate the world of men and women and are powerful so long as men and women believe in them and render them allegiance. But when their minds are liberated by faith in the crucified and risen Christ, then bondage imposed by those forces is broken, their power is dissolved and they are revealed as the "weak and beggarly" nonentities that they are in themselves.[8]

Two of the most potent of these, he says, are the strength of sin and the fear of death.

It is good, furthermore, to contemplate the effect of such exaltation upon Christ's inner life and subjective experience. We often consider the joy communicated to believers by the Holy Spirit, but too rarely think of it as being Christ's joy shared with His church from His heavenly session. Our exultation is the result of His exaltation, the outflow of His own triumphant joy in having accomplished the work He was sent to do, in being in glory at His Father's right hand, and in seeing His church gathered in. In His self-humbling He had been wedded to weakness and limitation and all the spoiled humanity of sinful flesh. He had known the pain of being confined within a world of sin, and had known the ultimate horror off taking sin upon Himself. Only the one who had allowed Himself to become the scorn of men and the victim of devils could know the exaltation of a triumph that rendered "angels, authorities and powers" subject to Him (1 Peter 3:22). Christ's ascension into heaven and His own jubilant emotions in the experience give new meaning to the ancient acclaim of the psalm: "God has ascended amid shouts of joy, the Lord amid the sounding of trumpets" (Psalm 47:5).

## WHAT HIS ASCENSION MEANS FOR US

Yet in the midst of all this—as the ascended Lord reigns in supreme exaltation and incomparable glory—He remains united to us and committed to us. He has not shed the human nature He once took, but He has taken it with Him into the holy of holies (Hebrews 9:24), into the central presence of God. There He abides, the God-man: everlastingly human now, as well as eternally divine.

In that human nature, He who shared "the same family" with us by His incarnation (Hebrews 2:11), who "shared in [our] humanity" (v. 14); is "not ashamed" to call us "brothers" (v. 11). Indeed, as the writer to the Hebrews so movingly puts it, recalling words of an ancient scripture, His attitude at the right hand of God is that He is there on behalf of His people and is not to be considered apart from the people He represents: "Here am I, and the children God has given me" (v. 13). He approaches the Unapproachable for us and He stands before the presence of the holy God on our behalf. For Him it is not only "here am I" (in the sense of John 17:5), but "here am I *and* the children."

With surprising regularity, however, the church's theologians and pastors have had to rescue this doctrine from neglect and remind people of its importance and relevance to us all. The "mediatory life" of Christ in heaven "is not so considered nor so applied as it ought to be,"[9] wrote theologian and preacher John Owen in the seventeenth century. Elsewhere he noted that "the darkness of our faith herein is the cause of all our disconsolations and most of our weakness in obedience,"[10] and called the ascension of our Jesus Christ into glory, and "His glo-

rious reception in heaven, with His state and condition therein
. . . a principal article of the faith of the church—the great foundation of its hope and consolation in the world."[11] Owen saw a
clear connection between Christ's exaltation and the church on
earth: "He leads not in heaven a life of mere glory, majesty and
blessedness, but a life of office, love and care also. He lives as
Mediator of the Church; as the King, Priest and Prophet there-
of. Herein do our present safety and our future eternal salvation depend."[12]

Torrance says that "The ascension means the exaltation of
man into the life of God and onto the throne of God. . . . We are
with Jesus beside God, for we are gathered up in Him and
included in His own self-presentation before the Father."[13]
However, lest this should be misunderstood or misused, he
adds the warning that this is solely in virtue of our sharing in
the humanity which the Son of God has, and that "we share in
the life of God while remaining what we were made to be, men
and not gods."[14]

Elsewhere Torrance explains such thinking further:

Since in Jesus Christ there became incarnate the very Son
of God whose life and being are eternally grounded in the
mutual relation between the Father and the Son. . . . The
mediation of divine reconciliation to mankind in and
through Christ means much more than the reconstituting
of holy relations between man and God, though it certainly
means that. Mediation of reconciliation which takes place
within the Person of the Mediator himself means that men
and women are singly reconciled to God by being taken up
in and through Christ to share in the inner relations of
God's own life and love.[15]

As the Father loves Christ in His divine nature so He also
loves Him in His human nature: and as Christ Jesus can no
more cease to be man than He can cease to be God, this is the
golden and *unbreakable* link between God and man. In Christ
deity and humanity, uncreated God and created man, yes even
Spirit and flesh, are everlastingly joined. There is a man in
heaven who is also God: eternally beloved, infinitely valued. He

now gives massive significance to us as human beings and to every part of our humanness. At a time in our race's history when the science of astronomy has made many feel so infinitesimally small as to be irrelevant in the universe, this setting of man in Christ in the position of supreme significance, even at the Creator's "right hand," is very important.

Consequently, because even in His glory Christ does not consider Himself apart from us, neither should we believers consider ourselves apart from Him. Christ is now living in a mode and on a level of existence that is the heavenly guarantee of our own future mode and level of existence. *Where* He is now we shall certainly one day be (John 14:1–3), and *as* He is now we shall one day be (John 17:22–24). Yet, lest we simply look forward to a time in the future when Christ's place in heaven will affect us and be decisive for us, the apostle Paul's words to the Colossian believers remind us that *even now,* in the midst of all our earthly struggles, temptations, contradictions, and challenges, we ourselves are crucially and centrally defined by Christ Jesus' place in heaven: "Since, then, you have been raised with Christ, set your hearts on things above, where Christ is seated at the right hand of God. . . . For you died, and your life is now hidden with Christ in God" (Colossians 3:1, 3; cf. Ephesians 2:4–6).

# 28

# THE GREAT HIGH PRIEST

One of the great themes developed in the book of Hebrews is that of the high priestly significance and activity of Christ. Most people today do not tend to think much in terms of priests or priesthoods, even when contemplating religion. If a man decides he will pray he tends to get on with the job himself, however fumblingly. The reason for his independence, however, is hardly theological, or even admirable. Modern man, sadly even many religious modern men and women, has little sense either of God's holiness or his own sinfulness.

Most people, used to measuring mass or energy and to computing distances in terms of miles or light years, are more likely to have a sense of God's power than His purity. They are more likely to feel their distance from Him in terms of physical contrast or locality in His universe than in terms of their spiritual fallenness and liability to His wrath. Consequently, as we saw in an earlier chapter, men need to learn again their need of a mediator: one who will stand between them and God to help them approach Him and to mediate His approach, in blessing, to them.

## A HIGH PRIEST

### Aaron: Israel's High Priest

In the world of the Old Testament no one taught God's lesson concerning the need and value of a mediator more colorfully or dramatically than the high priest of Israel. According to the laws that Yahweh gave to Moses, Aaron and his successors were to be, quite literally, clothed with His significance. Philip Edgcumbe Hughes summarizes their appearance:

> The most eloquent symbols of the intercessory function of the high priest are found in the prescriptions for the sacerdotal garments which Aaron was to wear. In the shoulder-pieces of the ephod two onyx stones were set on which the names of the sons of Israel were engraved. These stones are designated "stones of remembrance," because Aaron bore "their names before the Lord upon his two shoulders for remembrance." And attached in front of the two shoulder-pieces of the ephod was the breastpiece in which were set twelve precious stones, in four rows of three, also engraved with the names of the twelve sons of Israel; so that Aaron bore "the names of the sons of Israel in the breastpiece of judgment upon his heart" when he went into the sanctuary, "to bring them to continual remembrance before the Lord (Exodus 28:6ff.; 39:1ff.). Thus the people of God were carried by name into the divine presence, supported, as it were, in their weakness on the strong shoulders of their high priest, and bound closely to his loving and compassionate heart. Their high priest was their remembrance.[1]

All this and much more, the writer of Hebrews tells us, foreshadowed Christ who, as well as being the supreme sacrifice that alone could take away sins (Hebrews 10:11–12), was also God's great high priest appointed to appear before God in heaven on our behalf (Hebrews 9:24).

### Christ: The Present High Priest

At the heart of Hebrews is its teaching about the priesthood of Christ, teaching that touches on each aspect of His person and each stage of His work. G. Vos notes three unique factors. The sonship of Christ is the "determining principle" of Christ's priesthood (Hebrews 7:3, 28); "the dignity of office follows the worth of personality" unlike any other priesthood. Second, the human nature He took to Himself is the "instrumental aspect" of that priesthood (Hebrews 2:14; 10:5–7) by which He is able to die, a sacrifice for sin, and to present that sacrifice to God for us. Third, the atonement for sin He offered by His death for us is the ground on which He exercises His office (Hebrews 7:27; 9:12, 26; 10:12, 14); and the heavenly courts—the innermost presence of God—is the sphere wherein He exercises that function (Hebrews 7:26; 9:11–12, 23–24).[2]

We are told that Christ has gone to heaven as God's great high priest for us. That is emphasized repeatedly. He has not gone to heaven only for Himself, but for us and as "the author and perfecter of our faith" (Hebrews 12:2; cf. 2:10). He stands before God in heaven as He lived and died on earth, not as a private person but as a public one. He is the representative of His people, saying, "Here am I, and the children God has given me" (Hebrews 2:13). With Him, now, it is always "I and the children." He is bound up with us and one with us, even in His greatest glory. He is our high priest in heaven.

## OUR HIGH PRIEST

As our high priest, Christ shows several human traits as He represents us before our heavenly Father. We will focus on three: His mercy, sympathy, and willingness to intercede in prayer.

### A Merciful High Priest

No greater encouragement for faith or assurance of grace could be given than this: Christ represents us with mercy. For the office of high priest was altogether an office of mercy and grace, concerned with the forgiveness of sins and a state of peace with God (Hebrews 5:1). The old high priests were meant to "deal gently with those who [were] ignorant and . . . going astray" (Hebrews 5:2); and they did so, not least because they themselves also were often ignorant and wayward in God's sight.

God's high priest, Jesus, is no less "merciful and faithful" (Hebrews 2:17) than they in meeting the needs of His people, though He does so from a sinless experience of human frailty and trial (Hebrews 4:15). Everything contributed to this supreme ministry of mercy that Christ has: His Father's will, His own character, His relationship with the church and each of His people, and, as we can see, His office of high priest itself.

## A Sympathizing High Priest

Yet the writer to the Hebrews takes the character of Christ's high priestly mediation even further. Mercy itself, though patient, may be perplexed; though tender and forgiving, it may be utterly unable to understand at the deepest level the object of its attentions. Hence our writer insists that we have not only a merciful but also a *sympathizing* high priest: "For we do not have a high priest who is unable to sympathize with our weaknesses, but we have one who has been tempted in every way, just as we are—yet was without sin" (Hebrews 4:15). We have here principally a reference to our Lord's experience of temptation to sin, especially temptation to ignore the commission given Him by the Father (that is, temptation to gain His end by some other way than the way of the Cross, Matthew 4:1–10). Yet we are also pointed to the inescapable fact that the Son's earthly life as Jesus of Nazareth gave Him personal experience of every typical human situation, condition, and encounter.

I like the sharp perceptive quality of Harry Blamires's comment:

> A God who knows exactly what it is to eat a meal and take a walk, to have a toothache or a stomach ache, to rejoice at a wedding or to mourn at a funeral, to be indebted to an earthly mother and her husband, to stand trial in a human court, to be flogged, to be cruelly executed, does not need to apologise to men and women for His immunity, still less for His existence.[3]

This is precisely the dimension of Christ's sympathy with us as our high priest. We only truly "understand" another's trouble when we "stand under" it with the person. He is able to stand alongside us in all our troubles because He who is still human in heaven remembers what it was like to be human on earth and with perfect recall can match all our changing moments with His own experiences. "Because he himself suffered when he was tempted, he is able to help those who are being tempted" (Hebrews 2:18). He is able to help because He has been there before; so He stands alongside us in the rough places of life. To Him it is familiar territory. As we bring to Him our fears and pain He can say to each one of us, "I know, I have been where you are now. I have been there and I know the way out. I *am* the way out!"

Nor should we allow ourselves to imagine that Christ, having been sinless throughout His earthly life, is unable to feel with us the weight and shame of our sin. After all, if this were so, His sympathy and understanding and consequently His help would be wanting in the very area of our lives where it was most needed. But it is far from being the case: for on the cross He bore our sins *as if they were His own.* In this sense He made them His own; hence He knew to the full the pain of them, the guilt and shame of them, the wrath and the loss of any sense of God's love and presence caused by them. There is no fundamental or typical human need which God's (and our) great High Priest, Jesus, cannot understand.

## A Praying High Priest

In His praying on our behalf, we find the heart of Christ's heavenly work. Indeed, it is the second part of His priestly work after His earthly sacrifice of Himself. The heavenly intercession of our Lord has from the start been given close attention, in both its theology and its devotion. Says Calvin:

> Since no man is worthy to present himself to God and come into His sight, the Heavenly Father himself, to free us at once from shame and fear, which might well have thrown our hearts into despair, has given us His Son, Jesus Christ our Lord, to be our advocate [1 John 2:1] and mediator with Him [1 Timothy 2:5; cf. Hebrews 8:6 and 9:15].[4]

This intercession of Christ in heaven for us is, according to Owen, "a fundamental article of our faith and a principal foundation of the church's consolation," and from it we receive "all mercy, all supplies of grace and consolation needful unto our duties, temptation and trials."[5]

Two points in particular, however, are emphasized by both Calvin and Owen. The first is that this heavenly work of our Lord in no way adds to or completes His finished work at Calvary, and the second is that Christ's prayer life in heaven is not a pleading uncertainty but an assured intercession. Calvin puts it thus: "But we do not imagine that He, kneeling before God, pleads as a suppliant for us; rather, with the apostle we understand He so appears before God's presence that the power of His death avails as an everlasting intercession in our behalf" (cf. Romans 8:34).[6] And Owen says more fully:

> It must be granted that the virtue, efficacy, and prevalency of the intercession of the Lord Christ depends upon and flows from his oblation and sacrifice. Wherefore nothing remains for his intercession but the application of the fruits of his oblation unto all them for whom he offered himself in sacrifice, according as their conditions and occasions do require.[7]

The Reformed tradition, both in order to preserve Christ's once-for-all work at the Cross and in order to correct a crude literalism here, has tended to stress Christ's very presence, in human nature, before the Father as where He stays in almost perpetual intercession for us. As the nineteenth-century theologian Charles Hodge puts it: "His perfect manhood, His official character, and His finished work, plead for us before the throne of God."[8] Yet it is still not enough, I think, to say that our Lord's *place* in heaven is His priestly ministry in this regard. The intercession is more than the session: it is a particular and mighty work in which He is actively and marvelously involved. The order of Paul's words in Romans 8:34 makes this clear: He speaks of "Christ Jesus, who died—more than that, who was raised to life—[who] is at the right hand of God and is also interceding for us." Sanday and Headlam's observation is worth quoting here:

> Stroke follows stroke, each driving home the last. . . . It is not only a living Christ, but a Christ enthroned, a Christ in power. It is not only a Christ in power, but a Christ of ever-active sympathy, constantly (if we may so speak) at the Father's ear, and constantly pouring in intercessions for His struggling people on earth. A great text for the value and significance of the Ascension.[9]

Some later (nineteenth-century) theologians in the Reformed tradition sought to preserve an important aspect of the intercession here. Hence R. L. Dabney, maintaining the important truth that Christ mediates the grace of God in His divine nature as well as in His human nature ("Only the Omniscient can intercede for all"),[10] sees the divine nature of our Lord as operating in His unique intercession as it had in His unique sacrifice at Calvary:

> His petitions and their wants are so numerous that unless he were endowed with sleepless attention, an omnipotence which can never tire, an infinite understanding, omnipresence and inexhaustible kindness, he could not wisely and graciously attend so many and multifarious calls.[11]

We have familiar examples in Luke (22:31–32) and in John (17:9–24) of Christ's intercessions for His people in their need, and concerning the first of these James Denney writes:

> If we see nothing unnatural in the fact that Christ prayed for Peter on earth, we need not make any difficulty about his praying for us in heaven. The relation is the same: the only difference is that Christ is now exalted and prays, not with strong tears but in the sovereignty and prevailing power of one who has achieved eternal redemption for his people.[12]

Nowhere are the force and power of those prayers brought out more clearly than in Hebrews 7:24–25: "Because Jesus lives forever, he has a permanent priesthood. Therefore he is able to save completely those who come to God through him, because he always lives to intercede for them." The Greek word for *completely* combines the ideas of *time* and *completeness*. The word can thus be translated either as "perpetually" or as "completely." Such a mediator makes all other mediators as unnecessary as they are unlawful (1 Timothy 2:5).

## OUR WILLING FATHER IN HEAVEN

None of this, of course, means that the Father is a reluctant member of the Trinity who has to be cajoled and persuaded, either by Christ or ourselves. It is the Father whose love and wisdom has provided such a mediator. Jesus' words in John 16:26–27 are meant to stress this fact: "In that day you will ask in my name. I am not saying that I will ask the Father on your behalf. No, the Father himself loves you. . . ." Those words do not deny the doctrine of this heavenly priestly intercession of the Son. They are meant to heighten and to intensify the idea of the close relation that believers have to God their Father as a result of Christ's death for us.

It is as if Jesus said, "Look, it's not just because *I* love you that the Father loves you, and it's not just because I want Him to do so that He will bless you." The "wounds yet visible above" of the once-crucified Son are not so much arguments as guarantees from the presence of God that the beloved Son, who was given up to death for us (Romans 8:34), would not be refused His desires for us, and that He who in the first place "gave him up for us all" will certainly, along with Him, "graciously give us all things" (Romans 8:32).

Jesus Christ in His mediation does not operate as a third party, *moving between* God and believers, as though God would always be unapproachable; rather, He operates as *one* with God and His people, in whom believers are brought face to face with a Father who loves them, and who rejoices to make their persons and their prayers, their worship and their lives accepted in the beloved Son.

I once heard of an artwork that dramatically illustrated this aspect of Christ's work. It was a large, typically Victorian religious piece, but the artist showed a striking degree of spiritual insight as well as originality in his composition. The scene was a storm on the lake of first-century Galilee. In the foreground Jesus' terrified disciples were rowing furiously through huge waves that threatened to engulf them at any moment.

There seemed at first to be nothing else—no relief in the scene of fear and extreme danger. Then one's eye was taken by a shaft of sunlight through the storm clouds to a rocky hillside on the shore. And there one saw, kneeling among the rocks, a praying figure. Many artists had painted the later scene—Christ walking on the water—but this artist had captured a reality just as profound when he depicted an earlier stage in the drama. Here was Christ praying in the hills (Matthew 14:23), while His followers were battling in the storm (v. 24). It is the story of the church militant as she works and wars for the Christ triumphant. She is never alone.

# 29

# THE APPOINTED KING

In these democratic days, we don't speak much of kings or their rule and reign. Republics are more common than monarchies, and even where monarchs reign, as in my own country of England, they reign as constitutional monarchs, with governments holding the real political power. However, power to rule remains as real, as potent and as dangerous as ever; indeed ever more so, concentrated as it is in the modern state: power to brainwash the minds and manipulate the lives of millions; power to impose the will of a Lenin or a Stalin or a Hitler on millions; power to rule as never before; power to destroy as never before.

The use of power can be attractive to the highest mind, and the possession of power is dangerous to the most honest heart. The growth of power to absolute proportions has proved more than any human being can handle properly. In our century we have found it still, as ever, to be true that "power tends to corrupt and absolute power corrupts absolutely."

## A POWER RENOUNCED

There was a time when power was contrary to Christ's messianic office. God's will for Him then lay through voluntary weakness and suffering and death. It was a time when Satan offered Him another power and an alternative empire (Matthew 4:9)—an offer Jesus adamantly refused. Now, however, He has been exalted by His Father to the highest honor and to universal rule: "Then Jesus came to them and said, 'All authority in heaven and on earth has been given to me'"

(Matthew 28:18). Indeed it is only by such a delegation of absolute power that the saving purposes of God can now be carried forward and the work of Christ applied.

The epistle to the Hebrews, as we have seen, has much to say about the heavenly high priesthood of Christ, but a main point, repeatedly expressed, is that He unites kingly power with appointed priesthood, that He is a priest-king "after the order of Melchizedek," who in Abraham's day was high priest and king in the old city of Salem (Jerusalem). As the ascended Son He makes His priesthood effective by "the power of an inde-structible life' (Hebrews 7:16). As T. F. Torrance puts it: "It is the coincidence of grace and power which makes it Royal or Sovereign Priesthood."[1]

## A POWER RESUMED

Christ's present sovereignty and future disclosure are nowhere more graphically portrayed than in the book of Reve-lation, where "the Lamb slain," who by resurrection became "the firstborn from the dead," becomes also "the ruler of the kings of the earth" (Revelation 1:5; 17:14). He who has been give God's own name of "Lord" (Philippians 2:9) has also been given God's own title of "King of kings and Lord of lords." Of that title Robert H. Mounce notes:

> This name emphasizes the universal sovereignty of the war-rior Christ in His eschatological triumph over all the ene-mies of God. The title, as it occurs here and elsewhere in Scripture (Rev 17:14; 1 Tim 6:15; Dan 2:47), goes back to Moses' declaration to Israel, "The Lord your God is the God of gods and the Lord of lords" (Deut 10:17).[2]

A sovereignty more complete or a kingship more divine could hardly be contemplated.

What is distinctive about the Christology of Ephesians, as Andrew T. Lincoln notes, is its emphasis on the exaltation of Christ and His cosmic lordship (Ephesians 1:20–23). He writes: "Christ's resurrection and exaltation mean that the center of gravity in God's cosmic drama of salvation has moved from the realm of earth to that of heaven and that a change in the power structures of this world has been brought about [Ephesians 4:10; cf. Psalm 8:6; 110:1; 1 Corinthians 15:25–27]."[3]

Most intriguing for Lincoln is "the relationship between Christ's cosmic lordship and His lordship over the church." "The two," he says, "are not simply set in parallel, but the former is subordinated to the latter, as, in both Ephesians 1 and Ephesians 4, cosmic Christology is made to serve the needs of the readers. . . . God has given Christ as head over the cosmos to the Church (1:22)."[4] He concludes:

> The readers are shown that the divine election which has grasped them also involves God's purpose for history: "to sum up all things in Christ, things in heaven and things on earth in him" (1:10). This unifying of the cosmos and restoration of its harmony were achieved in principle when God exalted Christ to heaven as cosmic Lord, thereby ensuring the inseparable connection between heaven and earth that enables both heavenly things and earthly things to be summed up in him. This part of the opening blessing is meant to help the readers to see that to be in Christ is to be part of a programme which is as broad as the universe, a movement which is rolling on toward a renewed cosmos where all is in harmony.[5]

## KING OF HEAVEN AND EARTH

Christ's sovereignty over the world is as real as it is over the church, but His sovereignty over the world in its unreconciled state is not *of* the same *order* as His sovereignty *over* the church. He is uniquely King of the church; but He is at the same time irresistibly King over the world. Over the world (considered as society organized apart from God), His power is sovereign but not saving, and there He exercises dominion in a hidden form that can be perceived only by faith.

The book of Revelation opens a window on world history through this doctrine. It shows the Lamb on the throne, overruling world history for the in-gathering of His church. Yet it is as Leon Morris puts it, a "peep behind the scenes," bringing to John's readers "a glimpse of the realities of power" behind the

earthly appearance of things, where the wicked seem to rule
and God's will is ignored.[6]

It is only because of the rule and purposes of Christ, above
and behind the rule of "those in authority," that society in a fall-
en world does not entirely succumb to chaos and judgment.
Neither unbelieving man nor demonic powers are wholly free
from Him, as if Jesus of Nazareth were a refugee from earth
whose writ and rule were only effective in heaven. G. C. Berkouwer shows that the world wherein Christ suffered is the same
world over which He reigns from heaven and in which He
secretly but irresistibly brings to pass the decrees of His Father:

> By His victory He de-throned the powers, made them a pub-
> lic spectacle, and conquered them. Scripture emphatically
> ridicules the powers which boast and resist the cross. . . . we
> observe something of the laughter of the holy, divine irony:
> "He that sitteth in the heavens will laugh: the Lord will have
> them in derision" (Ps. 2:4). This divine laughter is . . .
> heard . . . throughout history. . . . Every power which refus-
> es to be a *serving* power becomes subject to the justice of
> Christ's glory.[7]

However, it is too easy to divorce the rule of Christ in heav-
en from the life of His church on earth; to so abstract the one
from the other that the effective outworking of Christ's sovereignty is left to mysterious forces quite unconnected with our
everyday Christian life. In this way we can make the reign of
Christ something too remote: invisible, inaudible, and eventually undetectable. Instead, society itself should be preserved
and invaded by this reigning Lord through the church's presence and power, by her work and witness.

The lives of Christian people in society at every level must
be the salt that preserves society from moral, social, and economic putrefaction. At the same, the church's prophetic witness—denouncing injustice and holding before leaders and
people concepts and standards of truth, value, and righteousness—must disturb the consciences and maybe redirect the
policies of governments and curb the permissiveness of society.
And above all the prayer life and preaching of the church must

invade Satan's territory, defeating "principalities and powers," bringing the gift and life of the gospel to societies in spiritual darkness, effectively calling men and women to Christ. By such means, as well as in unseen and independent ways, Christ Jesus exercises His rule, extends His kingdom, and fulfills God's eternal purposes. Torrance writes:

> So far as the Church in history and on earth is concerned, therefore, the great connecting link between world history and the heavenly session of Christ is to be found in *prayer and intercession*. [It] is in prayer that through the Spirit the heavenly intercessions of the risen and enthroned Lamb are made to echo in the intercessions of mankind and the people of God are locked with Christ in the great apocalyptic struggle with the forces of darkness. But because He who rules from the throne of God is the Lamb . . . the Church's engagement in prayer is already a participation in the final victory of the Kingdom of Christ. Thus the life, mission, and worship of the church on earth and in history are, as it were, in counterpoint to the victorious paeans of the hosts above who surround the throne of the Lamb and worship and glorify God.[8]

We dare not leave Christ to do alone what He has ordained to do through His church. The exercise and spread, the conflicts and conquests of God's kingdom are not put forth with such consideration for the church's comfort (not to say her laziness!). The church that shares the rule of Christ here, challenged and opposed though it is, is the church that will share the reign of Christ in her final, unchallenged, and full glory upon His return to earth. This is her promise and her reward, described by the apostle Paul: "if we endure, we will also reign with him" (2 Timothy 2:12; see also Revelation 2:26; 3:21).

# PART 6

## CHRIST
## THE COMING KING

# 30

# THE PERSONAL
# RETURN OF CHRIST

I have never been to Washington, D.C., but I have read that in the dome of the Capitol there is an inscription which few see. It is a line from the English poet Tennyson and reads simply: "One far off divine event to which the whole creation moves." When the Capitol was built, someone who believed the biblical revelation about Christ's rule over human history and His second coming to end this phase of it had ordered that those words be inscribed above the seat of government of what has become the most powerful nation on earth. It is a witness, humbling and encouraging, that "the kingdom of the world" will in that day become "the kingdom of our Lord and of his Christ" (Revelation 11:15).

## CHRIST'S PERSONAL RETURN

The Christian hope of the Second Coming looks forward to a great event that will end world history as we know it, consummating the promises of God as we now have them. The Second Coming will usher in a new and endless age: the age of the new heavens and the new earth. Yet the true greatness of this event, and its full significance, does not lie in its magnitude nor its ultimacy for world history. It is an event dominated by a person: Jesus Christ, the Son of God and the church's Lord. He shall come in love for His own as well as in judgment for the world. His return to earth is described as that of the bridegroom coming for His bride (Matthew 25:1–13; Revelation 22:17).

Therefore we should be less taken up with the details and

form of events than the knowledge that we shall meet the Lord, face-to-face (1 Thessalonians 4:17; 1 Corinthians 12:12). The meeting is more important than the mechanics, the "how" must give way to the "who" of the Second Coming. Before the fact of our Lord's personal return all other "facts" of tribulation, millennium, Armageddon, rapture, etc., fade into a truly subordinate place. And where Christians write on the great event they should not be alienated from one another by the current orthodoxies of evangelical opinion. Our Lord, our Savior, and our love is coming—and coming for us. In that we can all rejoice.

To speak of His "return," however, obviously implies His absence; and Scripture is quite clear about this. Jesus told His disciples that He was "going away" and that they would see Him no more (John 16:5, 7, 10), but that He would one day "come again" and take them to be where He Himself was going (John 14:3). Peter speaks of Him as the one "raised . . . to life" and "exalted to the right hand of God," abiding in heaven until the appointed day of judgment (Acts 2:32–33; 3:20–21). And Paul recognizes that the Lord is seated with God "in the heavenly realms," from which He shall one day come (Ephesians 1:20; 2:6; 1 Thessalonians 4:16). There is thus a real absence of her Lord for the church to understand.

Yet, though real, this absence is not absolute. It is a departure but not a desertion. Christ is absent in body yet present in awareness and power by His Holy Spirit, whom He has sent. The Spirit has been sent to console and guide the church in the absence of her Lord (John 14:17). From Christ's side, however, the Holy Spirit is so much one with Him in the Godhead, and so much united with Him in His mediatorial expectation, and so much His spirit commissioned from the throne (Acts 2:33; 2 Corinthians 3:17), that where the Spirit has come to live Christ can say, "surely I am with you always, to the very end of the age" (Matthew 28:20). The Spirit is not here instead of Him, but as a living link with Him. The Spirit is a way of being present for Him; Christ's presence is mediated by the church by the Holy Spirit. There is therefore both a real absence and a real presence of Christ.

The return, however, ends forever the period of relative absence. That is why it is variously described as our Lord's *parousia* (meaning "presence" or "arrival," as in 1 Corinthians 15:23; 1 Thessalonians 2:19), His appearing (e.g., 2 Thessalonians 2:8; Titus 2:13), His revealing (e.g., 1 Corinthians 1:7; 2 Thessalonians 1:7), or simply His coming (1 Corinthians 16:22).

The final "coming" will be quite distinct and decisive, no interim rescue and no temporary respite: "so Christ was sacrificed once to take away the sins of many people; and he will appear a second time, not to bear sin, but to bring salvation to those who are waiting for him" (Hebrews 9:28). His arrival will be visible not only to the church of that generation but to the whole world (Acts 1:11; Revelation 1:7), since it will be Jesus in bodily form who will appear. As Donald G. Bloesch puts it: "It will not be simply the spirit of Christ but Jesus Christ in his glorified humanity who will confront humanity in the last days."[1]

## THE PROMINENCE OF THE
## SECOND COMING IN THE NEW TESTAMENT

If the New Testament landscape is dominated by the cross of Jesus, the New Testament horizon is dominated by the return of Jesus. Next to the complex of events that lie at the climax of the gospel story, namely, the Cross, the Resurrection, the Great Commission, and Pentecost, the New Testament is dominated by another complex of events—the Second Coming, the resurrection of the dead, the general judgment, and the new heavens and the new earth. Of course there are no rivals contesting with one another for attention. As we shall see, they are all related, the first group leading to and looking toward the second. We ourselves are pilgrims, journeying from the empty tomb of Easter Sunday to the advent morning of God's new age: and our hearts are to be full of both.

It is said that there are over three hundred verses in the New Testament that refer explicitly to the Second Coming. Certainly there are well over two hundred outside the book of Revelation that do so. However, the importance of the doctrine is not to be judged simply by counting verses. There is hardly an area of the Christian life that is not affected by it, and the Christian life itself can be described and even defined in terms of it. In one of his earliest epistles Paul addresses the Thessalonian

Christians as those who "turned to God from idols to serve the living and true God, and to wait for his Son from heaven, whom he raised from the dead—Jesus, who rescues us from the coming wrath" (1 Thessalonians 1:9–10). And toward the end of his life and work he reminds his colleague Titus of the decisive influence of this doctrine upon all Christian teaching and living.

> For the grace of God that brings salvation has appeared to all men. It teaches us to say "No" to ungodliness and worldly passions, and to live self-controlled, upright and godly lives in this present age, while we wait for the blessed hope—the glorious appearing of our great God and Savior, Jesus Christ, who gave himself for us to redeem us from all wickedness and to purify for himself a people that are his very own, eager to do what is good. (Titus 2:11–14)

This perspective should affect everything in the Christian life. It is a great encouragement to day-by-day godliness.[2] The doctrine of the second coming of Christ gives the Christian confidence in spiritual warfare (Romans 13:11–13; 16:20; 1 Corinthians 6:3; 1 Thessalonians 5:2–8; 2 Thessalonians 2:8–12). It is a focus in all church life and worship (1 Corinthians 1:7; 11:26; Hebrews 10:25). The personal return of Christ also is the believer's comfort in times of persecution (Romans 8:18–25; 2 Thessalonians 1:6–10) and a great consolation during the loss of loved ones (1 Thessalonians 4:13–18). "Hope in the appearing of Christ is accordingly the distinguishing mark of the Christian life."[3]

Also prominent in the New Testament is the note of warning associated with the Second Coming. There is to be a "day of Christ" (1 Corinthians 1:8; Philippians 1:10), which will be the "Day of the Lord" of Old Testament prediction. This will be a day in which the secrets of all hearts will be judged (Romans 2:16) and the work of all believers tested (1 Corinthians 3:10–15). With a view to that fast-approaching day of judgment, believers are to "put aside the deeds of darkness and put on the armor of light" (Romans 13:11–12; cf. 1 Thessalonians 5:4–5). Only as the love of Christ Jesus establishes Paul's converts' hearts "blameless and holy in the presence of our God and Father when our Lord Jesus comes with all his holy ones" will he be "proud"' of them, and proud that he "did not run or labor for nothing" (1 Thessalonians 3:13; 2 Corinthians 1:14; Philippians 2:16).

We should remember too that the first-century church was a suffering church, in which "the cross" that believers bore was not arthritis or difficult children, but imprisonment, loss of goods, suffering of all kinds, and even death "for Christ's sake" (e.g., Hebrews 10:32–34). Their suffering was in fact avoidable suffering—but only avoidable at the expense of betraying and losing the Savior. It was out of love for Him that they suffered in a world alien and hostile to both Him and them (Matthew 5:10–11; 10:17–18; John 15:18–21). In return, He would not forget to reward them (1 Thessalonians 2:3, 6; Hebrews 6:10; Revelation 3:10–12).

Consequently, it is notable that again and again throughout the New Testament the second coming of Christ for the destruction of His enemies and the rescue and vindication of His church is held out to suffering Christians for their consolation (e.g., Romans 8:19–23; 2 Corinthians 4:17; James 5:7–9; 1 Peter 1:7; 4:13; Revelation 3:10–11).

## THE EXPECTATION OF THE SECOND COMING

Matching the prominence given to the Second Coming in the New Testament is the expectation it provokes in the Christian community. When teaching His disciples about His return, Jesus urged them to watchful expectation and readiness: "Therefore keep watch, because you do not know on what day your Lord will come," and "When these things begin to take place, stand up and lift up your heads, because your redemption is drawing near" (Matthew 24:42; Luke 21:28). The churches of the New Testament were notably communities of people who were "eagerly awaiting" their "blessed hope," when they would at last see their Lord and would be "like him" (Hebrews 9:28; Titus 2:13; 1 John 3:2). Hence the canon of Scripture closes with the promise, "I am coming soon," and the responsive cry, "Amen. Come, Lord Jesus" (Revelation 22:20).

Anthony Hoekema is surely justified when he admonishes

some sections of the contemporary Christian church for losing this sense of expectancy and longing:

> This same lively expectation of Christ's return should mark the church of Jesus Christ today. If this expectation is no longer present there is something radically wrong. It is the unfaithful servant in Jesus' parable who says in his heart, "My lord delays his coming" (Luke 12:45). There may be various reasons for the loss of this sense of expectation. It may be that the church of today is so caught up in material and secular concerns that interest in the Second Coming is fading into the background. It may be that Christians no longer believe in a literal return of Christ. It may also be that many who do believe in a literal return have pushed that event so far into the distant future that they no longer live in anticipation of that return.[4]

This reference to a tendency to push the event "into the distant future" brings us to the crucial matter of the *imminence* of the return of Christ, which is obviously closely connected with the church's expectation of it. Few aspects of the doctrine of the Second Coming are as plagued as this one with disputes, misunderstandings, and doubt. Yet it ought surely to be clear enough that the New Testament consistently (and not only in the earlier parts) speaks of the coming as imminent. "The Lord is near," Paul tells the Philippians; "the Judge is standing at the door!" James warns his readers; "Yes, I am coming soon," John records as Jesus' last words to the church on earth (Philippians 4:5; James 5:9; Revelation 22:20).

It is, of course, a commonplace of modern theology simply to dismiss as sincere but mistaken the expectations of an imminent return shared by Jesus and the New Testament writers. But this is not so easily done when due weight is given to Jesus' disclaimer concerning precise knowledge of the time (Mark 13:32; cf. 1 Thessalonians 5:1–2), His hints at delay (Matthew 25:1–13), His call to watchfulness (Matthew 24:36–44), and Paul's evident awareness that death might intervene between his present life and the Second Coming (e.g., 1 Thessalonians 5:9–11; Romans 8:10–11; 14:7–9; 2 Corinthians 4:12).

It is crucial to understand that there are theological reasons why the New Testament writers consistently emphasize the nearness of the return of Christ. These are closely bound up with the utterly decisive event of Christ's death and resurrection. On the Cross sin was effectively dealt with and its effects were in principle neutralized. There, a victory was won that could wholly and in a moment repair the devastation that sin and the Fall had caused. But that would involve the instant dismissal of every contrary power, including the unconverted, leaving no space for repentance. Consequently, in the goodness and patience of God (Romans 2:4–5) that glorious end that already has been won is delayed in order that more men and women, in both present and future generations, might enter it and enjoy its blessings. I have not found this matter of biblical imminence and historical delay put more memorably than by John Henry Newman:

> Though time intervene between Christ's first and second coming, it is not *recognised* (as I may say) in the Gospel scheme, but is, as it were, an accident. For so it was, that up to Christ's coming in the flesh, the course of things ran straight toward that end, nearing it by every step; but now, under the Gospel, that course has (if I may so speak) altered its direction, as regards His second coming, and run, not towards the end, but along it, and on the brink of it; and is at all times near that great event, which, did it run towards it, it would at once run into. Christ then is ever at our doors; as near eighteen hundred years ago as now, and not nearer now than then, and not nearer when He comes than now.[5]

We may want to qualify the word "accident" (as indeed Newman does), for this is a divinely ordained time, full of purpose, as we shall see; and certainly Newman does not mean to speak in dispensationalist terms. The value of his illustration is that it impresses upon us the continual imminence of the return, which is never far away but is always near. It is as if time and the long course of the years between the two comings form a corridor against the sides of which, and all around, the future of God—already fully purchased and wholly guaranteed by Christ's death and resurrection—is pressing, being held back from breaking in and demolishing the present, with all its corruption, only by the commanding patience of God.

"The conclusion is inescapable," writes G. C. Berkouwer, "that 'nearness' is an absolutely essential component of the eschatological proclamation of the New Testament."[6] Consequently, when Paul uses the first person plural in speaking of the return—"After that, *we* who are still alive and are left will be caught up together with them in the clouds to meet the Lord in the air" (1 Thessalonians 4:17, emphasis added; cf. 1 Corinthians 15:51)—he is not at all committing himself to the prediction of a date or a time-scale, but is speaking about the event in the only way he can, the only theologically proper way, and the only way that is consistent with the facts of the matter. He naturally and unhesitatingly takes into account the possibility that the Lord will come again within his lifetime; nothing could be more likely. As. F. F. Bruce says: "Each successive generation occupies the place of that generation which will witness the denouement, just as the first Christian generation so consciously did."[7]

## THE DELAY OF THE SECOND COMING

The delay in the personal return of Christ has enormous significance for ongoing human history. It not only gives purpose in regard to the future, it also gives meaning for the present. In his book *The Return of Christ,* Berkouwer has a chapter entitled "Crisis of Delay?" The question mark in the title is significant. There should be no crisis of delay for the church, however long that delay continues, for two chief reasons: the faithful God has promised, and the promised Christ has come! Berkouwer writes: "The Archimedean point in Paul's thinking is not . . . a futuristic one, but one founded squarely on what has already occurred."[8] The second coming of Christ is wholly conditioned by His first coming; therefore, our attitude to the former should be conditioned by our knowledge and understanding of the latter. The great, decisive, and determining deed has been done; at Calvary the victory has been secured. At the Second Coming the victory will be fully demonstrated.

For the church that awaits the coming of her Lord, the time

that remains is to be one of watching and working. It is not to
be a time of watching without working, an idle gazing into
heaven (Acts 1:11). Jesus' command to "watch" (Matthew
25:13; Mark 13:33–37) does not mean to "look for" or to
"observe," but to "be awake." G. E. Ladd remarks that the word
"does not denote an intellectual attitude but a moral quality of
spiritual readiness for the Lord's return"[9] (see, e.g., Romans
13:11–14). "Watchfulness and activity are two sides of the same
coin," says Berkouwer. "The true congregation may never be
like the servant whose affairs were in chaos because he did not
expect the coming of his master."[10]

This activity will include both the church's direct evangelism in the world and her more general work and witness. In
his second letter Peter recognizes the fact of the delay and the
use being made of it by the church's critics (2 Peter 3:3–4). But
he sees the delay as being determined by Christ's patience, not
caused by impotence: "He is patient with you, not wanting anyone to perish, but everyone to come to repentance" (2 Peter
3:9). Similarly, Paul speaks of God's "tolerance and patience" in
spite of the world's abuse of His kindness in delaying the judgment: a kindness meant to lead them toward repentance
(Romans 2:4).

The church is to fill up this time, fulfilling Christ's mandate
to "make disciples of all nations" (Matthew 28:19) and to be His
witnesses "to the ends of the earth" (Acts 1:8). This global mission of the church leaves no time for any "crisis of delay." Those
in the church are grateful for every year given them and every
tribe evangelized and every soul won. Indeed they can have no
passion left for any sullen frustration: it calls upon all its
resources for the commission given, and cries, like Paul, "Woe
to me if I do not preach the gospel!" (1 Corinthians 9:16).

The delay of Christ's second coming to salvation and to
judgment is not, after all, the failure of God's plan, but is the
condition of its success. As Berkouwer says: "If this is a time of
waiting, it is a period of divine waiting to which human waiting
must correspond."[11] And God waits and works (in the church's
waiting and working) so that the harvest might be full and glorious (James 5:7).

However, it is not only for the sake of evangelism and sav-

ing the lost that Christians live thankfully in God's world. There
is meaning and beauty and happiness in God's world even now.
We are not to have a tunnel vision that sees only the new earth
and ignores the old, for it is a world that is still preserved and
blessed by its Creator, even in the time of the Fall and the curse.
There is no inconsistency in a Christian who is a pilgrim journeying to the next world enjoying and appreciating this one.
We have work to do for this present age (2 Thessalonians
3:6–10), and our duty is to do it. We should say with Luther: "If
Christ were coming back tomorrow, I would plant a tree today."

The church must continually be aware of this great task,
and of its urgency. If the church loses the dominant note of
proclamation and soul-winning, it will lose its bearings and
even its character. It will either become quite desperate about
"the problem of the delay," with its charts and dates, or be lost
in internal disputes or resigned to fulfilling a merely social role
in the world.

This does not mean that the Christian church is to have no
interest in this world and its secular institutions. The compassion of Christ never allows that. The church has been and
always will be a prophetic voice and witness against cruelty
and injustice, because its members know that this is still rightly
God's world and that world is hastening towards His judgment.
Similarly, the church's members are to minister in compassion
to every kind of need and to encourage in hope every stumbling
discovery of a better way forward that man and his civilization
may make. In this respect there need be no opposition between
a watching and a working church. The Victorian social
reformer Lord Shaftesbury is reported to have said that for
thirty years not a single day had passed when he did not consciously recall that Christ was coming. It is not a church with-
drawn into the desert which is ready to give account to her
master.

Yet the church must never forget that this is a world in
process of passing away, a world under judgment, a world
doomed in its alienation from God. Helmut Thielicke cautions
us about our attitudes to "progress" in a world that resists
God's kingdom:

Any progress will be marked by profound ambivalence. Man subdues the earth (Genesis 1:28) and thus fulfils the Creator's command but he does so with the methods of the fallen world: tyranny, force, competition, and self-interest, so that as the light of creation increases its shadow also increases. . . . Yet to accept the permanence of historical structures is no reason for resignation. It cannot mean that we must believe in fate and mark time. It cannot mean that every effort to change the perverted conditions of the world is a hopeless initiative. . . . What it does mean is that modesty is enjoined. It tells us that attempts to change things can produce only gradual improvements. We can undertake partial modifications. We can make the world a little more just and prosperous and free. We can try to replace dictatorships by slightly less bad democracies. We live within the limit of comparatives. We will be proof against utopian superlatives.[12]

In this way the people of God can act as salt amid what Thielicke calls "the decay of history," stemming its decline, retarding the process of putrefaction, encouraging progress, setting up what Karl Barth calls "small steps" and "parables of what shall be,"[13] in prospect of the day when Christ shall come and God will make all things new (Revelation 21–22).

## THE SIGNIFICANCE OF THE
## SECOND COMING FOR WORLD HISTORY

The fact of our Lord's second coming to end world history as we know it, to judge the generations of both past and present, and to renew the heavens and the earth, tells us that human history is going somewhere—that it is moving towards a God-appointed goal.

This perspective is in stark contrast to much of the thinking of the ancient world (the ancient exception being the nation of Israel). The Greeks, for instance, had a cyclical view of history in which it endlessly repeated itself, whatever personal goals the individual might reach. There was no purpose or meaning in history, and man's only hope was to be rescued from time and brought into eternity by a power, or powers, that belonged to the Beyond: "For the Greeks, the idea that redemption is to take place through divine action in the course of events in time is impossible,"[14] Oscar Cullmann writes. The divorce between God and time, God and history, God and the world was considered absolute.

It may seem odd to us that the Greeks, whose gods were all too human, should eschew the idea of a real incarnation of God in which time and eternity, God and man, creation and Creator would be brought into a perfect reconciliation and harmony. But so it was. God was outside history and therefore there could be no real meaning in history. History had no goal because God was not operating within it, leading it to a goal.

The biblical teaching, including the Old Testament perspective, stands in outstanding contrast to this. From the day God called Abraham to become the father of a nation that would bless "all the families of the earth," his people were pointed towards a future hope that would embrace the world (Genesis 12:1-3, RSV). Their journey under Moses' leadership to a land that was promised to Abraham but only possessed under Joshua became the parable of a pilgrimage, both personal and historical, to a "rest" that could never be perfectly or permanently found in the present order of things (Hebrews 4:8-9).

Therefore Israel's prophets pointed beyond their own days to a time when mankind would be redeemed from the chaos sin had brought into the world. But that future would lie with God, the true and only God, the God of the Jews. It would not be a man-made utopia, but a God-given deliverance and kingdom. It would be a time when a new David (Isaiah 9:6-7) would bring with him a new era, a new heaven and a new earth (Isaiah 65:17-18), making the people of God all they were meant to be—a new Israel, a new Jerusalem, a new and living temple for God to dwell in. This was the great Old Testament hope: a hope and a message that embraced all peoples, even Israel's traditional enemies (Isaiah 19:18-25), and called the distant coastlands to repentance and peace (Psalm 96; Isaiah 66:18-23).

Many of the elements of the New Testament's vision of the future are therefore already present in the Old Testament hope. But they are there in a hidden form, often obscured by apparent contradictions and setbacks, always in fragmented form, with vital elements missing. Indeed, much is said of the coming age, but little of the one who would bring it to pass or the strange means whereby He would establish and extend the kingdom of God (Isaiah 53:12).

The New Testament, on the other hand, loudly proclaims that God Himself has entered the course of human history in a new way: as Jesus of Nazareth (Acts 2:22; Hebrews 2:14). In Jesus all the hopes of the Old Testament prophets and New Testament apostles find their focus. He in whom "the whole fullness of the Deity lives in bodily form" (Colossians 2:9) has achieved at a decisive point in human history an irreversible victory over sin and death. He has entered a fallen world and accomplished its redemption from chaos and corruption. He has established "for all time" (Hebrews 10:11–14) a victory whose ensuing effects are spreading throughout human history. He Himself, as the God-man, the Mediator and King, governs the world and superintends the effects of that victory from the throne of Godhead.

History is now dominated by Jesus Christ. Calvary, His own act of atonement, is the fulcrum by which He will raise the earth to its destiny in God. Pentecost witnessed the beginning of that work, and ensuing history and the expansion of the church has seen its unstoppable continuance. Jesus sometimes spoke of the spread of the kingdom as being like yeast or leaven in dough, its rise and spread being irresistible, unstoppable, until He came again to bring it to completion.

Similarly Paul likens the world in its sin to a pregnant woman whose time of delivery pain and birth is inevitable. The world has judgment in the midst of it; judgment is growing in the womb of history. All things, and people, hasten to their appointed goal.

Though at present characterized by incompleteness, ambiguities, and contradictions, human history is a conquered chaos, an overruled confusion in which Christ the Lord of history secretly, and even in some cases openly, rules and overrules for the sake of His church. As Augustine long since indicated in his *City of God*,[15] amidst the clash of empires, the rise and fall of kingdoms, one ultimate purpose is being fulfilled, one hidden kingdom is being extended. It is in the kingdom of God that the real meaning of history is to be found.

Where God's future for man and His world is ignored or denied, everything is touched with frustration and meaninglessness. If God is denied man cannot be affirmed. If the meaning of history is only to be found *within* history (as Marxism claims), then history will soon lose both its meaning and its way.

Stephen H. Travis reminds us that for the Christian too history loses meaning without this great event as its goal:

> The hope of Christ's coming at the end of history is the logical and necessary outcome of our faith that God has already acted for our salvation in the historical events of Jesus' life, death and resurrection. To remove the hope of a final consummation of what Jesus Christ began in history is to undermine the whole idea of God acting in history. God's plan of salvation worked out through history is left with a beginning and no end. As Emil Brunner puts it: ". . . Faith in Jesus without the expectation of His Parousia is a cheque that is never cashed, a promise that is not made in earnest. A faith in Christ without the expectation of a Parousia is like a flight of stairs that leads nowhere but ends in the void."[16]

# 31

# THE RESURRECTION
# OF THE DEAD IN CHRIST

The doctrine of the resurrection of the dead is a New Testament doctrine. This does not mean, however, that it has no connection with important Old Testament insights and aspirations. Certainly by Jesus' time the doctrine was widely taught among the Jews, especially in Palestine among the Pharisees. Nevertheless, it was Jesus Christ who "brought life and immortality to light" in His own person, atonement, and resurrection (2 Timothy 1:10).

## THE OLD TESTAMENT HOPE

### A Place Called *Sheol*

The hope of Old Testament peoples for resurrection after death began with a belief in sheol. The Hebrew Old Testament gives the name *sheol* to the state of men and women after death. According to D. K. Stuart *sheol* has a wide range of meanings, including "death, the grave, hell, the next world and the nether world," and it appears in poetic as well as descriptive passages. Consequently, writes Stuart, in the sixty-six references that occur, "the picture of Sheol that emerges is multifaceted but not contradictory." He informs us that "Not until the Hellenistic era (after 333 B.C.) was sheol (hades) conceived of as compartmentalized, with places of torment and comfort."[1]

The Greek Old Testament, the Septuagint, uses the word *hades* to translate *sheol*. Joachim Jeremias notes that in its use in the New Testament (ten times only) *hades* covers both the older view (denoting "the whole sphere of the dead") and its later emphasis as the place of "the temporary sojourn of the souls of the ungodly" who are awaiting final judgment.[2]

A striking feature of the Old Testament writings is their reticence about speaking of life after death. This is strange when we consider that Israel as a nation grew up in Egypt under the shadow of a sophisticated religious system which was lavish in its attention to the subject of the afterlife. By contrast, the Old Testament teaching is modest to the point of obscurity in expressing its hope, and is profoundly aware of the seriousness of death as the expression of God's wrath upon mankind (Psalm 90:5–10). It refuses to lighten the grim picture of death reigning in man's world, eschewing extravagant or even bright pictures of the possibilities "beyond"; instead, it consistently paints the picture of life after death in dark colors, firmly retaining the abnormality of death even when hinting at the continuance of life.

In much twentieth-century biblical scholarship we encounter the conviction that there is no doctrine of life after death in the Old Testament writings, at least not before the seventh or sixth century B.C. and the Exile. However, dissenting voices have long been raised. At the turn of the century S. D. F. Salmond pointed out that the idea of *extinction* "is foreign to the Old Testament,"[3] notwithstanding its fears. And a generation later Paul Heinisch made the same point: "Israel at all times firmly believed that the soul, when separated from the body, does not cease to exist."[4] Whatever unresolved difficulties and tensions this created when considered alongside the other elements of Hebrew thought about man and God, sin and death, the biblical teaching about sheol showed that after death man continued to exist, and existed for a purpose, albeit unspecified. Sheol is, after all, a place of *waiting*.

Similarly, the Old Testament writers resisted ideas that life after death entailed a loss of personal identity, a state of being swallowed up by nature. However reduced by death his life might become, a man remained individually and recognizably himself, and while social distinctions might be irrelevant there (Job 4:13–19), personal and even moral ones were not (Job 19:25–27; Isaiah 14:9–22).

## Muted Old Testament Teachings

Notwithstanding these two important points, it remains true and significant that for all the hopes and fears of the people no clear light from heaven shone into the forbidding darkness of the grave. No clear prophetic word, no further revelation, no formal doctrine was given to Israel. That is why our Old Testament, even with its early hints, growing convictions, and eventual assurances, is so profoundly unsatisfactory with regard to this matter of life after death, muted as its teaching is and shadowed over, even in its persistent hope, with a deep sadness (Job 14:7–17).

But there is a crucially important reason for this, a reason bound up with the whole spiritual education of this elect nation to whom belonged "the adoption as sons . . . the divine glory, the covenants, the receiving of the law, the temple worship and the promises" (Romans 9:4). The religious convictions and elaborate speculations of the other nations (notably the Egyptians) concerning life after death were fundamentally flawed in that they failed to take adequate account of the holiness of God and the sin of man. Only in Israel was the true God truly known: a holy God who was Judge of all the earth. And the vantage point of being placed alongside *this* God as His sons gave the Israelites a unique perspective upon all of life and upon its universal end—death. Only the chosen people learned—by prophetic speech *and* prophetic silence—the seriousness of sin, the true nature of death and its full horror as the divine curse upon sin (Genesis 2:15–17; 3:19). Consequently, only they understood how wonderful, how undeserved and faithful was the love of God for Israel (Deuteronomy 7:6–11). And only as these lessons were deeply engraved upon the nation's heart was Israel taught the personal implications of an undying love and an indestructible covenant (e.g., Psalm 16:10–11; 49:15; 73:24).

Colin Brown, surveying some of the more recent studies on these verses and on the Old Testament hope concerning life beyond death,[5] notes that what underlies them is not a Greek view of the intrinsic immortality of the soul, but a recognition that God, for whom nothing is impossible, will not let the fellowship that exists in the covenant die or even diminish. Thus on Psalm 49:15 ("God will ransom my soul from the power of

Sheol, for he will receive me"[RSV]) he writes: "Psalm 49 clearly does not teach a positive doctrine of resurrection. On the other hand, it envisages an ongoing life with Yahweh in which the believing Israelite is saved from the ongoing power of Sheol."[6] As G. C. Berkouwer puts it: "Nothing of the radical gravity of death is discounted. . . . But this seriousness of death remains subject to divine possibilities . . . Sheol does not have the last word" (Isaiah 25:7–8; 26:19).[7]

Yet still there remained a deep ambiguity about any kind of existence after death, and for a further reason: the loss of the body. Unlike many later Greeks, for instance, most Hebrews did not make a wide division between the physical and the spiritual elements in man. They would use the terms *flesh* and *soul* interchangeably to denote the whole of a man. They did not think of a soul *in* a body, but of man as a bodily being who *was* a soul. Nor did they speculate about the soul as being intrinsically indestructible and consequently immortal, as did the Greeks. They believed that man had been created by God as a unity, comprising body and soul together. Man was a bodily being, "fearfully and wonderfully made" for the concrete world of beauty and goodness (Psalm 139:14; Genesis 1:31)—made to enjoy it and dominate it (Genesis 1:26). Hence they were unable to contemplate life beyond the grave, out of the body, as being "life" in any fullness (Job 10:20–22; Ecclesiastes 9:1–10). Man without his body was a reduced being cut off from his proper environment. Edmond Jacob rightly asserts that "the Old Testament never presents death as a liberation or as a gateway giving access to perfect felicity."[8]

There was thus something of a tug-of-war in Hebrew thought. On the one hand they could not conceive of God's people forever ceasing to have a relationship with Him (see, e.g., the endings of Psalms 16 and 73). But, on the other hand, crucial and urgent questions were left unanswered. What was man, banished by death from the world he was made for, a half-alive being living an almost wholly negative existence (Job 3:11–26), and above all banished from the covenant community where God had His dwelling to a shadowy region where God hid Himself, at least to the gaze of the living (Isaiah 38:18–19)? How could the dead equal the praise of the living (Psalm 115:17)?

Snatches of hope there seemed to be. Not so much words, as whispers of hope to show that for all this, in the omnipotence of God a full salvation and even a bodily future beyond death was possible.

### Snatches of Hope from Enoch, Elijah, Job, and Others

There was the taking up of Enoch (Genesis 5:24; cf. Hebrews 11:5). There was the bodily ascension of Elijah (2 Kings 2:1–12). There were from time to time poetic-prophetic outbursts such as Isaiah's cry: "Your dead will live; their bodies will rise. You who dwell in the dust, wake up and shout for joy. Your dew is like the dew of the morning; the earth will give birth to her dead" (Isaiah 26:19); and the psalmist's statement: "You will not abandon me to the grave, nor will you let your Holy One see decay" (Psalm 16:10), singled out by Peter when proclaiming the resurrection of Jesus and God's foreordained plan of salvation (Acts 2:30–31).

Job's famous cry of faith, wrung out of him by the pressures of the hour, is especially well known and treasured: "I know that my Redeemer lives, and that in the end he will stand upon the earth. And after my skin has been destroyed, yet in my flesh I will see God" (Job 19:25–26). Francis Andersen challenges much fashionable thinking when he writes: "The argument that Job does not expect personal reconstitution as a man, because this idea entered Judaism only towards the very end of the biblical period, can be dismissed in the light of much recent research that shows interest in the after-life as an ancient concern for Israelite faith."[9]

Eventually, however, there came one clear and indisputable shaft of light to break the encircling gloom. Among the prophecies of Daniel, so futuristic and so aware of forces beyond our human world, the ultimate vindication and full salvation of God's people is assured in a strong and clear promise:

Multitudes who sleep in the dust of the earth will awake: some to everlasting life, others to shame and everlasting contempt. Those who are wise will shine like the brightness of the heavens, and those who lead many to righteousness, like the stars for ever and ever. But you, Daniel, close up and seal the words of the scroll until the time of the end. (Daniel 12:2–4)

It is noteworthy that even here, in the clearest and most advanced Old Testament statement about resurrection and immortality, there is still a reminder of reserve, a mark of secrecy. It is not yet time to reveal all.

Nor would it be, until "the appearing of our Savior, Christ Jesus, who has destroyed death and has brought life and immortality to light through the gospel" (2 Timothy 1:10). The true revelation of God's plan for man's salvation could never be taught adequately, or its foundations clearly uncovered, apart from the person and achievement of Jesus Himself, who by His death as a ransom and His resurrection as a total victory showed eternal life to be the costly gift of a loving Father and not the inevitable progress of the human soul. Nor are immortality and the resurrection products of innate qualities and impersonal forces, but exist for us through the personal authority and power of Him who said, "I am the resurrection and the life" (John 11:25). So, from the Old Testament half-light we come into the New Testament's clear teaching on the future of man and the resurrection of the dead.

## THE NEW TESTAMENT REVELATION

### Our Valued Bodies

It is with the bodily resurrection and subsequent glorification of Jesus that man's place in God's abiding purpose is fully revealed. It is repeatedly made plain in the New Testament that the body, and not just the soul, has a sacred and central place in God's plan for man. It is the object of value, compassion, and healing in the ministry of Christ and the apostles (Matthew 4:23–24; 8:17; 10:1), and it is the focus of particular care where the poor and needy are concerned, especially among God's people (2 Corinthians 9:1–15). The body is the temple of the Holy Spirit (1 Corinthians 6:19) and the theater of God's glory in our lives (Romans 12:1; 1 Corinthians 6:20). Even now it is mystically united to the incarnate Son (1 Corinthians 6:15) and will one day be glorified with Him in a resurrection and exaltation like His (1 Corinthians 6:14–15).

Hence no part of the body or of bodily existence can be despised, neglected, or detached from the demands of godliness (Romans 12:1). In the body we share the life of Christ: His sufferings (2 Corinthians 4:10–11) and His reward (Philippians 3:10–11). All areas of bodily life are therefore to be yielded up to God in view of this future and the historic death and resurrection of Christ which is its foundation (Romans 6:12–14). It is this *total* bodily existence as it stands in the will and purposes of God that has been purchased by the death of our Lord and reclaimed by the power of His resurrection (Romans 6:4–5).

Throughout the New Testament the salvation of believers is never simply a matter of the salvation of their souls, but is a full salvation that includes their bodies also: the totality of their humanness is redeemed. Man in his bodily existence—"fearfully and wonderfully made" (Psalm 139:14), yet frail and temporary as "the flowers of the field" (Isaiah 40:6, 8)—is lifted, body and soul, into the life of God, who, like His promise, endures forever. Hence Paul writes to the saints at Rome: "we wait eagerly for our adoption as sons, the redemption of our bodies" (Romans 8:23). Note that it is definitely not, as in so much contemporary thinking, redemption *from* our bodies of which he speaks, but the redemption *of* our bodies. As joint heirs with Christ we shall enjoy a deliverance as total as His from the effects of death; "we shall certainly be united with him in a resurrection like his" (Romans 6:5, RSV; 2 Corinthians 4:14).

## Our Bodily Resurrection and 1 Corinthians 15

The single most sustained passage in the New Testament about this subject is 1 Corinthians 15. Here Paul is protesting not against a denial of the physical resurrection of Christ (something all the Corinthians obviously accepted), but against a denial that *Christians* are similarly raised. This denial came from super-spiritual Corinthians who had in fact imbibed a pagan and not a Christian concept of spirituality, and who denied the need for or the truth of any physical, bodily aspect to the age to come. Paul opposes such a disembodied piety as being untrue to the past, unreal to the future, and unhelpful to the present.

The apostle argues in general from the resurrection of Christ to the resurrection of believers, from a fact that is not doubted to a fact that should not be doubted, since the one follows on from the other. But first he argues backwards from their position: "But if it is preached that Christ has been raised from the dead, how can some of you say that there is no resurrection of the dead? If there is no resurrection of the dead, then not even Christ has been raised" (1 Corinthians 15:12–13). Of course, if this is so then Christ is dead, and with Him all our hopes of atonement and justification (Romans 4:25; 5:10), of forgiveness and eternal life with God, and we are left hopeless (1 Corinthians 15:14–19). Berkouwer rightly says: "With the denial of the resurrection from the dead everything is denied; life sinks into the abyss and its meaning becomes illusory: 'If the dead are not raised, let us eat and drink for tomorrow we die'" (1 Corinthians 15:32).[10]

Like a trumpet blast, however, the controlling statement of the whole chapter is sounded in verse 20: "But Christ has indeed been raised from the dead." For Paul the resurrection of Jesus is the basis, the guarantee, and the pattern of the resurrection of all who are joined with Him. By raising Christ, whom He appointed the head and representative of His people, God has, in the words of Gordon Fee, "set in motion the events of the End in such a way that they must of divine necessity be brought to consummation."[11] His resurrection was decisive for them, Christ's resurrection being "the firstfruits of those who have fallen asleep" (1 Corinthians 15:20). The firstfruits of the old Hebrew harvest times (Deuteronomy 26:1–4) was the first installment of the crop which foreshadowed and pledged the whole. So the resurrection of Christ not only foreshadows or even indicates but actually *begins* the process which will end with the resurrection and glorification of all believers in the Last Day. Furthermore, Christ's resurrection body will be the pattern and pledge of our own resurrection bodies. Ours will be a resurrection like his (Romans 6:5; cf. 2 Corinthians 4:14).

However, what occupies Paul for much of 1 Corinthians 15 (but only because it occupies the thoughts and questioning of some of his readers) is the *nature* of this resurrection body. Here, as Donald Guthrie suggests, Paul's main aim "seems to be to show that the believer will receive a spiritual body which will be entirely appropriate to existence in the after-life."[12] The resurrection state is not a return to flesh and blood (1 Corinthians 15:50), but is nevertheless a return to an embodied state (v. 44) from a disembodied one. No longer will the body be patterned after Adam, "the man of dust," but after the risen embodied and glorified Christ, "the man of heaven" (v. 49, RSV). What was "sown in dishonor" will be "raised in glory . . . a spiritual body" (vv. 43–44)—but a body nonetheless: spiritual but not spectral (cf. Luke 24:39). The resurrection body will be a physical reality, but one wholly dominated by the Spirit who enlivens it (Romans 8:11; cf. 1:4).

Of course the precise nature of the glorified body is bound to be a mystery that is incomprehensible to us in our present state. Yet it is not to be thought of simply as a new (in the sense of another) body. It is a resurrection and therefore not simply a further creation. On the one hand, it is not the resuscitation of dead corpses or the restoration of a previous fragile existence, as if it were a matter of gluing molecules together again. It will in fact be the most profound and radical renewal, a transformation of the old embodied state, and one which surely involves, as Donald Bloesch says, "the transfiguration of matter itself."[13] On the other hand, however, it is not simply another creation. It is indeed a renewed creation: that is, a new creation in some respects, but one that is in other respects determined by the previous life and its bodily existence. It is in fact in continuity with the old body in some way; different in form, but not in identity. It will still be our mortal body (Romans 8:11): at one time given up to corruption, it shall be raised incorruptible (1 Corinthians 15:42–44).

Paul prepares the way for what he is to say about the spiritual body by means of the analogy of seeds which become transformed as they enter a new stage of their life (vv. 36–38); and he then illustrates it further by pointing out that there are different kinds of bodies for different levels of existence and different "splendors" for different heavenly bodies (vv. 39–41). His aim is to show that the transformed nature of the resurrection body will be suitable to the new mode of life after the resurrection, and indeed part of it. At this point Paul's concern, says Fee, "is to emphasize that each is adapted to its own peculiar existence, that 'body' does not necessarily mean one thing (=flesh and blood) since there are many kinds of bodies."[14]

The apostle further illustrates His point by contrasting the Christians' present share in the earthly body of the first man, Adam, with their future share in the heavenly body of the second man, Christ (vv. 45–49). Paul then concludes his argument with verses 50–57: a "magnificent crescendo," writes Fee, in which Paul emphasizes "the absolute necessity of transformation in order to enter the heavenly mode of existence"[15] and shows how certain and complete and final that transformation will be. Nothing, absolutely nothing, of mortality will remain about us, and death shall be "swallowed up in victory"—the shared victory of Jesus Christ over sin and death and hell (vv. 54–57).

Yet even here—and typically—Paul intrudes an ethical note (v. 58) that touches the present. This is not a remote hope for the Christian. The power that raised our Lord is already working within us (Ephesians 3:20), and has been from the beginning of our new life in Christ. We believe, says Paul, "according to the working of his great might which he accomplished in Christ when he raised him from the dead" (Ephesians 1:19–20, RSV). This same power is changing us even now "with ever-increasing glory" (2 Corinthians 3:18) as we persevere in faith and obedience. This is no impersonal 'force', but the personal power of the Holy Spirit.

## Our Bodily Resurrection and 2 Corinthians 4:16–5:10

The other major Pauline passage on this subject is 2 Corinthians 4:16–5:10. In 2 Corinthians 4:16 we enter what Philip Edgcumbe Hughes calls "one of the most important eschatological passages of the New Testament."[16] Here Paul speaks of his mortal physical body holding the precious treasure of a gospel ministry (4:7) but decaying with age and weakness even while his spirit is growing in grace and joy (4:16). Yet as he looks in faith upon eternal realities (4:18), he knows himself to be united in destiny with his risen glorified Savior, and knows that he will share fully in the resurrection victory of Christ.

Death would destroy the tent of his body (5:1), but God would raise up a "house in heaven, not built by human hands," heavenly and spiritual in contrast to what is earthly and physical. Hughes argues strongly that if "house" in the first part of the sentence refers to the body, then it is most natural to find the same meaning of "body" in the second part. Paul is therefore clearly speaking of the resurrection body, and not just of a "heavenly mansion" or a blessed (and disembodied) state.[17] Moreover, the Christian's physical body is repeatedly in view in the context of this passage (see particularly, 4:7, 10–11, 16).

In the fragile, decaying body which he has, Paul even now longs for the appearing of Christ and the experience of placing over that body his heavenly resurrection body that will transfigure it (5:2). True, he is prepared to be absent from the body and in a disembodied state in order to be at home with the Lord (5:6–8), but it is not his ideal, nor is it his (or our) final destiny.

## SOUL-SLEEP?

A further word should be said concerning the believer's interim state between earthly death and final resurrection. It is again becoming common to meet theories of soul-sleep or of temporary annihilation that have always been on the edge of orthodoxy. Luther entertained this idea for a time but then dismissed it; Calvin wrote his first theological work against it (*Psychopannychia*); and in our own day Donald Bloesch has referred to it as "a profound misunderstanding."[18] Among other things, the soul-sleep theory fails to see that the metaphorical use of the term *sleep* for death is a convenient way of pointing to a state not only of rest from sorrow and toil (even the rest of God), but also of waiting, of incompleteness, of waiting to begin a new day. Sleep is an interim term.

Jeremias contends that the idea of soul-sleep is "foreign to the entire New Testament as well as to late Judaism."[19] It cannot stand before Christ's words to the thief on the cross (Luke 23:43) or Paul's wish: "I desire to depart and be with Christ, which is better by far" (Phillipians 1:23). The book of Revelation, for all its symbols, does not lead us to a picture of an empty heaven waiting for dead saints to awaken, but of a

crowded interim with worshipping and even passionate multitudes (Revelation 6:9–11; 8:3–4) aware of the realities of heaven
and earth and awaiting their final and full redemption.

Murray Harris concludes from his own study of the issue:

> The state of the Christian dead is one of unconsciousness or
> sleep only in the sense that they are no longer active in, and
> therefore conscious of, the earthly world of time and space.
> But they are conscious of their heavenly or spiritual envi-
> ronment, in that they "live to God" (Luke 20.38b) "'in the
> presence of Christ" (Philippians 1:23), evidently having the
> ability (at least) to recall the past and to think rationally.[20]

This, says Harris, in spite of its incompleteness, should not
at all be looked upon as diminished existence, but on the contrary as one of "enriched fellowship with Christ" in great glory
and joy. Believers between the events of death and the final resurrection are with Christ, which is "far better," but without a
resurrection body which awaits the Last Day and is one of the
greatest glories.

This conviction about the human body and its destiny has
lain at the root of Christian concern with and respect for the
bodily needs of men and women, especially the disabled, the
sick, and the aged. It has been said strikingly, though not without reason, that Christianity is the most materialist religion in
the world. And we shall see that emphasis carried beyond this
particular doctrine of the bodily resurrection of believers when
we examine the larger context of the physical renewal of the
whole earth at the second coming of Christ, who makes it an
eternal home for Himself and His church (Revelation 21:1–5;
cf. Romans 8:18–23; 2 Peter 3:13).

# 32

# THE FINAL
# JUDGMENT BY CHRIST

The concept of judgment is prominent throughout the Bible, from Genesis to Revelation. It is, furthermore, an essential part of the teaching of Scripture concerning God and the world He created. All history is moving toward a "general judgment," the inescapable destiny of each human being. At that time God will exhibit His supreme righteous character one final time. As Judge He will then acquit, and He will condemn. The judgment also will serve as the public vindication of Christ in His glory and of the church, His bride. It is the climactic end of the old order and the beginning of a new. Such judgment traces back to Old Testament times, and its approach should fill us with a certain fear and respect, as well as anticipation.

## JUDGMENT IN THE OLD TESTAMENT

In the Old Testament the basic concept of judgment is, from the start, a religious concept; it never is a purely secular or even simply an ethical one. Such judgment goes far beyond any view of intrinsic or even absolute right and wrong. Judgment is first and foremost *God's* activity, asserting His order in the midst of a disordered world and maintaining His standards of truth, righteousness, and justice amid all confusion and against all contradiction.

Leon Morris maintains that the fundamental meaning of the Hebrew word-group for judgment "is that of discrimination, of distinguishing between parties" such as "the innocent and the guilty, those who are wronged and those who deny them jus-

tice" (e.g., Exodus 18:16; Deuteronomy 1:16; 1 Kings 3:9).[1]
However, Yahweh's judgment was not cold and technical, a
mere mental sifting of evidence leading to an impartial
announcement. "Judging, whether by God or man," says Morris, "was essentially dynamic," and where Yahweh was concerned "it implied a passion for right."[2] God was personally
involved in every case, the companion of the injured party and
the opponent of the guilty one. In matters of judgment, of
truth, and of justice, He is the God who acts.

### Judgment Directed Toward God's People, Israel

One arresting feature of the doctrine is that while God's
judgment will reach to all mankind, it is singularly directed to
His own people. Chiefly and most searchingly, judgment applies
to Israel. We should not be surprised at this, since Israel was
taught from the beginning that privilege implies responsibility.
The obligations of justice and righteousness were heightened in
the covenantal relationship which Israel enjoyed (Deuteronomy 27–28).

However, there were provisions equal to the demands made
upon the chosen people. If judgment began in Israel, so did
grace. From the start Yahweh's laws were embedded in grace,
in a covenantal relationship (e.g., Exodus 20:2), and He would
give grace to keep them. He had given Israel His laws not simply as a set of regulations, but as the outcome and implication
of *a shared existence* in which God's standards and priorities
become Israel's standards and priorities. God would dwell in
the midst of His people, with all the encouragements and all
the demands which that implied.

One implication of that partnership was startlingly brought
into focus by Amos: "You only have I chosen of all the families
of the earth; therefore I will punish you for all your sins" (Amos
3:2). While Israelite nationalists looked forward to Yahweh's
day of judgment as a time when the heathen nations would be
judged, the true prophets in Israel warned that Israel herself
would be in the very epicenter of the judgment of God upon all
sin and wrongdoing. V. Herntrich writes:

If the day of Yahweh had originally been envisaged as a day

of victory over Israel's foes, the concept changes in the presentation of [Amos] 1 and 2, and the day of Yahweh now becomes a day of judgment on Israel, cf. Ho. 4:1ff.; Is. 1:2, 18ff.; Mi. 1:2–4; Zeph. 3:8; Jl. 3:2; Mal. 3:2. Indeed, the judgment on Israel stands at the very heart of the general judgment on the nations. Israel's only privilege of election at the judgment is to be judged with particular severity, Am. 3:1ff.; Is. 5:1ff.[3]

The modern Western mind frequently claims to have a problem with the emphasis and even the concept of God as Judge as we find it in the Old Testament. However, it is to be doubted if this "problem" issues from a "higher" conception of God. The Old Testament believer was taught that Yahweh's judgment was the demonstration of His righteous character in mercy and in wrath, in deliverance of the innocent and in punishment of the guilty. It had two sides—judgment *and* mercy, wrath *and* grace—but neither was in contradiction of the other. Both were consistent with God's righteousness. In fact the same characteristic of justice underlay salvation for His much-tried people (Isaiah 30:18–19) and retribution for His (and their) enemies. He was, after all, the faithful God, always true to His covenant of grace. As. E. W. Heaton says: "The righteousness of Yahweh embraced both His judgment on wickedness and His salvation from wickedness."[4]

## Faith in a World of Injustice

For the Israelite believer, the great difficulty was not God's part in concrete judgments upon sinful men, for this was consistent with His holy character. What *was* problematic for the Israelite mind was God's apparent *inactivity* in the face of injustice (e.g., Psalm 44; Habakkuk 1). We are likely to agonize over the ferocious end of Sodom and Gomorrah; the Israelite agonized over the peaceful prosperity of Nineveh or Babylon or Rome. For him God's activity in judgment was essential to His true nature, and God's office and function as judge was essential to His very being.

This sensitivity to God's character, this awareness of His zeal in championing righteousness, led to a further and deeper inquiry into His ways of working in the matter of judgment. If God was not at present exercising to the full His right to condemn and destroy the wicked, He was nevertheless storing up wrath for a time reserved in the future, a day when He would "ease Himself" of the present tensions. The prophets declared this, and many of the Hebrews believed this. Morris notes that of the sixty-five occurrences of the verb *shaphat,* to judge, in the Old Testament, forty-one times the word is used to look to the future. He concludes, "While some of these refer to temporal judgments like the exile, the conclusion is inescapable that to the men of the Old Testament the most significant thing about judgment was the eschatological judgment of the Lord."[5] This ultimate day of judgment would involve not only Israel but all the nations, for there was only one true God over all the earth whose character as Judge made universal judgment inevitable: "He will judge the world in righteousness and the peoples in his truth" (Psalm 96:13; cf. Psalm 98; 110; Isaiah 62–66, etc.).

So, in a world of injustice and many contradictions, Old Testament believers lived by faith and looked in faith to God's future. That future, including its aspect of judgment, is clarified for us in the New Testament teaching.

## JUDGMENT IN THE NEW TESTAMENT

Whenever reference is made to the Second Coming in the New Testament, attention is drawn to the fact of judgment, which is central to it. That judgment will affect all men and nations, the living and the dead, the good and the bad, believers and unbelievers, and Jesus Christ Himself will be its central and presiding figure.

### Jesus and Judgment

There are few subjects on which Jesus spoke more frequently or with greater urgency than that of judgment. Whether preaching to the crowds, addressing His own disciples, or debating with the Pharisees, it was a subject that He repeatedly brought to their attention. A brief survey of Matthew's gospel will show this.

Men are warned, "Do not judge, or you too will be judged"

(Matthew 7:1). False disciples are warned, "Then I will tell them plainly, 'I never knew you. Away from me, you evildoers!'" (7:23). Timid witnesses to Christ are spurred on with the words, "Do not be afraid of those who kill the body but cannot kill the soul. Rather, be afraid of the One who can destroy both soul and body in hell" (10:28). Christ Himself will acknowledge or disown before His Father those who have confessed or denied Him before men (10:32–33). Whole cities and their populations will be caught up in the catastrophic event of the day of judgment (11:20–24), none more so than those which have heard most of Jesus and failed to respond to Him: "But I tell you that it will be more bearable for Sodom on the day of judgment than for you" (11:24). Men will have to account for every careless word spoken in dismissal of Christ (12:36–37).

The imagery of judgment assumes common, yet vivid terms for those listening to Jesus. At the harvest of the generations, when present history ends, weeds will be separated from wheat and burned (13:29–30); the good fish from the bad (13:47–51); the sheep from the goats (25:31–46). On that day of judgment, faithful servants will be separated from those who have abused their trust (24:45–51; cf. 23:13–15). On that great day of reckoning every man will give account of his life and how he has used what has been entrusted to him (25:14–30).

All should be ready for the coming of the Judge of all the earth, who is also the bridegroom of the church. Those unprepared, those without His love in their hearts, those without a wedding garment will be excluded decisively and forever (25:1–13; cf. 22:1–14).

One is left wondering if any shall or can survive that day, but with His warnings Jesus also gives hope and assurance. His words are not meant to reduce men to despair, but to cast them on God and open them to God's way of forgiveness and salvation: "With man this is impossible, but with God all things are possible" (19:26). F. Buchsel writes:

> The only ground of deliverance in the judgment is God's remission, not man's achievement. But the believer may have assurance of this forgiveness. The divine forgiveness is wholly grace and miracle. But Jesus promises it to man

(Mk. 2:9) notwithstanding the severity of His guilt, Lk.
7:36–50 . . . He promises His disciples that He will confess
them before the divine Judge and that He will thus assure
them against condemnation, Matthew 10:32. Hence the last
judgment will mean their deliverance, and they can look
forward to it with longing, the more so as their discipleship
entails persecutions, Lk. 21:28, cf. 18:6–8.[6]

However, it is in the event of Calvary and His own sin-bearing act of atonement that Jesus' promises find their rationale,
and God's remission of punishment its ground and justification. At the cross we see what G. Schrenk calls the same
"unsparing seriousness of God" in the matter of sin, righteousness, and judgment that we see in the final judgment itself.
Indeed, says Schrenk,[7] at Calvary Christ bore the judgment of
God upon sin, so that all who are in Him might go free of condemnation. In the final judgment, finding no adequate shelter
in themselves, those who are outside of Christ must bear the
judgment that nothing else can divert.

To deny Jesus' preaching on judgment is to dismiss a great
part of His teaching as historically redundant. To ignore it is to
set it aside as irrelevant. The outcome of such an attitude is
that Jesus' unique and authoritative position as the Son and
only Revealer of the Father (Matthew 11:27; John 1:18; 5:20) is
undermined. He becomes more and more just another religious
thinker, a figure on the landscape, a face in the crowd. His word
is no longer definitive for our faith. In turn, we undermine all
His sayings and He becomes as fallible on heaven as on hell, on
mercy as on judgment. In this case He too is groping in the
dark towards the light—with no real assurance to give that
there is any light. Such a Jesus is nowhere near the Jesus of the
Gospels or the Christ of Christianity.

## Jesus in the Judgment

Jesus demands to be taken seriously in what He has to say
about judgment, because Jesus Himself is crucial to it. Men's
relation to *Him* now will be the decisive thing on that day, and
men will face *Him* in His sovereign majesty as the one by whom
God will judge the whole world. From both points of view,

therefore, His word on this matter is supremely weighty and we must attend it.

Again and again Jesus stands forward in the Gospels as the one hope of the world, the dividing line between light and darkness (John 9:39; cf. 8:12), life and death (John 5:24), forgiveness and condemnation (Mark 2:5; Luke 7:47). This is no small indication of His self-conscious deity, His place in the Godhead alongside the Father. There is no thought of the possibility of a man or woman being right with God but wrong with Jesus (John 5:23).

Those who deny Him here will themselves be denied in the Last Day; those who refuse His testimony concerning Himself will die in their sins. The word He has spoken will judge them; a word of truth, of warning and of hope:

> "Whoever acknowledges me before men, I will also acknowledge him before my Father in heaven. But whoever disowns me before men, I will disown him before my Father in heaven." (Matthew 10:32–33)

> "You are from below; I am from above. You are of this world; I am not of this world. I told you that you would die in your sins; if you do not believe that I am the one I claim to be, you will indeed die in your sins." (John 8:23–24)

> "There is a judge for the one who rejects me and does not accept my words; that very word which I spoke will condemn him at the last day." (John 12:48)

These are not empty words, for Jesus Himself will be the Judge on the great day of judgment and will make good all His threats and promises. Men will not be tried by a different standard, for they will not be tried by a different judge. Jesus Christ will act then in consistency with His words now. He will personally validate His claims and character.

Although at His first coming Christ came not to condemn the world but to save it (John 3:17; 8:15; 12:47), at His second coming He will come in the role of Judge. Invested with His Father's prerogative as Judge of all the earth (John 5:22, 27, 30),

He will raise the dead, vindicate His people, and condemn the guilty (John 5:19–30; 6:39, 54). Again, Jesus' own words proclaim that truth:

> "The Father judges no one, but has entrusted all judgment to the Son, that all may honor the Son just as they honor the Father." (John 5:22–23)

> "Do not be amazed at this, for a time is coming when all who are in their graves will hear his voice and come out— those who have done good will rise to live, and those who have done evil will rise to be condemned." (John 5:28–29)

The central position that Jesus would occupy in the judgment of the world was clearly stated in the apostolic preaching from the beginning. Peter tells Cornelius and his household: "He [Jesus] commanded us to preach to the people and to testify that he is the one whom God appointed as judge of the living and the dead" (Acts 10:42; cf. 1 Peter 4:5). Paul warns the Athenians that God "has set a day when he will judge the world with justice by the man he has appointed. He has given proof of this to all men by raising him from the dead" (Acts 17:31). In 2 Timothy 4:8 Paul gives to Christ the title of "the righteous Judge," whose future coming is the present encouragement of His saints (e.g., 1 Corinthians 1:8; 2 Corinthians 1:14; Philippians 1:6, 10; 1 Thessalonians 4:18), and their present spur and warning too (e.g., 1 Corinthians 3:10–15).

Thus the Old Testament "Day of the Lord [Yahweh]," the great day of universal and apocalyptic judgment (e.g., Isaiah 2:12–13; Joel 3; Zechariah 12; Malachi 4:5), becomes in the New Testament "the Day of the Lord [Jesus]" (1 Thessalonians 5:2; 2 Peter 3:10), "the day of our Lord Jesus Christ" (1 Corinthians 1:8; cf. 5:5; 2 Corinthians 1:14; Philippians 1:6), "the day of Christ" (Philippians 2:16). Jesus has both God's name of "Lord" (Philippians 2:9; 1 Thessalonians 5:2) and His prerogative as "Judge of all the earth" (Genesis 18:25; Psalm 50:4–6; 96:13; 98:9; Romans 2:16; 2 Timothy 4:1; 2 Peter 3:10, 12; Jude 14–15). As Christ and the Father are one, the New Testament writers continue to speak of the "Father" as judging (e.g., 1 Peter

1:17; cf. Revelation 20:11) and of the judgment seat of "God" (e.g., Romans 14:10; cf. John 14:10). But the judgment seat of God is also the judgment seat of Christ (2 Corinthians 5:10), just as the judgment of Jesus is itself the judgment of God (John 5:22; 2 Peter 3:10, 12). There is no higher court to which appeal can be made.

### Judgment as Both Present and Future

One note clearly sounded in John's gospel is that judgment is present as well as future:

> Whoever believes in him [Jesus] is not condemned; but whoever does not believe stands condemned already, because he has not believed in the name of God's one and only Son. This is the verdict: Light has come into the world, but men loved darkness instead of light, because their deeds were evil. (John 3:18–19; cf. v. 36)

Jesus' very presence among men and women is a kind of judgment, since it stirs up their resentment of Him and of what He so perfectly represents, and exposes their deep-seated enmity to God (Romans 8:7). The *process* of judgment has begun and is under way, even before the *verdict* has been finally and publicly given (John 12:48). It is the church's task to warn, as it is the Spirit's work to convince men of this (Acts 24:25; John 16:8–11).

This gives great seriousness to the present, and a more than temporal dimension to human life and history. Judgment, says John, is already a fact for Satan and the unbelieving world (John 12:31; 16:11). Yet this judgment is partial and provisional, and must one day merge with the full judgment of God, the supreme crisis of history. Consequently, judgment is also a future reality in its fullness and finality (John 5:28–29; Romans 2:5–6; 2 Thessalonians. 1:7–10; 2 Peter 3:7; Revelation 20:12).

Judgment is more than history and it is more than the inexorable outworking of laws such as sowing and reaping (Galatians 6:7–8). It is an appointment every man and woman will keep with God. They will be judged according to the purpose for which he and she were created in the image of a righteous

God (Genesis 1:26–27). The failure of men and women and the fact of death will not alter the certainty or the standard of their Creator's judgment. Thus "man is destined to die once, and after that to face judgment" (Hebrews 9:27). Inasmuch as Christ has been received as the last Adam (1 Corinthians 15:21–22), God's new and perfect Man for us (Romans 5:15–17), we may eagerly await our vindication: for He is now all-sufficient for us (Hebrews 2:8–9; 9:27–28). But outside of Him people are only fallen and corrupt humanity, liable to the avenging judgment of a just and holy Judge. As the writer warns, "It is a dreadful thing to fall into the hands of the living God" (Hebrews 10:31).

It is crucial that we recognize both of these possibilities, for if there is no danger in being outside Him, then there is no possibility of being lost and there is no real meaning in being saved. If there was no judgment unto condemnation at the cross, and if there will be no judgment of condemnation at the appearing of Christ, then judgment itself becomes an empty and irrelevant concept, both to God and man. But, in the words of Buchsel, "The concept of judgment cannot be taken out of the New Testament gospel. It cannot even be removed from the centre to the periphery."[8] It is essential to the integrity of the biblical teaching on man, Christ, and God.

### Judgment According to Works

That judgment will be according to works is repeatedly and consistently taught in the New Testament. For example, Jesus says: "For the Son of Man is going to come in his Father's glory with his angels, and then he will reward each person according to what he has done" (Matthew 16:27); Paul teaches: "God 'will give to each person according to what he has done'" (Romans 2:6); Peter speaks of God as "a Father who judges each man's work impartially" (1 Peter 1:17); John of Revelation records: "And I saw the dead, great and small, standing before the throne. . . . The dead were judged according to what they had done as recorded in the books" (Revelation 20:12). Finally, among Christ's last recorded words is the promise: "Behold, I am coming soon! My reward is with me, and I will give to everyone according to what he has done" (Revelation 22:12).

G. C. Berkouwer is entirely right when he observes, "Judgment according to works is declared with sharp and sustained accents and we simply must listen with deep earnestness."[9]

But are we not clearly told that we are justified by faith and not by works or by a mixture of faith and good works? There is no inconsistency here. Throughout his letters Paul emphatically teaches that a man is justified by faith; yet he is uncompromisingly clear that all men, including those who have been justified by faith, will be judged by their works:

> For we will all stand before God's judgment seat . . . So then, each of us will give account of himself to God. (Romans 14:10, 12)

> For we must all appear before the judgment seat of Christ, that each one may receive what is due him for the things done while in the body, whether good or bad. (2 Corinthians 5:10)

> Therefore judge nothing before the appointed time; wait till the Lord comes. He will bring to light what is hidden in darkness and will expose the motives of men's hearts. At that time each will receive his praise from God. (1 Corinthians 4:5; cf. Romans 2:6–11)

Here the true believer is assessed as a justified man or woman, justified by faith; yet what is revealed is the quality and character of the obedience that has followed that gift of faith and the divine act of free justification. The reason for this repeated New Testament emphasis on the assessment of the believer's life of works at the judgment seat of Christ is that by it is shown the vital and intimate connection between faith and works. As Calvin long ago pointed out, "It is . . . faith alone which justifies and yet the faith which justifies is not alone."[10] Paul recognizes only that faith which works by love (Galatians 5:6), and James teaches that faith without works is dead (James 2:26). For Paul, no less than for James, dead faith is not justifying faith. A living faith will demonstrate both its divine author and its intrinsic nature by producing good works (Ephesians 2:8–10; cf. James 2:18).

## Rewards and Loss at the Judgment Seat of Christ

Yet even in Christian lives there are failures, backslidings, and impoverishing compromises with the godless world around. True, there is no condemnation for those who are in Christ Jesus (Romans 8:1; cf. John 5:24), but there may yet be real loss. Paul speaks to the Corinthians (and especially their church leaders) of the fiery testing of a life's work which is built upon the immovable foundation, Christ, but which is reduced to ashes on that foundation because the believer has built with inferior materials (1 Corinthians 3:11–15). The Christian involved will at the end be saved, "but only as one escaping through the flames." That is, as a man might run from a burning home, all his goods lost, and his body only barely saved and with the smell of burning on it. Though the immediate reference of Paul's words is to the teaching of true or false doctrine, the implications are much wider. What will be judged on that day are the deeds and the motives, the words and the thoughts of men.

We must approach with the same care the entire question of rewards. These are mentioned frequently by Christ for His followers' encouragement (Matthew 5:11–12; 6:4, 6, 18; 10:41–42; 19:29), and by Paul for his own as well as others' encouragement (e.g., 2 Corinthians 4:17; Galatians 6:7–8; Philippians 2:16; Colossians 3:24; 2 Timothy 4:8). God's approval, and Christ's "Well done," can be looked for by those whose lives have been marked by faithfulness, true priorities, and fruitful service. The reward is not forgiveness or salvation, but God's demonstrated approval of those already forgiven on the basis of Christ's once-for-all sacrifice for sin. It expresses His delight in those whose response to a salvation already won has been grateful service and lifelong dedication. At the judgment seat of Christ, the Lord Jesus will judge rewards and loss by how we have used or neglected[11] the privileges and resources we had. As Jesus explained while on earth, "From everyone who has been given much, much will be demanded" (Luke 12:48; cf. Romans 2:12–13). Properly speaking, even here merit has no place, for God gives us grace to do what pleases Him. As Augustine put it, "God crowns His own gifts in us." On the other hand, the debt we owe and the sin that mixes with our best duties compel us to say, when we have done everything we were told to do, "We are unworthy servants; we have only done our duty" (Luke 17:10).

Helmut Thielicke is concerned that we should so understand the concept of reward that it cannot "come independently between God and us":

> The kingdom does not consist of what we acquire but of what we come to be. This "being" is not characterised by a material something which is increased by reward. . . . We shall have as our reward, not something, but God himself . . . the reward is identical with God and with the fellowship which binds us to Him.[12]

The reward of a close walk with God is a closer walk with God; the reward of great obedience is greater trust, calling for further obedience; always the reward is more of the same, and essentially more of God in the same; always it is, in C. S. Lewis's words, "higher up and farther in."

## JUDGMENT AND CONFIDENCE

It was a cardinal article of faith in Judaism that God would one day judge the world, rewarding obedience to His holy law and punishing evil, bringing redemption to Israel as a nation and to the truly righteous within its bounds. However, this often produced in the loyal Pharisee a great anxiety. Unlike the Sadducean party, the Pharisee was confident of judgment to come. Yet he was fearful of his own destiny in it. Notwithstanding his unwearying attempt to achieve merit sufficient to outweigh his sins and ensure his acquittal, he tended, says Buchsel, to vacillate between an arrogant confidence in his good works that blinded him to his sinfulness and a hopeless fear of God's wrath. "In the last resort," Buchsel concludes, "his religion was not the force which sustained his life, it was the open wound from which he suffered."[13] More recent studies suggest that this may be somewhat overstated (see, e.g., Philip-

pians 3:6–7), but it does seem true to say that while the Pharisee insisted on the fact of judgment to come, he was by no
means sure that he would survive it.

In contrast to this the vindication of the Christian believer
at the day of judgment is an assured fact. Then the acquittal we
have already received (Romans 5:1) will become the verdict
that God will pronounce in the hearing of all creation. Then the
righteousness that we have received by faith (Romans 1:17; cf.
Galatians 5:5) will be fully and finally revealed in its imperishable perfection. It is God who judges justly; but it is this same
God who provided for the justification of sinners: therefore His
own justification will survive His own judgment (Romans
3:24–26).

Paul shows no anxiety about this. He knows that at the
cross Christ bore the condemnation of God for him, and that
"Therefore, there is now no condemnation for those who are in
Christ Jesus" (Romans 8:1). He already lives in the echo of that
day's "not guilty."

The sixteenth-century Heidelberg Catechism vividly cap-
tures this same attitude when it answers the question, "What
comfort hast thou by the coming again of Christ to judge the
quick and the dead?" It replies: "That in all my miseries and
persecution I look with my head erect for the very same who,
before, yielded Himself unto the judgment of God for me and
took away all malediction from me." No Pharisee ever achieved
such a righteousness that he could thus await the final judgment of God. Nor can we. Yet, because of the justification of
God on the basis of His Son's finished work, we can look
towards that day "with head erect."

# 33

# HEAVEN, HELL, AND
# THE NEW CREATION

Speculation about life after death has fascinated and fright-
ened men and women for millennia. Poets, painters,
philosophers, and preachers have communicated their
hopes and fears on a subject that touches us all. We might
therefore expect to find definitive information on this matter in
the Bible. Yet if with the help of a concordance we would examine all the New Testament references to *heaven*, we might soon
be surprised to learn that outside the book of Revelation few
details are given and the picture is modestly outlined. The Bible
stresses repeatedly that heaven is where God is, where Christ is,
and where the dead in Christ have gone. Heaven is a place of
great glory and rest, and a place in that glory and rest is prepared for us. Yet no details are given and no great space is given
to it. In fact the main focus of the Bible is not on heaven "up
there" at all, but upon the full and final coming of the kingdom
when Christ returns, and on the new creation that will be part
of it.

This interim period, when "the spirits of just men and
women made perfect" are in heaven awaiting that final consummation, is graphically (and symbolically) described only in
the last book of the New Testament: Revelation. Even there the
picture of a victorious, worshipping, purified multitude with
the heavenly host before the throne of God and of the Lamb
shares the canvas with the ongoing action on earth. There the
final purposes of God are being worked out in tribulation and
judgment.

Yet the hearts of believers and their hopes in all periods of the Christian era have been drawn to the subject of heaven and its rest, its glory, and its joys—and to heaven as it is now, as well as to the final state of those in it who accompany Christ at His coming. As the great pastor, evangelist, and theologian of the seventeenth century, Richard Baxter, says in his classic *The Saint's Everlasting Rest,* "Christ brings the heart to heaven first and then the person."[1] This is not surprising since heaven is, first and foremost, the dwelling place of God. We long for heaven because we long to be nearer God our Father. Once we were rebels running away from God; but we have been reconciled to God by the death of His Son, and now we cannot get close enough.

However, sin seems to keep us from feeling as warmly or thinking as clearly as we should. Even Paul, who knew so much by the Spirit (1 Corinthians 2:9–10, 12–13), confessed that "the perfect" had not yet come and that "we see but a poor reflection"; only when "face to face" would he—or we—understand fully (1 Corinthians 13:10–12). In heaven we shall know God in a direct way, involving a face-to-face intimacy (1 John 3:2) which we cannot at present imagine. There the sight will not frighten us as it did Isaiah, Ezekiel, Daniel, and John. Then the light will not blind us as it did Saul on the Damascus road. For there we will be in our proper element, in it and of it, touched by its glory; with nothing in us that is allergic to the holy God; nothing of sin or reserve, but only a perfect openness before God, a total surrender to God, and an entire compatibility with God.

## AN ETERNAL HOME

The only one who stood among men and women who had ever had that experience was Jesus. Only He could speak with authority of such things, because, although "No one has ever gone into heaven" (John 3:13), there was one who had come down from there and who belonged there, "the Son of Man" who is in heaven and of heaven: "No one has ever gone into heaven except the one who came from heaven—the Son of Man" (John 3:13). As Leon Morris notes: "Men cannot raise themselves to heaven and penetrate divine mysteries . . . Jesus, however, really has been in heaven and He has brought heavenly realities to earth."[2]

Moreover, He has come not only to tell us of heaven, but to bring us to heaven. He is "the living bread that came down from heaven" (John 6:51). By His self-sacrifice at Calvary we may live forever, and at His second coming He will raise us up at the Last Day (John 6:51, 54). Meanwhile He has gone to prepare a place for us in His Father's house and has left His Word as the antidote for doubt in a world where death seems so final: "If it were not so, I would have told you. I am going there to prepare a place for you" (John 14:2). On these words Donald Guthrie comments, "We may perhaps be permitted to deduce that in the mind of Jesus the primary idea of heaven for believers is the idea of an eternal home."[3] James Montgomery Boice agrees, and, asking the question "Why is John 14 so popular?" suggests that

> The answer is probably because of the warm image that is found there: heaven is a home. We need a home. We long for a home. Jesus calmly told His disciples that we have one. . . . Our need for a home arises from the fact that we have lost one. We had a home once in Eden. But sin caused the loss of that home and ever since the history of the human race has been one of wandering.[4]

Heaven is the end of our wandering and the beginning of our rest. As Millard J. Erickson notes: "The writer of the letter to the Hebrews makes much of this concept. Rest, as the term is used in Hebrews, is not merely a cessation of activities, but the experience of reaching a goal of crucial importance."[5] The attainment of this goal will still mean activity, but activity in the full flower of our manhood and womanhood; to change the metaphor slightly, and using the words of John Baillie, it will be "development in fruition" as opposed to "development *towards* fruition."[6]

## WHERE JESUS IS

If Jesus stresses that heaven is where His Father dwells ("my Father in heaven"; "your Father in heaven"), the New Testament writers often stress that heaven is where Jesus is. Peter announces the exaltation of Jesus "to the right hand of God" in Acts 2:33, and in Acts 3:21 adds that heaven must receive Him until the establishment of the new creation. Paul longs to "depart and be with Christ" (Philippians 1:23), and John in Revelation sees Him in the central glory of heaven as the Lamb once slain and now forever victorious (Revelation 5:9, 13; 14:1). On this last point Guthrie writes:

> What is most characteristic of this book is the presence of the slain Lamb in heaven. The numerous references to Christ under this figure are intended to set Him in the centre and indeed to portray Him in the same terms as God. The throne is described as the throne of God and of the Lamb (22:1) and the heavenly temple is described in a similar way (21:22). Heavenly worship is directed to Him on the throne and to the Lamb (5:13). The exalted state of the Lamb is seen as the dominating theme in heaven and the Apocalypse gives no indication that it will not continue to be in the ultimate heavenly state.[7]

The Christ who is the link between heaven and earth (Matthew 3:16–17; John 1:51), who is of heaven and from heaven (John 8:23, 42), has come to take His people to heaven (John 17:3, 5, 24), to see and to share His glory. This last element is as crucial as any, since the believer's entry into heaven and the heavenly state is the fulfillment of God's plan to conform us to the image of His Son (John 17:2, 4, 22; Romans 8:29–30; Ephesians 1:9–12), that He might be "the firstborn among many brothers" (Romans 8:29; cf. Colossians 1:18). The promise is not only that we shall go to heaven *because of* Christ, and not only that we shall go to heaven to be *with* Christ, but that we shall go to heaven and *be like* Christ. The apostle John sees this in its most developed stage at the Second Coming: "Dear friends, now we are children of God, and what we will be has not yet been made known. But we know that when he [Christ] appears, we shall be like him, for we shall see him as he is" (1 John 3:2).

When the last elect soul is saved and all opposition to the

spread of His kingdom destroyed, then the end will come (1 Corinthians 15:24); then the full number of the redeemed will be presented to the Father (Hebrews 2:13); then the mediatorial order will end (1 Corinthians 15:28), and the full consummation of God's reconciling work in Christ be achieved.

Guthrie observes: "The most significant event related about the future of God's people is the marriage supper of the Lamb (Revelation 19:6ff.; cf. 21:2). In the well-known apocalyptic imagery of the messianic banquet, the completion of the mission of the Lamb is portrayed."[8] This, however, lies at the end of the interim period. The interim period itself consists of present heavenly glory and bliss short of the full redemption of the church in the resurrection of the dead at the second coming of Christ out of heaven to be the judge of all, the vindicator of the suffering church on earth (Revelation 15:1–5; 16:4–7) and the waiting church in heaven (Revelation 6:10–11).

That coming will, however, involve not only glory for some, but final judgment, everlasting loss, and eternal punishment for others. And to this we must turn.

## THE DOCTRINE OF ETERNAL PUNISHMENT

The doctrine of eternal punishment troubles us more, perhaps, than any other. We often feel insecure when challenged about it, and we may feel persistently uncertain about its reality or even its justice. *Does anyone deserve this? Short of the worst criminals in history, are people that bad?* Perhaps we ought to ask ourselves, in approaching this subject, why it is that our main focus is on the punishment of sin and not on sin itself. Is it not that we are conditioned to sin and little realize its true character or full consequences, not only because we ourselves are sinners, but because we, even now, scarcely appreciate the utter holiness of God, from which perspective alone sin can be adequately assessed? Let us at least begin with an unspoiled mind in this regard—the mind of Jesus; and let us listen to and weigh His words, which are neither uncertain nor apologetic.

### The Warnings of Jesus

In His preaching, Jesus gives frequent and forceful warn-

ings to men and women of the judgment to come on account of
sin. The only way out, He warns, is to believe and repent. However, these warnings go beyond the act or pronouncement of
judgment; they indicate a degree and duration of loss and suffering that shock and even frighten:

> The Son of Man will send out his angels, and they will weed
> out of his kingdom everything that causes sin and all who
> do evil. They will throw them into the fiery furnace, where
> there will be weeping and gnashing of teeth. (Matthew
> 13:41–42)

> Then he will say to those at his left, "Depart from me, you
> who are cursed, into the eternal fire prepared for the devil
> and his angels." . . . Then they will go away to eternal pun-
> ishment, but the righteous to eternal life. (Matthew 25:41,
> 46)

> If your hand causes you to sin, cut it off. It is better for you
> to enter life maimed than with two hands to go into hell . . .
> where "their worm does not die, and the fire is not quenched."
> (Mark 9:43, 48)

> The rich man also died and was buried. In hell, where he
> was in torment, he looked up . . . (Luke 16:22–23)

Such passages can be multiplied (e.g., Matthew 7:22–23;
10:28; 23:16, 33), and it is clear that we have more frequent
warnings and more terrifying images of future punishment
from the lips of Jesus than anywhere else in the New Testament. Harry Buis makes the salutary point that "The fact that
the loving and wise Saviour has more to say about hell than any
other individual in the Bible is certainly thought-provoking."[9]
Jesus nowhere exhibits a cruel, unfeeling, or gloating attitude,
but only one of urgency and sorrow (e.g., Matthew 5:29–30).
Hell is to be avoided at all costs: and He was to meet the highest
cost (Matthew 27:46; Galatians 3:13). But what shocks us most,
perhaps, is that these predicted sufferings are neither remedial
nor temporary, but retributive and never-ending. It is a sober-

ing fact that Jesus Christ is responsible for the Christian doctrine of eternal punishment.

This is not to say that the idea may not have been widespread before Christ's coming, among both Jews and pagans of various kinds. Jesus' use of the name *Gehenna* referred to the Valley of Hinnom, bordering Jerusalem on the south, an area infamous for pagan rites, especially child-sacrifice and burning, that had taken place there in a dark time in Judah's history (2 Kings 16:3; 23:10; 2 Chronicles 28:3; 33:6). Just as the prophet Jeremiah designated it a place of judgment in his time (Jeremiah 19:6), it came to represent the place of judgment for all time.[10]

Jesus urges His hearers to avoid Gehenna at all costs (Matthew 5:29–30; 18:9; Mark 9:43–47). His phrase "child of hell," used to describe false teachers of the law and Pharisees (Matthew 23:15), is literally "child of Gehenna." G. A. Lee notes an important distinction in New Testament vocabulary:

> The New Testament seems to distinguish Gehenna from Hades. Gehenna is the place of final judgement, and Hades is the intermediate place where the ungodly await their final judgement (cf. Revelation 20:14, where Death and Hades are cast into the lake of fire at the last judgement). As the place of final punishment, Gehenna receives both body and soul (Matthew 10:28 par. Luke 12:5) whereas Hades receives only the soul (Acts 2:27, 31).[11]

The idea that this valley was used as a rubbish dump in Jesus' time does not seem to be evidenced earlier than the twelfth century A.D. It represented a place not only of rejection, but of retribution, and had by His day become a term of endless torment, as *Paradise* and *Abraham's bosom* had become terms for endless blessedness.

The nature of this punishment and the sufferings that accompany it are most often expressed in metaphorical and symbolic terms. But they are terms that *mean* something—and something as terrible as anything imaginable by men and women. The two aspects to this suffering are those of loss of good and infliction of pain.

The destiny of those who die in their sin is loss of the (common) presence of God, all sense of well-being, enjoyment of life, of earthly human company, and of divine favors. The banishment from the divine presence is expressed as being expelled from or being cast out of the presence of Christ into utter darkness (Matthew 7:23; 25:30); being cast out or shut out from the marriage feast of Christ and His people (Matthew 22:11, 13; 25:10–11).

## A Place of Loss and Pain

Loss alone, however, is clearly not the full burden of the pictures, or of the more explicit warnings. Those who are cast out into darkness are also cast into pain. (Again, see Matthew 25:41, 46 and Mark 9:47–48.) The element of retribution is unmistakable, as is the ingredient of pain (cf. Matthew 8:12).

The duration of this final punishment is repeatedly described as eternal, unending, and unchanging. Jesus speaks of everlasting fire and everlasting punishment (Matthew 18:8; 25:41, 46); of the fire that is not quenched and the worm that does not die (Mark 9:47–48). In one saying the same word is used of punishment for the wicked as of life for the righteous: "Then they will go away to eternal punishment, but the righteous to eternal life" (Matthew 25:46).

It is sometimes suggested with regard to the metaphors used by Jesus, and of those used elsewhere in the New Testament, that only the "fire" is everlasting. But besides emasculating the image of its real force and point, this ignores Jesus' reference to the "eternal fire" as having been "prepared for the devil and his angels" (Matthew 25:41). In Jewish and biblical thought, they were quite clearly and explicitly thought to be destined for an experience of unending torment. Hence in Revelation 20:10 we read, "And the devil, who deceived them, was thrown into the lake of burning sulphur, where the beast and the false prophet had been thrown. They will be tormented day and night for ever and ever."

The clear message is that what was prepared for rebels among the angelic order of beings will be shared by those of humankind who ally themselves with them. This is a warning given clearly elsewhere (Revelation 14:11), and is the final exposure and punishment of an alliance that involves, in varying degrees, all mankind (Ephesians 2:1–3; cf. 2 Corinthians 4:4). Those who reject God's holy lordship over their existence, whether demonic or human, will share in varying degrees one fate.

In Matthew 25:46, when Jesus speaks of "eternal punishment," He uses the active noun *kolasis,* which might be better translated "punishing" than "punishment." What is in view is an ongoing process, not a summary execution. The same idea (and the same Greek word in its verbal form, *kolazomenous*) is found in 2 Peter 2:9, which states that for the "unrighteous" the time between death and the last judgment is filled with punishments. The final public exposure of their ungodliness will occur on "the day of judgment."

This raises the question of the use of the term *aionios,* "eternal." It is derived from the word *aion,* "age," and may have a variety of senses, from "while the age lasts" to "for all ages"; that is, it can have a restricted or an indefinite or an infinite sense (as in regard to God). In the Old Testament, "forever" can denote limitless duration (e.g., Genesis 3:22; Exodus 3:15; Psalm 146:6, 10), or it can denote unbroken duration within a fixed span of time (e.g., Exodus 21:6). The context decides whether or not *eternity* in the strict sense is meant. One thing ought to be clear, however: that *eternal* is a *time* word. Murray J. Harris writes:

> It is sometimes claimed that the adjective is fundamentally qualitative in meaning ("having the characteristics of the age" in question) and that the quantitative or temporal sense is secondary. Such a thesis would be difficult to sustain either from secular Greek literature or from the LXX, where temporal considerations predominate.[12]

It is, of course, well known that John speaks of eternal life as a quality of life in relation to God, which we can enjoy here and now (e.g., John 17:3; 1 John 5:11, 13). But this same life is also unending and has a future (John 4:14, 36; 6:27; 12:25), and the temporal aspect is still present. The qualitative sense of the term "eternal life" belongs rather to the noun *life* than to the adjective *eternal*.

S. D. F. Salmond, in an older work entitled *The Christian Doctrine of Immortality*, points out that the idea of extinction is "foreign to the Old Testament" and "inconsistent with the general conception of a realm of the dead, distinct from the grave, which pervades the Old Testament." He insists that "The problem which pursues the mind of Israel is not the possibility of a future existence, but the nature of that existence."[13] However, the knowledge of the true God, His Sovereign power, and His covenant of grace and love sustained in the Old Testament believer the hope of a relationship that not even death would dissolve (e.g., Psalms 16; 49; 73; and Job 19; cf. Daniel 12:1–3).

In our own time Murray Harris has concluded that "Neither the Old Testament nor the New Testament entertains the possibility of the total extinction of persons,"[14] and that the concept of *destruction* (Gk. *apōleia*) or *perishing* (Gk. *appollusthai*) "does not imply annihilation," as "is clear from the use of the verb *perish* (*apollusthai*) in John 11.50; Acts 5.37; 1 Corinthians 10.9–10; Jude 11."[15] Similarly, while *apollymi* has a variety of meanings (including "to destroy," "to kill" [Matthew 2:13], and "to lose," "to perish," and "to be lost" [Luke 15:4, 8]), A. A. Hoekema writes: "*Apollymi* in the New Testament, however, never means annihilation."[16] When used to describe the ultimate destiny of those who are not in Christ (as in Matthew 10:28; 18:14; Luke 13:3; 2 Peter 2:1; 3:16), it means "everlasting perdition, a perdition consisting of endless loss of fellowship with God, which is at the same time a state of endless torment or pain."[17]

It is in fact not eternal torment which is the metaphor, but the words "destruction and death." This perspective is maintained throughout the New Testament (e.g., Romans 2:5–10; 2 Thessalonians 1:8–10; Hebrews. 10:26–31; 2 Peter 2:4–9; Jude 5–13; Revelation 20:7–15; 21:8; cf. 14:10).

## ATTEMPTS TO SOFTEN
## THE DOCTRINE OF HELL

Faced with such terrible and uncompromising statements, and with an almost unthinkable situation, it is not surprising that today, as ever, there should be attempts to soften the doctrine and lessen the "scandal" of believing in the conscious, eternal punishment of human beings who die unreconciled to God. Even among evangelical scholars and preachers, where universalism is clearly rejected, are those who hope for a "conditional immortality" that eventually means extinction for the impenitent and everlasting existence only for the people of God.

### Is an Immortal Soul a Biblical Idea?

It is true that the idea that the soul is immortal by nature, that immortality is an innate quality of the human soul, is a Greek idea and not a biblical one. However, we can claim the idea of the immortality of the soul as a biblical one, and not merely a philosophical idea, if we are clear that immortality is a gift of *creation* (not simply of redemption), and is bound up with God's intention of what human beings should be. Hence when God says, "Let us make man in our image, in our likeness" (Genesis 1:26), He is announcing a decision to share His own everlasting existence with men and women.

Immortality, then, is intrinsic to what it is to be human in God's sight, and is a gift. The tragedy of the Fall is that what was potentially our greatest joy has become our greatest terror; the promise has become a curse, and not because of any change in God, but because of a change in us. We have elected the darkness, we have sought distance from God; and in such distance there is neither light nor life, only death without nonexistence, destruction without annihilation.

This gifted immortality seems to be clear even in the Old Testament, where the teaching on life beyond death seems so unsatisfactory. While life in sheol is life in a reduced state, it is still a version of life. Nowhere is the complete annihilation of the person supposed: not even when their bodies are destroyed.

Against this background we have Jesus' urgent warnings and vivid (even terrifying) metaphors. But metaphors *mean* something, and Jesus' words about hell would have been clearly understood by His hearers in the light of well-known Old Testament and rabbinic teaching.

## Is Eternal Punishment Just?

But is it just of God to requite even a lifetime of sins with an eternity of punishment? Among several factors, we should consider that sin is an offense against God, corrupting His creation, insulting His authority and hateful to His holiness to an infinite degree. It is not from the person sinning but from the God who is sinned against that sin acquires its full significance. The punishment of sin must be understood in terms of the character of God. As J. H. Thornwell put it long ago:

> His holiness is declared by banishing the guilty from His presence—His hatred of sin by pouring out upon them the vials of His wrath. . . . In the penal fires of hell we contemplate the inextinguishable hatred of God to all the forms of iniquity. They result from the purity of infinite holiness in terrible collision with guilt.[18]

Furthermore, sin does not cease at death, but the person goes on in the life beyond death in a state of rebellion: hating God as much as hell, finding the light even more unbearable than the darkness, and cursing God without repentance. Those who have not softened towards God on earth do not do so in hell; there is not more grace there than here. Consequently, ongoing sin fuels ongoing punishment; endless antipathy to God means endless exile from God; hell has locks on the inside too.

We shudder to think of this, and cannot think about it long or hard. We tend to ask, "Is there any mitigation for thousands who at any rate are not the worst of sinners?" Jesus' words in Luke 12:47–48 do indicate some mitigation of their condition. The difference in the severity of the beating inflicted cannot be taken as a reference to varying lengths of time, since hell is eternal, everlasting, without end for all who are there. However, the suggestion is that every consideration will be given to the sinner, that the degree of suffering will be less for many than for some. Perhaps for some it will be a place of dull sorrow and dreary discontent, while for others the rage and pain will be terrible indeed. It may be objected that Jesus' metaphors of fire and worm, etc., do not allow for any recognizable mitigation of pain. But the consciousness that one's life, without happiness, without company or the many comforts of earthly life, will quite literally go on forever, without improvement or end, contains within itself such horror and anguish that the sharpest and most fearful metaphors do not seem out of place in describing the deepest reality of hell. If hell were to consist of lying on a feather bed in darkness and loneliness without God, it would still be terrible and at all costs to be avoided. Moreover, Jesus' use of such descriptions in His warnings is clearly meant to persuade His hearers to avoid such a future and to turn them to God and safety in repentance, faith, and salvation.

### Can God's People Feel Happy If Hell Exists?

Finally, to the objection that neither God nor His saints could be happy with hell still in defiant existence, it should be replied that no hint of that appears in God's Word or among Christ's many uncompromising warnings. Perfect holiness can only be at ease, in blessedness, as it thrusts away from itself corruption, as it expresses its pure nature perfectly, uncompromisingly and perpetually—and hell is a perpetual combination of man's rebellion and God's revulsion.

Although he bases his story on a kind of second-chance concept that is found nowhere in Scripture, C. S. Lewis ends his book *The Great Divorce* with the solemn recognition that there are those who will be lost forever, and gives a sharp retort to those who object that God and the saved could not be happy if any were everlastingly lost. Lurking behind such an apparently high-minded consideration he sees, as one of his characters says,

> "The demand of the loveless and the self-imprisoned that they should be allowed to blackmail the universe: that till they consent to be happy (on their own terms) no one else shall taste joy: that theirs should be the final power; that Hell should be able to *veto* Heaven."[19]

## A NEW HEAVEN, A NEW EARTH

God is the Creator of all creation; Christ is the Redeemer of all creation; the people of God are the inheritors of all creation.

No doctrine of heaven can be fully biblical that is content to leave this (yes, even this) creation behind forever. In our study of the resurrection of the dead we saw that the disembodied condition of the dead in Christ was an interim condition and that the final state of glory involved a glorious resurrection and embodied state. That final, physical condition will be the crowning part of a larger materiality involving the whole created order that suffered fracture and damage and corruption with the entrance of sin into the universe (Romans 8:19–25), and which "will be liberated from its bondage to decay" (8:21) through the reconciling work of Christ in His atonement (Colossians 1:20). It is the will of God, "to be put into effect when the times will have reached their fulfillment—to bring all things in heaven and on earth together under one head, even Christ" (Ephesians 1:10).

## A *Renewed* Heaven and Earth

The creation which God pronounced "very good" in the beginning (Genesis 1:31) will not be superseded or replaced. It will share "the glorious freedom of the children of God" (Romans 8:21). In this connection R. H. Mounce comments on God's declaration, "I am making everything new!" (Revelation 21:5): "The transformation which Paul saw taking place in the lives of believers (2 Corinthians 3:18; 4:16–18; 5:16–17) will have its counterpart on a cosmic scale."[20]

In old prophetic imagery, the desert will blossom as a rose, the trees of the field shall clap their hands, the lion will lie down with the lamb, and all the world will be the promised land, God's holy mountain. Paul depicts the whole creation as waiting "in eager expectation" (Romans 8:19) for the birthday of the new era; or as J. B. Phillips paraphrases it, standing "on tiptoe," waiting for this to happen.

Peter's use of terms like "destruction," "disappear," and "melt" (2 Peter 3:5–13) must be understood against this background and in the light of his own use, where for instance the term "destroyed" (v. 6) means wiped clean, purified, cleansed. Similarly the "new heaven" and "new earth" that John sees (Revelation 21:1, 5) are really a *renewed* heaven and a *renewed* earth, and what has "passed away" is really the debris of sin and the corruption that characterized the old order. Anthony Hoekema points out that in both 2 Peter 3:13 and Revelation 21:1 the Greek word used to designate the newness of the cosmos is not *neos* but *kainos*, and writes: "The word *neos* means new in time or origin, whereas the word *kainos* means new in nature or in quality." The expression "a new heaven and a new earth" means, therefore, "not the emergence of a cosmos totally other than the present one, but the creation of a universe which, though it has been gloriously renewed, stands in continuity with the present one" (cf. Matthew 19:28; Acts 3:21).[21]

However, Richard Bauckham stresses the fact that salvation for humankind and its world is not simply a return to the Genesis beginning, but the completion of an interrupted work that God will bring to an as-yet-unseen perfection: "Salvation is both restorative (repairing the damage done by sin) and progressive (moving the work of creation on to its completion)."[22] The continuity, however, is quite as important in its way as the change. It vindicates God's covenant with Noah and *all* living creatures (Genesis 9:16), a promise that He was committed still, and forever, to the world(s) He had made (Genesis 8:21–22; 9:8–17). And it also forms the biblical rationale of a Christian approach to ecology. By our care of this planet and its treasures, by our proper use (not exploitation) of its resources, and by our concern to repair past damage done to its structure and life forms, Christians are making a prophetic and eschatological statement. First they are saying, "The earth is the Lord's and everything in it"; and they are also saying, "What we are doing provisionally and imperfectly, God is going to do perfectly at the coming of Christ Jesus His Son."

The biblical view of heaven is not a vision of disembodied spirits forever sitting on clouds and plucking harps. It is neither ethereal nor static. True, the interim time before the coming of the Lord does involve a disembodied state in heaven—but not for long. God has appointed earth as the proper place for mankind, and the Bible both opens and closes with this statement (Genesis 1–2; Revelation 21–22). This does not mean we shall one day leave heaven behind us, but that we shall one day bring heaven with us. As Hoekema writes:

Since God will make the new earth his dwelling place, and since where God dwells there heaven is, we shall then continue to be in heaven while we are on the new earth. For heaven and earth will then no longer be separated, as they are now, but will be one (see Rev. 21:1–3).[23]

## The "New Jerusalem": The People of God

There the "new Jerusalem," which John sees "coming down out of heaven from God, prepared as a bride beautifully dressed for her husband," is of course not a literal city, but the people of God (cf. Hebrews 11:10; 12:22; 13:14; Philippians 3:20) in their spiritual unity and physical perfection. In this New Jerusalem they take their appointed place on the planet God made for them, and there He will live with them in complete intimacy forevermore (Revelation 21:3). Martin Kiddle writes that the heart of the symbol is a community of men and women: "It is a city which is a family. The ideal of perfect community, unrealisable on earth because of the curse of sin which vitiated the first creation, is now embodied in the redeemed from all nations."[24]

This social aspect of Christian religion, witnessed throughout the New Testament epistles, is continued in its perspective on the future. A. M. Hunter rightly asserts: "The consummation of the Christian hope is supremely social. It is no 'flight of the alone to the Alone' but life in the redeemed community of heaven."[25]

There—at last—the meek shall inherit the earth (Psalm 11; Matthew 5:5). There at last they shall reign on the earth, a kingdom and priests to our God (Revelation 5:9–10). There at last Old Testament visions will become new world realities (Isaiah 17–25; 66:22–23). There we shall live as we have never lived before and serve God as we have never served before, in the full flowering of all our human powers. For if mountains, trees and brooks, plant life and animal life on land and in the sea shall flourish, how much more will human devotion and delight, skill and song, ingenuity and creativity, conservation and counsel, with adventures on earth and beyond in human and angelic company.

## In the Midst of It All—Jesus

And in the midst of it all will be Jesus, the Son of God: the Shepherd who "will guide them to springs of living water" (Revelation 7:17, RSV), which flow from God and from Him (Revelation 22:1)—Jesus who is forever Immanuel, God with us. As the Temple He is supremely the place of God's presence on earth; as the Lamp (Revelation 21:23) He will be in every sense the "light of the world" and "the true light that enlightens every man" (John 1:9, RSV; 8:12). Above all else, by His light we shall "see his face" (Revelation 22:4). What no one could do and live (Exodus 33:20), everyone shall do and adore.

Though in a glorious event Jesus has delivered the kingdom so dearly bought, so carefully gathered to His Father in willing subjection as the mediator of the kingdom (1 Corinthians 15:24–28; cf. Hebrews 2:13b), yet He does not cease to be God and King in a kingship that will last forever (Psalm 89:4; Isaiah 9:7; Luke 1:33; Hebrews 10:12; 2 Peter 1:11) and a lordship that shares the throne of God (Revelation 22:3).

The cry of the earth is for that kingship and that kingdom to come in all its fullness with the coming of Christ. He promises: "Yes, I am coming soon," and the answering cry of the church He saved is: "Amen. Come, Lord Jesus" (Revelation 22:20).

# NOTES

## Abbreviations Used in the Notes

| | |
|---|---|
| Calvin, *Institutes* | *Calvin: Institutes of the Christian Religion,* trans. Ford Lewis Battles (Philadelphia: Westminster, 1960). |
| ICC | *The International Critical Commentary* (Edinburgh: T. & T. Clark, 1958 et al.). |
| ISBE | G. W. Bromiley, ed., *The International Standard Bible Encyclopedia,* 4 vols. (Grand Rapids, Mich.: Eerdmans). |
| NBD | J. D. Douglas, ed., *The New Bible Dictionary* (Leicester: InterVarsity, 1982). |
| NDT | Sinclair B. Ferguson and David F. Wright, eds., *New Dictionary of Theology* (Leicester: InterVarsity, 1988). |
| NICNT | *New International Commentary on the New Testament* (publishers vary depending on volume). |
| NICOT | *New International Commentary on the Old Testament* 12 vols. (Grand Rapids, Mich.: Eerdmans). |
| NIDNTT | Colin Brown ed., *The New International Dictionary of New Testament Theology* (Exeter: Paternoster Press, 1976–78). |
| NIGTC | *New International Greek Testament Commentary* (Exeter: Paternoster Press, 1978 et al.). |
| TDNT | G. Kittel and G. Friedrich, eds., *Theological Dictionary of the New Testament,* 10 vols. (Grand Rapids, Mich.: Eerdmans, 1964–76). |
| TNTC | *Tyndale New Testament Commentaries*, 20 vols. (Leicester: InterVarsity). |
| TOTC | *Tyndale Old Testament Commentaries*, 23 vols. (Leicester: InterVarsity). |

WBC       *Word Biblical Commentary* (Dallas: Word, 1982 et al.).

WEC       *The Wycliffe Exegetical Commentary* (Chicago: Moody Press, 1988 et al.).

## Introduction

1. C. S. Lewis, *Mere Christianity* (London: Collins Fount, 1977), 52.

2. C. S. Lewis, *God in the Dock* (London: Collins Fount, 1979), 81.

3. David F. Wells, *The Person of Christ* (London: Marshall, Morgan & Scott, 1984), 35.

4. Ibid., 35–36.

5. Ibid., 36.

6. R. T. France, "The Worship of Jesus: A Neglected Factor in Christological Debate?" in Harold H. Rowdon, ed., *Christ the Lord: Studies in Christology Presented to Donald Guthrie* (Leicester: InterVarsity, 1982), 25.

7. P. T. Forsyth, *The Person and Place of Jesus Christ* (London: Independent Press, 1961), 152.

8. Ibid., 160.

## Chapter 1: Jesus Stands Among Us

1. D. A. Carson, *Matthew*, in Frank E. Gaebelein, ed., *The Expositor's Bible Commentary*, vol. 8 (Grand Rapids, Mich.: Zondervan, 1984), 109.

2. William L. Lane, *The Gospel According to Mark*, NICNT, 57–58.

3. Ibid., 58.

4. George R. Beasley-Murray, *John*, WBC (1987), 14.

5. Lane, *Mark*, 58.

6. James Denney, *The Death of Christ*, R. V. G. Tasker, ed. (London: Tyndale, 1951), 22.

7. C. F. D. Moule, *The Origin of Christology* (Cambridge: CUP, 1978), 145–46.

8. David J. Bosch, *Transforming Mission* (New York: Orbis Books, 1991), 109–10.

9. Ibid., 110.

10. I. Howard Marshall, *The Gospel of Luke: A Commentary on the Greek Text*, NIGTC (1978), 185–86.

11. Ibid., 186.

12. Bosch, *Transforming Mission*, 111.

13. Ibid., 111–12.

## Chapter 2: Jesus and the Kingdom of God

1. G. R. Beasley-Murray, *Jesus and the Kingdom of God* (Grand Rapids, Mich.: Eerdmans, 1986), 24.

2. Ibid.

3. R. T. France, "The Church and the Kingdom of God: Some Hermeneutical Issues," in D. A. Carson, ed., *Biblical Interpretation and the Church* (Exeter: Paternoster Press, 1984), 41.

4. G. R. Beasley-Murray, *The Coming of God* (Exeter: Paternoster Press, 1983), 24; cf. his *Jesus and the Kingdom of God*, 73.

5. R. T. France, *Divine Government* (London: SPCK, 1990), 24.

6. Ibid., 25.

7. Beasley-Murray, *Jesus and the Kingdom of God*, 227.

8. Ibid., 102.

9. Quoted in ibid., 121.

10. D. A. Carson, *Matthew*, in Frank E. Gaebelein, ed., *The Expositor's Bible Commentary*, vol. 8 (Grand Rapids, Mich.: Zondervan, 1984), 170.

11. Beasley-Murray, *Jesus and the Kingdom of God*, 152.

12. Ibid., 172.

13. Carson, *Matthew*, 380.

14. Ibid., 370.

15. Richard Bauckham, *The Bible in Politics: How to Read the Bible Politically* (London: SPCK, 1989), 142.

16. Ibid., 143.

17. Eddie Gibbs, *I Believe in Church Growth* (London: Hodder & Stoughton, 1985), 142.

## Chapter 3: Jesus and the Holy Spirit

1. John V. Taylor, *The Go-Between God: The Holy Spirit and the Christian Mission* (London: SCM, 1972), 48.

2. C. K. Barrett, *The Holy Spirit and the Gospel Tradition* (London: SPCK, 1975), 157–58.

3. Ibid., 158.

4. Ibid., 23.

5. John Owen, *A Discourse Concerning the Holy Spirit,* in *The Works of John Owen,* William H. Goold, ed., vol. 3 (London: Banner of Truth, 1966), 161.

6. George Smeaton, *The Doctrine of the Holy Spirit* (London: Banner of Truth, 1958), 125–26.

7. Leon Morris, *The Gospel According to John,* NICNT, 152.

8. Herman Ridderbos, *The Coming of the Kingdom* (Philadelphia: Presbyterian & Reformed, 1976), 86–87.

9. Morris, *John,* 385.

10. Raymond E. Brown, *The Gospel According to John,* vol. 1 (London: Geoffrey Chapman, 1971), 300.

11. John Murray, *The Epistle to the Romans,* NICNT, vol. 1 (Grand Rapids, Mich.: Eerdmans, 1959), 11.

12. Richard B. Gaffin, Jr., *The Centrality of the Resurrection* (Grand Rapids, Mich.: Baker, 1978), 89.

13. Ibid., 89–90.

14. Ibid., 97.

15. Ibid., 95.

16. M. M. B. Turner, "The Spirit of Christ and Christology," in Harold H. Rowdon, ed., *Christ the Lord: Studies in Christology Presented to Donald Guthrie* (Leicester: InterVarsity, 1982), 180.

17. Ibid., 183.

18. David J. Bosch, *Transforming Mission* (New York: Orbis, 1991), 84.

## Chapter 4: The Son of Man

1. William L. Lane, *The Gospel According to Mark,* NICNT (London: Marshall, Morgan & Scott, 1974), 297.

2. See I. Howard Marshall, *The Origins of New Testament Christology* (Leicester: InterVarsity, 1976), 64.

3. C. F. D. Moule, *The Origin of Christology* (Cambridge: CUP, 1978), 13.

4. Robert D. Rowe, "Is Daniel's 'Son of Man' Messianic?" in Harold H. Rowdon, ed., *Christ the Lord: Studies in Christology Presented to Donald Guthrie* (Leicester: InterVarsity, 1982), 89–90.

5. Ibid., 95.

6. Leon Morris, "Weather," NIDNTT, vol. 3, 1003.

7. R. T. France, *Jesus and the Old Testament* (London: Tyndale Press, 1971), 187–88.

8. G. R. Beasley-Murray, *Jesus and the Kingdom of God* (Grand Rapids, Mich.: Eerdmans, 1986), 229.

9. Richard N. Longenecker, *The Christology of Early Jewish Christianity* (London: SCM, 1970), 87–88.

10. Beasley-Murray, *Jesus and the Kingdom of God*, 226.

11. Vincent Taylor, *The Gospel According to Mark* (London: Macmillan, 1952), 199.

12. Ibid., 201.

13. Donald Guthrie, *New Testament Theology* (Leicester: InterVarsity, 1981), 280.

14. Beasley-Murray, *Jesus and the Kingdom of God*, 233.

15. D. A. Carson, *The Gospel According to John* (Grand Rapids, Mich.: Eerdmans; Leicester: InterVarsity, 1991), 200–201.

16. Guthrie, *New Testament Theology*, 285.

17. Carson, *John*, 257.

18. J. Jeremias, quoted in Beasley-Murray, *Jesus and the Kingdom of God*, 282.

19. Lane, *Mark*, 384.

20. M. J. Harris, "Appendix: Prepositions and Theology in the Greek New Testament," NIDNTT, vol. 3, 1179.

21. Ibid., 1180.

22. Lane, *Mark*, 383.

23. Carson, *John*, 482.

24. Ibid., 345.

25. Ibid., 482.

26. Ibid., 445.

27. H. Schlier, quoted in W. Grundmann, *"dexios,"* TDNT, vol. 2, 39.

28. Ibid., 39–40.

29. France, *Jesus and the Old Testament*, 141.

30. R. T. France, *Divine Government* (London: SPCK, 1990), 77; his note 17 (120–21) gives references demonstrating this "shift of opinion."

31. France, *Jesus and the Old Testament*, 141–42.

32. Ibid., 227–34, See also R. T. France, *The Gospel According to Matthew: An Introduction and Commentary*, TNTC (1985), 333–49.
33. France, *The Gospel According to Matthew*, 288.

## Chapter 5: The Only Revealer of the Father

1. Benjamin B. Warfield, *The Lord of Glory* (London: Evangelical Press, 1974), 82.
2. Herman Ridderbos, *The Coming of the Kingdom* (Philadelphia: Presbyterian & Reformed, 1962), 90.
3. D. A. Carson, *Matthew*, in Frank E. Gaebelein, ed., *The Expositor's Bible Commentary*, vol. 8 (Grand Rapids, Mich.: Zondervan, 1984), 277, quoting G. E. Ladd, *A Theology of the New Testament* (Grand Rapids, Mich.: Eerdmans, 1974).
4. Ibid., 277.
5. Ridderbos, *The Coming of the Kingdom*, 90.

## Chapter 6: The "I Am" Sayings of Jesus

1. Leon Morris, *The Gospel According to John*, NICNT (Grand Rapids, Mich.: Wm. B. Eerdmans, 1971), 350, n. 43.
2. D. A. Carson, *The Gospel According to John* (Grand Rapids, Mich.: Wm. B. Eerdmans; Leicester: InterVarsity, 1991), 343–44.
3. Raymond E. Brown, *The Gospel According to John*, vol. 1 (London: Geoffrey Chapman, 1971), 367.
4. George R. Beasley-Murray, *John*, WBC (1987), lxxxiv.
5. Ibid., 94.
6. Ibid., 128.
7. Carson, *John*, 337–38.
8. Beasley-Murray, *John*, 169–70.
9. Carson, *John*, 385.
10. Ethelbert Stauffer, "Ego," TDNT, vol. 2, 344.
11. Brown, *John*, vol. 1, 394.
12. Carson, *John*, 385.
13. Ibid., quoting Roy Clements, *Introducing Jesus* (Eastbourne: Kingsway, 1986), 103.
14. Ibid., 387.
15. Ibid., 386.
16. Morris, *John*, 550.

17. A. D. Thiselton, "Truth," NIDNTT, vol. 3, 889.

18. Ibid., 892.

19. Ibid.

20. Beasley-Murray, *John*, 272.

21. D. A. Carson, *Jesus and His Friends: His Farewell Message and Prayer in John 14 to 17* (Leicester: InterVarsity, 1986), 90.

## Chapter 7: God Is with Us

1. D. A. Carson, *The Gospel According to John* (Grand Rapids, Mich.: Eerdmans; Leicester: InterVarsity, 1991), 87–95.

2. G. Fries, "Word," *NIDNTT*, vol. 3, 1084.

3. Ibid.

4. B. Klappert, "Word," *NIDNTT*, vol. 3, 1116.

5. Ibid., 1087.

6. Ibid., 1087–88.

7. Ibid., 1116–17.

8. J. H. Bernard, *A Critical and Exegetical Commentary on the Gospel According to St. John*, ICC, vol. 1, 2.

9. Ed L. Miller, "The Logos Was God," *Evangelical Quarterly* 3, no. 2 (1981): 76.

10. Ibid., 68–69.

11. C. K. Barrett, *The Gospel According to St. John* (London: SPCK, 1978), 156.

12. Raymond E. Brown, *The Gospel According to John*, vol. 1 (London: Geoffrey Chapman, 1971), 24.

13. Carson, *John*, 117.

14. George R. Beasley-Murray, *John*, WBC (1987), 11.

15. Ibid.

16. Leon Morris, *The Gospel According to John*, NICNT (Grand Rapids, Mich.: Eerdmans, 1971), 80.

17. Ibid., 84.

18. Carson, *John*, 119.

19. Ibid.

20. Morris, *John*, 85. But see Beasley-Murray, *John*, 11.

21. Carson, *John*, 124.

22. Brown, *John*, vol. 1, 31.

23. A. C. Thiselton, "Truth," NIDNTT, vol. 3, 890.

24. Carson, *John*, 130.

25. Ibid., 135.

26. Beasley-Murray, *John*, 3–4.

## Chapter 8: God Has Spoken

1. Oscar Cullmann, *The Christology of the New Testament* (London: SCM, 1963), 305.

2. Ibid.

3. F. F. Bruce, *A Commentary on the Epistle to the Hebrews*, NICNT (London: Marshall, Morgan & Scott, 1965), 4.

4. For example, see Exodus 24:15ff.; 33:9ff.; 40:34–8; and Ezekiel 43:1–5 in the Old Testament, and compare with Mark 9:22ff. and Acts 9:3.

5. Bruce, *Hebrews*, 6.

6. Philip Edgcumbe Hughes, *A Commentary on the Epistle to the Hebrews* (Grand Rapids, Mich.: Eerdmans, 1977), 43.

7. William L. Lane, *Hebrews 1–8*, WBC (1991), 12.

8. Ibid., 18.

9. Ibid., 13.

10. Ibid., 14–15.

11. Ibid., 15. Note also Exodus 29:37; 30:10; Leviticus 16:19, 30; Hebrews 9:13–14, 22–23; 10:2, 22.

12. Martin Hengel, *The Cross of the Son of God* (London: SCM, 1986), 85.

13. Hughes, *Hebrews*, 47.

14. H. Bietenhard, "Angel," NIDNTT, vol. 1, 101.

15. Ibid.

16. Ibid., 102.

17. Bruce, *Hebrews*, 24.

## Chapter 9: The Doctrine of the Incarnation

1. St. Athanasius, *The Incarnation of the Word of God*, sec. 17.

2. Calvin, *Institutes*, 2.13.4.

3. Helmut Thielicke, *The Evangelical Faith*, vol. 1 (Grand Rapids, Mich.: Eerdmans, 1974), 292–93.

4. Calvin, *Institutes,* 2.14.1.

5. Henry Bettenson, *Documents of the Christian Church* (Oxford: OUP, 1963), 51–52.

6. G. C. Berkouwer, *The Person of Christ* (Grand Rapids, Mich.: Eerdmans, 1954), 85.

7. Ibid., 88. See also A. N. S. Lane, "Beyond Chalcedon," in Harold H. Rowdon, ed., *Christ the Lord* (Leicester: InterVarsity, 1982), 257–81.

8. Benjamin B. Warfield, *The Works of Benjamin B. Warfield,* vol. 3: *Christology and Criticism* (Grand Rapids, Mich.: Baker, 1981), 263. See also Bruce Demarest, "Creeds," NDT, 180.

9. Klaas Runia, *The Present-Day Christological Debate* (Leicester: InterVarsity, 1984), 103.

10. Berkouwer, *The Person of Christ,* 195.

11. P. T. Forsyth, *The Cruciality of the Cross* (London: Hodder & Stoughton, 1909), 27.

12. H. D. McDonald, "Docetism," NDT, 202.

13. Runia, *Present-Day Christological Debate,* 115.

14. See B. B. Warfield's outstanding and beautiful essay, "On the Emotional Life of Our Lord," in his *The Person and Work of Christ,* ed. Samuel G. Craig (Philadelphia: Presbyterian & Reformed, 1950), 83–145.

15. James Stalker, *Imago Christi,* quoted in Warfield, "On the Emotional Life of Our Lord," 100.

16. Os Guinness, *The Dust of Death* (Downers Grove, Ill.: InterVarsity, 1973), 385.

17. A. Bengel quoted in Warfield, "On the Emotional Life of Our Lord," 131.

## Chapter 10: The Significance of the Virgin Birth

1. I. Howard Marshall, *The Gospel of Luke,* NIGTC (1978), 58.

2. Ibid., 70.

3. Ibid., 71.

4. A. N. S. Lane, "Virgin Birth," NDT, 709–10.

5. Millard J. Erickson, *Christian Theology* (Grand Rapids, Mich.: Baker, 1986), 752.

6. Karl Barth, *Church Dogmatics,* vol. 4 (Edinburgh: T. & T. Clark, 1956), 207.

7. G. C. Berkouwer, *The Work of Christ* (Grand Rapids, Mich.: Eerdmans, 1965), 129.

8. T. M. Dorman, "The Virgin Birth of Jesus Christ," ISBE, vol. 4, 992–93.

9. John N. Oswalt, *The Book of Isaiah: Chapters 1–39*, NICOT (1986), 206.

10. Ibid., 208.

11. Ibid., 213.

12. D. A. Carson, *Matthew*, in Frank E. Gaebelein, ed., *The Expositor's Bible Commentary*, vol. 8 (Grand Rapids, Mich.: Zondervan, 1984), 77–81.

13. Ibid., 79.

14. F. F. Bruce, "Genealogy of Jesus Christ," NBD, 411.

15. Joachim Jeremias, *Jerusalem in the Time of Jesus* (London: SCM, 1969), 294.

16. Marshall, *Luke*, 161.

17. J. Gresham Machen, *The Virgin Birth of Christ* (Grand Rapids, Mich.: Baker, 1965), 202–9.

18. Erickson, *Christian Theology*, 757.

## Chapter 11: "You Are the Messiah"

1. Oscar Cullmann, *The Christology of the New Testament* (London: SCM, 1963).

2. David F. Wells, *The Person of Christ* (London: Marshall, Morgan & Scott, 1984), 67.

3. C. F. D. Moule, *The Origin of Christology* (Cambridge: CUP, 1978), 7.

4. Ibid., 47.

5. G. R. Beasley-Murray, *Jesus and the Kingdom of God* (Grand Rapids, Mich.: Eerdmans; Exeter: Paternoster Press, 1986), 24.

6. The Promised Land itself was an idealized symbol of this future kingdom, and the prophets of Israel, from their highest vantage points of inspiration, saw it and proclaimed it would be a time of blessing for Israel (Isaiah 65:17–25) and peace for the whole earth (Isaiah 66:20–24; cf. Psalm 96; 100; Isaiah 19:19–25; Habakkuk 2:14).

7. R. T. France, *Jesus and the Old Testament* (London: Tyndale, 1971), 79–80. A good example of the OT references to the coming Messiah can be found in Psalms 22, 41, 42 and 118, which contain an extraordinary mixture of what are either types or prophecies. Christ refers to or quotes from many of these during His ministry. (See, for instance Matthew 27:46; John 13:18; and concerning Psalm 118:22, see Matthew 21:42; Mark 12:10–11; Luke 20:17–18.)

8. Beasley-Murray, *Jesus and the Kingdom of God*, 146.

9. William L. Lane, *The Gospel According to Mark*, NICNT (London: Marshall, Morgan & Scott, 1974), 288.

10. Ibid.

11. France, *Jesus and the Old Testament*, 120; see 116–32.

12. According to Joachim Jeremias, "he emptied himself" is "an exact translation" of "He poured out His soul" in Isaiah 53:12. See Joachim Jeremias, *"Pais theou,"* TDNT, vol. 5, 711. W. D. Davies, *Paul and Rabbinic Judaism* (London, SPCK, 1970), 274, usefully tabulates the parallels between the Philippian 2 hymn and Isaiah's last servant song.

13. C. E. B. Cranfield, *A Critical and Exegetical Commentary on the Epistle to the Romans*, ICC, vol. 1 (1975), 59 n. 1.

14. R. T. France, *Matthew: Evangelist and Teacher* (Exeter: Paternoster Press, 1989), 285.

## Chapter 12: "Jesus Is Lord"

1. C. F. D. Moule, *The Origin of Christology* (Cambridge: CUP, 1978), 35.

2. Donald Guthrie, *New Testament Theology* (Leicester: InterVarsity, 1981), 292.

3. I. Howard Marshall, *The Gospel of Luke: A Commentary on the Greek Text*, NIGTC (1978), 274.

4. Leon Morris, *The Gospel According to John*, NICNT (Grand Rapids, Mich.: Eerdmans, 1971), 495.

5. Ibid., 496.

6. F. F. Bruce, *This Is That* (Exeter: Paternoster Press, 1968), 80.

7. George R. Beasley-Murray, *John*, WBC (1987), 385.

8. John Murray, *The Epistle to the Romans*, NICNT, vol. 2 (Grand Rapids, Mich.: Eerdmans, 1965), 182.

9. Consider these dozen verses written by the apostles: Acts 2:33; 5:31; 7:55–56; Romans 8:34; Ephesians 1:20; Colossians 3:1; Hebrews 1:3, 13; 8:1; 10:12; 12:2; and 1 Peter 3:22.

10. Benjamin B. Warfield, *The Lord of Glory* (London: Evangelical Press, 1974), 210–11.

11. J. Gresham Machen, *The Origin of Paul's Religion* (New York: Macmillan, 1925), 308.

12. C. E. B. Cranfield, *A Critical and Exegetical Commentary on the Epistle to the Romans*, ICC, vol. 2 (1979), 529.

13. Herman Ridderbos, *Paul and Jesus: Origin and General Character of Paul's Preaching of Jesus* (Philadelphia: Presbyterian & Reformed, 1958), 72.

14. D. R. deLacey, "'One Lord' in Pauline Theology," in Harold H. Rowdon, ed., *Christ the Lord: Studies in Christology Presented to Donald Guthrie* (Leicester: InterVarsity, 1982), 200.

15. Ibid., 201.

16. Gordon D. Fee, *The First Epistle to the Corinthians*, NICNT (Grand Rapids, Mich.: Eerdmans, 1987), 375.

17. Warfield, *The Lord of Glory*, 231.

18. Cranfield, *Romans*, vol. 2, 529.

## Chapter 13: "He Is the Son of God"

1. Martin Hengel, *The Cross of the Son of God* (London: SCM, 1986), 12.

2. Ibid., 22.

3. Ibid., 88.

4. O. Hofius, "Father," *NIDNTT*, vol. 1, 618.

5. Ibid., 620.

6. D. A. Carson, *The Gospel According to John* (Grand Rapids, Mich.: Eerdmans; Leicester: InterVarsity, 1991), 249 n. 1.

7. Hofius, "Father," 614.

8. Ibid., 620.

9. R. T. France, *Matthew: Evangelist and Teacher* (Exeter: Paternoster Press, 1989), 292.

10. Donald Guthrie, *New Testament Theology* (Leicester: InterVarsity, 1981), 308–9.

11. D. A. Carson, *Matthew*, in Frank E. Gaebelein, ed., *The Expositor's Bible Commentary*, vol. 8 (Grand Rapids, Mich.: Zondervan, 1984), 112.

12. Guthrie, *New Testament Theology*, 310.

13. France, *Matthew: Evangelist and Teacher*, 293.

14. Ibid., 294.

15. William L. Lane, *The Gospel According to Mark*, NICNT (London: Marshall, Morgan & Scott, 1974), 44 n. 23.

16. I. Howard Marshall, *The Gospel of Luke: A Commentary on the Greek Text*, NIGTC (1978), 129–30.

17. George R. Beasley-Murray, *John*, WBC (1987), lxxxiii–lxxxiv.

18. Ibid., lxxxiv.

19. Carson, *John*, 254–55.

20. Ibid., 395.

21. Beasley-Murray, *John*, 294.

22. Guthrie, *New Testament Theology*, 305.

23. Lane, *Mark*, 130.

24. P. T. Forsyth, *The Person and Place of Jesus Christ* (London: Independent Press, 1961), 271.

25. Guthrie, *New Testament Theology*, 286.

26. Herman Ridderbos, *Paul: An Outline of His Theology* (London: SPCK, 1977), 68.

27. Helmut Thielicke, *The Evangelical Faith*, vol. 2 (Grand Rapids, Mich.: Eerdmans, 1977), 344.

28. C. E. B. Cranfield, *A Critical and Exegetical Commentary on the Epistle to the Romans*, ICC, vol. 1 (1975), 61–62. See also C. K. Barrett, *A Commentary on the Epistle to the Romans* (London: A. & C. Black, 1962), 18. For Murray, see below.

29. John Murray, *The Epistle to the Romans*, NICNT, vol. 1 (Grand Rapids, Mich.: Eerdmans, 1959), 7.

30. I. Howard Marshall, *The Origins of New Testament Christology* (Leicester: InterVarsity, 1976), 120.

31. Ridderbos, *Paul*, 77.

32. Beasley-Murray, *John*, 2.

33. Ibid., 16.

34. Ibid., 15.

35. Carson, *John*, 135.

36. Kittel, quoted in Carl F. Henry, *God, Revelation and Authority,* vol. 3 (Waco, Tex.: Word, 1979), 181.

37. Ridderbos, *Paul,* 77.

38. Ibid.

39. P. E. Hughes, *A Commentary on the Epistle to the Hebrews* (Grand Rapids, Mich.: Eerdmans, 1977), 51.

## Chapter 14: The Last Adam

1. John Henry Newman, "Praise to the Holiest in the Height," *The English Hymnal* (Oxford: OUP, 1906), no. 471. Public domain.

2. C. E. B. Cranfield, *A Critical and Exegetical Commentary on the Epistle to the Romans,* ICC, vol. 1 (1975), 282.

3. C. K. Barrett, *From First Adam to Last* (London: A. & C. Black, 1962), 15.

4. C. K. Barrett, *A Commentary on the Epistle to the Romans* (London: A. & C. Black, 1962), 112.

5. Cranfield, *Romans,* vol. 1, 286.

6. John Murray, *The Epistle to the Romans,* NICNT, vol. 1 (Grand Rapids, Mich.: Eerdmans, 1959), 203.

7. Leon Morris, *The Epistle to the Romans* (Grand Rapids, Mich.: Eerdmans; Leicester: InterVarsity, 1988), 241.

8. Herman Ridderbos, *Paul: An Outline of His Theology* (London: SPCK, 1977), 59.

9. Millard J. Erickson, *Christian Theology* (Grand Rapids, Mich.: Baker, 1986), 952–53.

10. Calvin, *Institutes,* 4.17.1.

11. Ridderbos, *Paul,* 60–61.

12. C. F. D. Moule, *The Origin of Christology* (Cambridge: CUP, 1978), 53, 95.

13. Donald Guthrie, *New Testament Theology* (Leicester: InterVarsity, 1981), 652.

14. Calvin, *Institutes,* 3.1.1.

15. Ibid., 3.1.2.

16. Anthony A. Hoekema, *Saved by Grace* (Grand Rapids, Mich.: Eerdmans; Exeter: Paternoster Press, 1989), 60.

17. James Stewart, quoted in ibid., 65.

18. Ridderbos, *Paul,* 45.

19. John Murray, *Redemption Accomplished and Applied* (London: Banner of Truth, 1961), 161.

20. Ibid., 165.

## Chapter 15: "There Is One Mediator"

1. A. Oepke, "Mesites," *TDNT*, vol. 4, (1978) 614.

2. Ibid., 613.

3. Ibid., 619.

4. John Murray, *The Epistle to the Romans*, NICNT, vol. 1 (Grand Rapids, Mich.: Eerdmans, 1959), 282.

5. Calvin, *Institutes*, 2.12.1.

6. Ibid., 2.12.2.

7. Carl F. Henry, *God, Revelation and Authority*, vol. 3 (Waco, Tex.: Word, 1979), 203.

8. Ibid., 205.

9. Ibid., 206.

10. Ibid., 207.

11. Thomas F. Torrance, *The Mediation of Christ* (Exeter: Paternoster Press, 1983), 64.

12. Ibid.

13. Ibid., 65.

14. Ibid.

15. Ibid., 66.

16. Ibid., 73–74.

17. F. F. Bruce, *A Commentary on the Epistle to the Hebrews*, NICNT (London: Marshall, Morgan & Scott, 1965), 134.

18. Torrance, *The Mediation of Christ*, 69–70.

19. Ibid., 70.

20. Ibid.

## Chapter 16: The Condescension of Christ

1. Benjamin B. Warfield, *The Person and Work of Christ*, Samuel G. Craig, ed. (Philadelphia: Presbyterian & Reformed, 1950), 563–75.

2. Ibid., 564.

3. R. P. Martin, *Carmen Christi* (Cambridge: CUP, 1967), 2.

4. Peter T. O'Brien, *The Epistle to the Philippians: A Commentary on the Greek Text,* NIGTC (Grand Rapids, Mich.: Eerdmans, 1991), 263–68.

5. Ibid., 209.

6. Ibid., 208, 210.

7. Ibid., 208.

8. The Nicene Creed; Henry Bettenson, ed., *Documents of the Christian Church* (Oxford: OUP, 1963), 26.

9. Moises Silva, *Philippians,* WEC (1988), 118.

10. See Roy W. Hoover, "The Harpagmos Enigma: A Philological Solution," *Harvard Theological Review* 64 (1971): 95–119.

11. N. T. Wright, "Harpagmos and the Meaning of Philippians 2:5–11," *Journal of Theological Studies* 37.2 (1986): 345.

12. Moule, quoted in O'Brien, *Philippians,* 213.

13. Augustine, quoted in Leon Morris, *The Gospel According to John,* NICNT (Grand Rapids, Mich.: Eerdmans, 1971), 114.

14. Augustine, quoted in F. W. Beare, *The Epistle to the Philippians* (London: A. & C. Black, 1959), 164.

15. Joachim Jeremias, *"Pais theou,"* TDNT, vol. 5, (1978), 711.

16. O'Brien, *Philippians,* 220.

17. John R. W. Stott, *The Cross of Christ* (Leicester: InterVarsity, 1986), 24.

18. Martin Hengel, *The Cross of the Son of God* (London: SCM, 1986), 93–178.

19. O'Brien, *Philippians,* 240.

20. Wright, "Harpagmos and the Meaning of Philippians 2:5–11," 346.

## Chapter 17: The Cosmic Christ

1. Peter T. O'Brien, *Colossions, Philemon,* WBC (1982), 32.

2. James D. G. Dunn, *Christology in the Making* (London: SCM, 1980), 187–94.

3. Herman Ridderbos, *Paul: An Outline of His Theology* (London: SPCK, 1977), 79.

4. O'Brien, *Colossians, Philemon,* 37–40.

5. John F. Balchin, "Paul, Wisdom and Christ," in Harold H. Rowdon, ed., *Christ the Lord: Studies in Christology Presented to Donald Guthrie* (Leicester: InterVarsity, 1982), 214.

6. Ibid., 215.

7. Ibid., 212.

8. Ibid., 218–19.

9. Ridderbos, *Paul*, 78–86, esp. 85.

10. G. Kittel, *"Eikong,"* TDNT, vol. 2, 395.

11. F. F. Bruce, *The Epistle to the Colossians, to Philemon, and to the Ephesians*, NICNT (Grand Rapids, Mich.: Eerdmans, 1984), 63.

12. J. Weiss, quoted in Paul Beasley-Murray, "Colossians 1:15–20: An Early Christian Hymn Celebrating the Lordship of Christ," in Donald A. Hagner and Murray J. Harris, eds., *Pauline Studies* (Exeter: Paternoster Press, 1980), 174.

13. C. K. Barrett, *From First Adam to Last* (London: A. & C. Black, 1962), 37.

14. Ridderbos, *Paul*, 380–81, lists eight good reasons why we should reject the common attempt to put the metaphors of "head" and "body" together.

15. Edmund P. Clowney, "Interpreting the Biblical Models of the Church: A Hermeneutical Deepening of Ecclesiology," in D. A. Carson, ed., *Biblical Interpretation and the Church: Text and Context* (Exeter: Paternoster Press, 1984), 81.

16. N. T. Wright, *The Epistles of Paul to the Colossians and to Philemon*, TNTC (Leicester: InterVarsity, 1986), 73.

17. O'Brien, *Colossians, Philemon*, 53

18. Bruce, *Epistle to the Colossians, etc.*, 75; see Colossians 2:15 and Galatians 4:9.

19. Ibid., 261.

20. R. P. Martin, *Colossians: The Church's Lord and the Christian's Liberty* (Exeter: Paternoster Press, 1972), 48–49.

21. John Calvin, *The Epistles of Paul the Apostle to the Galatians, Ephesians, Philippians, and Colossians* (Edinburgh: Saint Andrew, 1965), 313.

22. Wright, *Colossians, Philemon*, 113.

## Chapter 18: The Shadow of the Cross: The Cross in the Old Testament

1. H. F. Lyte, "Praise, My soul, the King of Heaven," *The English Hymnal* (Oxford: OUP, 1906), no. 470. Public domain.

2. Carl F. Henry, *God, Revelation and Authority*, vol. 6 (Waco, Tex.: Word, 1983), 341.

3. Geerhardus Vos, "The Scriptural Doctrine of the Love of God," *Redemptive History and Biblical Interpretation: The Shorter Writings of Geerhardus Vos*, R. B. Gaffin, Jr., ed., (Phillipsburg, N.J.: Presbyterian & Reformed, 1980), 425–57.

4. Ibid., 440.

5. E. Stauffer, *"Agapao," TDNT*, vol. 1, 38.

6. John N. Oswalt, *The Book of Isaiah: Chapters 1–39*, NICOT (1986), 180–81.

7. Ibid., 162, 180–85.

8. O. Procksch, *"Hagios," TDNT*, vol. 1, 93.

9. Henry, *God, Revelation and Authority*, vol. 6 (Waco, Tex.: Word, 1983), 327.

10. Gordon J. Wenham, *The Book of Leviticus*, NICOT (1979), 19–20.

11. Ibid., 22, 26.

12. Ibid., 26.

13. Ibid., 33.

14. Ibid., 28.

15. Derek Kidner, "Sacrifice—Metaphors and Meaning," *Tyndale Bulletin* 33 (1982): 128.

16. Ibid., 130.

17. R. K. Harrison, *Leviticus: An Introduction and Commentary*, TOTC (1980), 31–32.

18. Leon Morris, *The Apostolic Preaching of the Cross* (Leicester: InterVarsity, 1965), 112–28; *The Cross in the New Testament* (Exeter: Paternoster Press, 1976), 219–20.

19. Wenham, *Leviticus*, 61; Harrison, *Leviticus*, 62.

20. Morris, *The Apostolic Preaching of the Cross*, 144–213; Wenham, *Leviticus*, 25–29.

21. C. H. Dodd, *The Epistle of Paul to the Romans* (London: Hodder & Stoughton, 1932).

22. Morris, *The Apostolic Preaching of the Cross*, 144–213.

23. Walther Eichrodt, *Theology of the Old Testament*, vol. 1 (London: SCM, 1961), 258.

24. Herman Ridderbos, *Paul: An Outline of His Theology* (London: SPCK, 1977), 108.

25. F. F. Bruce, *A Commentary on the Epistle to the Hebrews*, NICNT (London: Marshall, Morgan & Scott, 1965), 41 n. 57.

26. Wenham, *Leviticus*, 236.

27. William L. Lane, *Hebrews 1–8*, WBC (1991), cxxxii.

## Chapter 19: The Light of the Cross: The Cross in the New Testament

1. T. Kelly, "We Sing the Praise of Him Who Died," *The English Hymnal* (Oxford: OUP, 1906), no. 510.

2. John Bunyan, *The Pilgrim's Progress*, Roger Sharrock, ed. (Harmondsworth: Penguin Books, 1987), 82.

3. See Alister E. McGrath, *Luther's Theology of the Cross: Martin Luther's Theological Breakthrough* (Oxford: Basil Blackwell, 1985).

4. Markus Barth, *Was Christ's Death a Sacrifice?* (Edinburgh: Oliver & Boyd, 1961), 48.

5. John R. W. Stott, *The Cross of Christ* (Leicester: InterVarsity, 1986), 134.

6. P. T. Forsyth, *The Cruciality of the Cross* (London: Hodder & Stoughton, 1909), 139.

7. P. T. Forsyth, *The Person and Place of Jesus Christ* (London: Independent Press, 1961), 271.

8. Quoted in Carl F. Henry, *God, Revelation and Authority*, vol. 6 (Waco, Tex.: Word, 1983), 327.

9. Forsyth, *The Cruciality of the Cross*, 39.

10. Ibid., 5.

11. Ibid., 134.

12. Ibid., 205.

13. Stott, *The Cross of Christ*, 112.

14. Ibid., 210.

15. Douglas Moo, *Romans 1–8*, WEC (1991), 228.

16. Leon Morris, *The Epistle to the Romans* (Grand Rapids, Mich.: Wm B. Eerdmans, 1988), 179.

17. See, for example, Mark 14:24; 1 Corinthians 11:25; Ephesians 1:7; Hebrews 9:11–14; 10:19, 29; 13:12; 1 Peter 1:2, 19; and 1 John 1:7; 5:6.

18. Moo, *Romans*, 246.

19. Ibid., 237.

20. C. E. B. Cranfield, *A Critical and Exegetical Commentary on the Epistle to the Romans*, ICC, vol. 1 (Edinburgh: T. & T. Clark, 1975), 216–17. See also Morris, *Romans*, 181–82; and John Murray, *The Epistle to the Romans*, NICNT, vol. 1 (Grand Rapids, Mich.: Eerdmans, 1959), 117.

21. J. I. Packer, *What Did the Cross Achieve?* (Leicester: Theological Students Fellowship, 1974), 25.

22. Morris, *The Cross in the New Testament* (Exeter: Patemoster Press, 1976), 220.

23. Philip Edgcumbe Hughes, *Paul's Second Epistle to the Corinthians*, NICNT (Grand Rapids, Mich.: Eerdmans, 1962), 211.

24. C. K. Barrett, *A Commentary on the Second Epistle to the Corinthians* (London: A. & C. Black, 1973), 180.

25. John Owen, *The Doctrine of Justification by Faith, the Works of John Owen*, William H. Goold, ed., vol. 5 (London: Banner of Truth, 1967), 203.

26. Stott, *The Cross of Christ*, 149.

27. Karl Barth, *Church Dogmatics* IV/I (Edinburgh: T. & T. Clark, 1956), 230.

28. Ibid., 231.

29. Ibid., 233, 237.

## Chapter 20: The Great Achievment: Redemption and Reconciliation

1. Leon Morris, *The Apostolic Preaching of the Cross*, 2nd ed. (London: Tyndale, 1960), 23.

2. O. Procksch, *"Luo,"* TDNT, vol. 4, 239.

3. Leon Morris, *The Apostolic Preaching of the Cross*, 3rd ed. (Leicester: InterVarsity, 1965), 26.

4. Ibid., 29.

5. T. R. Schreiner, "Sacrifices and Offerings in the OT," ISBE, vol. 4, 271.

6. Ibid.

7. Ibid.

8. James Denney, *The Death of Christ,* R. V. G. Tasker, ed. (London: Tyndale Press, 1960), 149.

9. Morris, *The Apostolic Preaching of the Cross,* 100–124.

10. Leon Morris, *The Cross in the New Testament* (Exeter: Paternoster Press, 1976), 216–24.

11. Morris, *The Apostolic Preaching of the Cross,* 114.

12. Ibid., 118.

13. Quoted in C. Brown, "Redemption," NIDNTT, vol. 3, 197.

14. In particular see Romans 1:18; 2:3; 5:10; 11:28; 1 Corinthians 15:25–26; and Ephesians 2:3, 5–6.

15. Calvin, *Institutes,* 2.17.2.

16. P. T. Forsyth, *The Cruciality of the Cross* (London: Hodder & Stoughton, 1909), 27.

17. G. W. Bromiley, "Reconcile; Reconciliation," ISBE, vol. 4, 56.

18. G. C. Berkouwer, *The Work of Christ* (Grand Rapids, Mich.: Eerdmans, 1965), 293.

19. John Calvin, *The Epistles of Paul the Apostle to the Galatians, Ephesians, Philippians, and Colossians* (Edinburgh: Saint Andrew, 1965), 313.

20. Markus Barth, "Christ and All Things," in M. D. Hooker and S. G. Wilson, eds., *Paul and Paulinism: Essays in Honour of C. K. Barrett* (London: SPCK, 1982), 165.

## Chapter 21: Justification in Christ

1. J. Barton Payne, *The Theology of the Older Testament* (Grand Rapids, Mich.: Zondervan, 1962), 155–61. The need for such conformity is clearly seen in such texts as Deuteronomy 25:1, Exodus 23:7, Isaiah 5:23, and Isaiah 43:9.

2. Morris, *The Apostolic Preaching of the Cross,* 3rd ed. (Leicester: InterVarsity, 1965), 259.

3. Ibid., 260.

4. Alister E. McGrath, *Justification by Faith* (Grand Rapids, Mich.: Zondervan, 1990); Colin Brown, "Righteousness, justification," NIDNTT, vol. 3, 352–77; R. A. Kelly, "Righteousness," ISBE, vol. 4, 192–95.

5. Douglas Moo, *Romans 1–8,* WEC (1991), 78.

6. Leon Morris, *The Epistle to the Romans* (Grand Rapids, Mich.: Eerdmans; Leicester: InterVarsity, 1988), 145.

7. Moo, *Romans 1–8*, 82.

8. C. E. B. Cranfield, *A Critical and Exegetical Commentary on the Epistle to the Romans*, ICC, vol. 1 (Edinburgh: T. & T. Clark, 1975), 438.

9. Moo, *Romans 1–8*, 584.

10. J. I. Packer, *God's Words* (Leicester: InterVarsity, 1981), 146.

11. J. I. Packer, "Justification," NBD, 683.

12. Moo, *Romans 1–8*, 83–84.

13. Ibid., 84.

14. Cranfield, *Romans*, vol. 1, 199.

15. C. E. B. Cranfield, *A Critical and Exegetical Commentary on the Epistle to the Romans*, ICC, vol. 2 (1979), 828.

16. For example, look at the following verses: Romans 1:2, 10; 8:3–4, 12–16; Galatians 5:6, 13–14, 16–24; 1 Peter 1:7, 13–16; 2:11–12, 13–17; 3:8–12; and 1 John 2:3–6; 3:4–10; 4:2–5.

17. Calvin, *Institutes*, 3.16.1.

18. Ibid.

19. G. C. Berkouwer, *Faith and Justification* (Grand Rapids, Mich.: Eerdmans, 1954), 86.

## Chapter 22: Sanctification from Christ

1. J. I. Packer, *God's Words* (Leicester: InterVarsity, 1981), 178.

2. Herman Ridderbos, *Paul: An Outline of His Theology* (London: SPCK, 1977), 26.

3. John Murray, "Definitive Sanctification," *The Collected Writings of John Murray*, vol. 2 (Edinburgh: Banner of Truth, 1977), 277.

4. Philip Edgcumbe Hughes, *A Commentary on the Epistle to the Hebrews* (Grand Rapids, Mich.: Eerdmans, 1977), 103.

5. F. F. Bruce, *The Epistle to the Galatians: A Commentary on the Greek Text*, NIGTC (1982), 75–76.

6. G. C. Berkouwer, *Faith and Sanctification* (Grand Rapids, Mich.: Eerdmans, 1952), 20.

7. Ibid., 41.

8. I. Watts, "When I Survey the Wonderous Cross," *The English Hymnal* (Oxford: OUP, 1906), no. 107.

## Chapter 23: Adoption Through Christ

1. G. Schrenk, "Pater," TDNT, vol. 5, 591.

2. O. Hofius, "Father," NIDNTT, vol. 1, 617.

3. Ibid.

4. Peter C. Craigie, *Psalms 1–50*, WBC (1983), 67.

5. C. E. B. Cranfield, *A Critical and Exegetical Commentary on the Epistle to the Romans*, ICC, vol. 1 (1975), 397.

6. Hofius, "Father," 614.

7. Those father references are found in Matthew 11:25; 26:39, 42; Mark 14:36; Luke 10:21; 22:42; 23:34; and John 11:41; 12:27–28; 17:1, 5, 11, 21, 24–25.

8. Schrenk, *"Pater,"* 985.

9. Ibid., 991.

10. R. A. Finlayson, "God," NBD, 429.

11. Hofius, "Father," 620.

12. Francis Lyall, "Roman Law in the Writings of Paul—Adoption," *Journal of Biblical Literature* 88 (1969): 458–66; Leon Morris, *The Epistle to the Romans* (Grand Rapids, Mich.: Eerdmans, 1988), 315.

13. Lyall, "Roman Law," 46.

14. D. M. Lloyd-Jones, *Romans. The Sons of God: An Exposition of Chapter 8:5–17* (Edinburgh: Banner of Truth, 1974), 151.

15. Ibid., 1.

16. Ibid., 285–399.

17. Cranfield, *Romans*, vol. 1, 407.

18. O. Becker, "Gift, Pledge, Corban," NIDNTT, vol. 2, 40.

19. F. F. Bruce, *The Epistle to the Colossians, to Philemon, and to the Ephesians*, NICNT (Grand Rapids, Mich.: Eerdmans, 1984), 266.

20. J. I. Packer, *Knowing God* (London: Hodder & Stoughton, 1975), 226–29.

21. Ibid.

22. Ibid., 256.

## Chapter 24: Believing the Resurrection

1. Carl F. Henry, *God, Revelation and Authority*, vol. 3 (Waco, Tex.: Word, 1979), 147.

2. Murray J. Harris, *Raised Immortal: Resurrection and Immortality in the New Testament* (London: Marshall, Morgan & Scott, 1983), 5.

3. Gordon D. Fee, *The First Epistle to the Corinthians*, NICNT (Grand Rapids, Mich.: Eerdmans, 1987), 721.

4. A. M. Fairbairn, *Studies in the Life of Christ*, 357, as quoted in W. H. Griffith Thomas, "The Resurrection of Christ," ISBE, vol. 4 (Chicago: Howard Severance Company, 1937), 2566.

5. Harris, *Raised Immortal*, 41.

6. Ibid., 42–45.

7. Ibid., 64–65.

8. Michael Green, *World on the Run* (Leicester: InterVarsity, 1983), 53. See also his *The Day Death Died* (Leicester: InterVarsity, 1982); and *Man Alive* (London: InterVarsity, 1967).

9. Frank Morrison, *Who Moved the Stone?* (Bromily: STL Books, 1987), 96.

10. Wenham, *Easter Enigma*, 79.

11. Michael Green, *You Must Be Joking: Popular Excuses for Avoiding Jesus Christ* (London: Hodder & Stoughton, 1981), 125–26.

12. See Gary Habermas and Antony Flew, "Did Jesus Rise from the Dead?" Terry L. Miethe, ed., *The Resurrection Debate* (San Francisco: Harper & Row, 1987), 20–27, 113–17.

13. George R. Beasley-Murray, *John*, WBC (1987), 40.

14. Ibid., 41.

15. D. A. Carson, *Matthew*, in Frank E. Gaebelein, ed., *The Expositor's Bible Commentary*, vol. 8 (Grand Rapids, Mich.: Zondervan, 1984), 296.

16. Thomas F. Torrance, *Space, Time and Resurrection* (Edinburgh: Handsel, 1976), 65, n. 4.

17. Ibid., 83.

18. Ibid.

## Chapter 25: Understanding the Resurrection

1. A. M. Ramsey, quoted in Thomas F. Torrance, *Space, Time and Resurrection* (Edinburgh: Handsel, 1976), 31.

2. Ibid., 74–75.

3. John Murray, *The Epistle to the Romans*, NICNT, vol. 1 (Grand Rapids, Mich.: Eerdmans, 1959), 10.

4. Richard B. Gaffin, Jr., *The Centrality of the Resurrection* (Grand Rapids, Mich.: Baker, 1978), 85–92.

5. Ibid., 97.

6. Murray J. Harris, *Raised Immortal: Resurrection and Immortality in the New Testament* (London: Marshall, Morgan & Scott, 1983), 73.

7. Ibid., 74.

8. Torrance, *Space, Time and Resurrection*, 51–52.

9. Quoted in Torrance, *Space, Time and Resurrection*, 48 n.2.

10. G. C. Berkouwer, *The Work of Christ* (Grand Rapids, Mich.: Eerdmans, 1965), 195.

11. Gaffin, *The Centrality of the Resurrection*, 34–35.

12. Herman Ridderbos, *Paul: An Outline of His Theology* (London: SPCK, 1977), 53–57.

13. Ibid., 55.

14. Ibid., 56.

15. C. K. Barrett, *A Commentary on the First Epistle to the Corinthians* (London: A. & C. Black, 1971), 358.

## Chapter 26: Entering the Resurrection

1. Thomas Jacomb, *A Commentary Upon Romans Chapter 8 verses 1–4* (ca. 1670; reprinted, Edinburgh: James Nisbet, 1867), 193–94.

2. Calvin, *Institutes*, 3.1.1.

3. Ibid., 3.1.3.

4. Ibid., 3.1.4.

5. D. A. Carson, *The Gospel According to John* (Grand Rapids, Mich. Eerdmans, 1991), 189.

6. Ibid., 195–96.

7. Andrew T. Lincoln, *Ephesians*, WBC (1990), 108.

8. Ibid., 105.

9. Ibid., 108.

10. Ibid., 285–86.

11. Herman Ridderbos, *Paul: An Outline of His Theology* (London: SPCK, 1977), 208.

12. Oliver O'Donovan, *Resurrection and Moral Order: An Outline for Evangelical Ethics* (Grand Rapids, Mich.: Eerdmans, 1986).

13. Ibid., 13.

14. Ibid., 58.

15. Ibid., 14–15.

16. See Gordon D. Fee, *The First Epistle to the Corinthians*, NICNT (Grand Rapids, Mich.: Eerdmans, 1987), 795.

## Chapter 27: The Ascended Lord

1. Brian K. Donne, *Christ Ascended* (Exeter: Paternoster Press, 1983), 60.

2. Ibid., 63.

3. Ibid.

4. F. F. Bruce, *A Commentary on the Epistle to the Hebrews*, NICNT (London: Marshall, Morgan & Scott, 1965), 8.

5. Donne, *Christ Ascended*, 32.

6. Paul does use the phrase "the right hand of God" in Romans 8:34, Ephesians 1:20 and Colossians 3:1 (cf. 1 Corinthians 15:25).

7. F. F. Bruce, *Paul, Apostle of the Free Spirit* (Exeter: Paternoster Press, 1983), 118.

8. Ibid., 119.

9. John Owen, *An Exposition of Hebrews*, vol. 3 (Marshallton, Del.: The National Foundation for Christian Education, n.d.), 535; cf. 536–42.

10. John Owen, "A Declaration of the Glorious Mystery of the Person of Christ," in *The Works of John Owen*, William H. Goold, ed., vol. 1 (London: Banner of Truth, 1967), 252.

11. Ibid., 235.

12. Ibid., 252.

13. Thomas F. Torrance, *Space, Time and Resurrection* (Edinburgh: Handsel, 1976), 74.

14. Ibid., 136.

15. Thomas F. Torrance, *The Mediation of Christ* (Exeter: Paternoster Press, 1983), 74.

## Chapter 28: The Great High Priest

1. Philip Edgcumbe Hughes, *A Commentary on the Epistle to the Hebrews* (Grand Rapids, Mich.: Eerdmans, 1977), 351–52.

2. Geerhardus Vos, "The Priesthood of Christ in the Epistle to the Hebrews" (1907), *Redemptive History and Biblical Interpretation: The Shorter Writings of Geerhardus Vos*, R. B. Gaffin, Jr, ed. (Phillipsburg, N.J.: Presbyterian & Reformed, 1980), 126–60.

3. Harry Blamires, *On Christian Truth* (London: SPCK, 1983), 71.

4. Calvin, *Institutes*, 3.20.17.

5. John Owen, *An Exposition of Hebrews*, vol. 3 (Marshallton, Del.: The National Foundation for Christian Education, n.d.), 538.

6. Calvin, *Institutes*, 3.20.20.

7. Owen, *An Exposition of Hebrews*, vol. 3, 540–41.

8. Charles Hodge, *Systematic Theology*, vol. 2 (London: James Clarke, 1960), 592.

9. William Sanday and Arthur C. Headlam, *A Critical and Exegetical Commentary on the Epistle to the Romans*, ICC (Edinburgh: T. & T. Clark, 1908), 221.

10. Robert L. Dabney, *Lectures in Systematic Theology* (Grand Rapids, Mich.: Zondervan, 1972), 474.

11. Ibid., 201.

12. Quoted in ibid., 774.

## Chapter 29: The Appointed King

1. Thomas F. Torrance, *Space, Time and Resurrection* (Edinburgh: Handsel, 1976), 114.

2. Robert H. Mounce, *The Book of Revelation*, NICNT (Grand Rapids, Mich.: Eerdmans, 1977), 347.

3. Andrew T. Lincoln, *Ephesians*, WBC (1990), xc.

4. Ibid., xci.

5. Ibid.

6. Leon Morris, *The Book of Revelation: An Introduction and Commentary* (Leicester: InterVarsity, 1987), 23.

7. G. C. Berkouwer, *The Work of Christ* (Grand Rapids, Mich.: Eerdmans, 1965), 233.

8. Torrance, *Space, Time and Resurrection*, 138–39.

## Chapter 30: The Personal Return of Christ

1. Donald G. Bloesch, *Essentials of Evangelical Theology*, vol. 2 (San Francisco: Harper & Row, 1979), 180–81.

2. In addition to the Titus 2 passage, see 1 Thessalonians 1:10; 2:13; 3:13; 5:23.

3. Herman Ridderbos, *Paul: An Outline of His Theology* (London: SPCK, 1977), 488.

4. Anthony A. Hoekema, *The Bible and the Future* (Grand Rapids, Mich.: Eerdmans, 1979), 110.

5. As quoted in C. Armerding and W. W. Gasque, eds., *Handbook of Biblical Prophecy* (Grand Rapids, Mich.: Baker, 1977), 9.

6. G. C. Berkouwer, *The Return of Christ* (Grand Rapids, Mich.: Eerdmans, 1972), 83–84.

7. As quoted in Armerding and Gasque, eds., *Handbook of Biblical Prophecy*, 9.

8. Berkouwer, *The Return of Christ*, 76.

9. George Eldon Ladd, *A Theology of the New Testament* (Grand Rapids, Mich.: Eerdmans, 1974), 208.

10. Berkouwer, *The Return of Christ*, 90.

11. Ibid., 214.

12. Helmut Thielicke, *The Evangelical Faith*, vol. 3 (Grand Rapids, Mich.: Eerdmans, 1982), 421–22.

13. As quoted in ibid., 417.

14. As quoted in Hoekema, *The Bible and the Future*, 24.

15. Augustine, *The City of God* (Harmondsworth: Penguin, 1972).

16. Stephen H. Travis, *I Believe in the Second Coming of Jesus* (London: Hodder & Stoughton, 1983), 105.

## Chapter 31: The Resurrection of the Dead in Christ

1. D. K. Stuart, "Sheol," ISBE, vol. 4, 472.

2. Joachim Jeremias, "Hades," TDNT, vol. 1, 149.

3. S. D. F. Salmond, *The Christian Doctrine of Immortality* (Edinburgh: T. & T. Clark, 1913), 136.

4. Paul Heinisch, quoted in R. B. Laurin, ed., *Contemporary Old Testament Theologians* (London: Marshall, Morgan & Scott, 1970), 206.

5. Colin Brown, "Resurrection," NIDNTT, vol. 3, 259–309.

6. Ibid., 262.

7. G. C. Berkouwer, *The Return of Christ* (Grand Rapids, Mich.: Eerdmans, 1972), 176.

8. Edmond Jacob, *Theology of the Old Testament* (London: Hodder & Stoughton, 1958), 299.

9. Francis I. Andersen, *Job: An Introduction and Commentary*, TOTC (1976), 194; see also his comment on John 14:13 on 172–73.

10. Berkouwer, *The Return of Christ*, 183.

11. Gordon D. Fee, *The First Epistle to the Corinthians*, NICNT (Grand Rapids, Mich.: Eerdmans, 1987), 746.

12. Donald Guthrie, "Transformation and the Parousia: Reflections on the Resurrection," *Vos Evangelica* 14 (1984): 44.

13. Donald G. Bloesch, *Essentials of Evangelical Theology*, vol. 2 (San Francisco: Harper & Row, 1979), 188.

14. Fee, *1 Corinthians*, 782.

15. Ibid., 797.

16. Philip Edgcumbe Hughes, *Paul's Second Epistle to the Corinthians* (Grand Rapids, Mich.: Eerdmans, 1962), 152.

17. Ibid., 163–65.

18. Bloesch, *Essentials of Evangelical Theology*, vol. 2, 187.

19. Jeremias, "Hades," 148.

20. Murray J. Harris, *Raised Immortal: Resurrection and Immortality in the New Testament* (London: Marshall, Morgan & Scott, 1983), 142.

## Chapter 32: The Final Judgment by Christ

1. Leon Morris, *The Biblical Doctrine of Judgment* (London: Tyndale, 1960), 14.

2. Ibid., 16–17.

3. V. Herntrich, *"Krino,"* TDNT, vol. 3, 928–29.

4. As quoted in Morris, *The Biblical Doctrine of Judgment*, 22.

5. Ibid., 24.

6. F. Buchsel, *"Krino,"* TDNT, vol. 3, 936.

7. G. Schrenk, *"Dikaiosune,"* TDNT, vol. 2, 208.

8. Buchsel, *"Krino,"* 941.

9. G. C. Berkouwer, *Faith and Justification* (Grand Rapids, Mich.: Eerdmans, 1954), 103.

10. Calvin, *Institutes*, 3.16.1.

11. Jesus describes the assigning of rewards according to how we use our privileges in Matthew 25:14–30; He describes the loss we

sustain by neglecting our privileges in Matthew 21:32 and Luke 12:47.

12. Helmut Thielicke, *The Evangelical Faith*, vol. 3 (Grand Rapids, Mich.: Eerdmans, 1982), 444–45.

13. Buchsel, *"Krino,"* 936.

## Chapter 33: Heaven, Hell, and the New Creation

1. Richard Baxter, *The Practical Works of the Rev. Richard Baxter*, W. Orme, ed., vol. 23 (London: James Duncan, 1830), 44.

2. Leon Morris, *The Gospel According to John*, NICNT (Grand Rapids, Mich.: Eerdmans, 1971), 223–24.

3. Donald Guthrie, *New Testament Theology* (Leicester: InterVarsity, 1981), 878–79.

4. James Montgomery Boice, *Foundations of the Christian Faith* (Leicester: InterVarsity, 1986), 714.

5. Millard J. Erickson, *Christian Theology* (Grand Rapids, Mich.: Baker, 1986), 1229.

6. John Baillie, *And the Life Everlasting* (New York: Scribner, 1933), as quoted in Erickson, *Christian Theology*, 1233.

7. Guthrie, *New Testament Theology*, 886.

8. Ibid.

9. As quoted in Anthony A. Hoekema, *The Bible and the Future* (Grand Rapids, Mich.: Eerdmans, 1979), 266.

10. For example, in Jewish literature of the intertestamental period, the evil inherit Gehenna (the Valley of Hinnom), according to D. J. Wieand. See Wieand, "Hinnom, Valley of," ISBE, vol. 2, 717.

11. G. A. Lee, "Gehenna," ISBE, vol. 2, 423.

12. Murray J. Harris, *Raised Immortal: Resurrection and Immortality in the New Testament* (London: Marshall, Morgan & Scott, 1983), 182.

13. S. D. F. Salmond, *The Christian Doctrine of Immortality* (Edinburgh: T. & T. Clark, 1913), 133, 136.

14. Harris, *Raised Immortal*, 183–84.

15. Ibid., 184.

16. Hoekema, *The Bible and the Future*, 269.

17. Ibid., 270.

18. J. H. Thornwell, "The Necessity of the Atonement," in *The Collected Writings of James Henley Thornwell*, vol. 2 (Edinburgh: Banner of Truth, 1974), 244.

19. C. S. Lewis, *The Great Divorce* (London: Collins Fount, 1977), 111.

20. Robert H. Mounce, *The Book of Revelation*, NICNT (Grand Rapids, Mich.: Wm B. Eerdmans, 1977), 373.

21. Hoekema, *The Bible and the Future*, 280.

22. Richard Bauckham, "First Steps to a Theology of Nature," *Evangelical Quarterly* 58.3 (1986): 240.

23. Hoekema, *The Bible and the Future*, 274.

24. As quoted in Mounce, *Revelation*, 370.

25. As quoted in Mounce, *Revelation*, 370.

# INDEX OF AUTHORS

Moody Press, a ministry of Moody Bible Institute,
is designed for education, evangelization, and edification.
If we may assist you in knowing more about Christ
and the Christian life, please write us without obligation:
Moody Press, c/o MLM, Chicago, Illinois 60610.